Master of
the Sacred Page

D1319324

Master of
the Sacred Page

ESSAYS AND ARTICLES

IN HONOR OF

ROLAND E. MURPHY, O.CARM.,

ON THE OCCASION OF HIS

EIGHTIETH BIRTHDAY

KEITH J. EGAN, T.O.CARM.
CRAIG E. MORRISON, O.CARM.
EDITORS

MICHAEL J. WASTAG, O.CARM.
TECHNICAL EDITOR

The Carmelite Institute
WASHINGTON, D.C.
1997

Library of Congress Cataloging-in-Publication Data

Master of the sacred page: essays and articles in honor of Roland E.
   Murphy, O. Carm., on the occasion of his eightieth birthday /
   Keith J. Egan and Craig E. Morrison, editors; Michael J. Wastag,
   technical editor.
       p.   cm.
   Includes bibliographical references.
   ISBN 0-9656910-0-4
   1. Bible–Criticism, interpretation, etc. 2. Murphy, Roland
   Edmund, 1917- . 3. Carmelites–History. 4. Theology.
   I. Murphy, Roland Edmund, 1917- . II. Egan, Keith J., 1930- .
   III. Morrison, Craig E., 1958- .
BS531.M36 1997
282–dc21   97-16137
                                            CIP

Published by The Carmelite Institute
1600 Webster St., N.E.
Washington, D.C. 20017-3145

Printed and bound in the United States of America

Contents

Master of
the Sacred Page

PART I

INTRODUCTION

The Young Scholar

CURIA GENERALIZIA DEI CARMELITANI

00184 ROMA (ITALIA) · VIA GIOVANNI LANZA, 138
TEL. 481.41.67 · 482.39.28 · 487.0016
TELEFAX 487.11.81
TELEGRAPHICE: CARMELCURIA

1 November 1996

Dear Roland,

With great pleasure I heard of the *Festschrift* planned in your honour to cel-ebrate your 80th birthday. Your love for the Sacred Scriptures has made you a "master of the sacred page" for many generations of Carmelites and students.

Happily in recent years we have witnessed a renewal among us of the ancient practice of *Lectio Divina*, the prayerful pondering on the Word of God which leads to a profound listening and a transformation of the human heart. We have also seen a renewed interest in the Carmelite Rule which is imbued with Scripture. St. Albert of Jerusalem had a love for the Word of God which is apparent from the many quotes and allusions to the Bible in our Rule.

The inspirational figures which our Carmelite charism offers to us in our fol-lowing of Christ are of course the Prophet Elijah and Our Lady. The prophet was a man of God who spoke God's Word to the people. Our Lady listened to the Word and put it into practice. St. Thérèse of Lisieux, whose centenary we cel-ebrate this year, would have greatly appreciated the opportunity to study He-brew and Greek in order to delve more deeply into the riches contained in the Word of God. In your life you have shown how a careful study of the sacred text can be combined with a profound love for what it contains and a desire to live its implications in daily life.

I thank you for all you have given to the Order throughout the years. May your 80th birthday be a time of great blessing for you. May the Word of God be always on your lips and continue to live in your heart so that you may proclaim the Good News of Jesus Christ for many more years to come.

Yours in Carmel,

Joseph Chalmers O. Carm.

Joseph Chalmers, O.Carm.
Prior General

ORDER OF CARMELITES

Roland E. Murphy, O.Carm.
Whitefriars Hall
1600 Webster Street, NE
Washington, DC 20017-3198

Dear Roland,

It is a special pleasure for me to extend my congratulations to you on the occasion of your eightieth birthday. Because you have honored us as brother, priest, friend and scholar, your Carmelite brothers wish to honor you with this *Festschrift,* a token of our admiration and respect for you. The Province of the Most Pure Heart of Mary has known many loyal sons since its formal beginning in 1890. Without exception, I do not know of anyone who has brought more genuine renown to our province than you.

I am sure that your many years at Whitefriars Hall contain mixed memories. There were the fun times of celebration, and the sad times as you saw men choose different paths. There were the bright lights of student scholarship, and the dim lights of disappointment. The Catholic University of America in the late sixties presented unique challenges. Through those difficult years you remained the gentleman and uncompromising scholar that so many of us appreciate. It is no wonder, then, that Duke University came to appreciate your gifts. Although many of us were not part of your Duke experience, we revel in the accolades which you receive from that community to this very day. Roland, you have touched the lives of so many Carmelites, and it is only proper that we celebrate your eighty years and more with this *Festschrift.*

You make the scriptures come alive for countless individuals, Roland. That is your most precious gift to us and to the Church. I pray that you will continue to unfold for us the hidden treasure of scriptures, the precious treasure of our relationship with the Lord.

Sincerely in Carmel,

Leo McCarthy, O.Carm.
Prior Provincial

1317 Frontage Road • Darien, Illinois 60561-5376
Telephone (630) 971-0050 • Telefax (630) 971- 0195

A Word from the Editors

The editors of this *Festschrift* have had ample opportunity to honor Roland Murphy elsewhere in this volume. This preface merely speaks a few words of gratitude and explanation. *Master of the Sacred Page* has been created by the Carmelite family to celebrate one of its most prominent members. It is a *Festschrift*— a composition (*Schrift*) to celebrate (*Fest*) the honoree's contribution to the Order and the Church. The Province of the Most Pure Heart of Mary graciously provided the subvention necessary to undertake this volume, and the authors responded enthusiastically and promptly to the request for contributions.

A note of thanks is owed to the Society of Biblical Literature and the Catholic Biblical Association for granting permission to publish their interviews with Roland Murphy. Thanks also to Monica Blanchard, librarian of the Semitics Department and the Institute of Christian Oriental Research at The Catholic University of America, to James Crenshaw of the Duke University Divinity School, and to Cathy Severns for their assistance in generating Roland Murphy's bibliography. Bruce Baker, O.Carm., is responsible for the picture of Roland at his computer (a contemporary Carmelite in his study!).

A heartfelt word of gratitude is owed to John Welch, O.Carm., President of the Carmelite Institute, for his assistance and to Michael Wastag, O.Carm., technical editor of this volume, whose tireless precision has resulted in a work fitting the one who is honored by it.

There are four sections in this *Festschrift*. Part I offers a few words of introduction followed by an updated bibliography of Roland's writings. The Society of Biblical Literature and the Catholic Biblical Association provided Roland an opportunity to reflect on his years as a biblical scholar. Part II presents these dialogues so that they may be enjoyed by a wider audience. His impact on the life of our province and the wider Church is presented in Part III as his students reflect on the friend, teacher, and colleague they meet in Roland. In Part IV his Carmelite brothers offer the fruits of their own scholarship in his honor. We invite the reader to celebrate with us Roland's eighty years by taking up and reading this *Festschrift* composed in his honor.

Keith J. Egan, T.O.Carm.   Craig E. Morrison, O.Carm.
St. Mary's College   Pontifical Biblical Institute
Notre Dame, IN   Rome, Italy

Editors

A Word of Introduction

Listen, my son, take my words to heart,
and the years of your life shall be multiplied.
I have educated you in the ways of wisdom....
Proverbs 4:10-11

This *Festschrift* honors Roland E. Murphy, O.Carm., in his eightieth year of life and sixty-seventh year of Carmelite community. His years have been multiplied, and his Carmelite family is grateful for the opportunity to honor him, a master of the sacred page.

Roland has spent his life taking God's "words to heart." Indeed, most of his eighty years have been dedicated to the scholarly study of God's Word and to the sharing of that knowledge and understanding. He has shared it with scholars, seminarians, and people of faith. He has moved comfortably between the worlds of the academy and church, communicating his great love of God's Word and encouraging others to listen to it in faith. The scholarly and pastoral worlds have honored Roland in the past, and the Carmelites are grateful for his powerful presence and generous contributions to those worlds and to their own.

This volume is a family tribute. It is an opportunity we take as his family, friends, colleagues, and students to recognize the contribution he has made to the Carmelite family. Roland's Carmelite roots are deep. Of the many gifts he has shared with us, two seem particularly important: community and scholarship.

Roland's sense of community has been an anchor for him and for us. For over twenty-five years, he taught generations of Carmelites from both North American provinces at Whitefriars Hall, inculcating a knowledge and love of Scripture that has been an important grounding in our lives as teachers and preachers of the Word. The experience of community gathered around the Word of God has been renewed and deepened by his commitment and his daily example. Even in his years at Yale, Princeton, and Duke, while not living in a Carmelite house, his sense of community was always strong and important to him. Whether staying with Carmelites when presenting lectures around the nation and world or making frequent visits to Whitefriars, he communicated his love of community life to us in many ways, educating us in the wisdom of this Carmelite value.

Scholarship has been an important part of Carmelite identity since 1247 when Carmel became a mendicant order. Roland's contribution to scholarly research has been immense, deepening that value for us as Carmelites. By his life and work he enabled many of us to see that the intellectual life can be a source of humanization and holiness. His encouragement of younger scholars, his commitment to sharing his technical knowledge in pastoral settings, and his integrity in pursuit of the truth have profoundly influenced our province and order.

Roland Murphy has educated us in the ways of wisdom—professionally and personally. His life as a member of our community and as a scholar has enriched us beyond our telling. I invite you to enjoy these remembrances and studies as a tribute to Roland and for your own enrichment. May his years and his influence continue to be multiplied.

Quinn R. Conners, O.Carm.
Prior Provincial 1990-1996

Bibliography of
Roland E. Murphy, O.Carm.

This bibliography of Roland E. Murphy's scholarly writing encompasses only a portion of his total contribution since it is limited to the books and articles he has authored. Book reviews (he has done over three hundred), book review articles, and abstracts (innumerable!) are not listed below. This bibliography covers publications through the end of 1996. A list of abbreviations used in this bibliography appears at the end of it.

1943

Marie, Sister of St. Thérèse; Her Life written by Pauline, another sister of the Little Flower. Co-translator with Joachim Smet, O.Carm. Englewood, NJ: Carmelite.

1948

A Study of Psalm 72 (71). Studies in Sacred Theology Series 2, 12. Washington: Catholic University of America.

1949

An Allusion to Mary in the Apocalypse. *TS* 10:565-73.

The Epistle for All Saints. *AER* 121:203-09.

The Structure of the Canticle of Canticles. *CBQ* 11:381-91.

1952

A Fragment of an Early Moabite Inscription from Dibon.
BASOR 125:20-23.

1953

Israel and Moab in the Ninth Century B.C. *CBQ* 15:409-17.

1954

The All Beautiful One. *Mary* 15:7-11.

The Canticle of Canticles and the Virgin Mary. *Carmelus* 1:18-28.

Recent Literature on the Canticle of Canticles. *CBQ* 16:1-11.

1955

The Canticle of Canticles in the Confraternity Version. *AER*
133:87-98.

Job in the New Confraternity Version. *AER* 133:16-29.

The Pensées of Coheleth. *CBQ* 17:304-14 (*Festschrift* for E.
O'Hara), paginated separately: 184-94.

1956

The Dead Sea Scrolls and New Testament Comparisons. *CBQ*
18:263-72.

The Dead Sea Scrolls and the Bible. Westminster, MD: Newman. = *Le couvent de la Mer Morte et la Bible.* Maredsous, 1957.

Insights into the New Testament from the Dead Sea Scrolls. *AER* 135:9-22.

Those Dead Sea Scrolls.... *AER* 134:361-73.

1957

The Dead Sea Scrolls—Ten Years After. *Extension* 52/2:12-13, 46-47.

Notes on Old Testament Messianism and Apologetics. *CBQ* 19:5-15.

1958

Šaḥat in the Qumran Literature. *Bib* 39:61-66.

Yēṣer in the Qumran Literature. *Bib* 39:334-44.

1959

BSR in the Qumrân Literature and Sarks in the Epistle to the Romans. In *Sacra Pagina.* J. Coppens et al., eds. 2:60-75. BETL 12-13. Paris: Lecoffre and Gembloux: Ducolot.

A New Classification of Literary Forms in the Psalms. *CBQ* 21:83-87.

Sharing the Same Book. *Worship* 34:53-54.

1960

The Book of Exodus with a Commentary by Roland E. Murphy. PPBS 4-5. New York: Paulist.

Élie (le prophète). *DS* 4:564-67.

The Old Testament for Seminarians. The Purpose of the Course. *NCEAB* 57/1:89-93.

Seven Books of Wisdom. Milwaukee: Bruce.

1961

The Book of Ecclesiastes and the Canticle of Canticles with a Commentary by Roland E. Murphy. PPBS 38. New York: Paulist.

GBR and GBWRH in the Qumran Writings. In *Lex Tua Veritas* (*Festschrift* for H. Junker). H. Gross and F. Mussner, eds. 137-43. Trier: Paulinus.

A New Theology of the Old Testament. *CBQ* 23:217-23.

1962

The Concept of Wisdom Literature. In *The Bible in Current Catholic Thought.* J. L. McKenzie, ed. 46-54. M. Gruenthaner Memorial Volume. New York: Herder and Herder.

The Old Testament: The Unfolding of Salvation History. *Ascent* 67-72.

Promise and Preparation. *The Gospel of Jesus the Christ: a Symposium by Roland E. Murphy, John Oesterreicher and David Stanley,* 11-19. Seton Hall University.

Where is the Wise Man? *TBT* 1:30-37.

1963

A Consideration of the Classification "Wisdom Psalms." *VTSup* 9:156-67. Reprinted in *SAIW* 456-67.

Divino Afflante Spiritu—Twenty Years After. *ChSt* 2:16-28.

The Incarnational Aspects of Old Testament Wisdom. *TBT* 9:560-66. Reprinted in *Contemporary New Testament Studies.* M. R. Ryan, ed. 77-83. Collegeville, MN: Liturgical, 1965.

The Problem of Authority: A Roman Catholic View. *C&C* 23:98-99.

Eclesiástico. In *EB* 2:1056-58.

Elías. In *EB* 2:1210-13.

Libro de los Proverbios. In *EB* 5:1318-20.

Libro de la Sabiduría. In *EB* 6:301-07.

Salvation History and the Bible. *MF* 3:74-79.

To Know Your Might is the Root of Immortality (Wis 15,3). *CBQ* 25:88-93.

1964

The Biblical Instruction. *Commonweal* 80:418-20.

The Old Testament Wisdom Literature and the Problem of Retribution. *The Scotist* 20:5-18.

The Relationship Between the Testaments. *CBQ* 26:349-59.

The Significance of the Bible in the Life of the Church. *MF* 4:23-33.

1965

The Human Reality of Sacred Scripture. P. Benoit, B. van Iersel and Roland E. Murphy, eds. Concilium 10. New York: Paulist.

The Wisdom Literature of the Old Testament. In *The Human Reality of Sacred Scripture.* P. Benoit, R. E. Murphy and B. van Iersel, eds. 126-40. Concilium 10. New York: Paulist.

Introduction to the Wisdom Literature of the Old Testament. Old Testament Reading Guide 22. Collegeville, MN: Liturgical.

Old Testament Studies. In *Theology in Transition.* E. O'Brien, ed. 41-77. New York: Herder and Herder.

The Relevance of Old Testament Studies for Ecumenism. In *Scripture and Ecumenism.* L. J. Swidler, ed. 95-109. Duquesne Studies, Theological Series 3. Pittsburgh, PA: Duquesne University.

The Dead Sea Scrolls. In *Catholic Youth Encyclopedia.*

1966

The Dynamism of Biblical Tradition. P. Benoit and R. E. Murphy, eds. Concilium 20. New York: Paulist.

Foreword to *Man Before God: Toward a Theology of Man.* D. Burkhard and W. T. Merten, eds. *vii-ix.* New York: P J. Kenedy.

The Kerygma of the Book of Proverbs. *Int* 20:3-14.

The Old Testament Canon in the Catholic Church. *CBQ* 28:189-93. Reprinted in *A Symposium on the Canon of Scripture* 247-52. 1969. Correction in *CBQ* 28:484-85.

Praying the Psalms. *Ascent* 14-18.

Present Biblical Scholarship as a Bond of Understanding. In *Torah and Gospel: Jewish and Catholic Theology in Dialogue*. P. Scharper, ed. 81-96. New York: Sheed and Ward.

1967

Alphabetic Psalms. In *NCE* 1:336.

Assumptions and Problems in Old Testament Wisdom Research. *CBQ* 29: 407-18. = published separately in L. Hartman *Festschrift*, 101-12.

Canticle of Canticles. In *NCE* 3:68-69.

A Catholic Foreword. In W. D. Wagoner, *The Seminary: Protestant and Catholic* ix-xiv. New York: Sheed and Ward.

How Does the Christian Confront the Old Testament? P. Benoit, B. van Iersel and Roland E. Murphy, eds. Concilium 30. New York: Paulist.

Penitential Psalms. In *NCE* 11:85-86.

Psalm. In *NCE* 11:935.

Book of Psalms. In *NCE* 11:935-39.

Sapiential Books. In *NCE* 12:1081.

Wisdom (in the Bible). In *NCE* 14:971-74.

1968

R. E. Brown, J. A. Fitzmyer and R. E. Murphy, eds., *The Jerome Biblical Commentary.* Englewood Cliffs, NJ: Prentice-Hall= *Comentario Biblico "San Jerónimo."* Madrid: Ediciónes cristiandad, 1971. *Grande Commentario Biblico.* Brescia: Queriniana, 1973.

Canticle of Canticles. In *JBC* 1:506-10.

Ecclesiastes (Qoheleth). In *JBC* 1:534-540.

A History of Israel. With Addison G. Wright and Joseph A. Fitzmyer. In *JBC* 1:671-702.

Introduction to the Wisdom Literature. In *JBC* 1:487-94.

Psalms. In *JBC* 1:569-602.

The Figure of Elias in the Old Testament. *Carmelus* 15:230-38. Reprinted as The Figure of Elijah in the OT in *Ascent* (1969) 8-15.

Salvation in History. *CBQ* 30:86-87.

1969

The Breaking of Bread. P. Benoit, B. van Iersel and Roland E. Murphy, eds. Concilium 40. New York: Paulist Press.

Form Criticism and Wisdom Literature (Presidential Address). *CBQ* 31:475-83.

The Interpretation of Old Testament Wisdom Literature. *Int* 23:289-301.

The Presence of God. P. Benoit, B. van Iersel and R. E. Murphy, eds. Concilium 50. New York: Paulist.

1970

Christian Understanding of the Old Testament. *TD* 18:321-32.

The Hebrew Sage and Openness to the World. In *Christian Action and Openness to the World.* J. Papin, ed. 219-44. The Villanova University Symposia. Villanova, PA: Villanova University. Reprinted in *Theological Folia of Villanova University: Biblical Studies.* J. Papin, ed. 11-36. Villanova University, 1975.

History, Eschatology and the Old Testament. *Continuum* 7:583-93. Reprinted as Geschichte, Eschatologie und das Alte Testament. In *Eschatologie im Alten Testament.* H. D. Preuss, ed. 325-341. Darmstadt: Wissenschaftliche Buchgesellschaft, 1978.

Immortality and Resurrection. P. Benoit and R. E. Murphy, eds. Concilium 60. New York: Herder and Herder.

Reading II: The Church's Attitude Toward the Old Testament. Alternate Reading No. 8, p. 346 of *Christian Readings VI*, Year 2 (Second Nocturn, Second Sunday of the Year).

The Relevance of the Old Testament for Preaching in the '70's. *Preach* 5:1-12.

1971

The Book of Joel. In *ICB* 461-64.

The Book of Jonah. In *ICB* 480-82.

The Book of Obadiah. In *ICB* 477-479.

The Role of the Bible in Roman Catholic Theology, Part I. *Int* 25:78-86.

Theology, Exegesis, and Proclamation. R. E. Murphy, ed. Concilium 70. New York: Herder and Herder.

1972

Biblical Theology (Bibliography). *DDSR* 37:74-75.

Office and Ministry in the Church. B. van Iersel and R. E. Murphy, eds. Concilium 80. New York: Herder and Herder.

1973

Deuteronomy—A Document of Revival. In *Spiritual Revivals.* C. Duquoc and C. Floristan, eds. 26-36. Concilium 89. New York: Herder and Herder. = Das Deuteronomium als Dokument einer Erweckung, in *Theologisches Jahrbuch*. W.Ernst et al., eds. 150-155. Leipzig, 1975.

Form-Critical Studies in the Song of Songs. *Int* 27:413-22.

Modern Approaches to Biblical Study. In *The New Oxford Annotated Bible* 1519-22. Oxford University.

1974

The Authority of the Scriptures. In *Seminar on Authority.* J. W. Angell, ed. 31-39. Winston-Salem, NC: Wake Forest University.

Focus on Faculty. *DDSR* 38:181-83.

A Form-Critical Consideration of Ecclesiastes 7. *SBL Abstracts and Seminar Papers* 1:77-85.

The Old Testament as Word of God. In *A Light unto My Path* (J. M. Myers *Festschrift*). H. N. Bream et al., eds. 363-74. Philadelphia: Temple University.

Mowinckel, Sigmund. In *NCE* Supplementary Volume 16:304-5.

Rowley, Harold Henry. In *NCE* Supplementary Volume 16:392-93.

1975

Israel's Psalms: Contribution to Today's Prayer Style. *Review for Religious* 34:113-20. Reprinted in *Scripture in Church* 7/24 (1976) 98-108.

Wisdom and Yahwism. In *No Famine in the Land* (J. L. McKenzie *Festschrift*). J. W. Flanagan and A. W. Robinson, eds. 117-126. Missoula, MT: Scholars.

The Theology of Hope: The Cardinal Cook Lecture. *The Camillan* (National Association of Catholic Chaplains, 11th Annual Convention Proceedings). Houston, TX.

Qohelet der Skeptiker. *Concilium* (German edition) 12:567-70.

Song of Songs. In *IDBS* 836-38.

Wisdom Theses. In *Wisdom and Knowledge* (J. Papin *Festschrift*). J. Armenti, ed. 2:187-200. Villanova, PA: Villanova University.

1977

Biblical Wisdom and Christian Ministry. *DDSR* 42:175-77.

"Nation" in the Old Testament. In *Ethnicity*. A. Greeley and G. Baum, eds. 71-77. Concilium 101. New York: Seabury.

The Psalms, Job. PC. Philadelphia: Fortress. = *Giobbe, Salmi.* Leggere oggi la Bibbia. Brescia: Queriana, 1977.

Symposium on Biblical Criticism. *TToday* 33: 364-65.

Towards a Commentary on the Song of Songs. *CBQ* 39:482-96.

What and Where is Wisdom? *CurTM* 4:283-87.

1978

Moral Formation. In *Moral Formation and Christianity*. F. Böckle and J.-M. Pohier, eds. 29-36. Concilium 110. New York: Seabury.

The Understanding of Revelation in Prophecy and Wisdom. *ChSt* 17:45-57. = Concetti di rivelazione nel libri prophetici e sapientiale. In *Catechismo Biblico*. G. Dyer, ed. Brescia: Queriniana, 1979.

Vatican III—Problems and Opportunities of the Future: The Bible. In *Toward Vatican III: The Work that Needs to Be Done*. D. Tracy, ed. 21-26. Colloquium at the University of Notre Dame, 1977. Concilium. New York: Seabury.

Wisdom—Theses and Hypotheses. In *Israelite Wisdom: Theological and Literary Essays in Honor of Samuel Terrien*. J. G. Gammie et al., eds. 35-42. Missoula, MT: Scholars.

1979

A Biblical Model of Human Intimacy: The Song of Songs. In *The Family in Crisis or in Transition: A Sociological and Theological Perspective*. A. Greeley, ed. 61-66. Concilium 121. New York: Seabury.

Interpreting the Song of Songs. *BTB* 9:99-105.

Qohelet's "Quarrel" with the Fathers. In *From Faith to Faith* (D. G. Miller *Festschrift*). D. Y. Hadidian, ed. 235-45. Pittsburgh Theological Monograph Series 31. Pittsburgh: Pickwick.

The Unity of the Song of Songs. *VT* 29:436-43.

Wisdom and Salvation. In *Sin, Salvation, and the Spirit.* D. Durken, ed. 177-83. Commemorating the Fiftieth Year of the Liturgical Press. Collegeville, MN: Liturgical.

1980

The Faith of the Psalmist. *Int* 34:229-39.

The Old Testament as Scripture. *JSOT* 16:40-44.

1981

Biblical Insights into Suffering: Pathos and Compassion. In *Whither Creativity, Freedom, Suffering?: Humanity, Cosmos, God.* F. A. Eigo, ed. 53-75. Proceedings of the Theology Institute of Villanova University. Villanova, PA: Villanova University.

The Faces of Wisdom in the Book of Proverbs. In *Mélanges bibliques et orientaux en l'honneur de M. Henri Cazelles.* A. Caquot and M. Delcor, eds. *AOAT* 212:337-45. Neukirchen-Vluyn: Neukirchener.

Hebrew Wisdom. *JAOS* 101:21-34.

Israel's Wisdom: A Biblical Model of Salvation. *StMiss* 30:1-43.

Patristic and Medieval Exegesis—Help or Hindrance? *CBQ* 43:505-16.

Wisdom Literature: Job, Proverbs, Ruth, Canticles, Ecclesiastes, and Esther. FOTL 13. Grand Rapids, MI: Eerdmans.

1982

Prophets and Wise Men as Provokers of Dissent. In *The Right to Dissent.* H. Küng and J. Moltmann, eds. 61-66. Concilium 158. New York: Seabury.

Qohelet Interpreted: The Bearing of the Past on the Present. *VT* 32:331-37.

1983

Wisdom Literature & Psalms. IBT. Nashville: Abingdon.

1984

A Response to "The Task of Old Testament Theology." *HIBT* 6/1:65-71.

The Theological Contributions of Israel's Wisdom Literature. *Listening* 19:30-40. Reprinted in *A Companion to the Bible.* M. Ward, ed. 269-83. New York: Alba, 1985.

1985

Cant 2:8-17—A Unified Poem? In *Mélanges bibliques et orientaux en l'honneur de M. Mathias Delcor.* A. Caquot et al., eds. 305-10. *AOAT* 215. Neukirchen-Vluyn: Neukirchener.

The Proverbs. In *HBD* 831-32.

Reflections on the History of the Exposition of Scripture. In *Studies in Catholic History in Honor of John Tracy Ellis* N. Minnich et al., eds. 489-99. Wilmington: Glazier.

Two Dangerous Books? *Duke University Letters* 69:1-4.

The Song of Solomon. In *HBD* 978-79.

Wisdom. In *HBD* 1135-36.

Wisdom and Creation (Presidential Address). *JBL* 104:3-11.

1986

Wisdom's Song: Proverbs 1:20-33. *CBQ* 48:456-60.

(with Burton Mack) Wisdom Literature. In *Early Judaism and Its Modern Interpreters*. R. A. Kraft and G. W. Nickelsburg, eds. 371-410; *The Bible and Its Modern Interpreters* 2. D. Knight, ed. Atlanta: Scholars.

The Song of Songs: Critical Scholarship vis-a-vis Exegetical Traditions. In *Understanding the Word: Essays in Honour of Bernhard W. Anderson*. J. T. Butler, et al., eds. 63-69. JSOTSup 37; Sheffield: JSOT.

Proverbs and Theological Exegesis. In *The Hermeneutical Quest: Essays in Honor of James Luther Mays*. D. G. Miller, ed. 87-95. Princeton Theological Monographs 4; Allison Park, PA: Pickwick.

History of Exegesis as a Hermeneutical Tool: The Song of Songs. *BTB* 16/3:87-91.

The Writings. In *The Biblical Heritage in Modern Catholic Scholarship*, J. J. Collins and J. D. Crossan, eds. 85-105. Wilmington, DE: Glazier.

1987

Medieval Exegesis of Wisdom Literature: Essays by Beryl Smalley, Roland E. Murphy, ed. Reprints and Translation Series. Atlanta: Scholars. Preface by Roland E. Murphy.

Dance and Death in the Song of Songs. In *Love and Death in the Ancient Near East: Essays in Honor of Marvin H. Pope*. J. Marks and R. Good, eds. 117-19. Guilford, CT: Four Quarters.

Update on Scripture Studies. *Religious Education* 82/4:624-36.

The Faith of Qoheleth. *Word and World* 7:253-60.

Proverbs 22:1-9. *Int* 41:398-402.

Scripture and Church History. In *Exodus—a lasting paradigm*. B. van Iersel and A. Weiler, eds. 3-8. Edinburgh: T&T Clark.

Religious Dimensions of Israelite Wisdom. In *Ancient Israelite Wisdom: Essays in Honor of Frank Moore Cross*. Patrick D. Miller, Paul D. Hanson and S. Dean McBride, eds. 449-458. Philadelphia: Fortress.

1988

Wisdom and Eros in Proverbs 1-9. *CBQ* 50: 600-603.

The Riddle of Love and Death. In *Mysteries of the Bible*. The Reader's Digest Association, Pleasantville, New York/Montreal, 229-30.

The Symbolism of the Song of Songs. In *The Incarnate Imagination: Essays in Theology*. Ingrid H. Shafer, ed. (Andrew Greeley Festschrift), 229-34. Bowling Green, OH: Popular Press.

The Listening Heart. In *Biblical People as Models for Campus Ministry*. M. Galligan-Stierle, et al., eds. 47-56. Dayton Ohio: Catholic Campus Ministry Association.

In Our Image. In *Biblical People as Models for Campus Ministry*. M. Galligan-Stierle, et al., eds. 201-10. Dayton Ohio: Catholic Campus Ministry Association.

The Psalms in Modern Life. *TBT* 25:231-39.

1989

Song of Solomon. In *The Books of the Bible*. B. W. Anderson, ed. 1:241-46. New York: Charles Scribner's Sons.

Foreword. In G. P. Fogarty, *American Catholic Biblical Scholarship*. San Francisco: Harper & Row, xii-xiv. See the references to Roland E. Murphy in the index of this book.

1990

R. E. Brown, J. A. Fitzmyer, R. E. Murphy, eds. *The New Jerome Biblical Commentary*. Englewood Cliffs, NJ: Prentice Hall.

Introduction to the Pentateuch. In *NJBC* 3-7.

(with Richard J. Clifford) Genesis. In *NJBC* 8-43.

Introduction to Wisdom Literature. In *NJBC* 447-452.

Canticle of Canticles. In *NJBC* 462-465.

(with R. A. F. MacKenzie) Job. In *NJBC* 466-488.

(with Addison G. Wright and Joseph A. Fitzmyer) A History of Israel. In *NJBC* 1219-1252.

The Tree of Life: An Exploration of Biblical Wisdom. Anchor Bible Reference Library. New York: Doubleday.

The Song of Songs. Hermeneia. Minneapolis, MN: Fortress.

The Old Testament/Tanakh—Canon and Interpretation. *The Hebrew Bible or Old Testament? Studying the Bible in Judaism and Christianity.* R. Brooks and J. J. Collins, eds. 11-29. Christianity and Judaism in Antiquity 9; Notre Dame, IN: University of Notre Dame.

The Song of Songs and St Thérèse. In *Experiencing St Thérèse Today.* J. Sullivan, ed. 1-9, 191-92. *Carmelite Studies* V; Washington: Institute of Carmelite Studies.

The Sage in Ecclesiastes and Qoheleth the Sage. In *The Sage in Israel and the Ancient Near East.* E. Gammie and Leo Perdue, eds. 263-71. Winona Lake, IN: Eisenbrauns.

1991

(with Bruce M. Metzger) ed. *The New Oxford Annotated Bible/New Revised Standard Version, with the Apocryphal/Deuterocanonical Books.* Oxford/New York/Toronto: Oxford University. (R. Murphy's contributions: Introduction to the OT, Introduction to the Poetical Books or "Writings," Modern Approaches to Biblical Study, and Introductions and Annotations to Job, Proverbs, Ecclesiastes, Song of Songs, Lamentations, Wisdom of Solomon, and Ecclesiasticus [Sirach].)

The Revised Psalms of the New American Bible. New York: Catholic Book Publishing (one of six editors).

Old Testament and Christian Unity. *Dictionary of the Ecumenical Movement.* N. Lossky et al., eds. 745-46. Grand Rapids, MI: W. B. Eerdmans.

On Translating Ecclesiastes. *CBQ* 53:571-79.

Qoheleth and Theology. *BTB* 21:30-33.

The Biblical Elijah: A Holistic Perspective. In *A Journey with Elijah.* Paul Chandler, O.Carm., ed. 21-27. Carisma e Spiritualità 2; Rome: Institutum Carmelitanum.

Proverbs in Genesis 2? In *Text and Tradition: The Hebrew Bible and Folklore.* S. Niditch, ed. 121-25. SBL Semeia Studies. Atlanta: Scholars.

Reflections upon Historical Methodology in Biblical Study. In *The Land of Carmel.* Paul Chandler and Keith J. Egan, eds. 19-25. Rome: Institutum Carmelitanum.

1992

The Psalms: Tune into the Original Soul Music. *U.S. Catholic,* February, 1992, 57:20-27. Edited and reprinted in *God's Word Today,* May 1993, 39-44.

Book of Song of Songs. In *The Anchor Bible Dictionary,* six volumes. D. N. Freedman, ed. 6:150-55. New York: Doubleday.

Wisdom in the OT. In *The Anchor Bible Dictionary,* six volumes. D. N. Freedman, ed. 6:920-31. New York: Doubleday.

Images of Yahweh: God in the Writings. In *Studies in Old Testament Theology.* R. L. Hubbard, et al., eds. 189-204. (David Hubbard *Festschrift)* Dallas: Word.

Ecclesiastes. Word Biblical Commentary 23A. Dallas: Word.

The Psalms and Worship. *Ex Auditu* 8:23-31.

The Fear of the Lord: The Fear to End All Fears. In *Overcoming Fear Between Jews and Christians.* James H. Charlesworth, ed.

172-80. Vol. 3 of Shared Ground Among Jews and Christians: A Series of Explorations. New York/Philadelphia: Crossroad/American Interfaith Institute.

Raymond E. Brown, Joseph A. Fitzmyer, Roland E. Murphy, eds., *The New Jerome Bible Handbook.* London: Chapman; Collegeville: Liturgical.

1993

Reflections on Contextual Interpretation of the Psalms. In *The Shape and Shaping of the Psalter*. J. Clinton McCann, ed. 21-28. JSOTSup 159. Sheffield: JSOT.

The Book of Psalms. In *The Oxford Companion to the Bible*. B. M. Metzger and M. D. Coogan, eds. 626-29. New York/Oxford: Oxford University.

Solomon. In *The Oxford Companion to the Bible*. B. M. Metzger and M. D. Coogan, eds. 707-8. New York/Oxford: Oxford University.

Recent Research on Proverbs and Qoheleth. In *Currents in Research: Biblical Studies* 1:118-40.

The Psalms are Yours. New York: Paulist.

L'albero della vita: una esplorazione della letteratura sapienziale biblica. Brescia: Queriniana. Translation of *The Tree of Life* (1990).

Fireside Chat II. Cassette Recording, Annual Meeting of the AAR/SBL.

1994

Watch Your Language: Why We Should Mind our Hes and Shes....
U.S. Catholic, February, 1994, 32-35.

Wisdom Literature and Biblical Theology. *BTB* 24/1:4-7.

The Psalms: Prayer of Israel and the Church. *TBT* 32:133-37.

Responses to 101 Questions on the Psalms and Other Writings.
New York: Paulist.

Israelite Wisdom and the Home. In *"Où demeures/tu?" (Jn 1,38).
La maison depuis le monde biblique* (Guy Couturier *Festschrift*),
199-212. Saint-Laurent, Québec: Fides.

Worship, Officials, Wealth and its Uncertainties: Ecclesiastes
5:1-6:9. In *Reflecting with Solomon: Selected Studies on the Book
of Ecclesiastes.* Roy B. Zuck, ed. 281-290. Grand Rapids, MI:
Baker (a reprint from R. Murphy's *Ecclesiastes*, 1992).

1995

The Personification of Wisdom. In *Wisdom In Ancient Israel:
Essays in Honor of J. A. Emerton.* J. Day et al., eds. 222-32.
Cambridge: Cambridge University.

1996

*Responses to 101 Questions on the Biblical Torah: Reflections on
the Pentateuch.* New York: Paulist.

The Tree of Life. 2nd rev. ed. Grand Rapids, MI: W. B. Eerdmans.

The Old Testament and the New Catechism. *TBT* 34/4:253-59.

Reflections on "Actualization" of the Bible. *BTB* 26/2:79-81.

Job. In *The Collegeville Pastoral Dictionary of Biblical Theology.* Carroll Stuhlmueller et al., eds. 492-93. Collegeville: Liturgical.

Proverbs. In *The Collegeville Pastoral Dictionary of Biblical Theology.* Carroll Stuhlmueller et al., eds. 796-98. Collegeville: Liturgical.

Wisdom. In *The Collegeville Pastoral Dictionary of Biblical Theology.* Carroll Stuhlmueller et al., eds. 1081-85. Collegeville: Liturgical.

Abbreviations Used in this Bibliography

AER	*American Ecclesiastical Review*
AOAT	Alter Orient und Altes Testament
BASOR	*Bulletin of the American Schools of Oriental Research*
BETL	*Bibliotheca ephemeridum theologicarum lovaniensium*
Bib	*Biblica*
BTB	*Biblical Theology Bulletin*
C&C	*Christianity and Crisis*
CBQ	*Catholic Biblical Quarterly*
ChSt	*Chicago Studies*
CurTM	*Currents in Theology and Mission*
DDSR	*Duke Divinity School Review*
DS	Denzinger-Schönmetzer, *Enchiridion symbolorum*
EB	*Enciclopedia de la Biblia.* 6 vols. Barcelona: Garriga, 1963.
FOTL	The Forms of Old Testament Literature
HBD	P. J. Achtemeier et al., eds. *Harper's Bible Dictionary.* San Francisco: Harper and Row, 1985.
HIBT	*Horizons in Biblical Theology*
IBT	Interpreting Biblical Texts
ICB	C. M. Laymon, ed., *The Interpreter's One-Volume Commentary on the Bible.*
Int	*Interpretation*
JAOS	*Journal of the American Oriental Society*
JBC	R. E. Brown, J. A. Fitzmyer and R. E. Murphy, eds., *The Jerome Biblical Commentary.* Englewood Cliffs, NJ: Prentice-Hall, 1968.
JBL	*Journal of Biblical Literature*
JSOT	*Journal for the Study of Old Testament*
MF	*Marian Forum*
NCE	*New Catholic Encyclopedia.* 15 vols. New York: McGraw-Hill, 1967. Supplementary Volume 16. Washington: Publishers Guild, 1974. Supplemen-

	tary Volume 17. Washington: Publishers Guild, 1979.
NCEAB	*National Catholic Education Association Bulletin*
NJBC	R. E. Brown, J. A. Fitzmyer, R. E. Murphy, eds. *The New Jerome Biblical Commentary.* Englewood Cliffs NJ: Prentice Hall, 1990.
PC	Proclamation Commentaries
PPBS	Paulist Pamphlet Bible Series
Preach	*Preaching Today* (prior to 1971); *Preaching: A Journal of Homiletics* (1971 and later)
SAIW	J. Crenshaw, ed., *Studies in Ancient Israelite Wisdom.* New York: Ktav, 1976.
StMiss	*Studia Missionalia*
TBT	*The Bible Today*
TD	*Theology Digest*
TS	*Theological Studies*
TToday	*Theology Today*
VT	*Vetus Testamentum*
VTSup	Supplements to Vetus Testamentum

PART II

DIALOGUES WITH
ROLAND E. MURPHY, O.CARM.

In Palestine, 1953

Dialogues with
Roland E. Murphy, O.Carm.

As a senior biblical scholar, Roland Murphy's scholarly achievements have caught the attention of the Society of Biblical Literature and the Catholic Biblical Association of America. These organizations invited him to share moments from his personal history and to reflect on the advancements of biblical scholarship in this century. With the permission of these scholarly societies, these interviews have been edited for presentation here.

The Fireside Chat

This interview with Roland Murphy by Robert K. Johnston from Fuller Theological Seminary took place on Sunday, November 21, 1993 during the Annual Meeting of the Society of Biblical Literature in Washington DC.

R. JOHNSTON: Welcome to this Fireside Chat. We have no easy chair, we have no fire, but we have an interesting person with whom we can dialogue and from whom we can learn. I was asked to say a word about the series and to make an announcement or two and then I want to introduce our guest for the evening, Roland Murphy. Then, after saying a word about myself, we will be off and running. We have a microphone down here in the front seat and,

35

at the appropriate time, Roland and I will invite questions from you so that you will also be able to participate in this informal conversation.

This year is the second year of what the SBL [Society of Biblical Literature] hopes will be an ongoing series of Fireside Chats in order to help give some impetus to an oral tradition or an oral history within the Association. I am Robert Johnston; I am the newly appointed Provost at Fuller Theological Seminary after spending the past eleven years at North Park Theological Seminary in Chicago where I was dean. I am a Protestant and an ordained minister in the Evangelical Covenant Church. I am also a "Dukie" and I studied with Roland in the early seventies. I am a theologian, however, so there is not only a certain ecumenical quality to this dialogue but also a cross-disciplinary breadth. I had a minor in wisdom literature, and Roland tried to keep me honest as a theologian. Though he hasn't always succeeded, he continues to try.

Roland has kept in close touch with a number of his students; I hope we can talk about that tonight. I am one of those students. Typically at a meeting like this we would have lunch together, often with a group of six or eight others. He would phone when he was in town (in Chicago) and we would get together. You will see, as the conversation progresses, that Roland is both a mentor and close friend of mine.

As a way of introducing my colleague and friend, I want to read a citation which was read in May at Loyola University in Chicago as Roland had conferred upon him a Doctorate of Humane Letters. Roland thinks that it is a little flowery, but it is accurate.

> Certain scholars stand out as giants among their peers. The Rev. Roland E. Murphy is clearly one of these giants in American Catholic Biblical scholarship. Fr. Murphy was trained in Semitic Languages, Philosophy and Theology at the Catholic University of America and received scriptural training at the Pontifical Biblical

Institute in Rome. At various times in his career he has
taught at Yale, Princeton, Notre Dame, and Duke University Divinity School where he was the George Washington Ivey Professor of Biblical Studies. Fr. Murphy is
among the first modern generation of Catholic Biblical
scholars in this country. He began teaching at the
Catholic University six years after Pope Pius XII issued
Divino Afflante Spiritu, the Magna Carta of Catholic
biblical studies. The fact that he was invited to teach at
Protestant institutions was indeed recognition for that
quality of his scholarship. His interest in serving was an
indication of his deep ecumenical interest. Fr. Murphy's
scholarly specialization is the study of the Wisdom
tradition in the Old Testament and Hebrew Scriptures.
He has authored numerous books and articles in this
area. Within the last decade he has authored *Wisdom
Literature in the Psalms, The Tree of Life, The Song of
Songs* (and they could have added *Ecclesiastes* in the
Word Biblical Commentary Series [see Roland's bibliography for further details]). He has served on the editorial
boards of scholarly journals and presses, for example,
Interpretation, Vetus Testamentum, Concilium, and as
President of the Catholic Biblical Association of America
and the Society of Biblical Literature. Fr. Murphy, along
with Fr. Joseph Fitzmyer and Fr. Ray Brown, was editor
of *The Jerome Biblical Commentary.* He was also coeditor
of the major revision of that fine commentary in 1990.
As a translator Murphy has contributed to the New
American Bible and the New Revised Standard Version.
With Dr. Bruce Metzger he has most recently been editor
of *The New Oxford Annotated Bible.* Reverend President,
for a life dedicated to the study of the word of God in a
way which has combined both scholarly interest and
religious conviction, for a life dedicated to Roman Catholic
tradition and to deeply held ecumenical convictions, for
a life of scholarship so distinguished as to place him not

only among the founders but among the giants of
American biblical scholarship, I am proud to recom-
mend that the degree of Doctorate of Humane Letters,
honoris causa, be conferred upon the Rev. Roland E.
Murphy of the Order of the Carmelites.

R. MURPHY: [interrupting] Do I stand up now and
receive....[laughter]

R. JOHNSTON: An introduction so you can see something
of the stature of this individual and the pleasure with which I
begin the conversation. They asked that we ask some questions
that allow Roland to reflect on his life, on his role in scholarship,
and on his role within the Society of Biblical Literature. I want to
begin with some questions of a personal nature. Your brother
David is also a priest and also a teacher. What was it that caused
two Irish Catholic boys in Chicago to take on this particular
vocational bent?

R. MURPHY: Well, we lived on Dante Avenue which is a
name you would not expect to find in South Chicago. On Dante
Avenue you had Mount Carmel High School and Mount Carmel
Monastery. We used to play ball with the Carmelite students and
when we finished grammar school both of us went to what we call
the minor seminary in Niagara Falls, on the Canadian side. There
we studied Latin and Greek and particular high school topics,
undisturbed by thoughts of girls, with a heavy emphasis on sports
and studies.

After four years of that you would go into the novitiate
which would be a year of preparation for the religious life of which
you had a vague inkling. You might say, you wanted to be a priest,
but you wanted to be a Carmelite priest—the kind you knew. Then
you studied something of Carmelite history and way of life and
after a year given entirely to that, you would begin college.
Fortunately, I was sent to Washington to Catholic University and
there I experienced a great stir intellectually. I did philosophy and
theology there and an M.A. in Semitics which saved me because
the theology I was taught was, shall I say, pre-Vatican II. But the

language and the reading of the text and the command of the text made a big difference for me.

In those days, when you received a commission from your superior, you would be called into the room and be told, "You are going to do this or that." And so the superior told me, "We are going to send you to Chicago to a parish to give you some experience, but you are going to come back and teach Scripture here. Well, I thank God every day that Providence illumined his mind that way, because it has been one happy year after another to be dealing with the Scriptures.

R. JOHNSTON: As a Carmelite you have pledged yourself to a life long rhythm of work and worship. How have you worked that vow out concretely as a scholar, as a person, and as a Christian?

R. MURPHY: As a Carmelite, I took a vow of poverty. When my superior told me that it was going to be Scripture, I was obliged to do what I could. If I had blundered and he had sent me into another area, that would have been alright too. Fortunately there was no blunder.

R. JOHNSTON: Roland, if you don't mind talking personally. I can remember conversations with you when I was a graduate student; you would reflect on the rhythm of reading the Bible devotionally and reading the Bible in a scholarly way and the combination of the two and the overlap. Could you talk about how you have been able to work out your own personal rhythm in the context of your vows?

R. MURPHY: Well, I don't think that there is too much difference between studying the Word of God and reflecting upon it in a meditative, religious way. I think of our Jewish brothers and sisters; for them the study of the Bible is a religious act. I remember teaching a graduate course in Job to a group, and among them was a rabbi. After a couple of weeks I said to them as we were breaking up on a Friday, "What are you going to do this weekend?" The rabbi responded, "I am going to study the Torah." This was a great answer because it showed me where his value was. Now, studying the Torah for him was a religious act, and I really think that studying the Bible for anyone who is of a religious bent would be so. I wouldn't distinguish very clearly between study and prayer.

R. JOHNSTON: You have written several books in which you have used the phrase: "the Psalms are a school of prayer." To what degree has your own use of the Psalms as a school of prayer influenced your scholarship? I think of Dahood's volume on the Psalms [Dahood, Mitchell, *Psalms*. The Anchor Bible 16-17A; New York: Doubleday, 1966-1970], there is lots of erudition there, but he had a different approach.

R. MURPHY: [interjecting] He said it in Ugaritic!

The difference [between the scholarly and religious approach] would be this. In religious life we say the office in which there are certain psalms and readings. In this situation you grow up being able to recite the Psalms somewhat by heart, but in Latin—I wish we had been brought up saying them in Hebrew. By saying them in Latin it was more difficult to absorb the prayer value because my Latin was not all that good. It took a little time for the Latin to become vital and real in life. But that itself had strong formative value in the way in which I would understand prayer and the presence of God. Now the office was divided into four or five points of the day for ten or fifteen minutes. A few key phrases helped toward a personal sense of the presence of God as one lived through the day; it is in that sense that the Psalms would be a school of prayer.

But now, the way I understand that phrase—one, after all, grows into an understanding of a phrase that one uses—is that my freedom as an individual in speaking to God, and speaking roughly to God, and emptying myself to God, has been very much inspired by the freedom of the language of the Hebrew Bible, of the Psalms, and of Job. That's what I mean by saying that the Psalms are a school of prayer.

R. JOHNSTON: Roland, you came to Catholic University to begin teaching in 1948, or rather, to begin teaching at Whitefriars.

R. MURPHY: I came to Whitefriars Hall in 1939 to do first year theology, and that's where I studied Hebrew for two years.

After I finished theology and I was sent out for a year, I was sent back to Washington in 1943 and told to get busy and to learn Scripture. Then I had the fortune of studying under Monsignor Skehan in the Semitics department at Catholic University where I really saved my soul from the point of view of teaching Scripture. Then I went on the faculty. That's when you learn your language—when you have to teach others.

R. JOHNSTON: In 1943 comes the encyclical that begins to move the Catholic Church beyond a condemnation of modernism.

R. MURPHY: I knew you were going to ask that. Now in 1943 I was just beginning, and that was during the war. It was not until the 1950's that the effects of *Divino Afflante Spiritu* came to be felt in the Church and in teaching [Bible]. So I came along at the right time, or the encyclical came along at the right time. I don't know which way to put it. This opened up an exciting new world, compared to the way it was before.

R. JOHNSTON: Let me ask you, I am an American evangelical and we don't have encyclicals behind us. But there was similar suspicion of biblical criticism. As those suspicions broke down, there was a movement among Bible scholars to become language experts. There was a sense that Wisdom literature was safer than Genesis. In my faculty, for example, we were experts on the Hurrians or on how the Ethiopians interacted with the Israelites. Was there a similar phenomenon [among Catholic scholars]? Were the concerns that you had different from the concerns that your mentor Fr. Patrick Skehan had? You were at the beginning.

R. MURPHY: First of all when I came to Catholic University, I joined the Semitics department. I remember one day that I was with Pat Skehan. I said to him, "I don't think you are picking the right man." He responded, "Let us decide that." One time, during my study of Christian Arabic, I asked Pat Skehan, "How do you work up enthusiasm for the Syriac and Arabic fathers?" He had a wonderful answer, "The Church has to have a memory." The more you ponder that—the idea of retrieval—it becomes more and more important. Then I went to teach Old Testament in the school of theology. I was already teaching Old Testament at Whitefriars Hall, so it wasn't a complete change. But having taught the language for seven years made all the difference in the world. Even today seminarians who do not take any Greek do not read the Bible in the same way as those who have taken some Greek.

The other part of your question is Modernism. The Catholic Church had real Modernism in its wake, and it was busy building churches to care for immigrants. The intellectual life was not first on the agenda. Modernism created an atmosphere of fear. This effected the European Catholic Biblical scholars more than Americans. Skehan's real love was the Christian Orient not the Bible. But, because the Bible took off in the 1950's and so many students came to him for Hebrew and he worked on the Dead Sea Scrolls, he naturally changed his field and sacrificed himself to give a great impetus to the study of these necessary tools.

In my own experience at Catholic University, the Mosaic authorship of the Pentateuch really didn't grab me and maybe that's why I got into Psalms and Wisdom which were more realistic and experiential than how Genesis was put together. I remember explaining in class what the Biblical Commission decrees were. Most of them were negative; you couldn't prove the opposite (that's an easy way to win an argument). Because Vatican II opened up so many questions, the biblical question was put into perspective and people weren't so ready to bang you on the head about the authorship of the gospels.

R. JOHNSTON: We were talking before this interview and I was reflecting on how evangelical biblical scholars trickled into the Society of Biblical Literature. Maybe that happened a decade or so before they trickled into the American Academy of Religion. Why in the 1950's wasn't the Society of Biblical Literature part of your world?

R. MURPHY: I thought I had all the truth. We had our own Catholic Biblical Association, which really had exciting papers and a great deal of cross conversation. It just didn't occur to me [to become a member of the Society of Biblical Literature]. Vatican

II changed that in 1965. In my own experience after 1965 I started teaching at various non-Catholic institutions such as Pittsburgh Theological Seminary (Presbyterian), where I would teach in the morning and take a plane out to teach a course in the afternoon, stay overnight, teach a course in the morning and come back on Tuesday afternoon. It made you feel very important. This was for me a great opening.

R. JOHNSTON: You talked about Patrick Skehan. What would you say was his contribution to you personally?

R. MURPHY: A tremendous contribution! A man of great patience in teaching. You could have great difficulty, but he would inspire you to study. Because he gave his precious time [to students], he wrote no book. I published a collection of his essays because I wanted to make sure that there would be some record of this man. He used to read the New Yorker. He was a confirmed New Yorker. I said to him, "Why do you read the New Yorker?" He responded, "It's good prose." His own prose was complicated; you had to read it carefully. Some of you who have read his essays in the CBQ [Catholic Biblical Quarterly] will appreciate what I am saying.

R. JOHNSTON: The late sixties was a time of turbulence in universities across the country. For some of us who were in a university at the time, the war was a focus. For Catholics it was also birth control. In 1968 you put your name on a petition in support of some openness.... Well, you tell the story.

R. MURPHY: To make the story short, there was an encyclical known as *Humanae Vitae* that approached the question of birth control. A number of priests signed the petition—not that they threw the encyclical out. I did not regard this act as being rebellious, I regarded it as being loyal opposition.

R. JOHNSTON: But it wasn't interpreted as loyal opposition by some.

R. MURPHY: Opposition is never interpreted as loyal opposition by the opposition. You know who the loyal opposition is when you are one of them. In my case it was interesting because, after it happened, the school of theology at Catholic University elected me dean. The first lay president that Catholic University had came on the scene and he couldn't support me. So I said to him—I was on good terms with him: "I will be dean if that's what you choose." He selected a committee of three people and I was one of the candidates. So I went to see him separately, and I said to him: "It's no easier for you to support me now than it was last summer." He said "No." I said "Fine, I have no scars, select your dean, but I think that, on principle, I should resign, because, if I can't be dean, neither should I be able to teach." So I resigned. Fortunately Bernie Anderson of Princeton was taking a sabbatical and he asked me to come up to Princeton to teach in 1970. Then Duke called and I went to Duke. It was a very opening experience—to be teaching with Methodists and Presbyterians and others. Going to Duke was one of the greatest experiences I have had. You never know how provincial you are until you are thrown into the healthy competition that comes from working with colleagues who were not brought up in a monastery as I was. Duke was a great experience for me—a priest of Irish descent teaching Bible to Protestant students so that they would be fired up with the Old Testament and be better preachers for it. It was quite a challenge.

R. JOHNSTON: Roland, as I was thinking of this conversation, I reflected on the fact that you have written for *Hermeneia* and for *The Jerome Biblical Commentary*. You have also written for the *Word Biblical Commentary*. I don't think I know of anyone else in the Academy who, as an insider, has been accepted by Protestants, Catholics, and Evangelicals at the highest level of scholarship. From your perspective, what caused you in your scholarship to move so easily between lines? That is still a rare gift within our Academy.

R. MURPHY: I think a basic knowledge of the ancient languages and modern foreign languages was a great help; then the ecumenical movement gathered steam from 1965 onward. I discovered that I could learn from my non-Catholic colleagues and be inspired by them.

R. JOHNSTON: Tell the group the story you told us last year at the dinner honoring David Hubbard. This had to do with the term "biblical commentary."

R. MURPHY: David Hubbard was President for twenty-five years at Fuller Theological Seminary where Rob [Johnston] is now. I had known David for many years. I wrote to him about my Ecclesiastes commentary which was going very slowly as far as publication was concerned. And I said to him, "David, only a brash Irishman would write such a letter as this, but when will you ever write your commentary on Ecclesiastes?" Now, he was editor of the *Word Biblical Commentary*, he was writing a commentary on Ecclesiastes, he was President of Fuller, and he was all over the United States on various activities. So I said to him, "When will you ever finish that commentary on Ecclesiastes?" Second paragraph: "I have a commentary to offer you!" So we met at the next meeting of the Society of Biblical Literature. He was pleased with my suggestion, but before I left, he said, "You should go down and look at the display on the *Word Biblical Commentary* and see whether or not the rationale of the *Word Biblical Commentary* really suits you." So I went down to the display and I read the rationale and I went back to David and said, "I am an evangelical too." He liked that!

R. JOHNSTON: You are still teaching.

R. MURPHY: One course a semester. This year I advertised the course as "Two Dangerous Books." The two dangerous books are Ecclesiastes and the Song of Songs. In Jewish and Christian tradition they had to be tamed. In the Christian tradition Jerome tamed Ecclesiastes—Vanity of vanities! All is vanity—with an ascetical interpretation. Jewish interpretation tamed it by making it Torah because of the last few verses of the book. And as for the Song of Songs, Jewish tradition in the Talmud interpreted it as a kind of history of Israel culminating in the messianic eschaton.

R. JOHNSTON: I recall the story of Jerome writing to a woman in Jerusalem, saying, "Yes, it's okay for your daughter to read the Song of Songs but only after she reads Kings and Chronicles three times."

R. MURPHY: Well, I'm all for Bible reading!

R. JOHNSTON: What do you enjoy most about teaching?

R. MURPHY: The idea of awakening persons to the value of the Bible as something to know and appropriate in their lives.

R. JOHNSTON: As a student I see you get charged up when you come into the room.

R. MURPHY: It's a question of believing in the book that I am teaching. Teaching the Word of God to people who are to be charged with preaching that Word–if anything would inspire you, that would.

R. JOHNSTON: You have had several outstanding graduate students. What have you learned from your students these years?

R. MURPHY: I have been lucky. My students have been so good that people think that the teacher of these students must be good! It is really your students who make you look good.

R. JOHNSTON: I would like to thank Roland for sharing with us tonight. Most of us have read his books, some of us have benefited from his teaching and friendship. You are welcome to come up now to greet Roland.

An Interview by the Catholic Biblical Association

Roland Murphy was interviewed by Carolyn Osiek, R.S.C.J., on May 8, 1995 at the University of St. Mary of the Lake, Mundelein, Illinois.

C. OSIEK: Today is May 8, 1995. This is an interview with Roland Murphy, O.Carm. We are in the seminary of Our Lady of the Lake in Chicago. Roland, you're on.

R. MURPHY: I went to Catholic University for college and theology. When I finished the provincial said, "You're going to study Scripture." I'd taken two years of Hebrew because I rather liked the language. I'd been inspired by Monsignor William Newton of Cleveland and then by Fr. Arbez who taught me second year Hebrew. So after a year in Chicago I came back to Catholic University and I received the S.T.D. which, at that time, had a major in theology. It was a somewhat inadequate program but, what made up for it, was a strong program in Semitics which eventually allured me into getting an M.A. in Semitics. By 1948, when I had finished, Monsignor Skehan asked me to enter the Semitics Department. I told him that I didn't think that was my strength. He said, "Let me be the judge of that." So I went into Semitics and developed a major in Christian Arabic. In 1950-51 the possibility of sending me overseas to the American School of Oriental Research to acquire some archaeological background for the good of the Department of Semitic Languages presented itself. I went there, took part in a couple of digs, and found out that I was not an archaeologist. But I had a whole year in Palestine which was a great advantage.

I returned in 1951 and started my research in Christian Arabic Literature until 1956 when there was a problem in the theology department regarding an Old Testament professor. The rector asked me if I would change over to theology. By this time Pat Skehan was in Jerusalem working on the [Dead Sea] Scrolls. I contacted Pat and he thought it would be a good idea. So I went over to theology and taught for a year. To become respectable, the university sent me to the Biblical Institute in 1957 where I acquired an S.S.L. [License in Sacred Scripture]. Then I came back and taught Scripture in the department of theology at Catholic University.

Now during that time *Divino Afflante Spiritu* [1943] had appeared but it took a long time for it to have an effect in the United States. Let me go back to the days when I taught Scripture, from 1945 on, at Whitefriars and then went into Semitics in '48, still teaching Old Testament at Whitefriars. The Biblical Commission statements were so carefully phrased: "Such and such doesn't prove that Isaiah was not the author." You could go along with statements like that. But it meant that you didn't take, for example, the Pentateuchal narratives and divisions of the JEPD [the four sources of the Pentateuch: Yahwist, Elohist, Priestly, and Deuteronomist] seriously. You just avoided questions of authorship because that's where most of the problems were.

The people I look back on are Arbez and Skehan, and Skehan inviting me to teach. You see, you had in the Semitic Department the ICOR, the Institute of Christian Oriental Research, founded by Hyvernat, one of the first faculty members. This is what Pat [Skehan] had given his life to. Since there were so were many new developments in Bible, he had to get into the biblical field.

In the late 1950's I was invited to Princeton University to take the place of R.B.Y. Scott, who was going on sabbatical. He had been in Jerusalem the year I was there. So, I took a leave of absence. The rector asked me, "Do you want me to write to the bishop of Trenton?" I said, "Alright. Do that." He received a letter back: "Under no condition is that young man to come to Princeton University." So I decided to write him a letter, a very polite letter in which I asked if I could come up and explain. I received a letter from him: it was not subject to discussion.

C. OSIEK: You never went to Princeton then?

R. MURPHY: I never went to Princeton. No. But after 1965...well, with the opening of Vatican II, the Council settled all that. The year 1964 saw the decrees on the formation of the New Testament. Then I was invited by Pittsburgh Theological Seminary to teach there. I did this for a year. It was a very interesting year, coming to know the Presbyterians in Pittsburgh. From there I went to Yale for a semester to teach for Brevard Childs as a visiting professor. In the meantime, Duke expressed an interest. So in '68 I went to Duke and taught in the college as a visiting professor and lived with students. I always kept my seat at the Catholic University and I returned there.

Then in 1968 came *Humanae Vitae*. In '68-'69 a judicial examination considered whether or not we had acted responsibly in our opposition—partial opposition—to the encyclical. Well it turned out that the committee of peers of the University said, yes, we had. So that was over. During that time I was elected dean of the School of Theology. The trustees would not approve. Normally this would have been simply automatic. They would not approve. Various people tried to take my side but to no avail. And so the school year began with no dean. The first lay president decided to have a search committee, and the search committee came up with three names including mine. He called us in separately. In December of '69 I said to him, "Well, it's no easier for you to support me now than it was last summer." He responded "No." And I said, "Fine, "I have no scars but, if I can't be dean, I shouldn't be allowed to teach. So, I'm going to resign in June." In the meantime, Duke got back on the line and said, "Would you consider coming to teach here?" "Yes," I said, "I'm out of a job." But, this wouldn't be until '71. Bernie Anderson was going on a sabbatical, so Princeton asked me to come as soon as I was free. So, in '70-'71 I was at Princeton Theological Seminary living on the grounds and teaching Bernie's introductory courses.

C. OSIEK: A different bishop I assume by this time.

R. MURPHY: He wasn't asked! But this was after the Council. All this was terribly exciting, illuminating, encouraging, and stirring. It was helpful for my own studies. Then at Duke I met very serious Methodists. Although I taught in the college, there were also graduate studies for Ph.D. candidates. That was a very valuable component.

C. OSIEK: Did you experience any inter-denominational tensions when you were teaching there? Your being a Catholic, did that make any difference?

R. MURPHY: No. It was really an illumination.

C. OSIEK: What was it like in the early years of the Catholic Biblical Association?

R. MURPHY: I didn't join until 1948. I felt I should have a doctorate before I'd enter that august group.

C. OSIEK: There were few who had doctorates at that point, right?

R. MURPHY: Most were from the Biblical Institute. And moreover, it had to be an ecclesiastical degree. One advantage [of the association] was that we read papers to each other. John McKenzie was there at the time, of course. He was always stimulating. We talked about teaching and established an *esprit de corps* that was very valuable for me.

The 1943 encyclical [*Divino Afflante Spiritu*] didn't take any effect until about 1950. We knew about the encyclical, but we didn't know what was going on. Gradually we became progressive. The importance of the Vatican II document *Dei Verbum* cannot be exaggerated. That saved us: the fact that it was changed and became a kind of pivot for the whole Council. That may be exaggerating a bit.

C. OSIEK: What have been the most significant changes in the Catholic Biblical Association?

R. MURPHY: Well, the most significant change is that trained scholars joined the society—that made all the difference— and wrote for the magazine [*the Catholic Biblical Quarterly*]. Today we should have more Catholic scholars writing for it but we don't. A good example of the growth in Catholic scholarship is discovered by comparing the scholars involved in the *JBC* [*The Jerome Biblical Commentary*] with those involved in the *NJBC* [*The New Jerome Biblical Commentary*]. The *JBC* was published in 1968 and the *NJBC* was published in 1990, a twenty year difference.

After twenty years we had a lot of horses to pick from, whereas in 1968 we used everyone.

The most significant change is the fact that there are more trained women, but that's been only in the last ten years, would you say?

C. OSIEK: Yes, I would say that. Which biblical scholars have been most influential?

R. MURPHY: Monsignor Newton, who was one of the first scholars of the Catholic Biblical Association, along with Arbez and Skehan. You know, here I was, an American and where were your best Catholic sources? They were in French—Lagrange and so on. In the past I had read German Catholic scholars, but I didn't read the German Protestants. So gradually, as the European Protestant scene opened up, and the whole ecumenical atmosphere grew, I became more open to other points of view.

C. OSIEK: In your graduate training was there no encouragement to read Protestants?

R. MURPHY: [laughs] No.

C. OSIEK: None whatsoever.

R. MURPHY: I don't know if there was any encouragement to read in theology. In Semitics it wasn't the same—you couldn't apply the same test. In Greek we had Marty Higgins. He was a Byzantine priest. I mean a priest, specialist in Byzantine history, but he taught Greek. He was an excellent teacher. But there wasn't an openness to Protestants; you didn't think of the Protestant scene when you were doing languages.

C. OSIEK: If you could do it all over again, what would you do differently?

R. MURPHY: I think I would do a Ph.D. in Semitic languages with an orientation toward the Bible. At the time when I wrote my dissertation (I did it on Psalm 72) I wanted to get rid of it and teach. I was naive. When I went into the university, I didn't know I was supposed to write articles for promotion. I had no idea what academic life was like. Probably a good thing.

C. OSIEK: You have a licentiate from the Pontifical Biblical Institute.

R. MURPHY: That was necessary to make myself respectable when I changed from the Semitics Department to the School of Theology. I had to go over to Rome. So I had one year there, and it was a lark.

C. OSIEK: Really?

R. MURPHY: I wrote papers. In the fine print it said you could write a paper instead of an exam. So I wrote papers and then published them.

C. OSIEK: That's not the general impression of the Biblicum, that it's a lark.

R. MURPHY: Well, I went over there after having taught Arabic, Syriac and Hebrew and having written articles. They really treated me well.

C. OSIEK: What is the future direction for Catholic biblical studies in North America?

R. MURPHY: Number one, I think we need more Catholics doing research. It occurred to me that we [the Catholic Biblical Association] provide money, a post doctoral program, but I think we should award money for people who write an important book in the field.

C. OSIEK: Now what else would you like to say?

R. MURPHY: Well, I guess I'm talked out. Do I have anything worthwhile to say after all this?

C. OSIEK: Any favorite stories?

R. MURPHY: Oh, faint memories. A famous story of mine, of course, is associated with Pat.

C. OSIEK: Pat Skehan?

R. MURPHY: Pat Skehan was invited by Albright to come and teach while Albright went off for a semester to Arabia to study inscriptions. So I asked him, "Hey, Pat, are you going to do it?" He said, "Yeah." He was very much a New Yorker. He said, "It's like being asked to pinch hit for Babe Ruth." Pat was a very humble man, very patient. I once asked him, "Why bother [to study Arabic and Syriac]?" He gave me a nifty answer: "Look, the Church has to have a memory, a memory of itself. All this work is to keep that memory alive." Wow, that was really a vision of faith that made a great impression on me. So I went ahead with studying Arabic.

C. OSIEK: Did you keep up your Arabic?

R. MURPHY: Not after a few years. I can still read it, but my vocabulary is weak. I didn't keep up with it.

C. OSIEK: That's a wonderful advantage to know Arabic; there aren't many biblical scholars who do.

R. MURPHY: No, no there aren't.

C. OSIEK: OK, anything else you want to say?

R. MURPHY: I can't think of anything else, Lyn. I've covered everything here.

PART III

REMEMBRANCES OF FRIEND, TEACHER, AND COLLEAGUE

In front of St. Peter's Basilica, Rome

Remembrances of Friend,
Teacher, and Colleague

The members of the Carmelite Order esteem Roland Murphy as a friend, as a teacher, and, indeed, as a Master of the Sacred Page. As part of the celebration of his eightieth birthday a few of his peers and students share their recollections of Roland.

Roland arrived in Chicago in 1944 fresh out of the seminary, ready for his first pastoral assignment as assistant in the Carmelite parish of St. Clara and teacher at nearby Mount Carmel High School. He had received the best seminary training that the Chicago province of Carmelites had been able to provide to this point in its history. His professional formation was to continue. After the interim year of "seasoning" he was slated for graduate studies in Scripture at Catholic University in Washington. He obtained the M.A. degree in Semitic languages and the S.T.D. in theology with a major in Scripture. This program prepared him well to be teacher, researcher, writer, and editor. Much of the reason for his success was the man himself. He took full advantage of every opportunity in academic training.

Roland had entered Mount Carmel Niagara as a high school freshman in 1931, the year Fr. Kevin Cahill became rector. He had taken the competitive scholarship examination for the seminary as only a seventh grader, and placed sixth in a field with five winners. His good showing led one of the priests in his Carmelite parish of St. Cyril's to encourage him to take the eighth grade exams immediately, and if he passed, to enter Niagara that fall. And so it was that the seventh grader entered Mount Carmel Niagara in September, 1931.

After high school and novitiate the next step was normally the three year college course at Mount Carmel Niagara. Roland, instead, was chosen as one of four in his class to do his college studies at Catholic University. This was a marvelous opportunity. His high school years had awakened Roland's intellectual appetite especially for languages and literature. The Catholic University college experience put him in touch with scholars like John Tracy Ellis, who fired his imagination and pointed him in the direction of an academic career. In summer school he took additional foreign languages instead of getting some required courses out of the way. Becoming multilingual was an invaluable asset for his future research and writing.

Before Roland reached his fourth year, the Province made the decision to move the theologate from Chicago to Washington, D.C. The first class, Roland's novitiate class, was to arrive in September, 1939. He had to return to Niagara for his final year of college to make room for the incoming theological students. This shift coincidentally placed him in the same class as his younger Carmelite brother David.

Whatever the disappointment for the collegians, the gain for the province was considerable. The theologate in Chicago had lacked the milieu and resources of a theological center that Catholic University and the surrounding religious seminaries now provided. In Chicago there were the distractions of part-time teaching in the high school and outside academic work at DePaul University. The opportunity to study theology full-time at a university, to have access to public lectures on campus, to meet scholars, and to mix with students from other seminaries offered a stimulating environment for doing theology. The move was definitely an advance in the Carmelite seminary system.

After his second year of theology at Catholic University, there was another interruption. The University withdrew its policy of reduced tuition for religious seminarians; the Carmelites countered by establishing their own independent faculty of theology at Whitefriars Hall. In the beginning religious of other local communities were engaged as teachers to augment the Carmelite faculty, which included Fr. Kilian Healy among others. Eventually the Province would train its own men, a necessity that was a blessing because it increased the number of trained Carmelite theologians.

Roland's sights on Scripture were set during the two years at Catholic University. He developed an intense interest in Scripture studies under the influence of one particular teacher, William L. Newton, S.S.D.; later his mentors would include Edward P. Arbez and Patrick W. Skehan, who were pioneers in the new approach to Scripture and models of painstaking and courageous scholarship. While at Catholic University Roland had taken a second year of Hebrew and continued to study the language at Whitefriars and in Chicago. When he returned to Catholic University for the S.T.D. in theology in 1945, he was ready to tackle Old Testament studies with a good grasp of the language.

The graduate studies took place between 1945 and 1948; his S.T.D. dissertation was on Psalm 72, and this concluded his formal studies. One could imagine an easier scenario with more continuity on the undergraduate level of college and seminary theology, followed immediately by Ph.D. studies in Semitics under a professor like William F. Albright at Johns Hopkins University or intensive biblical studies at Rome or Jerusalem. But then, Roland would have been less "homegrown," and his achievement less remarkable.

Coincident with the graduate studies Roland began his twenty-five year career as teacher of Scripture at Whitefriars Hall. This direct contact with a whole generation of Carmelite students was the single most important feature of his influence on the intellectual life of the Carmelites. His achievements and reputation outside the community as university professor, researcher, writer, and editor, gave him a high profile and were a source of pride and admiration among his Carmelite brethren. But the teaching put the man in living contact with the students, where he touched minds and hearts. Here students experienced his contagious enthusiasm for Scripture, his competence as a scholar, his rigorous honesty in both academic and practical matters, his high standards and expectations, and his undeviating commitment to truth. Roland was a giant: physically, mentally, and spiritually. In his religious life he followed the *strictior observantia* and taught by silent example rather than word.

Roland launched his public career in 1948, when he accepted an appointment on the faculty of the Semitic Department at his alma mater: his field was Christian Arabic literature. He remained in that department until 1956. At that time he transferred to the School of Theology as Scripture professor where he taught until 1970.

Through the fifties and sixties Roland was identified with Catholic University; it was the springboard for multiple workshops, lectures, and writing. His role as an editor of *Concilium* placed him on the international scene and involved him in projects inside and outside the Order. He became editor of the *Catholic Biblical Quarterly* in 1958. Roland excelled in networking with other scholars, knowing hundreds of them on a first-name basis and collaborating with them in various ways. He began his scholarly writing early, writing two interpretive articles on New Testament passages in his first year of teaching at the University. His prolific writings have continued to the present day and have been catalogued by admiring students (see my review of books that he wrote or edited between 1987 and 1995 in *The Sword* 55 (1995) 77-81).

A mutually beneficial relationship between Professor Roland Murphy and the Catholic University ended when he resigned in 1970 over a policy decision. After a visiting professorship at Princeton Theological Seminary, he accepted an appointment as a full-time professor at Duke University in 1971. Duke later awarded him the George Washington Ivey Chair of Biblical

Studies, which he occupied until his retirement in 1986. In previous years he had been visiting professor at Pittsburgh Theological, Yale Divinity, and Duke Divinity School, so that working with predominantly Protestant students, many of whom were preparing for the ministry, was not new to him. The opportunity was an enriching ecumenical experience for all concerned. Since retiring Roland has spent his time in writing and in part-time teaching at the Washington Theological Union.

What precisely did Roland contribute to the intellectual life of the Carmelite Order? As a genuine intellectual he inspired individuals both inside and outside the classroom and he raised consciousness and maintained high standards wherever he taught. His presence bore witness to intellectual integrity and gave added credibility to faculties where he served. His word was his bond. His recommendation of a teacher or speaker was warranty enough for most administrators. I received invitations to summer school teaching positions and to full-time employment as a professor at Catholic University on the strength of Roland's recommendations. Painfully honest in his evaluations he promoted his own generously but judiciously. Here as elsewhere he spoke the truth as he saw it, unambiguously and without dissimulation.

Roland was the apostle of higher education in the Province, encouraging those with aptitude and promise, mentoring those interested in biblical studies, and lobbying superiors for greater commitment in this area. For those already involved in studies he was their conscience in promoting research and writing. Publication for him was a sure way of growth and enhancement in the teaching profession.

I want to end this tribute with two vignettes that illustrate the ways in which he influenced Carmelites young and old. The first is a memory of Roland at sports. In the forties he played regularly in the athletic games at Whitefriars. Once the football or baseball game ended, however, he literally ran for the showers. He never wasted a minute. No matter how quickly we tried to get ready for the 3:00 p.m. study period, he would beat us to the desk.

His lamp would be burning brightly and reflecting in his window before the rest of us were quite organized. His discipline was not lost on us.

The second incident took place in October, 1995, at a meeting of Senior Carmelites. Roland brought to the floor a well-prepared statement calling the attention of the provincial council to the fact that the men involved in Carmelite studies were getting older and fewer in number. It was imperative that new people be assigned to studies in Carmelite history and spirituality, so that the momentum of recent years would continue. The motion received attention and immediate approval, largely because it came from Roland. He was the wisdom figure of this group, who spoke with authority both in his field of specialization and in the broader terrain of the Order's life. This great scholar did not forget his roots. Because he is a public authority and a faithful Carmelite, the Order has profited immensely by his life and work. He is gift in our midst.

Ernest Larkin, O.Carm.

The ordination class of 1948 that arrived at Whitefriars Hall in August of 1945 took their first Scripture classes from young Fr. Roland Murphy that September. I believe this was the beginning of his teaching career. He was twenty-eight years old, ordained for two and a half years, and was working on his degree at Catholic University. Tuition fees there had just been doubled, so the seminarians from both Carmelite provinces began to take their theology at "The Hall."

Those of us in first year didn't realize that our introduction to Scripture coincided with an extraordinary turning point in the history of Scripture studies. On Sept. 30, 1943, Pius XII promulgated *Divino Afflante Spiritu* which inaugurated a new day for Catholic biblical scholarship. The historical critical method was declared not only appropriate, but even necessary, and Catholic scholars were now free to explore all facets of scriptural inquiry. It was the dawning of an exciting era in scriptural studies. Thanks to Fr. Roland our class was the first to benefit from the changes that were emerging. Against this background I wish to share a few personal stories, my reflections of Roland as the person, the Carmelite, and the teacher he was in 1945.

Somehow I never quite got used to Roland's size. While teaching he would often relax his six foot four frame by resting his arm on top of the portable chalk board. He always stood tall and seemed to be looking at us from on high. I can still picture Roland's large hands, his long bony fingers balancing a Bible in one hand and a tome in some strange language in the other. He didn't seem to stand still much in class. Pacing back and forth, pausing now and then in serious thought, and occasionally leaning forward to make a point, there was gesticulating, grimacing, frowning, smiling, and in general an energetic movement that riveted our attention to the matter at hand. Laughter came easily and often. His energy and enthusiasm was matched only by his devotion to the Scriptures. Even after 50 years some incidents stand out. One year he assigned the entire Pentateuch over the Christmas holidays. We were to read it, study it, and be prepared for an exam when the new year started. He always seemed to assume I had more time to study than I did.

Early that first year we learned a valuable lesson. Roland was going to great lengths to introduce the Patriarchs. He began by trying to "date Abraham." As he presented more and more tentative and speculative material he kept using the phrases: "If you want to date Abraham...," "To date Abraham...," and so forth. Well, to us, the thought of dating Abraham, as he had been dead for centuries, seemed a bit humorous. We started to grin and even giggle a bit. Suddenly Roland bellowed, "What's so funny?" We meekly tried to explain why we reacted the way we did fearing that he would grab a desk and use it to wipe us out like Samson did with the jawbone of the ass.

Another incident a few years later has become part of Carmelite lore from those days at the Hall. Roland was mapping out the journeys of Paul and had come to a rather sticky part. We were to decide whether Paul had taken the northern route or southern route on the next leg of his journey. There was much discussion, lots of pros and cons. The atmosphere was really intense. Then right at the critical moment, while there was a brief lull, Leon 'Chum' Battle, who was sitting up in the front row, said aloud, "It's clear, Rollie, he took the southern route." Roland stopped, came over to Chum, leaned down and asked, "How do you figure that, Chum?" Leon explained, "It's clear. He went by the southern route. Listen to the way he begins his next epistle, 'Greetings to y'all'." The class exploded with laughter. Roland went into momentary shock, totally stunned, but eventually he regained enough poise to continue the rest of the lesson.

I had great admiration for Roland's tremendous mental self-discipline. He could play a rough game of touch football and minutes after the game be showered and at his desk absorbed in serious study. Sometimes we would take on a team from another seminary. One game stands out in my memory. Always a fierce competitor, and, of course, a good basketball player, Rollie had agreed to play for the Carmelite 'frats' against our arch rivals from Holy Cross. When the O.Carms met 'the Cross,' both sides brought only the best they could find. On this particular day Fr. Ed Joyce, future vice president of Notre Dame University, had suited up for Holy Cross. As I recall, we played in Catholic University Gym. The game was marked by so much pushing, shoving, and hacking that it had to be cut short before there was serious injury. Rollie was in the thick of the fray.

Those days were full of contrasts. For example, after just such a strenuous game, Roland would be our most popular confessor as we lined up for our weekly confessions. There, the sweaty giant we were so proud of would be our Father Confessor. He was patient, calm, understanding, full of encouragement, and able to give sound spiritual guidance.

Rollie, before I close, let me give one quick glance back to that first course in the Old Testament fifty years ago. Yes, numerous biblical passages still nourish me to this day. Among these I list 1 Kings 19:12 where Elijah experiences the Lord's presence in the gentle breeze. Perhaps it was because of the Carmelite connection, or because of your zeal in passing on the motto: "With Zeal am I Zealous..." that the passage has remained part of my prayer. Then there is Ezekiel's vision of the dry bones in chapter 37. It was you who first opened up my heart to the deep meaning of that exciting story. I can recreate this story and tell it dramatically: "Now hear the word of the Lord!" has become a mantra for me. It is the theme for my closing talk when I preach a mission. I am proud to say that, after forty-seven years in the pulpit I still base my preaching on the Word of the Lord.

So, Roland, I offer these thoughts from your first class 50 years ago. I hope I have stirred up a few memories from my generation of Carmelites. None of that first class ever became Scripture scholars, but I hope that each of us has, in our own way, made you proud. You can look back with satisfaction and be pleased with the results of your earliest teaching efforts. We do! *Ad multos annos.*

Myles Colgan, O.Carm.

The Psalms, Roland's favorite book of the Hebrew Scriptures, tell us: "Seventy are the sum of our years, or eighty, if we are strong" (Ps 90:10). Roland is among the strong.

Having known him for over sixty years, and having lived together in community many of our younger years, I ask myself: Who were some of the people who played an important part in shaping and developing his scholarly life? I do not pretend to know all of them or even the most important. I mention some whom I know from personal experience: his mother, his scholarly friends, and his Carmelite community.

His mother. Throughout his life Roland has been known for his exuberant energy. During his academic career at Duke University I recall asking him, "Where do you get all the energy?" He answered, "From my mother." Anyone who knew his mother knows that all her life she was a person of astonishing ability. Even in her Golden Years Mrs. Marian Murphy, the beloved wife of John Murphy, was still working for the Church and the Carmelites. It was from his mother, Roland tells us, that he received the energy that for over sixty years has served him well in biblical studies as student, teacher, lecturer, workshop presenter, and author. Energy has been his trademark.

His scholarly friends. Many scholars have had an impact on Roland's career. I would not presume to single out the most influential. However, on various occasions I heard him speak of his teachers at Catholic University. He had great admiration and respect for Monsignor William Newton, a Semitic languages and Old Testament professor. Monsignor Patrick Skehan, another Semitic languages and biblical scholar, offered great encouragement to Roland. After Roland defended brilliantly his doctoral dissertation, a study of Psalm 72, which I witnessed as a guest, he joined the faculty at Catholic University. In the years following, his friendship with Monsignor Skehan deepened. Only Roland can tell us of the profound impact this outstanding priest and scholar had on his personal and scholarly life.

Although I was only a spectator of the Catholic biblical movement that enriched the Church in the middle of this century, Roland's enthusiasm kept me informed. Together we visited the highly esteemed scholars, Bruce Vawter, C. M., in Rome, and H. H. Rowley, a British Old Testament scholar in London. He would often refer to his friends at the Biblical Institute in Rome, especially Fr. Roderick MacKenzie, S.J. Through correspondence I also knew of his high esteem for Fr. Raymond Brown, S.S., and Fr. Joseph Fitzmyer, S.J. Among those who played a significant role in Roland's scholarly career, and I have mentioned only those known to me, was Monsignor John Tracy Ellis, professor of Church History at the Catholic University. Their friendship began, I believe, when Roland was a seminarian. John Tracy Ellis preached the homily at Roland's first Mass in Chicago in May 1942. Their friendship blossomed through the years while they both were on the faculty of the University, and afterwards when they taught at different schools. During the last days of Monsignor Ellis, when he was confined to a nursing home in Washington, D.C., Roland visited him frequently. He would sit at his bedside and read the Psalms, both of them pondering the Word of God in their hearts. The Psalter was their prayer book.

His Carmelite Community. It is the liturgical life of the community, the daily recitation of the liturgy of the Hours, and the celebration of the Eucharist that plays an important part in Roland's life. The Word of God which he studies each day and proclaims in the classroom has became the soul of his prayerful life. In this he is faithful to the Carmelite Rule that exhorts its members: "Each one of you is to stay in his own cell or nearby, pondering the Lord's law day and night and keeping watch at his prayers unless attending to some other duty" (ch. 7). "The sword of the spirit, the Word of God, must abound in your mouths and hearts. Let all you do have the Lord's Word for accompaniment" (ch. 14).

It has been a grace to know Roland over sixty years and to have had the pleasure of living in community with him. I cannot begin to count the many benefits of our friendship, in particular, the reverence he taught me, unknown to him, for the written Word of God. I learned from him to take up the Scriptures, especially the Psalms, with a "listening heart." May the Lord grant him many more years to proclaim the Word of God.

Kilian Healy, O.Carm.

For how many people has Roland Murphy been an unforgettable teacher? My own recollections date from the early years of his teaching Scripture at Whitefriars Hall, 1949 to 1953. One of those years he spent in Palestine, and in the postcards he wrote to us he related his joy to be studying the Word of God at the very site of Jesus' lifework.

Roland livened his classes by dramatizing the biblical stories and by taking on the different personages. He was the first in my experience to use the term "Yahweh" for God. It wasn't long before the students pinned on him, outside of class of course, the very title he used for God, "Yahweh."

When Roland taught the prophets, he could play the prophet as he resoundingly condemned the kings of Israel and Judah, echoing the judgment of Yahweh. He paced back and forth with those giant strides that his six foot four frame permitted. More than once he had to grab the toppling blackboard as he went on his pursuit of God in history. We left class breathless from his physical and psychic energy.

I recall his treatment of Wisdom, the Song of Songs, Ben Sirach, and Ecclesiastes. He delighted in the concrete imagery of wisdom literature: "As a door turns on its hinges, so does the sluggard in his bed" (Prov 26:14). He'd scrutinize the room as if looking for an example in class.

As I read his recent book on the Psalms, I realized how far the studies in his own field had advanced. I admire his flexibility in handling authors with whom he disagrees. He repeats their thought in a way, it seems to me, that situates his own opinion as one among equals. He labors so that the dialogue with God's Word continues.

I have engaged Roland in an on-going, albeit intermittent, dialogue regarding the use of Scripture among Latin American theologians of liberation such as Carlos Mesters, O.Carm. It has been exciting for me to see in recent decades the convergence of American and European Scripture studies with Latin American theology, one coming more from scientific research and the other from the faith-practice of a people living the drama of oppression, persecution, torture, and martyrdom.

I always dreamed of hiking around the Holy Land with Roland as a guide and interpreter. His enthusiasm is contagious. He wouldn't need to take the Bible along, since he knows it by heart. Somehow we have traveled the land of Israel together, even though these feet have never trod that soil. There but remains a short time for us to walk together through the land where the Word-Spirit is moving in the holy people and places of El Salvador.

Peter C. Hinde, O.Carm.

"Ha!"

The sound comes from the depths of the man. Sometimes it says, "Aren't we foolish to underestimate the power and wonder of God?" Sometimes it says, "Oh, you missed the point entirely." And sometimes it says, "You understand the deeper meaning, good for you." But, it is a constant, sounding forth almost daily, or at least daily when classes are in session. One begins to wonder: Does Roland say "Ha!" when, alone in his room studying the Scriptures, he comes to a deeper understanding of the Word of God?

We arrived at Whitefriars Hall in the summer of 1960. There we heard many stories about Roland and his love of Scripture and study. During the hot summer months we would hook the doors of our rooms and closets together to allow a bit of cross ventilation into the rooms. Roland would walk the corridor and peer over the doors to make sure we were studying. He was our prior.

It is told that during a meeting with one of the students, Roland's phone rang. On his way to answer the phone, he looked quickly around the room, then, grabbing a Bible (what else!), gave it to the student with the injunction: "Here, read!" Many of his students from the early 60's remember the final exam in which for the first hour they were told to outline Salvation History from the Garden to candles glowing in the Temple after the Maccabeean revolt. During the second hour of the exam they were to fill in the outline!

Still, not too many years ago a Carmelite in the Jersey Valley offered a course to his parish on the Psalms. When asked what book he was using for the course, he responded, "Oh, I use Roland's work on the Psalms; it is not necessary to look any further."

The neuroscientist, Eric R. Kandel, in his article in the *LIFE* issue of *The Living Pulpit*, wrote, "a newborn infant is extremely vulnerable and cannot grow into a normal adult...without nourishment for the brain, which comes only with continuing social interaction with caring human beings." We were infants in the study of Scripture when we arrived at Whitefriars Hall in 1960; most people in the Church were in that same boat in those days. But, we were lucky. At Whitefriars Hall we came into contact with Christian Ceroke and Roland Murphy. We were helped to grow into an adult relationship with the Scriptures through the nourishment and stimulation for our brains, which came from continuing interaction with caring human beings. Roland loved his subject matter and loved to share his knowledge of the Scriptures with all comers, and he knew how to say "Ha!" with enthusiasm.

Simon Kenny, O.Carm.

On April 28, 1996, I was privileged to preside over the inaugural initiation of a chapter of Kappa Delta Pi, the International Education Society, in the School of Education at Loyola Marymount University. One of the highlights of this meeting was the address given by our President, Thomas O'Malley, S.J. One specific point he made stuck with me as I reflected on this paper for Roland Murphy, a teacher and scholar. Fr. O'Malley spoke of the importance of teaching and learning in our lives. Great teachers have stamped us indelibly, not for a semester, not for a year, not for a specific course but for all of our lives. Research surveys tell us only 10% of our teachers are considered memorable or excellent. However, Fr. O'Malley continued, our memory is fallacious. What we remember is very often not the way it really was. So we think that some teachers were truly great because we recall what they said. In fact, for the great teachers, we have assimilated that learning so completely, that the teacher lives in what they learned. For that teacher, for that scholar, for that mentor, we have one responsibility: Say thank you! In this essay I say thank you to Roland Murphy, a teacher, a scholar, and a true mentor for hundreds of Carmelites over the past fifty years.

When I left Whitefriars in 1960 to begin a teaching career at Crespi Carmelite High School (rather ill-prepared I might add), I took with me the models of excellent teachers I had experienced through the thirteen years in the seminary. Most of us in those years were destined to teach at Crespi, at Mount Carmel in Chicago or Los Angeles, at Joliet Catholic, or at Salpointe. We went forth with very little training to teach religion, English, Latin, biology and so on. All we had were some models to look back on and to emulate in whatever way we could. For me, a certain few jump out: Jude Cattelona in math, Malachy Smith in history, Philotheus Boener, a Franciscan philosopher teaching biology at St. Bonaventure's during the summer, Chris Ceroke in New Testament and, above all, Roland Murphy in Old Testament. I believe the list for every Carmelite who went through the seminary system would vary considerably (remember memory is fallacious). However, I do believe Roland would make most lists.

I taught high school math, religion, Latin and science for twelve years, and have taught at the university level for twenty years. However, neither of these accomplishments necessarily qualify me to write about excellence in teaching and scholarship. Rather, I will try to incorporate some of the research on teaching excellence with personal reflections from a few Carmelites who experienced Roland in the classroom at Whitefriars.

Joseph Lowman in his excellent book, *Mastering the Techniques of Teaching*, speaks of the qualities that a university professor must possess. Interestingly, he points out that our own natural instincts to portray the masterful teacher often give pictures of the awe-inspiring scholar lecturing to a massive group of students. Or we might picture the warm, very approachable, gentle professor discussing issues of great concern with a seminar group of ten or twelve. Or we may even portray the masterful teacher as the likable Mr. Chips type, meeting with two or three students in his cluttered and messy office. Note right away these images of great teachers are always *with students*. Never do we think of the excellent teacher spending hours and hours in isolation, in reading, in preparing and planning, in reflecting on the best ways for knowledge to come alive for students. Nor do we think of the masterful teacher presenting to colleagues at a conference, completing research, publishing new journal articles or books. Yet both aspects, both pictures—the one that comes easily to mind and the one that comes less easily—define a truly excellent instructor who is both teacher and scholar. As John Russell wrote me:

> I met Roland when I went to study in Rome in 1957. Roland was in Rome to obtain an S.S.L. In that year I came to understand the cost of serious scholarship. One must be willing to submit to six to eight hours a day of study, research and writing. Roland never took a siesta after the mid-day meal. Years later when I observed the many hours each day that professional tennis players give to their conditioning and skills, I was reminded of Roland's dedication. You simply cannot be expert in your field unless you spend many hours each day in a regimen of self-discipline.

On the other hand, if we asked randomly a hundred people, who had attended college, for the qualities of the excellent teacher, we would no doubt get characteristics like these:

Enthusiastic
Well prepared, well organized
Good ability to stimulate and motivate
Knows (and has a passion for) the subject matter

Having all four of these characteristics probably applies to only 10% of university or graduate professors. Do they apply to Roland? I think so. Robert Colaresi remembers Roland's enthusiasm in this way:

His classes were like theophanies—there was power and energy, thunder storms of outbursts, lightning bolts of insights—and Yahweh himself, standing tall before us, booming divine insights and commandment expectations: study, learn, embrace, chew on it and eat it! The classroom was Sinai, and we shivered in fear, hoping to grasp the verbal manna dropping from his lips.

Ben Hogan adds:

Roland's classes were scintillating because of his energy, enthusiasm and conviction. The Medium was the Message. One day, gesturing dramatically, he put his fist through the ceiling.

That's enthusiastic!

Few would argue that Roland was not always totally prepared and organized. It was our job to be the same. Not a minute of class was ever wasted. His exams stressed his preparedness, his organization. We had to know everything. In fact, we often had to give him back everything. As Ben put it so well:

His exams were horrible—he asked for *everything*.
I remember getting ready for my first final, making
what I thought was the supreme effort by translating footnotes from the Jerusalem Bible, then available in French only. I got a "C" and decided I would
never be a Scripture scholar.

Vernon Malley remembers the event a little more facetiously:

In 1956-57, after we completed the survey course
on the Jewish Scriptures, one of Roland's final
exam questions was: outline the history and events
covered by the Old Testament, beginning with
creation—in fifty words or less. (Or, at least, so it
seemed...)

I too remember that exam. Coming from a mathematical
approach, I had outlined the history, the dates, the persons, the
events, all in one gigantic sheet of paper. I figured I could answer
any question and fit it into this massive outline. As it turned out,
he asked for the entire outline. The memorized outline allowed me
to write up *everything* rather easily, though not in fifty words or
less.

Roland's ability to stimulate and motivate was beyond
comparison in terms of teachers I had before and after. Granted,
part of the motivation was based on fear, but who of us has not
used that weapon sometime in our teaching career. Who of us has
not told students that passing the next exam will go a long way in
determining the grade for the semester. Learn it, you pass; do not
learn it, you will fail. But Roland's own commitment and dedication to his subject were the major motivators for his students. As
Maslow would say, certainly our deficiency needs were pretty well
met. We were ready to be motivated by intellectual curiosity, by
interest in understanding the wisdom and Word of God in the Old
Testament. I think Ben put it well:

I do not think I am exaggerating when I say that every young Carmelite dearly hoped to be like Roland Murphy as priests. He was the complete man, the Renaissance Man. He embodied all the virtues of the Carmelites we learned about, from the University of Paris in the Middle Ages to Vatican II. He is the Carmelite who would be at home with St. Jerome, Karl Rahner, and Pope John XXIII.

Lastly, in the survey view of excellent teaching, we think of the teacher "knowing the subject matter" and "having a passion for it." If any characteristic fits Roland to perfection in describing "the excellent or masterful teacher," we have found it here. His research, his publications, the respect of his colleagues world-wide, all point to his passion for the Old Testament and his knowledge of it. In all the Jesuit Universities I have visited over these past twenty years, the one Carmelite everyone knew and respected was Roland Murphy. He made Scripture come alive in the Church. Bob Colaresi put it best:

Roland demanded (he did not ask) the best—the best from himself, and the best from us as his students. He had a grand passion for learning and an incredible zeal that we learn—and learn to love the Bible, especially the Hebrew Scriptures and Wisdom Literature, as he did. He wanted us to get passionately involved with God's Word, so that we could understand and serve the Church. It was almost as if he were personally hurt if we did not love and embrace the Hebrew Scriptures as he did—so much did he seem to identify with Yahweh!

In his book, *Masters: Portraits of Great Teachers*, Joseph Epstein summarizes well the Roland Murphy that we all remember:

> What all the great teachers appear to have in common is love of their subject, an obvious satisfaction in arousing in their students, and an ability to convince them that what they are being taught is deadly serious.

Returning to Lowman, he reduces all the characteristics of the masterful teacher to a two dimensional model where the quality of instruction results from a professor's skill at "creating both intellectual excitement and positive rapport in students, the kinds of emotions and relationships that motivate them to do their best work."

The first characteristic of creating intellectual excitement has already been addressed. The second, creating positive rapport in students, is slightly different and perhaps a characteristic we do not always relate to the excellent teacher. Yet for motivation, for long term learning, for a life-commitment to the knowledge imparted, I do believe it is essential in the great teacher. I quoted Fr. O'Malley in the beginning of this essay as saying that, when we have assimilated the learning so completely to ourselves, the teacher lives in the thing learned. This was Roland's way. He, as well as knowledge and passion, would live on in his Carmelite students. As Tom Batsis wrote me, Roland's rapport started very early with students:

> What I remember most about Roland was the first time I met him. We frats had all arrived back from Camp Maria and were settling in for the school year. One day as I was sitting in my room I heard someone with a rather loud, booming voice making his way down the corridor, stopping at each door to greet the occupant. Finally he made it to my

door and I met Roland for the first time. He made
a serious effort to get to know each of us. And of
course there is no forgetting the laughter that filled
the third floor that afternoon.

Ben Hogan wrote me that on his return to Whitefriars
some forty years after his first arrival, Roland greeted him with
"Ben, welcome! We are delighted you will be here with us." Bob
Colaresi too remembers Roland when he and his classmates were
at Whitefriars in the mid 60's: "When we were students in
formation, he always had time when we had a question (about the
Bible or otherwise) or a concern. Roland stopped what he was
doing—he attended well—he listened intently and gave solid wise
advice. He had that human respect which is life-giving, and we
knew he was a natural for Wisdom literature."

Since the Hall, I have not lived near Roland except a few
summers at Notre Dame University while I was completing my
master's degree and he was teaching summer school. We saw a
little more of the human side of him there: his love for the
outdoors, for the cottage at Long Beach, for just relaxing and
exercising his great sense of humor. Roy Conry wrote me that he
had spent much time with Roland in those summers and always
remembered that he was first in line, after the last bell on Friday
afternoon, to head to the lake. No matter how cold and cloudy the
day, he would immediately head down to the beach, and pacing
back and forth, he would read the Psalms, looking up occasionally
to see if the sun were breaking through.

According to Lowman, outstanding instructors are those
who excel in both these dimensions of teaching effectiveness:
creating intellectual excitement and positive rapport in students.
From what we have discussed thus far I think Roland more than
qualifies as a masterful teacher.

Roland's work as a scholar fits well with the recent (1991)
special report of Ernest Boyer for the Carnegie Foundation for the
Advancement of Teaching. Boyer, recently deceased, was an
impressive leader in higher education for many years. At Loyola

Marymount we are proud that he began his university teaching career with us. His work, *Scholarship Reconsidered, Priorities of the Professoriate*, has been an influential document in higher education these past five years. Very briefly, Boyer advocates for our present day that the work of the professoriate might be thought of as having four separate, but overlapping, functions. These would be scholarship of *discovery*, the scholarship of *integration*, the scholarship of *application*, and the scholarship of *teaching*. Reading Boyer's explanations of the various types of scholarship, they all fit Roland well—and have for fifty years.

Roland's most obvious commitment was to the scholarship of *discovery*. This involves traditional scholarship, normally what is meant when we speak of "research." This scholarship is the commitment to knowledge for its own sake, the commitment to follow, in a disciplined way, an investigation wherever it may lead. Roland and his fellow Scripture scholars through the 50's, 60's, 70's and 80's paved new frontiers in the pursuit of the meaning of God's Word in the Scriptures. This scholarship contributes not only to the wealth of human knowledge but also to the intellectual climate of an institution. So Whitefriars, with its faculty of scholars, brought "the frats" along, sometimes willingly, sometimes not so willingly. But we all learned it is a wonderful endeavor, even if it was not totally for us.

By the scholarship of *integration*, Boyer points out the need for scholars to give meaning to isolated ideas, facts, and issues, putting them in perspective with the rest of one's studies. In this research, the scholar begins to ask "what do the findings mean?" Is it possible to interpret what has been discovered in ways that provide a larger, more comprehensive understanding? I believe our Old Testament courses were constantly geared to this commitment. Making the Wisdom literature come alive was only part of the message. Making the Old Testament a lead-in, so to speak, to the New Testament gave more meaning and more understanding to the gospel message. Even moral theology, dogmatic theology, and canon law had their roots in the classes and discussions of the Old Testament. Integration was the heart of studying God's Word in the Old Testament.

Likewise, the third element of Boyer's *Scholarship Reconsidered*, the Scholarship of *Application*, was essential to Roland's teaching career at Whitefriars. Clearly here, Roland was helping to prepare future priests to go out into schools and parishes to preach and teach the Word of God. Understanding the Scriptures enabled Carmelites to be recognized in every area of the country as marvelous preachers and teachers. What we learned of Roland's massive scholarship of discovery and integration, we were able to carry into our communities and apply it.

Lastly, Roland's scholarship of *teaching* certainly was a high priority. To consider teaching as a scholarly activity, Boyer says we must realize that teaching begins with what the teacher knows. This type of scholarship both educates and entices future scholars. We may think of Aristotle's statement that "teaching is the highest form of understanding." I believe for all of us Carmelites over the years, Roland's teaching held a very high priority in his life. He loves research, he loves Bible, he is passionately committed to sharing his knowledge in print and at conferences, but most of all, I believe, he loves sharing his knowledge in the classroom, educating and enticing future priests to be scholars in their own way.

Even though these ideas of Ernest Boyer are fairly new, I believe Roland has been living all four elements of scholarship for many years. As I look back on my four years at Whitefriars, as I listen and read the comments of other Carmelites who passed through Whitefriars, there is no doubt that Roland's scholarship included discovery, integration, application and teaching. And for us, his students, the benefits were immeasurable. We had ourselves a model, a mentor, a colleague, a fellow Carmelite who would always be there to advise, to council, to encourage, and to entice.

I would like to end with one last personal note. Over the years, I have always felt close to both Roland and his brother, Dave. Roland helped inspire me to go on in higher education, to receive my doctorate and to work in a university. Dave, on the other hand, made all of it possible, first by naming me principal of Crespi in 1966 and by allowing me to begin the pursuit of a doctorate at the University of Southern California shortly afterwards. To them both I say thank you very much. I am most grateful to them and to their inspiration, dating all the way back to being fellow graduates of St. Cyril's elementary school on Chicago's South Side.

Al Koppes, O.Carm.

It was in 1954 or 1955, I don't remember the exact year, that I was sent to Rome from Brazil to study Philosophy. I asked permission not to study Hebrew because I thought that I would not need it for philosophical studies. But, after some time, a request came from the new Provincial asking me to study Sacred Scripture. By then I had already missed the first few weeks of the Hebrew course.

Roland Murphy had just arrived in Rome to do his doctoral thesis. There was a rumor among the students that he was an expert in Semitic languages. So I and Brocardo Ribera, from the Province of Catalonia, went to ask if it were possible for him to give us a course in Hebrew. (Both of us were planning to continue with biblical studies after priestly ordination.) Fr. Roland accepted, but he made it clear that he was quite busy. He agreed to give the Hebrew classes twice a week immediately after lunch on the roof terrace of the house. And so it was, twice a week, during his siesta time, in cool or warm weather, Roland, Brocardo Ribera, and I used to walk on the terrace at Sant'Alberto under the shadow of the dome of St. Peter's. As we paced we chanted Hebrew words and phrases. I am indebted very much to Roland's kindness; he gave up his siesta so that two younger confreres, who, at the time, were unknown to him, might improve their Hebrew. He has remained interested in the progress of our studies.

During the 60's, when I was back in Brazil, Roland was invited to speak at one of the universities in South Africa. On his trip he stopped in Brazil and stayed a week with us in Rio de Janeiro. I picked him up at the airport and spent a few days with him. We walked along the beaches and through the streets of Rio de Janeiro talking about the Bible and biblical studies. He read the notes I had prepared for my classes and commented on them. One day we took a bus to Angra dos Reis, a city near Rio de Janeiro, where the Carmelites have had a monastery for 400 years. We walked through the small streets of this city and discussed the poverty in which the people lived. We also discussed how to bring the Bible to the poor. I remember that as Roland looked upon this poverty he commented, "The Bible must be a light to this people. Certainly, it is not the scientific exegesis that we do in universities that can bring this light. Keep searching because I do not have the answer to this question!"

Carlos Mesters, O.Carm.

When I was first approached about contributing to this *Festschrift*, my reaction was one of considerable puzzlement. Surely this would be a project for heavyweights. However, after a bit of deliberation and discussion, a feeling emerged that some trivia may also be in order to put a human face on one recognized as a legend in biblical studies. These recollections surely differ from those of other contributors. Not to worry, that is a recognized problem of exegesis: finding the *ipsissima verba* or analyzing the *sitz im leben* of any tale in which the memories of times past vary from person to person and are dimmed with the passage of years. Whether told by a Parson Weems or a reputable historian such as

Roland's close friend, John Tracy Ellis, the story is often worth the telling without regard to accuracy of date and place.

Whether it was at the Jersey Shore, Wautoma in Wisconsin, or Long Beach in Indiana, when the world was much younger, several Carmelites were on vacation with Rollie. Already he had a routine. After early Mass and breakfast, the budding scholar lathered his fair Irish skin with appropriate sun lotion; when he gave special attention to his nose with a liberal dose of zinc ointment, he instantly became "Wax Nose" after a Dick Tracy villain of the time. He would launch a row boat into the deep, ship the oars, lie down in the boat and float wherever the wind took him. Then, for what seemed hours, Roland diligently pored over a much-thumbed Hebrew text. When his companions were moved by hunger, one of them would blow a whistle. Whereupon the boatman popped up and vigorously rowed ashore. After hamburgers and hot dogs, the whole tribe would descend on the local golf course for 18, 27, or 36 holes of duffer play. We never knew which Big Ed (Roland) loved the most, the boat ride with the book, the lunch, or the golf. They were all done with his unique zest.

There was the time, not too long after ordination, when Roland was at what is today an inner city parish. The pastor, a good humored veteran of parish life, was much given to practical jokes. The neophyte priest was fair game. Called to the front office one afternoon, Roland found a young woman on the verge of hysteria with a woeful tale of soap opera magnitude. Things became so emotional and complicated as her story unfolded that Roland excused himself to seek advice from his elders. The lady in distress was an actress put to this task by the pastor, and, as Roland was outside getting counsel, the woman was simultaneously being briefed on what he would propose. How long this went on depends on the narrator, but finally a much relieved young priest was happy to go back to real life with the Psalms and to the uncertainties of interpreting Wisdom literature.

In seminary days at Catholic University basketball and touch football were not especially gentlemanly pursuits. Aided and abetted by moral theologians and spiritual guides, who believed that vigorous contact sports significantly decreased libido, seminarians used to look forward to the games played between different religious communities. At one football game, the two ends from Whitefriars were directed to cross over the middle, one five yards deeper than the other. Unfortunately, when the pass was thrown, the two receivers were on the same track, and the ball, Roland and Scotty McCulloch met in their own version of the Big Bang. After a brief time-out, in which it was determined that the participants could still name the books of the Pentateuch, action resumed. There were "giants" in those days.

In more recent years, while serving as Director of Judeo-Catholic Relations in the Diocese of Venice, Florida, I invited Roland for a day with the local American Jewish Committee. The main event was his talk entitled, "Jews and Catholics Read the Bible Together." As usual, it was style and substance with wild gesticulation, sonorous tones, and the Charleton Heston Mosaic presence that amazed the audience. Afterwards there were questions. The first of these could have been interpreted as mildly hostile. Grinning broadly while balancing the Hebrew text in one hand, Roland expressed his delight at a good question. With extensive quotations in the original language, he proceeded to respond with a disarming gentleness that drew a spontaneous round of applause.

Ordained in 1942, Roland has lived through one of the most change-filled epochs in the history of the church. Beginning in his own field with the about-face of *Divino Afflante Spiritu*, he experienced the window opening of Pope John XXIII, the hope-filled tensions of Paul VI, the shattered expectations of John Paul I, and the return to a traditional ecclesiology of John Paul II. He was there for the interplay between subsidiarity and centralized authority, collegiality and infallibility, and clericalism and a more Catholic vision where women, men, religious and clergy strive to identify and claim their own roles.

In such turbulent times certain individuals are vulnerable as turned out to be the case for Roland. Without rehashing old stories, we can stand in solidarity with him. In a healthy pluralism, not all Carmelites are cast in the same mold, nor are all his friends and colleagues. But despite nuances of disagreement or even broader ecclesiological differences, the church has always held Roland's deepest loyalty. May the peace and understanding that Roland has given to his students and his friends return and remain with him at least twice as long as the Lord will remember his covenants.

Joel Schevers, O.Carm.

After skipping eighth grade at St. Cyril Grammar School in Chicago, Edmund Murphy, together with a group of aspiring seminarians, journeyed by train to Mt. Carmel College, the Carmelite Seminary located in Niagara Falls, Ontario. After an all night ride in a coach car, the boys arrived at Falls View where, for the first time, they viewed the magnificent grandeur of Niagara Falls. The sun was shining that early morning in September, 1930, as they walked the short distance to the Seminary.

The freshman class to which Edmund belonged was composed of some 50 boys, most of whom were from Chicago, Pittsburgh, and New Jersey. The newly appointed seminary rector was Fr. Kevin Cahill. The classes began at once with two periods each day devoted to the study of Latin. Although there was a number of bright students in the class, Edmund (now known as "Ed," "Eddie," or just "Murph") stood out, since invariably he received a mark of 100 on the daily vocabulary test. Thus began his career in foreign languages which eventually would lead to his mastery of Latin, Greek, Hebrew, German, French, Italian, Spanish, Aramaic, Syriac, Akkadian, Arabic, and Ugaritic.

During his high school years Ed distinguished himself in various sports, especially in basketball, where his height aided his natural ability. During the summer vacations at home in Chicago, I recall playing tennis with him in Jackson Park and swimming in Mt. Carmel High's ice-cold pool with a bit of boxing at poolside to warm up between plunges in the pool. Afterwards, we walked down the block to Ed's house, where Mrs. Murphy's home-made cake was always available.

After high school came the novitiate year at Niagara with Fr. Leo Walter as our Novice Master. Shortly after profession on August 15, 1935, five of the newly professed were sent to Washington to begin their college education at nearby Catholic University. The Carmelite students already at the University had acquired a fine reputation as scholars. The new arrivals were expected to maintain this tradition; Joachim Smet, Romaeus O'Brien, and Roland Murphy (Roland is Ed's religious name) did very well.

The first year European History course was taught by Fr. John Tracy Ellis who recognized Roland's talent and encouraged him in his study. Out of that relationship between teacher and student, developed a strong, life-long friendship.

One memory from those years may help to explain how Frater Roland developed his unique teaching style. I had developed a serious eye condition which resulted in my inability to read. So Frater Roland and I would go for a daily afternoon walk, during which, referring occasionally to his notes, he would review the material presented in that day's classes. This practice may have been a factor in developing his forthright, personal, and engaging manner of presentation which his audiences have enjoyed to this day.

After finishing his four years of theology, Fr. Roland was assigned as an assistant at St. Clara's Church in Chicago, with a part-time position at Mt. Carmel High School teaching Spanish. His first year as a teacher was in foreign languages, a presage of things to come. The following year, 1944, he was chosen to work for an advanced degree at Catholic University in the Department of Semitic Languages. With enthusiasm he began his career in Oriental languages and Sacred Scripture. Many years of diligent study, teaching, and writing have brought credit to his Carmelite Order and to his beloved Catholic Church, and have given him

international recognition as one of the foremost Scripture scholars of our day

Leander Troy, O.Carm.

About half a century ago, there was a classroom at Mt.
Carmel College set aside for the study of philosophy. Bookshelves
laden with hundreds of volumes lined its walls. Tomes written by
the great thinkers waited to impart insight or inspiration to eager
Carmelite seminarians. But no student, whether intent on the
lecture or dozing now and then, could have failed to notice high
above the blackboard a framed scroll with the admonition: NON
LICET NOBIS ESSE MEDIOCRIBUS. What was an ideal nailed to
the wall became for many of us a way of life incarnated in self-
discipline, integrity, and talents employed to the fullest. In the
1940's at Whitefriars Hall we met the paradigm of this expression
in Roland E. Murphy.

We were his first class of students at "The Hall." Though
most seminary instructors had a thorough knowledge of their
subjects, not all could fire up their hearers with enthusiasm. And
Holy Writ was not an area of study regarded with great interest by
the general run of Catholics in that era. As for teaching the
subject, it was not unknown for an instructor to read aloud from
notes—on the various senses of Scripture, on canonicity, etc.—
pausing at intervals to ask, "Any questions?" with only polite
silence as a reply. But teaching does not require an arid recitation,
but rather, enthusiasm, competence, and dedication to the
subject matter. Roland was the epitome of these virtues.

He proved at once to be a font of water in what might
otherwise have been a desert. He led us to the actual texts and we
plunged right in. Endowed with resonant voice and prophetic
stature, Roland highlighted a text with gestures and facial
expressions. Scripture had color, nuance, and spiritual depth. He
would invite us to find passages that most intrigued each one of

us and then tell us to write our own comments and add whatever insights we might draw from scholarly commentators. In this way we examined the Psalms, Proverbs, and Ecclesiastes. We explored a text and personally appropriated favorite passages. Proverbs, for example, was a mine of wisdom and wit; it also provided an insight into the parallelism of Hebrew poetry. We shared not only Roland's insights, but also his enthusiasm for the Word of God.

If a student raised a question for which Roland did not have the answer, there was no evasion, no hedging, no "Wait until we come to it." He was absolutely honest: "I don't know," followed by the assurance, "but I'll look it up and let you know at the next class." He did so invariably. Mastery of subject was enhanced by utter honesty. So was our confidence in this towering instructor. And so was our respect.

After we had moved on, he received his doctorate and continued biblical studies in Rome and at the École Biblique in Jerusalem. As any of us could testify who found him at his desk for hours during our years at "The Hall," self-discipline has characterized his life. Now, fifty years after he taught us, Roland is still at his desk for hours each day. A course has to be prepared, an article researched, a book reviewed ... or written. The tempo of his day is constant. There he is, working in his room with classical music in the background. No doubt, there are many who owe their charisma as teachers, scholars, speakers, or dedicated religious to the example of this teacher par excellence. There are also those who, at the end of the day, will settle down with the Word and, as they put themselves in the presence of the Lord, will for a moment remember Roland, who turned the Word into a flame.

Eugene Kilkenny

PART IV

ARTICLES

Awards and Honorary Degrees Conferred on
Roland E. Murphy, O.Carm.

1980
George Washington Ivey Professor of Biblical Studies, Duke University

1984
Cuthbert E. Allen Award for outstanding contribution to Ecumenism
from the Ecumenical Institute of Wake Forest University
and Belmont Abbey College

1985
John A. O'Brien Visiting Professor of Theology
at the University of Notre Dame

1986
Distinguished Service Award from The Washington Theological Union

McCarthy Professor of Theology, The Washington Theological Union

1987
Doctor of Humane Letters, *honoris causa*, Belmont Abbey College

1990
Doctor of Humanities, *honoris causa*, Saint Mary's College, Indiana

1993
Doctor of Humane Letters, *honoris causa*, Loyola University, Chicago

1994
Visiting Paluch Professor of Theology
University of Saint Mary of the Lake, Mundelein, Illinois

1995
Doctor of Theology, *honoris causa*, Assumption College

1996
The Jerome Award for excellence in Scholarship
from the Catholic Library Association

A Carmelite Master
of the Song of Songs

How does one say thank you for a gift that shapes one's faith, one's very existence? Not easily. From the time I was a student of Roland Murphy's the Scriptures have been a dear and challenging friend. The essay below is a quite modest attempt to express to Father Roland my gratitude for a gift beyond measure.

In 1987 Roland Murphy edited a volume of four essays by the renown scholar of medieval biblical interpretation Beryl Smalley. In the preface Father Roland quoted the following statement by the historian R. W. Southern: "In 1927, when Beryl Smalley began to study the Bible in the Middle Ages, I think it should be true to say that the Bible had almost had no place in the minds of medieval historians."[1] In 1949, when Roland Murphy published his first study of the Song of Songs,[2] this enigmatic book of the Hebrew Bible suffered mostly from neglect, left largely unread. In that era scholars seldom turned their attention to the Song of Songs, and preachers felt no impulse to bring the Song to the attention of their audiences. Those who prayed the Little Office of the Blessed Virgin, like Carmelite novices, knew some few snippets from the Song of Songs because these selections appeared in the Little Office. Otherwise the liturgy and Christian spirituality in the early post-World War II era were barely touched by the Song of Songs. This blatant neglect had not always been the case. In fact, the Middle Ages produced numerous commentaries on this book of the Bible with many of them still surviving. E. Ann Matter has written that there were "nearly one hundred extant commentaries and homilies on the Song of Songs...between the sixth and the fifteenth centuries...."[3] Moreover, the Song of Songs provided the symbolism and language for the bridal mysticism which became full blown in the Christian tradition under the influence of twelfth century Cistercians, especially as that Cistercian tradition was shaped by Bernard of Clairvaux's widely disseminated *Sermons on the Song of Songs.*[4]

Near the end of the second millennium Father Roland Murphy leaves the academy and the church much richer not only because of his extensive research into wisdom literature but, in particular, for what he has done to retrieve the meaning of the Song of Songs and its tradition. Roland Murphy did not leave the Song of Songs in the same state as he found it at the beginning of his career as a biblical scholar. Today is a new day for the Song of Songs. Credit for this new day belongs in no small measure to Roland Murphy.

No modern scholar can lay better claim to the title of this essay, Master of the Song of Songs, than Father Roland Murphy whose students have long been the beneficiaries of this mastery. I recall sending, on behalf of the Joliet Catholic High Carmelite community in the late 1950's, a telegram to Father Roland on the occasion of an honor that he had recently received. This telegram contained merely these words from Roland's beloved Canticle of Canticles: "the song of the turtle dove is heard in the land."[5] Students at Whitefriars Hall heard this line and others from the Canticle proclaimed in class by Roland with great enthusiasm. Indeed, having been marched through ten chapters of the Old Testament during each class, the students at Whitefriars Hall were exposed to the Hebrew Scriptures in so lively and insightful a way that Roland's students will never forget the impact of this teacher who so loved his text and who so cared for those whom he taught. The remembrances elsewhere in this *Festschrift* amply testify to this textual mastery and pedagogical virtuosity. Perhaps the passion of the Song of Songs has been so congenial because of his own passionate nature that made every class period a tour de force where daydreaming was impossible.

The Song of Songs in the Carmelite Tradition

Roland Murphy came to the Song of Songs not only as a scholar but as a Carmelite friar, an identity that has obviously been very dear and important to him. Carmelite Spirituality in time came to claim the Song of Songs as its primary biblical resource in the expression of its mystical tradition. That was not always the case. There is neither a quotation nor an allusion to the Song of Songs in the formula of life given to the Carmelites between 1206 and 1214 by Albert of Jerusalem, nor in the revision of that formula that made the Carmelite hermits into friars in 1247.[6] Nicholas the Frenchman's *Fiery Arrow* (1270 or 1271), a jeremiad against the mendicant life adopted by the Carmelites, has only two allusions to the Song of Songs. Nicholas advocated the solitary life, and one would have expected him to cite more extensively from the Song of Songs especially if the Carmelites had by then turned to the bridal mysticism that had been articulated by Bernard of Clairvaux.[7]

In 1989 the Dutch Carmelite historian Adrianus Staring published a superb critical edition of Carmelite documents from the late thirteenth and from the fourteenth century. The only citations from the Song of Songs found in these documents concern not Carmel's mystical tradition but are exercises in the Marian interpretation of the Song of Songs by Carmelite writers John Baconthorpe (d. 1348), John of Cheminot (fl. 1340's) and John of Hildesheim (d. 1375).[8]

When Felip Ribot (d. 1391) produced the *Institution of the First Monks* which explicitly introduced the mystical element into the Carmelite literature of the fourteenth century, one would have expected to find in this work significant citations from the Song of Songs. However, there are only four incidental references to the Song in this seminal work of Carmelite spirituality.[9] Clearly the Song of Songs and bridal mysticism were not central to the mysticism which Felip Ribot articulated in a work of far-reaching consequence.

More research needs to be done on the development of medieval Carmelite mystical texts before it will be known to what extent the bridal mysticism so central and primary to Teresa of Avila and John of the Cross made its effective appearance. Did bridal mysticism come to the Spanish mystics from Carmelite sources or external sources? What place did bridal mysticism have in the Touraine Reform that took place among the Carmelites of the Ancient Observance, a reform that effectively got under way in the seventeenth century and is seen as a counterpart to the Teresian Reform?

Whatever the sources, Carmelite mysticism became a bridal mysticism under the influence of the two saints and doctors of the church, Teresa of Avila and John of the Cross. From the Song of Songs came the basic symbolism for Teresa's descriptions of her mystical experience especially in her masterpiece *The Interior Castle*. Teresa, no shrinking violet, was so bold as to imitate the biblical commentators by composing a commentary on the Song of Songs. In the prologue to this commentary on the Song of Songs Teresa wrote that "[f]or a number of years now the Lord has given me great delight each time I hear or read some words from Solomon's Song of Songs."[10] Teresa realized that she was doing a daring deed with this commentary. Near the end of her commentary she wrote somewhat facetiously, I think: "May it please the Lord that what I have said may not have been bold."[11] With Teresa of Avila classical Carmelite mysticism became identified with the bridal mysticism of the Middle Ages. To that tradition Teresa added descriptions of her own experience that brought new vividness and explicitness to this bridal mysticism.

If possible, Teresa's collaborator, John of the Cross, was even more dependent on the Song of Songs for his experience[12] and for the expression of his mysticism. John wrote hardly a poem or a page of commentary that was not laced through and through with the symbolism of the Song of Songs. The bridal mysticism of John's "Spiritual Canticle" is more than self-evident, and it does not take much reflection to find the presence of the Song in John's poem "Dark Night." Elsewhere I have shown how indebted the poem "The Living Flame of Love" and its commentary are to the Song of Songs.[13] John of the Cross was a poet whose primary resource was the Bible and within the Bible the Song of Songs holds pride of place for its overall impact on John's biblical imagination. In his prologue to the "Spiritual Canticle," John calls the Song of Songs "the divine Song of Solomon" where along with "other books of Sacred Scripture...the Holy Spirit, unable to express the fullness of his meaning in ordinary words, utters mysteries in strange figures and likenesses."[14] When John was dying, he requested that the Song of Songs be recited for him. As he listened to the poetry that had so shaped his spiritual experience and message, he exclaimed: "Oh, what precious pearls."[15] Teresa of Jesus and John of the Cross set Carmelite spirituality on a course in which the Song of Songs and the bridal mysticism it informed became the principal fabric of Carmelite mystical doctrine.

In the last quarter of the nineteenth century, a young French woman reinterpreted in simple terms the classical Carmelite spirituality of her patroness Teresa of Avila[16] and she, who had very little education, home-schooled herself in the mystical teachings of John of the Cross. Thérèse wrote "Ah! How many lights have I not drawn from the Works of our holy Father, St. John of the Cross! At the ages of seventeen and eighteen I had no other spiritual nourishment...." Without a full Bible of her own, Thérèse may have learned the Song of Songs primarily from her study of John of the Cross. In any case Thérèse was devoted to the Song. She said that "[i]f I had the time I would like to comment on the Canticle of Canticles; in this book I have discovered such profound things about the union of the soul with the beloved."[17] In this desire and others Thérèse had a daring comparable to that of her patroness, the Spanish Teresa. Thérèse of Lisieux like Teresa and John discovered in the Song of Songs the symbolism and language with which she could better understand the powerful and beautiful dynamics of divine love. For her, for Teresa and

John, for Carmel, and for much of Christian mysticism since them, the Song of Songs is the font from which wells up lyrical wisdom about the journey to God in love. Were these three Carmelite saints alive, they would, indeed, read avidly and applaud heartily the many contributions that the Carmelite Roland Murphy has made to a deeper understanding of the Song of Songs.

Scholarly Contributions to the Understanding of the Song of Songs

Father Roland's writings on the Song of Songs have spanned his life as a scholar. As early as 1949 he published an essay in *the Catholic Biblical Quarterly* on "The Structure of the Canticles," as well as three reviews of publications on the Song.[18] Roland has been researching and writing about the Song ever since. Over the intervening years there have been seventeen essays or chapters of books on the Song, a pamphlet commentary and a full length commentary on the Song. The translation of the Song in the New American Bible is by REM and that in the New Revised Standard Version of the Bible was reviewed by him. The sheer quantity of scholarship on the Song of Songs by Roland is staggering especially when one takes into account the large number of publications he has authored on other biblical books and aspects of the Old Testament such as his major focus on the Wisdom of Israel and the Psalms. He truly is a master of the Song and much else besides.

The culmination but not the end of Roland's lifelong study of the Song of Songs came in 1990 with the publication of his commentary on the Song in the Hermeneia Series. This volume contains an extensive introduction (102 pages), an original translation of the Song by Roland accompanied by extensive notes, eighty one pages of commentary, seventeen pages of bibliography, and various indices. REM's Hermeneia commentary on the Song of Songs is an *opus magnum* that gave Roland Murphy an opportunity to synthesize the scholarship on the Song of Songs that he had produced over the years. With this commentary he was writing for a worldwide audience in a highly respected series that has an extensive ecumenical readership. Do you want a sophisticated but straightforward commentary on the Song that is as devoid of technical parlance as possible? Take up and read this commentary, as the voices said to Augustine in the garden. Every Carmelite sister, brother, priest or lay Carmelite, should know the Song of Songs through and through, first of all for the sheer pleasure of reading this beautiful biblical book and so that the Carmelite mystical tradition as it was appropriated into Carmelite spirituality by Teresa of Avila and John of the Cross may be better understood. Roland Murphy's Hermeneia Commentary answers nearly every question about the Song of Songs that may come to mind, and it communicates an understanding and an appreciation for this love poetry that comes right from the heart and mind of the author of this commentary.

Marvin Pope, the author of the massive Anchor Bible Commentary on the Song of Songs, reviewed REM's Hermeneia Commentary. There amidst other high praise, Pope wrote that "[i]n the amazing history of interpretation of Solomon's Song, the role of Roland Murphy has been and will long remain seminal." Of Roland's translation, Pope wrote: "Sensitive readers will savor the elegant simplicity of M[urphy]'s 'Englishing' of the sublime Song." Pope concluded his review with these words: "Long ago Solomon's Super Song was one of the most preached-on parts of Scripture. Recently it has been for the most part studiously ignored. M[urphy]'s *great commentary* will help restore theological perspective to the perennial problem of sex."[19] Roland's friends and students will chuckle at Pope's last observation.

Another outstanding scholar, Bernard McGinn, professor at the Divinity School of the University of Chicago, reviewed recent literature on the Song of Songs in the *Journal of Religion.* McGinn compared Roland's commentary with that of Marvin Pope. McGinn wrote:

> ...Roland Murphy's commentary has the
> advantages of greater conciseness, wider sympathy

with different forms of exegesis, and (at least to
this outsider) a more convincing argument. Given
the growing interest in the study of the Song and
its influence, the book should form a necessary
starting point, even for those who might not share
its interpretive perspective.[20]

Like Marvin Pope, Roland Murphy is a highly trained
master of the historical-critical method which is part and parcel
of the modern study of biblical texts. As a practitioner of this
methodology, Roland Murphy has made significant contributions
to the study of the Bible. In doing so Murphy and other Catholic
biblical scholars have not always escaped adverse reaction from
certain quarters despite the church's stance that there is nothing
to fear from history (Leo XIII) and that critical methods have an
important role in the interpretation of the Scriptures as was
stated in Pius XII's encyclical *Divino Afflante Spiritu*, the Pontifical
Biblical Commission's Instruction in 1964 and in Vatican II's
Dogmatic Constitution on Divine Revelation.[21] Creative scholarship, even with the kind of fidelity to the church that Roland
Murphy has so vigorously displayed throughout his career, runs
the risk of this kind of opposition. Hindsight so often finds these
courageous scholars to have been right on track as it did the
buffeted Thomas Aquinas.

The historical-critical method practiced over the last few
centuries has not been kind to the traditional Jewish and
Christian interpretation of the Song of Songs. Both of these
traditions interpreted the Song of Songs, not as panegyric of
human sexuality, but as a text to be interpreted spiritually, as a
description of the loving relationship between God and Israel,
then by Christians as the love between Christ and the Church or
Christ and the person on her or his journey to God. Interestingly
the new Catechism sees in the Christian tradition an honoring of
human love, an insight that seems overly generous to the tradition but may, in fact, be an anachronism that ironically may be

the result of work on the Song done by scholars like Roland Murphy.[22]

I want to point out that Father Roland Murphy has drawn the two methods of interpretation—historical critical and spiritual—into what I would call a creative tension and he has done so without giving up in the least his allegiance to his historical-critical training and commitment. It is precisely in this regard that Roland Murphy, the Carmelite, has made a truly major contribution to the understanding of the Song and its place in the Carmelite mystical tradition. Roland has, in fact, enabled Carmelites to read their mystics without forgoing the wonderful insights that the modern critical methods have discovered. Thus Carmelites and Christians of all stripes have no apologies to make about turning to the wisdom of that long Christian tradition initiated by Origen with his commentaries on the Song of Songs and continued by such luminaries as Gregory of Nyssa, Ambrose of Milan, Gregory the Great, Bernard of Clairvaux, William of St. Thierry and a host of other Christian interpreters of the Song of Songs. To this tradition and the late medieval bridal mysticism, Teresa of Jesus and John of the Cross owed a debt which they in turn amplified and expressed in their unique way. Bernard McGinn has succinctly described how the mystical tradition has adopted the Song of Songs as its own narrative: "the Song of Songs had played a central role in Christian mysticism since the time of Origen, who established the exegetical foundation for the transformation of eros that allowed the Song to be read as both the story of God's love affair with his people in the Old and the New Testament and the guidebook for the soul's inner encounter with the Divine Lover."[23]

The healing of the divorce between the historical-critical method and the spiritual or mystical interpretation of the Song of Songs is no mean achievement, and it has come gradually to Roland Murphy who has been willing to exercise his acumen in discerning what value might lie in the spiritual tradition. REM recognizes that the historical-critical method must read the Song of Songs as "[h]uman sexual fulfillment, fervently sought and consummated in reciprocal love between woman and man: yes, that is what the Song is about, in its literal sense and theological relevant meaning." But, with an appreciation for the mystical tradition which his order so thoroughly appropriated, Roland Murphy, goes on to ask: "But does the marvelous theological insight that the Song opens up have broader significance?" He adds: "Having reappropriated the literal meaning, can we still give any credence to those who have heard the poetry speak eloquently of celibate love as well as connubial bliss, of divine human covenant as well as male-female sexual partnership, of spiritual as well physical rapture?"[24]

These few lines tell a large story. They reveal a major modern scriptural scholar exploring historically and critically the Song of Songs. In so doing he could have maintained a rigid critical stance in firm opposition to the seemingly undisciplined spiritual interpretation of the Song. Bernard McGinn attributes this openness to that wonderful humanity for which Roland is so well known by his fellow Carmelites and scholarly colleagues: "What is most striking about Murphy's presentation is its humaneness and balance—his willingness to admit the value in the wide variety of readings of the Song, while still being willing to defend the priority of the book as fundamentally 'a theology of human sexuality.'"[25] Does not that kind of courage, honesty and long years of hard work make one think of what Thomas Aquinas called magnanimity which the Dominican said "denotes stretching forth of the mind to great things."[26] Generosity of mind may well be responsible for Roland's reconciliation of the critical with the spiritual. His insights, as always, are stated simply and straightforwardly. They have, however, a very important message not only for Carmelite women and men but for all Christians who find inspiration in the Carmelite mystical tradition. This tradition now has no reason to be intimated by modern scholarship about the Song or for that matter about any book of the Bible.

Roland Murphy has shown that modern scholarship, done with the due modesty that must be its guide, can lead one to the wisdom of the mystical tradition. He has, in fact, found in critical scholarship insights that lead him to this wisdom of the spiritual interpretation of the Song. Because he explains himself so directly and plainly, we can profit from his own statements about the relationship between critical scholarship and spiritual interpretation. He has written:

> The understanding of the Song in the light of modern scholarship is clearly a gain, because past interpreters glossed over the human dimension in the Song. Now the community of faith can respond to a level of meaning that deals directly with human love, the mutual fidelity between love[r] and beloved, and the strength of the love that unites them. It is no exaggeration to say that we owe this understanding of the Song to the efforts of critical scholarship.

Roland goes on to ask: how then can the traditional spiritual understanding of the Song such as is found in the writings of the Carmelite mystical tradition be "both reasonable and even convincing to the modern reader? His response to his own question is written with his usual conciseness.

> The first is the fact that any text comes to have more meaning tha[n] the literal historical sense given to it by the author(s). This is true of all literary texts, and the Bible is no exception. The text comes to have a life of its own within the community that preserves it, and thus acquires a surplus meaning. This is an inevitable hermeneutical process; as time passes, new horizons emerge. ... Hence one may not simply dismiss past exegetical traditions as 'precritical' and invalidated by the superiority of the historical-critical approach. This does not mean that the vagaries in the history of the exegesis of the Song need be

accepted. Rather, the basic insight that the Song also refers to God and people remains at the center of this issue.

Roland continues this line of thought:

The surplus meaning of the Song, or any piece of literature, can be defended by modern hermeneutical theory, but this would require extensive development. It is more interesting and important here to review the tools of critical historical scholarship which suggest the validity of a surplus meaning for the Song.

Roland then speaks to the symbolism of sex in the Bible as a description of "the covenant love between the Lord and Israel...," and states that he does not mean "to prove that the surplus meaning was intended by the original author(s) of the Song (else, how could it be surplus?). Rather, the subject itself, human love, had the intrinsic potential of expressing divine love." Father Roland finds in the Song itself warranty for this point of view when, in Song 8:6, love is said to be "as strong as death."

The concluding paragraph of Roland's essay from which I have been quoting reveals why I find that Roland Murphy has managed through long years of study and patient research to bring the traditional spiritual interpretation into creative tension with critical scholarship. He has been an ambassador of good will between polarities that seemed to many to be irreconcilable. This is Roland's conclusion.

The title of this essay is not meant to suggest an adversary relationship. The modern interpreter cannot do without historical-critical methodology. Negatively, it serves to cut away what is arbitrary in the traditional interpretation, such as the use of inappropriate allegory. Positively, it lays down the lines along which the original meaning can be apprehended and extended into another level of meaning. This is not an either/or situation. Pride of place may be given to one meaning over the other. The literal historical meaning, where it can be reached, is normative and hence determinative in assessing the various levels of meaning in a literary work. The traditional understanding of the Song complements the literal historical sense by extending it along certain paths which, as we have seen, can themselves be illumined by means of modern scholarship.[27]

Father Roland Murphy has thus set the stage for those who explore the use of the Song of Songs in the mystical and Carmelite traditions so that they may make use of his and the scholarship of others in expanding the horizons of the spiritual understanding of the Song of Songs. The small sampling of Father Roland's work above has, I believe, promising evidence for an ongoing fruitful dialogue between modern critical scholarship and a tradition of spiritual interpretation that seemed doomed to a disdained and uncritical place in the history of biblical exegesis. What a difference the scholarship of Roland Murphy has made in lifting that sentence of disregard from a tradition that has wisdom to share with a new conversation partner, one who adheres to the historical-critical method. Roland has reconciled these two partners to each other.

For one thing, this dialogue between critical scholarship and spiritual interpretations may well throw light on why the celibate community through the centuries has found the erotic symbolism of Song of Songs so congenial to their articulation of the search for God through love. Psychological suppositions suggesting sublimation do not explain the mystery of the great fascination of celibates for the Song of Songs. In the surplus of meaning in the Song there may be evidence that reveals what the power of human sexuality can say about its Maker and the women and men created by that Maker. Sexuality may be, as I think Roland Murphy's scholarship suggests, a powerful revelation of the God of Abraham, Isaac, Jacob and Jesus.

Roland's scholarship on the Song of Songs has made much possible. The following example comes to mind. Padre Ricardo Falla has used the Song of Songs to tell the story of his love for the people whom he has served in Guatemala. Scholars like Roland Murphy have made it possible for missionaries like Falla, in his book called *Historia de Gran Amor*, (The Story of a Great Love), to tell his story of his service to his people and their love in return through the powerful imagery of the Song of Songs.[28] Not only does Father Murphy's scholarship on the Song of Songs have implications for the mystical tradition, his identification of the Song's literal meaning as a celebration of human sexuality has many pastoral implications[29] that should be drawn from his work to broaden the church's wisdom about sexuality.

As Teresa and John and Thérèse found the Song of Songs a rich mine for their understanding of God's love, once again Carmelites have an invitation to return with confidence to the Song for which no apologies need be made. Bridal mysticism is not a treasure only of the past. It has a power to add energy to the search for ways in which the Carmelite Order and the Church may become more contemplative. Father Roland Murphy who works still in this rich mine has led the way for those who seek to live and understand the Carmelite contemplative tradition in the upcoming millennium.

Keith J. Egan, T.O.Carm.

Endnotes

1. *Medieval Exegesis of Wisdom Literature: Essays by Beryl Smalley.* Atlanta, GA: Scholars Press, 1987, [1] quoting *The Bible in the Medieval World: Essays in Memory of Beryl Smalley,* K. Walsh and D. Wood, eds. Studies in Church History: Subsidia 4 (Oxford: Blackwell, 1985), essay: pp. 1-16.

2. Roland E. Murphy, The Structure of the Canticle of Canticles, *Catholic Biblical Quarterly* 11 (1949) 381-91.

3. E. Ann Matter, *The Voice of My Beloved: The Song of Songs in Western Medieval Christianity* (Philadelphia: University of Pennsylvania, 1990) 3.

4. Bernard of Clairvaux, *On the Song of Songs.* 4 vols. (Spencer, MA and Kalamazoo, MI: Cistercian Publications, 1971).

5. The translation above has been updated to Roland's own translation: Roland E. Murphy, *The Song of Songs: A Commentary on the Book of Canticles or the Song of Songs;* "Hermeneia Series," (Minneapolis: Fortress Press, 1990) 138. Henceforth: Hermeneia.

6. See the two texts in Latin and English in *Albert's Way: The First North American Congress on the Carmelite Rule;* M. Mulhall, ed. (Rome and Barrington, IL: Institutum Carmelitanum, Province of the Most Pure Heart of Mary, 1989) 2-21; p. 1 has references to Latin texts. See also Le Fonti Bibliche della Regola Carmelitana, *Ephemerides Carmeliticae* 2 (1948) 65-97.

7. *Nicholai prioris generalis Ordinis Carmelitarum Ignea Sagitta,* Adrianus Staring, ed., *Carmelus* 9 (1962) 237-307. English translation: The Flaming Arrow, Bede Edwards, tr. *The Sword* 39 (1979) 3-52.

8. *Medieval Carmelite Heritage: Early Reflections on the Nature of the Order,* Adrianus Staring, ed. Textus et Studia Historica Carmelitana 16 (Rome: Institutum Carmelitanum, 1989) 462.

9. The Liber de Institucione et Peculiaribus Gestis Religiosorum Carmelitarum in Lege Veteri Exortorum et in Nova Perserverancium ad Caprasium Monachum by Felip Ribot, O.Carm. A Critical Edition with an Introduction by Paul Chandler, O.Carm. Unpublished Dissertation, Centre for Medieval Studies, University of Toronto. (1991), see index, p. 292.

10. "Meditations on the Song of Songs," *The Collected Works of St. Teresa of Avila*, vol. 2; Kieran Kavanaugh and Adela Rodriquez, trans. (Washington, DC: Institute of Carmelite Studies, 1980) 215.

11. Ibid. 260.

12. I suggest here that John's familiarity with the Song of Songs tradition predisposed him for the kind of divine experiences that he had.

13. Keith J. Egan, The Biblical Imagination of John of the Cross in The Living Flame of Love, *Juan de la Cruz, Espiritu de Llama*, Otger Steggink, ed. (Rome, Kampen, the Netherlands: Institutum Carmelitanum, Kok Pharos, 1991) 507-21.

14. *The Collected Works of St. John of the Cross;* rev. ed., Kieran Kavanaugh and Otilio Rodriquez, trans. (Washington, DC: Institute of Carmelite Studies, 1991) *The Spiritual Canticle*, Prologue 1.

15. *God Speaks in the Night; The Life, Times, and Teaching of St. John of the Cross* (Washington, DC: Institute of Carmelite Studies, 1991) 369.

16. Thérèse of Lisieux, *The Story of a Soul;* 2nd ed., John Clarke, trans. (Washington, DC: Institute of Carmelite Studies, 1976) 42.

17. Guy Gaucher, *The Story of a Life;* Anne Marie Brennan, trans. (San Francisco: Harper and Row, 1987) 141. See *La Bible avec Thérèse de Lisieux*, Textes de Sainte Thérèse.... (Paris: Editions du Cerf and Desclée de Brouwer, 1979) 101-16; see also Roland E. Murphy, "The Song of Songs and St

Thérèse," *Experiencing St Thérèse Today; John Sullivan ed., Carmelite Studies* 5 (1990) 1-9, 191-92.

18. Publications by REM until 1985 are listed in *The Listening Heart: Essays in Wisdom and the Psalms in Honor of Roland E. Murphy, O.Carm.*; Kenneth G. Highland, Elizabeth F. Haler, Jonathan T. Glass and Roger W. Lee, eds. *The Journal for the Study of the Old Testament, Supplement Series, 58* where the bibliography was compiled by Elizabeth F. Haler, Jonathan T. Glass, Catherine Fox Sevens.

19. *The Catholic Biblical Quarterly* 54 (October 1992) 758-61. Emphasis in the last quote added.

20. Bernard McGinn, With "the Kisses of the Mouth": Recent Works on the Song of Songs, *Journal of Religion* 72 (April 1992) 270.

21. See Roland E. Murphy, Divino Afflante Spiritu—Twenty Years After, *Chicago Studies* 2 (1963) 16-28. On Roland Murphy's significant role in American biblical Studies see index of Gerald P. Fogarty, *American Catholic Biblical Scholarship: A History from the Early Republic to Vatican II* (Foreword by Roland E. Murphy), (San Francisco: Harper & Row, 1989).

22. *Catechism of the Catholic Church* (Washington, DC: United States Catholic Conference, 1994) #1611.

23. Bernard McGinn, *The Growth of Mysticism: Gregory the Great through the 12th Century* (New York: Crossroad, 1994) 297.

24. Hermeneia 103.

25. McGinn, With "the Kisses of the Mouth".... 270.

26. *Summa theologiae* 2.2.129.1.

27. Roland E. Murphy, The Song of Songs: Critical Biblical Scholarship vis-à-vis Exegetical Traditions, *Understanding the Word: Essays in Honor of Bernhard W. Anderson*; J. T. Butler, E. W. Conrad, B. C. Ollenberger, eds., *Journal for the Study of the Old Testament*, Supplement Series 37 (Sheffield, England, 1985) passim. In the last decade or so Roland Murphy has written a number of essays exploring the

exegetical tradition as it relates to the Song of Songs. It seems to this writer that these explorations have been instrumental in leading him to the place where he can so persuasively argue for the compatibility of the historical-critical method and the spiritual tradition. These essays are noted in the bibliography elsewhere in this *Festschrift*.

28. Ricardo Falla, *Historia de un Gran Amor: Recuperación Autobiográfica de la Experiencia con las Comunidades de Problación en Resistencia Ixcán, Guatemala* (n.p.,n.d., 90pp.). I owe my copy of this book to the kindness of Father Peter Hinde, O.Carm.

29. Roland Murphy has greatly enriched Saint Mary's College, Notre Dame, IN., academically and pastorally. In September 1984, he addressed a crowd of more than one thousand at Saint Mary's and Notre Dame University with a lecture on the Song of Songs in O'Laughlin Hall, Saint Mary's College. In the following September he addressed the same audience, now over 1,400 students on the Psalms and Prayer. Both of these lectures were published as audio Cassette Tapes by Ave Maria Press. REM also lectured in 1988 at the Carmelite Forum's Summer Seminar on Carmelite Spirituality: "The Song of Songs and the Spiritual Canticle." This lecture was published by Alba House Communications (Audio cassette). Saint Mary's College awarded Father Murphy an honorary doctoral degree in the humanities in 1990. In that year he was the homilist for the baccalaureate Eucharist.

Handing on the Mantle: The Transmission of the Elijah Cycle in the Biblical Versions

In the Provincial's Room of the unrenovated Whitefriars Hall I met with Roland Murphy some eleven years ago to discuss further studies in Scripture. Throughout our hour long conversation he chanted a singular refrain: "Acquire the biblical languages first." With Roland's enthusiastic encouragement I frequented the Semitics department at Catholic University where he had studied and taught many years earlier. In gratitude to him for his fraternal support throughout my years of study, I wish to offer to him this exploration of the transmission of the Elijah cycle in the biblical versions.[1]

The Question

The Carmelite imagination has been intrigued by the figure of Elijah ever since the first community located itself within his ancient environs. The frescoes in the Basilica of San Martino ai Monti in Rome[2] that depict the life of Elijah present him wearing the Carmelite habit, thus reminding us that he was the first Carmelite! Our Carmelite traditions regarding Elijah are, however, late contributions to the world of Elijan interpretation. Centuries earlier, receivers of the biblical tradition were already busy elucidating the events of Elijah's life as the Hebrew text was translated into different languages. Because the biblical story preserved in Hebrew had to be rendered understandable for peoples who no longer knew this language, the biblical versions (the Greek, Syriac, Aramaic, and Latin translations) were composed between the third century B.C. and the fifth century A.D. Scribes and translators had the opportunity to clarify and explain biblical stories with the addition of a single word, or, as in the Aramaic Targum, with lengthy expansions. These translations preserve the biblical story as it was interpreted by successive generations within and beyond the borders of Israel. They are valuable for Carmelites because in them we discover some of the earliest traditions regarding Elijah.

This paper will focus on three verses of the Elijah Cycle (1 Kgs 19:3,12; and 18:21) in which at least one of the biblical versions contains an interpretation that diverges from the Hebrew text (hereafter MT, Masoretic Text). In each case the translations that appear in the Greek version (hereafter LXX, "the seventy"),[3] the Syriac version (hereafter Syr),[4] Targum Jonathan (hereafter TJon),[5] and the Vulgate (hereafter Vg) are presented.[6] From these examples some of the primitive interpretations of the Elijah Cycle will be recovered.

1 Kings 19:3: Elijah Fears and Flees

1 Kings 19:1-3 recounts that Elijah, upon learning that Jezebel was threatening his life, became afraid and fled to Beer-sheba. That Elijah *feared* is reported by most translations,[7] and rightly so, since this is most likely the original meaning. However, the MT and TJon record a different interpretation. The biblical texts read as follows:

MT: וַיַּרְא וַיָּקָם וַיֵּלֶךְ אֶל־נַפְשׁוֹ

He **saw** and got up and fled for his life

LXX: καὶ ἐφοβήθη Ηλιου καὶ ἀνέστη καὶ ἀπῆλθεν
κατὰ τὴν ψυχὴν ἑαυτοῦ
Elijah **feared** and got up and fled for his life

TJon: וחזא וקם ואזל לשיזבא נפשיה
He **saw** and got up and fled to save himself

Syr: ܘܕܚܠ ܐܠܝܐ ܘܩܡ ܐܙܠ ܕܢܦܠܛ ܢܦܫܗ
Elijah **feared** and getting up he fled to
escape with his life

Vg: timuit ergo Helias et surgens abiit
quocumque eum ferebat voluntas
Elijah **feared** and getting up, he fled to
where he wanted

These alternative readings (*he saw* or *he feared*) derive from two sound interpretations of the Hebrew consonants וירא (wyr'). The MT reads וַיַּרְא (wayyar'), "he saw," while the LXX, the Syr, and the Vg read וַיִּירָא (wayyirā'), "he feared." Not surprisingly, the interpretation in the Hebrew Bible is followed by TJon, the official Aramaic translation for Judaism. By accepting the LXX reading, "he feared," our modern English translations necessarily bury the Masoretic and Targumic interpretation that avoids characterizing Elijah as one who feared Jezebel.[8]

Medieval commentators, as noted by Paul Chandler, disdained Elijah's fearful flight from Jezebel. Chandler believes that the failure of the *Institutio* to mention Elijah's journey to Horeb is because medieval commentaries "were strongly critical of Elijah," particularly because he was afraid of a woman.[9] As the MT and TJon indicate, this concern was already felt in Jewish tradition. The antiquity of this interpretation is confirmed by TJon.

1 Kings 19:12: A Sound of Thin Silence

Elijah's encounter with God (1 Kgs 19:8-18) on Mount Horeb is a point of departure for Carmelite reflection on God's presence in the world. The phrase in 1 Kgs 19:12, קוֹל דְּמָמָה דַקָּה (*qôl dĕmāmâ daqqâ*), "a sound of thin silence," inspires us, even though its meaning is far from clear, and biblical exegesis is not all that helpful. One finds a full range of opinions, from scholars who consider the "sound of thin silence" entirely insignificant,[10] to those perceive in it the heights of mystical experience.[11] Others offer a more moderate approach that neither dismisses the event nor overstates its import.[12] Every translator, whether ancient or modern, has had to tackle the phrase *qôl dĕmāmâ daqqâ*. As the inventory of English translations below indicates, there is debate as to whether the Hebrew term *qôl* is best rendered "voice/whisper" or simply "sound." Translators also submit various attempts to capture the Hebrew terms *dĕmāmâ* and *daqqâ*.

English translations of *qôl dĕmāmâ daqqâ*:

a soft murmuring sound (Tanakh)
a still small voice (RSV)
a sound of sheer silence (NRSV)
a faint murmuring sound (REB)
a tiny whispering sound (NAB)
the sound of a gentle breeze (JB)
a light murmuring sound (NJB)
a gentle whisper (NIV)
the soft whisper of a voice (GNB)
a sound of a light whisper (Montgomery,[13] Burney[14])
a sound of thin silence (Gray,[15] Murphy[16])
a thin petrifying sound (De Boer[17])
a roaring and thunderous voice (Lust[18])
a thin silent sound (Coote[19])

The biblical versions translate as follows:

MT: קוֹל דְּמָמָה דַקָּה
a sound of thin silence

LXX (BNoc$_2$*e$_2$): φωνὴ αὔρας λεπτῆς
a sound of a gentle breeze

Gk mss (Ac$_2$[b] rell[20]): φωνὴ αὔρας λεπτῆς κακεῖ[21] κύριος
a sound of a gentle breeze; the Lord was there

Syr: ܡܠܐ ܕܡܡܠܠܐ ܕܚܒܝܒܐ
a voice of gentle speaking

TJon: קל דמשבחין בחשי.
a sound of those praising in silence

Vg: sibilus aurae tenuis
a whisper of a fine breeze

The LXX reading in the Codex Vaticanus (B) and Jerome's Vulgate appear to agree with the Hebrew, which is thought to preserve the original reading. The cryptic character of this phrase compelled some Greek scribes to add κακεῖ κύριος ("and the Lord was there") which suggests that for them[22] the presence of God in the shorter text, φωνὴ αὔρας λεπτῆς ("a sound of a gentle breeze") was not sufficiently explicit. The addition makes clear that, in the gentle breeze, Elijah has an experience of God.

The Syriac reports that Elijah heard a voice that was speaking gently[23] to him. The clue for understanding this interpretation lies in Deut 4:12 where Moses, while exhorting the Israelites, announces: "The Lord spoke to you from the midst of the fire and you heard *a sound of words* (קוֹל דְּבָרִים) but you did not see any form, there was only a voice." The phrase "sound of words" is translated into Syriac with the same expression that

renders דְּמָמָה קוֹל (*qôl dĕmāmâ*) in 1 Kgs 19:12: ܡܠܐ ܕܫܬܠܐ.
Deut 4:12 is the only instance where Hebrew דָּבָר קוֹל is rendered
ܡܠܐ ܕܫܬܠܐ in the Syriac Bible.[24]

Aside from the obvious parallels between Elijah and
Moses,[25] specific lexical choices link these two verses in the Syriac
version, suggesting that the Syriac translator, perplexed by the
phrase *qôl dĕmāmâ daqqâ* in 1 Kgs 19:12, associated it with Deut
4:12. In both verses there is a <u>theophany</u>, both refer to <u>fire</u> (though
in Deut 4:12 God *is* present in the fire), both occur on <u>Mount
Horeb</u>,[26] and both emphasize the <u>voice</u>. Thus, the Syriac interpretation for the Hebrew phrase *qôl dĕmāmâ daqqâ* in 1 Kgs 19:12
as a "voice of gentle speaking" alludes to the same voice that
instructed Moses and the Israelites on Mount Horeb in Deut 4:12.
This voice now instructs Elijah who finds himself on Mount
Horeb.

The interpretation in TJon, קל דמשבחין בחשי (a sound of
those praising in silence), is part of a larger expansion in 1 Kgs
19:11-12 that deserves extended treatment. The translations of
the MT and TJon are given below. The instances where TJon
diverges from the MT are underlined and the expansions are
written in italics:

MT	TJon
Then [the Lord] said, "Go out and stand on the mountain before the Lord. The Lord is going <u>to pass by</u>.	Then [the Lord] said, "Go out and stand on the mountain before the Lord. The Lord is going <u>to be revealed</u>.
There was a strong and powerful wind rending the mountains and smashing the rocks before the Lord.	*Before the Lord were hosts of angels of* wind rending the mountains and smashing the rocks before the Lord.
But the Lord was not in the wind.	But *the Shekinah of* the Lord was not in *the hosts of angels of* wind.
And after the wind, there was an earthquake.	And after *the hosts of angels of* wind, there *were hosts of angels of* earthquake.
But the Lord was not in the earthquake.	But *the Shekinah of* the Lord was not in the *hosts of angels of* earthquake.
After the earthquake there was fire.	After the *hosts of angels of* earthquake there *were hosts of angels of* fire.
But the Lord was not in the fire.	But *the Shekinah of* the Lord was not in *the hosts of angels of* fire.
After the fire there was <u>a sound of thin silence</u>.	After the *hosts of angels of* fire there was <u>a sound of those who were praising in silence</u>.

As expected, the expression יְהוָֹה עֹבֵר, "the Lord is about to pass by," is rendered "the Lord is going to be revealed" in order to provide a more explicit theological portrait of God. Two other motifs in TJon's interpretation, (1) the *Shekinah* of the Lord and (2) the angels, demand further attention.

1. The *Shekinah*

The concept of *Shekinah* is related to the Hebrew word שכן (√ŠKN) "to dwell," which, as a noun, simply refers to a dwelling place. The term then receives a more theological sense in Exodus 25-27 where it refers to the tent in which the Lord dwells. The relevant verses are Exod 40:35-36:

> Moses could not enter the meeting tent, because the cloud *dwelt* (שָׁכַן/*šākan*) upon it and the glory of the Lord filled the *Dwelling* (מִשְׁכָּן/*miškān*). Whenever the cloud rose from the *Dwelling*, the Israelites would set out on the next stage of their journey.

The "Dwelling," the *miškān*, represents God's presence that "tabernacled" among the Israelites, guiding them to the promised land. *Targum Neofiti* translates Exod 40:35 to make explicit that it was God's *Shekinah* that descended:

> And Moses could not enter the meeting tent because he made the glory of the *Shekinah* of the Lord dwell upon it and the glory of the *Shekinah* of the Lord filled the dwelling.[27]

The term *Shekinah* in targumic literature is an expression for the Divine Presence dwelling among the Israelites.

God's *Shekinah* is a fundamental concept for the rabbis. "Rabbinic literature in general, and the Targumim in particular, employ the term Shekinah (lit. Divine Presence) either as an alternative to God (especially where anthropomorphic expressions must be avoided) or to describe the numinous immanence of God in the created universe."[28] According to rabbinic tradition the Shekinah dwelt on the earth before Adam's sin. Because of his sin and the sins of subsequent generations the Shekinah withdrew to the seventh heaven. Abraham succeeded in bringing it down to the sixth heaven and his descendants drew it down to the first heaven, but it was Moses who brought it back down to earth and therefore he built the tabernacle for it.[29]

In the Hebrew text of 1 Kgs 19:11-12 God is not present in the first three theophanies, the wind, the earthquake, and the fire. Since TJon interprets these verses as a manifestation of God's Shekinah,[30] it is the Shekinah that is not present in the first three phenomena. But in the fourth, when Elijah hears "the voice of those praising in silence,"[31] God's Shekinah has arrived and he experiences the immanence of God.

Of particular interest for Carmelites is the role that the Shekinah plays in Jewish mysticism. Kudashin, in his foundational study of Rabbinic literature, discusses the Shekinah as part of what he calls "normal mysticism" and prayer.[32] The Babylonian Talmud, he notes, teaches that the one who prays should behave as if the Shekinah were before him.[33] "Shekinah is a name for God used only in statements having to do with God's nearness. It is therefore to be found in statements and ideas that reflect normal mystical experience, in statements and ideas about prayer, study of Torah, [and] God's love."[34] The experience of God's Shekinah transcends the day to day, guiding the person to a profound awareness of God's action in the world. Thus Elijah arrives at Mount Horeb after a long journey and, according to TJon, enjoys a deep experience of God's presence, a presence that "tabernacled" with Moses and the Israelites in the desert. At this critical juncture in his own mission, the experience of the Shekinah spurs him to decision and action.

2. Angels

In 4QShirot ʿolat Ha-Shabbat ("Songs of the Sabbath Sacrifice," a manuscript found at Qumran) there appears the phrase קול דממת אלוהים (*qol demamat ʾelohim*) which resembles *qôl děmāmâ daqqâ* in 1 Kgs 19:12. The Shirot is a liturgical text of thirteen compositions which "invoke angelic praise, [and] describe the angelic priesthood and the heavenly Temple."[35] Relevant to my discussion is the text of 4Q405 20-21-22 lines 7-8, presented by Newsom[36] as follows:

ורומ[מו]הו ... הכבוד במשכן אלוהי[ן] דעת יפול[ו]
לפני ה[כרו]בים ובנ[ר]כו בהרומם קול דממת אלוהים
[נשמע] רהמון רנה ברום כנפיהם קול[ן] דממ[ת אלוהים

> wondrous [...] exalt Him ... the Glory in the tabern[acle of the *God of*] knowledge. The cherubim fall before Him and bless. As they rise, the sound of divine stillness [is heard], and *there is* a tumult of jubilation as their wings lift up, the sound of divine [*stillnes*]s.

The phrase קול דממת אלוהים (*qol demamat ʾelohim*) is, Newsom believes, modeled after the biblical phrase *qôl děmāmâ daqqâ* in 1 Kgs 19:12. In the Shirot it is associated with the sound made by the wings of the cherubim. Schiffman reaches a similar conclusion, rendering *qol demamat ʾelohim* with "the gentle voice of the angels." He also cites rabbinic parallels for *qôl děmāmâ daqqâ* and *qol demamat ʾelohim* that refer to "praise uttered by angels."[37]

The Shirot, dated to around 60 B.C., offer an early interpretation of the *qôl děmāmâ daqqâ* as the sound of angels worshipping before the "glory in the tabernacle" (משכן/*miškān*). This Qumran text sheds light on TJon's interpretation of 1 Kgs 19:11-12 in which Elijah takes his stand on Mount Horeb to wait the coming of the *Shekinah*, the Lord's glorious presence. After the angels of wind, earthquake, and fire, the "sound of those who were praising in silence" signals that the *Shekinah* has arrived with angelic praising.

1 Kings 18:21: Limping Around

Elijah's challenge to the prophets of Baal in 18:21 receives various translations into English, alerting the reader to a difficulty in the Hebrew text:

NRSV: "How long will you go limping with two different opinions?"
REB: "How long will you sit on the fence?"
NAB: "How long will you straddle the issue?"
NJB: "How long do you mean to hobble first on one leg then on the other?"

As one might expect by this point, each of the versions registers its own interpretation of this phrase.

Hebrew: עַד־מָתַי אַתֶּם פֹּסְחִים עַל־שְׁתֵּי הַסְּעִפִּים
          How long will you limp about on two opinions?

LXX: Ἕως πότε ὑμεῖς χωλανεῖτε ἐπ' ἀμφοτέραις ταῖς ἰγνύαις
          How long will you limp on both legs?[38]

Syr: ܠܐܡܬܝ ܦܠܝܓܝܢ ܐܢܬܘܢ ܠܬܪܬܝܢ ܦܠܓܘܢ
          How long will you be divided in two divisions?

TJon: עד אמתי אתון פליגין לתרתין פלגון
          How long will you be divided in two divisions?

Vg: usquequo claudicatis in duas partes.
How long will you limp in two divisions?

Though the context (Elijah's accusation) allows the translator to be sure of the meaning, the precise metaphor is obscure. The meaning of פֹּסְחִים (pōsĕḥîm), "to limp," is relatively clear from 2 Sam 4:4 ("he fell and became lame" [וַיִּפֹּל וַיִּפָּסֵחַ]). It may also allude to the Israelite participation in the Baal cult since √PSḤ appears five verses later (1 Kgs 18:26: "and they limped [וַיְפַסְּחוּ] around the altar") in reference to the religious movement by the prophets of Baal as they implore their god.

The meaning of הַסְּעִפִּים (hassĕʿippîm), translated above as "opinions," is obscure. Gray and De Vries link it to the denominated *piel* form of √SʿP "to cut off boughs" and the substantive סָעִיף, "cleft or branch." Gray suggests the translation "hobbling between two forks (at a cross-roads),"[39] while De Vries renders it with "hobble about on two crutches."[40] Gerleman, referring to Judges 15:8,11,[41] submits the following interpretation: "Der dunkle Ausdruck meint nicht, daß die Israeliten 'auf beiden Seiten hinken', geschweige denn 'sich auf Krücken stützen', sondern daß sie gegen beide Seiten anprallen und — das gehört mit zum Prallen — abgewiesen, zurückgestoßen werden."[42] Keel accepts the translation "crutches" for הַסְּעִפִּים.[43]

The predicament that confronts modern translators also confronted their ancient counterparts. The LXX interprets the Hebrew with the image of a person limping on both legs. Jerome also accepts the limping metaphor (*claudicatis*), but simplifies הַסְּעִפִּים with the translation "two divisions." The Syriac and TJon, in near perfect agreement (only the word order differs: אתון פליגין/ ܐܢ̈ܬܘܢ ܡܦܠܓܝܢ), submit a free and lucid interpretation of Elijah's accusation.[44] The Syriac passive participle ܡܦܠܓܝܢ ("be divided") may imply a state of religious vacillation. Though in its simplest sense the Syriac √PLG means "to divide," the passive participle is glossed by R. Payne Smith[45] with the sense "doubting, wavering, or irresolute." This form appears in James 1:8[46] to translate the phrase "a man of two minds" (ἀνὴρ δίψυχος: ܓܒܪܐ ܕܬܪܬܝܢ ܢ̈ܦܫܢ).

Perhaps the Syriac is best rendered: "How long will you be wavering in two factions," to underscore the indecisive behavior of the Israelites.

TJon presents an Elijah that is more determined in his confrontation with the Israelites than the Elijah in the MT. The New American Bible for 18:21 reads as follows (instances where the two texts diverge are written in italics):

MT	TJon[47]
Elijah approached the whole assembly and said:	Elijah approached the whole assembly and said:
"How long will you limp about on two opinions?	*"How long will you be divided in two divisions?*
	Is not the Lord God?
If the Lord is God *go after him.*	*Serve the Lord alone. Why are you going astray after Baal in whom there is no profit.*
If Baal, go after him.	
The people had no response.	The people had no response.

In the Targum, Elijah refuses any allusion to the existence of Baal. "Serve the Lord," he thunders, echoing the following motifs of covenantal language:

1. "Serve the Lord" (Deut 10:12;[48] and Josh 24:12,21) is a regular refrain in Deuteronomy and the deuteronomistic history.
2. "Serve the Lord *alone*". The covenant stipulates that the Israelites must serve the Lord God *alone* and no other (Exod 22:19; Deut 6:4; 13:5 and 1 Sam 7:3).
3. The commandment not to go "astray" after false gods appears in Deut 30:17 and Jer 4:1.
4. False gods are of no profit (1 Sam 12:21; Isa 44:9; and Jer 2:8).

Elijah does not ask the people whom they wish to follow, but, like the later prophets, he exhorts them to renounce Baal worship, reminding them of their covenant with God.

TJon's translation in 18:21 ("how long will you be divided in two divisions?") is clarified by another expansion in TJon in 18:37.

Hebrew Text	TJon
Answer me, Lord.	*Receive my prayer* Lord *with the fire.*
	Receive my prayer Lord *with rain.*
Answer me	May this people know, *by your working*
so that this people may know	*for them a sign,* that you, Lord, are God
that	and that you, *in your mercy for them,*
you, Lord, are God and you have	*are asking them by your Memra* to bring
	themselves back *to fear of you. But they*
turned back	*gave their* **divided** hearts.
their hearts.	

In this expansion in TJon we encounter an Elijah who piously pleads before the Lord. He does not demand a response from God with the abrupt expression, "Answer me," as in the MT, but instead he implores the Lord to receive his prayer.

Prescinding from the fundamental themes of the theology of the Targum that appear in this expansion (i.e., God's mercy and God's *Memra*), I want to focus on the last phrase, וְאַתָּה הֲסִבֹּתָ אֶת־לִבָּם אֲחֹרַנִּית, ("you have turned back their hearts"). In TJon's interpretation of 18:37 Elijah reminds the people that they gave God their **divided** heart (ואנון יהבו ית לבהון פליג), using again the same passive participle (√PLG) that occurs in 18:21. This expansion suggests that TJon interprets the "two divisions" in 18:21 as an expression of Israel's *divided heart*.

In their covenant with the Lord the Israelites were to love the Lord with their *whole heart* (Deut 4:29; Josh 22:5; 23:14; 1 Sam 7:3; 12:20,24; 1 Kgs 8:23) and the prophets beseeched the people to return to the Lord with their *whole heart* (Jer 24:7 and Joel 2:12). In Hos 10:2, where Hosea accuses the people of idolatry, the Targum translates the Hebrew חָלַק לִבָּם with אתפליג לבהון ("their heart is divided") a phrase not unlike that

which appears in 1 Kgs 18:37 (לבהון פליג). According to TJon in
18:37, Elijah prays that the people might surrender their divided
hearts, abandon their idolatrous hearts, and return to fear of the
Lord. When Elijah refers to the two divisions in 18:21 he is
alluding to the Israelites' divided heart, a notion made explicit in
18:37.

Conclusion

The portrait of Elijah transmitted through the biblical
versions preserves some of the earliest traditions regarding the
legendary "founder" of the Carmelites. In 1 Kgs 19:3 TJon
excludes the mention of a frightened Elijah, opting to interpret the
Hebrew consonants with the innocuous meaning "he saw." For
biblical scholars the "sound of thin silence" in 1 Kgs 19:12 is a
puzzling phrase, for the Greek translators it was an expression of
God's presence, and for the Syriac translators it referred to the
moment in which God spoke to Elijah just as God spoke to Moses
and the Israelites at Horeb centuries earlier. For the Targum it
meant an experience of God's *Shekinah*, absent in the wind,
earthquake, and fire, but present in the quiet praising of angels.
And finally, in 18:21, during the contest on Mount Carmel, TJon
presents Elijah as a man of prayer who intercedes with God for the
people and challenges them to return to the covenant. This rich
heritage of Elijan interpretation, preserved in the biblical versions, reveals how the figure of Elijah teased the imaginations of
those who composed the biblical versions just as it did for the first
hermits who came to Mount Carmel.

Craig E. Morrison, O.Carm.

Bibliography

Barthélemy, D. *Critique textuelle de l'Ancien Testament,* OBO 50/1. Fribourg 1982.

Biblia Sacra iuxta Latinam Vulgatam Versionem ad Codicum Fidem, Cura et Studio Monachorum Abbatiae Pontificiae Sancti Hieronymi in Urbe. 16 vols. Rome: Polyglottis Vaticanis 1926-1981.

Burney, C. F. *Notes on the Hebrew Text of the Books of Kings.* Oxford: Clarendon, 1903.

Coote, Robert B. "Yahweh Recalls Elijah." In *Traditions in Transformation,* ed. Baruch Halpern and Jon D. Levenson, 115-20. Winona Lake: Eisenbrauns, 1981.

De Vries, S. J. *1 Kings.* WBC 12. Waco: Word Books, 1985.

Díez Macho, Alejandro. *Neofiti 1,* Tomo II, Éxodo. Madrid, 1970.

Dirksen, P. B. *La Peshitta dell'Antico Testamento.* Studi Biblici 103. Translated by P. G. Borbone. Paideia: Brescia, 1993.

Epstein, I. *The Babylonian Talmud.* London, 1935-52.

Gelston, A. *The Peshitta of the Twelve Prophets.* Oxford: Clarendon, 1987.

Gerleman, G. "Was heißt חַסֶפ." *ZAW* 88 (1976): 409-13.

Gottlieb, H., ed., with Hammershaimb, E., *Kings.* II/4. *The Old Testament in Syriac.* Leiden: Brill, 1976.

Gray, John. *I and II Kings.* OTL. Westminster: Philadelphia, 1970.

Hayward, R. "Memra and Shekhina: A Short Note." *JJS* 31 (1980): 210-213.

Kadushin, Max. *The Rabbinic Mind,* 2d ed. New York: Blaisdell, 1965.

Keel, O. "Erwägungen zum Sitz im Leben des vormosaischen Pascha und zur Etymologie von חַסֶפ." *ZAW* 84 (1972): 414-434.

Lust, J. "A Gentle Breeze or a Roaring Thunderous Sound?" *VT* 25 (1975): 110-115.

Masson, Michel. *Élie ou l'appel du silence.* Paris: Cerf, 1992.

Montgomery, James. *The Book of Kings.* ICC, ed. Henry Snyder Gehman. Edinburgh: T & T Clark, 1951.

Muñoz Leon, Domingo. *Gloria de la Shekina en los Targumim del Pentateuco.* Madrid: Santa Rita - Monachil, 1977.

Murphy, Roland. "The Figure of Elias in the Old Testament." *Carmelus* 15 (1968) 230-8.

Nelson, Richard. D. *First and Second Kings.* Atlanta: John Knox, 1987.

Newsom, Carol. *Songs of the Sabbath Sacrifice: A Critical Edition.* HSS. Atlanta: Scholars, 1985.

The Old Testament in Greek According to the Text of Codex Vaticanus Vol. I: The Octateuch, Vol II: The Later Historical Books, Vol III, Part I: Esther, Judith, Tobit. ed. A. E. Brooke and N. McLean with H. St. J. Thackeray for Vols. II-III. Cambridge, 1917-1940.

Prickett, Stephen. "What do the Translators Think They are Up To?" *Theology* 80 (1977) 403-10.

Schiffman, Lawrence H. "Merkavah Speculation at Qumran: The 4QSerekh Shirot 'Olat ha-Shabbat." In *Mystics, Philosophers, and Politicians.* Jehuda Reinharz and Daniel Swetschinski, eds., with the collaboration of Kalman P. Bland. Duke Monographs in Medieval and Renaissance Studies no. 5. Durham, NC: Duke University, 1982.

Smelik, Willem. F. *The Targum of Judges.* OTS 36. Leiden: Brill, 1995.

Smith, R. Payne. *Thesaurus Syriacus.* Oxford: Clarendon, 1879.

Smolar, Leivy, and Aberbach, Moses. *Studies in Targum Jonathan to the Prophets.* LBS, ed. H. M. Orlinsky. New York: KTAV, 1983.

Sperber, A., ed. *The Bible In Aramaic* 4 vols. Leiden: Brill, 1992.

Urbach, Ephraim E. *The Sages: Their Concepts and Beliefs,* 2d ed. Jerusalem: Magnes, 1979.

Weitzman, M. P. "Lexical Clues to the Composition of the Old Testament Peshitta." In *Studia Aramaica: New Sources and New Approaches.* M. J. Geller, J. C. Greenfield, and M. P. Weitzman, eds., 217-246. JSSSup 4. Oxford: Oxford University Press, 1995.

Endnotes

1. For the abbreviations of the journals cited in this article see S. Schwertner, *International glossary of abbreviation for theology and related subjects* (Berlin - New York, 1974).
2. Executed by Gaspare Dughet between 1640 and 1655.
3. The LXX dates to the second or third century B.C. and therefore it is the primary witness to the Masoretic Text.
4. Since the Syriac text is close to the Masoretic Text, scholars date it to the first part of the second century A.D. (see P. B. Dirksen, *La Peshitta dell'Antico Testamento*, P. G. Borbone, ed., Studi Biblici 103 [Brescia: Paideia, 1993], 24; A. Gelston, *The Peshitta of the Twelve Prophets* [Oxford: Clarendon, 1987], 192). Regarding the origins of the Syriac version Weitzman speculates: "[i]t may be that in the period of the translation the Jews were reeling from the wretched outcome of the uprising under Trajan and the Bar-Cochba revolt" (M. P. Weitzman, "Lexical Clues to the Composition of the Old Testament Peshitta," in *Studia Aramaica: New Sources and New Approaches*, M. J. Geller, J. C. Greenfield, and M. P. Weitzman, eds., JSSSup 4 [Oxford, 1995], 245). The citations from the Syriac version are taken from H. Gottlieb, ed. in collaboration with E. Hammershaimb, *The Old Testament in Syriac: Part II/4; Kings* (Leiden: Brill, 1976).
5. Targum Jonathan and Targum Onqelos are the authoritative Aramaic translations of the Bible for Judaism. Most scholars date TJon between 70 A.D. and the end the second century. For a recent discussion on its dating see W. F. Smelik, *The Targum of Judges*, OTS 36 (Leiden: Brill, 1995) 41-75. The citations of TJon are taken from Sperber's edition (A. Sperber, ed., *The Bible In Aramaic*, 4 vols. [Leiden: Brill, 1992]).

6. Jerome was called to Rome in 382 and commissioned to work on the Latin translation. He completed the Old Testament in 405.

7. NRSV: Then he was afraid; REV: In fear he fled; NAB: Elijah was afraid; NJB: He was afraid; EÜ: Elija geriet in Angst; La Bible de Jerusalem: Il eut peur.

8. See also D. Barthélemy, *Critique textuelle de l'Ancien Testament*, OBO 50/1 (Fribourg, 1982) 371-2.

9. P. Chandler, "*Princeps et exemplar Carmelitarum*: The Prophet Elijah in the *Liber de institutione primorum monachorum*," in *A Journey with Elijah*, P. Chandler, ed. (Rome: Carmelite Institute, 1991) 117-8.

10. Richard D. Nelson, *First and Second Kings* (Atlanta: John Knox, 1987), 124.

11. See the work of M. Masson, *Élie ou l'appel du silence* (Paris: Cerf, 1992). He writes: "La formule *qol demama daqqa* pourrait donc se référer non à un quelconque phénomène externe à caractère météorologique mais bien à une expérience mystique de type interne — celle de l'extase suprême où le mystique, vidé de ce qui fait son moi, accède ardemment à Dieu" (p. 40).

12. See J. Gray, *I and II Kings*, OTL (Westminster: Philadelphia, 1970). He writes: "The meaning of the theophany seems to us rather to be an admonition to the prophet to expect, not the supernatural and spectacular inbreaking of Yahweh into history anticipated in the traditional liturgy of the cult with the accompaniments of storm, earthquake, and fire..., but rather an intelligible revelation to find God's direction in the ordinary course of daily life and to communicate it regularly and constructively.

13. James Montgomery, *The Book of Kings*, ICC, Henry Snyder Gehman, ed. (Edinburgh: T & T Clark, 1951) 314.

14. C. F. Burney, *Notes on the Hebrew Text of the Books of Kings* (Oxford: Clarendon, 1903) 231.

15. Gray, *I and II Kings*, 406.

16. R. Murphy, "The Biblical Elijah: A Holistic Perspective," in *A Journey with Elijah*, P. Chandler, ed. (Rome: Carmelite Institute, 1991) 25.

17. P. A. H. de Boer, "Notes on Text and meaning of Isaiah 38,9-20," *OTS* 9 (1951) 179.

18. J. Lust, "A Gentle Breeze or a Roaring Thunderous Sound?" *VT* 25 (1975) 110-115.

19. Robert B. Coote, "Yahweh Recalls Elijah" in *Traditions in Transformation*, Baruch Halpern and Jon D. Levenson, eds. (Winona Lake: Eisenbrauns, 1981) 115.

20. rell: see *The Old Testament in Greek According to the Text of Codex Vaticanus*. This abbreviation refers all the cursive Greek manuscripts cited in this edition other than those that agree with Greek manuscript B (Vaticanus).

21. Some Greek manuscripts read καὶ ἐκεῖ.

22. It is also possible that some Hebrew manuscripts already contained the expansion וְשֵׁם יהוה.

23. The word ܪܘܚܐ appears in Prov 18:23 in opposition to ܥܘܬܪܐ:
תַּחֲנוּנִים יְדַבֶּר־רָשׁ וְעָשִׁיר יַעֲנֶה עַזּוֹת
ܒܥܘܬܪܐ ܡܡܠܠ ܚܣܝܪܐ ܘܥܬܝܪܐ ܡܡܠܠ ܥܙܝܙܐ.

24. The phrase קוֹל דָּבָר appears in Deut 1:34
אֶת־קוֹל דִּבְרֵיכֶם; 5:28 (ܡܠܐ ܕܚܠܦܝ); אֶת־קוֹל דִּבְרֵיכֶם;
לְקוֹל דִּבְרֵי יְהוָה; 1 Sam 15:1 (ܡܠܐ ܕܦܬܓܡܝܗܘܢ;
ܠܩܠ ܦܬܓܡܘܗܝ, ܕܝܗ); Ps 103:20 (בְּקוֹל דְּבָרוֹ; > Syr);
Dan 10:6 (וְקוֹל דְּבָרָיו; ܡܠܐ ܦܬܓܡܘܗܝ); 10:9 (ܡܠܐ ܕܚܠܦܗ; אֶת־קוֹל דְּבָרָיו).

25. For an inventory of these parallels see R. Murphy, "The Figure of Elias in the Old Testament," *Carmelus* 15 (1962) 234-5.

26. Deut 4:10-15 records the theophany that occurred at Horeb.

27. ולא יכל משה למיעל למשכן זימנא ארום אשרי עלוי
איקר שכינתה דייי ואיקר שכינתה דייי מלא משכנה

28. Leivy Smolar and Moses Aberbach, *Studies in Targum Jonathan to the Prophets*. LBS, H. M. Orlinsky, ed. (New York: KTAV,

1983) 221. For a recent review of the literature on *Shekinah* see Smelik, *The Targum of Judges*, 107-9.

29. Ephraim E. Urbach, *The Sages: Their Concepts and Beliefs*, 2d ed. (Jerusalem: Magnes, 1979) 51-52.

30. See D. Muñoz Leon, *Gloria de la Shekina en los Targumim del Pentateuco* (Santa Rita - Monachil: Madrid, 1977). He offers a careful study of the phrase "the Glory of the Shekinah." TJon in 1 Kgs 19:11-12 has only the word *Shekinah*, which Muñoz Leon interprets in Targum Onqelos as an abbreviation of the longer expression: "El empleo de Shekiná como sujeto es sustitutivo y parece una reducción de la expresión palestinense Gloria de la Shekiná. Probablemente la reducción se debe a una norma oficial que aconsejaba evitar el empleo del sintagma Gloria de la Shekiná" (p. 492). For a critique of his conclusions see R. Hayward, "Memra and Shekina: A Short Note," *JJS 31* (1980) 210-213.

31. The oxymoron should be preserved in the Targum translation for the same reason that Prickett argues it should preserved when translating the Hebrew (Stephen Prickett, "What do the Translators Think They are Up To?" *Theology* 80 [1977] 403-10).

32. Max Kadushin, *The Rabbinic Mind*, 2d ed. (Blaisdell: New York, 1965) 222-229.

33. *b. Sanh.* 22a המתפלל צריך שיראה עצמו כאילו שכינה כנגדו (I. Epstein, *The Babylonian Talmud* 18 vols. [London: 1935-52]).

34. Max Kadushin, *The Rabbinic Mind*, 228. By the term "normal mysticism" Kudashin refers to the experience of God's presence in day to day activity.

35. Carol Newsom, *Songs of the Sabbath Sacrifice: A Critical Edition*, HSS (Scholars: Atlanta, 1985) 306-314.

36. Ibid., 313.

37. Lawrence H. Schiffman, "Merkavah Speculation at Qumran: The 4QSerekh Shirot ʿOlat ha-Shabbat," in *Mystics, Philosophers, and Politicians*, Jehuda Reinharz and Daniel Swetschinski, eds., with the collaboration of Kalman P.

Bland, Duke Monographs in Medieval and Renaissance Studies, no. 5 (Durham, NC: Duke University, 1982) 36-37.

38. The interpretation of ἰγνύα ("the hind part of the thigh and knee"), a *hapax legomenon* in the LXX, is confirmed by the Vetus Latina which reads "femoribus" ("upper part of the thigh").

39. Gray, *I and II Kings*, 396.

40. S. J. DeVries, *1 Kings*, (WBC 12; Waco: Word Books, 1985) 223; HALAT: Krücken.

41. Judges 15:8: ‏וַיֵּשֶׁב בִּסְעִיף סֶלַע עֵיטָם‎.

42. G. Gerleman, "Was heißt ‏פֶּסַח‎," *ZAW* 88 (1976): 410.

43. O. Keel, "Erwägungen zum Sitz im Leben des vormosaischen Pascha und zur Etymologie von ‏פֶּסַח‎," *ZAW* 84 (1972) 428. Keel explains: "weil in den beiden Krücken schon die beiden Gottheiten mitschwingen, deren das lahme Israel sich als Krüchen bedient."

44. Though this agreement is provocative, no conclusion can be drawn regarding the relationship between these two versions without first analyzing all the agreements between them in 1 Kings.

45. R. Payne Smith, *Thesaurus Syriacus* (Oxford: Clarendon 1879) 3135: *dubitans, anceps*.

46. ἀνὴρ δίψυχος, ἀκατάστατος ἐν πάσαις ταῖς ὁδοῖς αὐτοῦ ("since he is a man of two minds, unstable in all his ways").

47. ‏קריב אליה לות כל עמא ואמר עד אמתי אתון פליגין‎
‏לתרתין פלגון הלא יוי הוא אלהים פלחו קדמוהי‎
‏בלחודוהי ולמא אתון טען בתר בעלא דלית ביה צרוך‎
‏ולא אתיבו עמא יתיה פתגם‎

48. Deut 10:12: "And now, Israel, what does the LORD, your God, ask of you but to fear the LORD, your God, and follow his ways exactly, to love and *serve the LORD*, your God, with all your heart and all your soul. See also Josh 24:12; 1 Sam 7:4; 12:20; Jer 30:9.

Stories of Naomi and Ruth

In 1957, when I entered the Carmelite Junior Seminary at Hamilton, MA, Roland Murphy was already a legend. It was four years before I met him. In 1961, a college course with Paul Kirchner, O.Carm., introduced me to the exciting way in which a new generation of Catholic scholars were reading the Bible. I wrote Roland and asked his advice on how I might prepare myself for a career in biblical studies. Even though I no longer have his letter, I can still see its tightly typed, single-spaced print which filled the page, margin to margin. His advice: Learn your languages. He also enclosed a flier for an upcoming workshop which Roland was teaching in East Aurora, NY. I did not ask permission to attend. It was for priests. Seminarians did not go to workshops. When Roland arrived at the workshop, and I was not there, he phoned. Suddenly, I was able to attend. Roland Murphy changed my life.

The book of Ruth combines the parable of the persevering widow (Ruth 1:1-22) and the parable of laborers in the wheat field (Ruth 2:1-23) with two ancestor stories (Ruth 3:1-18, 4:1-21).[1] Naomi is the protagonist in one parable, Ruth in the other. Ruth is also the protagonist in both ancestor stories.

There are four changes of scene in the book of Ruth: the road to Bethlehem, the field of Boaz, the threshing floor, and the gates of Bethlehem.[2] Action, however, is more important than place in the development of most plots, and action marks the most significant divisions in the book of Ruth. The action which causes

131

the greatest conflict in a plot is the climax episode (Ruth 3:1-18). Actions which lead up to the climax are crisis episodes (Ruth 1:1-21, 2:1-23). Action which restores harmony or shalom is the denouement episode (Ruth 4:1-22). At the outset, the household of Elimelech leaves the dying land of Judah for the refugee camps of Moab only to be discovered and ambushed there by an epidemic. Naomi and Ruth come back to Judah and initiate legal action to reclaim their land when Ruth exercises the widows' right of gleaning. The action reaches a climax when Ruth sues Boaz for marriage entitling her to full legal status with an heir, thus reclaiming the land and children of her household.

The Parable of the Persevering Widow (Ruth 1:1-22)

The coherence of the book of Ruth in the Bible today does not deprive the original parables and ancestor stories of their independence as traditions in their own right. Parables challenge the values of the establishment, who are people with land and children, the two things widows, orphans, and strangers lack. Without the political and economic power which land and children confer on members of the establishment, widows, orphans, and strangers are easy targets for discrimination (Exod 22:20-23). The intention of the parable of the persevering widow (Ruth 1:1-22) is to make its audience think about the same problem which nags Job and Qoheleth: "What are the advantages of believing in Yahweh if it does not get you land and children (Ruth 1:21)?"

Crisis: Famine, Migration, and Death (Ruth 1:1-7)

The words with which parables begin are as predictable as the questions with which they end. "In the days when the judges ruled..." (Ruth 1:1) is a good example. Like "...once upon a time" and "...many years ago in a far off place...," this introduction makes no reference to particular dates, times or places. It is a broad, universal orientation which is as sweeping and inclusive as possible. Parables catch audiences in the most ecumenical moments of their lives, moments which they have in common with people of any time and place.

Characters in parables are also generic rather than specific. Because parables are a class action form of tradition, they introduce their audiences to "...a farmer...sowing" (Mt 13:4-17) rather than "...farmer John." The parable of the persevering widow introduces the audience to "...a certain man of Bethlehem in Judah ...and his wife" (Ruth 1:1). Although later storytellers gave the man and his wife names such as Elimelech and Naomi, the typecasting remained. They named the characters in this parable for virtues and vices, like characters in medieval morality plays in Western Europe. Thus Naomi (Hebrew: *naomi*) means blessed, Mahlon (Hebrew: *mahelon*) means a critical patient, Chilion (Hebrew: *kilion*) mean a terminal patient, Ruth (Hebrew: *ruth*) means a companion and Orpah (Hebrew: *'orpah*) means one who returns home.

Parables regularly employ hyperbole, a literary technique which uses deliberate exaggeration for emphasis. The parable of the persevering widow outrages its audience by using hyperbole to exaggerate the suffering of the household of Elimelech. Famine in Judah is a difficulty, not a crisis. Even in Bethlehem, the breadbasket of Judah, famine is a predictable part of life. Just as famine drives the household of Jacob into Egypt in the book of Genesis, famine drives the household of Elimelech east into Moab in the book of Ruth. Hyperbole, however, turns hunger into a hound which relentlessly pursues the household of Elimelech. Famine, migration and then death after death changes his status from landowner to migrant worker, and plummets Naomi from society lady to welfare mother. Will the widow, the orphan, and the stranger find hospitality in Judah, or in Egypt, or in Moab?[3] Only those who are hospitable to the poor will enjoy the blessings of land and children.

Climax: A Covenant Between Ruth and Naomi (Ruth 1:8-18)

In the climax of the parable of the persevering widow, Naomi ritually degrades or humiliates herself. Although Orpah and Ruth attempt to console Naomi, just as Eliphaz, Bildad and Zophar attempt to console Job (Job 1:11-13), she abrogates the covenant which binds them to her. Naomi uses a variation of the divorce, dispensation or annulment formula to dismiss her daughters-in-law: "you are not my people and I am not your God" (Hos 1:8). Her dispensation of Ruth and Orpah directs them "to go back ...to your mother's house" (Ruth 1:7). The standard formula is "your father's house" (Gen 38:11; Lev 22:13; Num 30:16; Deut 22:21). "Your mother's house" appears only four times in the Bible and always in reference to the ability to bear a child (Gen 24:28; Ruth 1:7; Song 3:4; 8:2). Naomi reminds Ruth and Orpah that, since they can have children, they can leave behind their condition as liminal women only by remaining in Moab. With this ritual degradation, Naomi strips herself of every last vestige of authority and social status and stands helpless on the border between Moab and Judah. She is a woman without a household. Without land and children she stands alone in no-man's-land. Naomi's daughters-in-law obey her when she annuls their covenant obligations to her which Ruth and Orpah acquired through marriage to her sons. Orpah returns home to Moab as Naomi tells her to do. Ruth obediently accepts her annulment, but, instead of leaving Naomi, Ruth negotiates a new covenant with her. Ruth clings (Hebrew: *dabaq*) to Naomi (Ruth 1:14) as a husband is expected to cling to his wife (Gen 2:24; Prov 18:24). Later Ruth will cling to the women harvesting in the fields of Boaz. The strength of these women is in their sisterhood to one another.[4]

In the world of the Bible, covenants were negotiated by rulers at the surrender of their enemies. For Ruth, a widow from Moab, to negotiate a covenant with Naomi, a widow from Judah, is ironic. It is not the power of rulers, but the perseverance of widows which blesses Judah and Moab with land and children (Sir 35:5-15). Like the friend who comes at midnight (Luke 11:5-

8) and the widow (Luke 18:1-8) in the gospel of Luke, Ruth and Naomi keep coming back until the promises are fulfilled. The Lord does not deliver Naomi the widow from suffering but, like Ruth, shares her suffering. The land belongs to the widow, the orphan, and the stranger whose title is suffering. Yahweh does not march with soldiers but travels instead with the poor who clog the roads and glean the fields. The powerful put the land and children to death, while the persevering widowing raises them to new life.

Only two components of a standard covenant appear here. They are the stipulations (Ruth 1:15-17) and the litany of blessings and curses (Ruth 1:17-18). The credential (Exod 20:2), the liberation story (Exod 20:2), the notarization (24:1-2), and the documentation (Exod 24:3-11) are missing. In the stipulations, Ruth describes her obligations to Naomi. The opening stipulations in a covenant are often arranged in a decalogue (Exod 20:3-17). There are only five components not ten. In the covenants of the books of Exodus and Deuteronomy, the stipulations in the decalogue are directives like "remember the Sabbath day, to keep it holy" and in the parable of the persevering widow (Ruth 1:15-17) the stipulations are promises patterned on the words of Yahweh to Israel: "I...will be your God, and you shall be my people" (Lev 26:12). In the litany, Ruth describes both the blessings which her household will enjoy if she fulfills her obligations to Naomi, and the curses which it will experience if she does not.

Denouement: Companionship, Not Deliverance (Ruth 1:19-22)

Parables are stories without a denouement. In place of a standard denouement which restores the shalom interrupted by the crisis, the denouement in the parable simply asks the audience a question. In the crisis episode of the parable of the persevering widow, Naomi begins her exodus deprived of land by a famine in Judah and of children by an epidemic in Moab. In the climax, Naomi completes her divestiture by emancipating her widowed daughters-in-law. In the denouement, Naomi asks:

"Why call me Naomi, when the Lord has afflicted me and the Almighty has brought calamity upon me?" (Ruth 1:21).[5] Is this what it means to be chosen by the Lord? To have no land and no children? How can a woman whose name means blessed be cursed with the loss of her land and her children? How can the Lord's chosen people loose their land and children?

The loss of land and children creates worry and doubt. It raises questions, and turns faith into cynicism. The Lord promised to bless the Hebrews with land and children (Gen 12:1-8; Deut 30:15-20). So, when the Lord was Abraham and Sarah's guest, the couple conceived a child (Gen 18:1-15). When the Lord left the land, famine and epidemic crippled its children and weakened its harvests. In ancient Israel, suffering put the covenant to a test. The parable of the persevering widow struggles with both the question of why the innocent suffer, a classic theme in the wisdom of Mesopotamia, Syria-Palestine and Egypt, and with the question of how the covenant between the Lord and Israel will be fulfilled, a classic theme in the Bible of ancient Israel.[6]

For the parable of the persevering widow, the power of land and children is permanent only when uncontested. Therefore, by continuing to tell the story and ask the question, tellers of these parables and their audiences deny the powerful an uncontested claim to the land and its children. The perseverance of the storytellers is like the perseverance of the widows in their parables. They continue to ask: "When will the promises of land and children be fulfilled?" They ask not because they doubt, but because they are absolutely confident that now is a good time.

A Parable of Laborers in a Wheat Field (Ruth 2:1-23)

A parable of laborers in a wheat field (Ruth 2:1-23) further heightens the crisis initiated by the parable of the persevering widow (Ruth 1:1-22). The parable of the persevering widow wants its audience to think about whether the Lord delivers Hebrews from evil, or simply shares their suffering. The parable of laborers in a wheat field asks its audiences to consider whether the hospitality of the Lord and Boaz to strangers is a blessing or a curse for the households of Judah. This parable asks: "Why should the last, like Ruth the Moabite, be first, and the first, like the harvesters of Judah, be last?" The book of Jonah is a parable with much the same intention, as are the parables of laborers in a vineyard (Mt 20:1-16) and the miracle story of the Syro-Ephraimite woman (Mt 15:21-28; Mk 7:24-30) in the New Testament.

Crisis: A Moabite Exercises a Widow of Judah's Right to Glean (Ruth 2:1-3)

Ruth is the protagonist (Ruth 2:2). By gleaning without being clearly eligible to do so, she provokes a crisis among the other laborers. They react to Ruth as a stranger (Hebrew: *nokriyah*).

Climax: An Outsider Confronts an Insider (Ruth 2:3-7)

By continuing to glean (Ruth 2:7), Ruth aggravates the situation until the laborers report her to the owner of the field, but this "man of wealth" (Ruth 2:1) treats Ruth like his heir instead of his enemy. Ruth meets Boaz in a wheat field, at a threshing floor, and at the city gate. Each is a threshold which leads to fertility. At each site, Ruth and Boaz ritually celebrate the intercourse which will bless the household of Elimelech and Naomi with an heir.[7] When a man comforts and speaks kindly to a woman as Boaz speaks to Ruth in the wheat field, he is courting her. When a man feeds a woman like Boaz feeds Ruth in the wheat field, he is marrying her. Today when the bride and groom give each other wine to drink or feed each other wedding cake, they continue a very old wedding tradition in which feeding one another was the ritual by which a man and woman consummated the marriage vows which they had spoken.

After a remarkably short bargaining session Boaz initially grants Ruth three employee benefits. First, he is legally obligated to allow Ruth the privilege of gleaning for only one day, but he extends her privileges for the duration of the harvest. Second, he guarantees Ruth's security. Third, he agrees to allow Ruth water-breaks and even agrees to provide the water.

Denouement: An Outsider Becomes an Insider (Ruth 2:8-23)

In the denouement, she asks: "Why have I found favor in your eyes, that you should take notice of me, when I am a stranger (Ruth 2:10)?" In the parable of the laborers in the vineyard in the gospel of Matthew, the owner asks: "Am I not allowed to do what I choose with what belongs to me? Or are you [other harvesters] envious because I am generous?" (Mt 20:15)? In the parable of laborers in the wheat field Ruth asks: "Why have I found favor in your eyes, that you should take notice of me, when I am a stranger (Ruth 2:10)?" Like the question in the parable of the persevering widow, the question in this parable asks: "Am I an insider or an outsider, blessed or cursed (Ruth 2:10)?"

The commentary on the benefits which Ruth negotiates from Boaz stresses that no act of kindness is forgotten. Ruth's loving kindness (Hebrew: *hesed*) toward Naomi is repaid by the loving kindness of Boaz to Ruth.[8] Ruth's response to Naomi is unexpected. Despite the fact that Naomi dispenses Ruth from any legal obligation to her, Ruth continues to care for her mother-in-law in excess of what even the law itself would require. Likewise, despite the fact that Boaz fulfills his legal obligation to Ruth as a widow, he continues to care for her in excess of what even the law itself would require. Boaz grants Ruth far more generous privileges in his fields than the law obliges him to grant. He adds a fourth, fifth and sixth benefit to the three he has already granted Ruth. Fourth, Ruth eats a hot lunch with Boaz rather than parched grain with the other workers. Fifth, Ruth gets to gather not only the dropped gleanings to which the law entitles her, but also from the standing sheaves. Sixth, the harvesters are to show Ruth which is the good grain. With these gestures, this parable reminds audiences that Israel does not deserve the Lord's favor anymore than Naomi deserves the favor of Ruth, or Ruth the favor of Boaz.

In the wheat field Boaz promises Ruth: "May you have a full reward from the Lord, the God of Israel, under whose wings (Hebrew: *kanap*) you have come for refuge" (Ruth 2:12). At the threshing floor, Ruth asks Boaz to keep his promise and "...spread your cloak (Hebrew: *kanap*) over your servant" (Ruth 3:9). The book of Deuteronomy uses the same idiom. "A man shall not marry his father's wife, and lift up the cloak (Hebrew: *kanap*) which his father spread over her" (Deut 22:30, author's translation). "Cursed be anyone who lies with his father's wife and lifts up the cloak (Hebrew: *kanap*) which his father spread over her" (Deut 27:20, author's translation). The imagery is sexual.[9] A woman's dress or cloak are like the wings of her husband. Boaz promises to take Ruth under his wing. He will cover her body with his cloak when he has intercourse with her.

Every human community must decide how to distribute its goods and services. Some communities establish very simple formats, others very complicated ones. Few formats for the distribution of goods and services satisfy all the members of the community for very long and challenges to the system emerge. Many traditional societies forestall protests against the system of distribution by allowing certain officials to suspend the system so that people will continue to believe in the system. These dispensations often take place when the powerful like Boaz give the powerless like Ruth a face-to-face audience. The official listens to their petitions and generally grants some form of immediate, although temporary, relief.

A Story of Ruth (Ruth 3:1-18)

Having used two parables to create a crisis, the book of Ruth uses a story of Ruth (Ruth 3:1-18) to reach a climax. This story is an ancestor story which defends the household of David against charges questioning its eligibility to rule Israel.[10] Just as the books of Samuel-Kings (2 Sam 9:1-20:26+1 Kings 1:1-2:46) assemble stories about Bathsheba and Nathan which portray them as responsible for Solomon becoming the heir of David, so the Book of Ruth assembles stories (Ruth 3:1-18; 4:1-22) which portray Ruth and Boaz as the Bathsheba and Nathan who support David as the heir of Saul.

Crisis: A Liminal Woman Gleans the Land (Ruth 3:1-9)

The crisis in this story of Ruth ends with the same question found in the parable of laborers in a wheat field. In the parable, Boaz asks: "Whose maiden is this?" (Ruth 2:5). In this story, Boaz asks: "Who are you? (Ruth 3:9). It is precisely because the people of Judah are asking "Ruth who?" that the stories of the successor of David and the Book of Ruth develop. The intention of the stories is to give Ruth, and therefore the household of David, a legitimate claim to the rule Israel. Cultures define strangers or outsiders in a variety of ways. The loyal opposition tried to disqualify the household of David on several grounds. Initially opposition to David centered on the charge that he ousted Saul, the chief he had sworn to serve. The people loved Saul who delivered Israel from the Philistines. Like Peter in the New Testament, the stories of Saul portray this chief as an impetuous and outspoken, but magnanimous human being. These qualities made him a wonderful chief but an inept monarch.[11] Even though Saul could not establish an effective state in Israel, and eventually alienated Samuel who nominated him, the people continued to love him. He died a tragic death, watching the Philistines slaughter his sons and then committed suicide. Not even his aide-de-camp obeyed him and put him out of his misery. No matter what Saul had done or failed to do, the people found this death excessive punishment and held the household of David responsible.

Opponents to the household of David also argued that because he was the youngest in age and smallest in stature, David should not have passed over his brothers to rule Israel. They also considered David a mercenary, who fought for the enemies of Israel, because the Philistines granted David asylum. They charged that David provoked an unnecessary war with the Ammonites, and betrayed the loyalty of his soldier Uriah and his wife Bathsheba. They objected to David's decision to move the capital of Israel from the sanctuary at Hebron to Jerusalem, which was not even a Hebrew city.[12] Jerusalem belonged neither to Judah nor Israel, but only to the household of David. Finally, they accused the household of David of being Moabite, not Hebrew.

The story of Ruth which serves as a climax for the Book of Ruth celebrates this woman of Moab who continues to embrace Judah until it bears a child to enjoy its harvest. Ruth is tenacious. She holds on to Naomi, and she holds on to Boaz like the household of David holds on to Judah. In the end there is a harvest, and there is a child. Like Naomi, Ruth is a persevering widow.

Ruth is a "worthy woman" (Hebrew: *'eset hayyil*; Ruth 3:11). She is a "woman, who...like Rachel and Leah ...built up the house of Israel" (Ruth 4:11). The household of David considers Ruth to be the ancestor who taught it how to survive and how to serve others. Her virtues are characteristic of the household of David as a whole. The power of an ancestor is not based on land and children, but rather on some virtue which compensates for land and children. As an ancestor, Ruth has neither land nor children, but she compensates for them by her perseverance which the clan that tells her stories wants its households to imitate. The household of David has no clear claim to the throne based on land and children, but compensates for it by Ruth's virtues of perseverance.

The story portrays Boaz as "the man" (Ruth 3:8) and the "kinsman more closely related" (Ruth 3:12) as elders or "people of the land." The people of the land played the role of monarch makers in Judah. They had no official power in Jerusalem, but they had a vested interest in the monarch who held power there. The household of Boaz opposes the "young men, whether poor or rich..." (Ruth 3:10), who were the warriors with whom these elders competed in the village assembly. Ruth must decide which of these elders would be a better patron for the household of Elimelech.

The threshing floor (Hebrew: *goren*) which appears in both the stories of David's rise to power (2 Sam 24:18-25) and here in this story of Ruth (Ruth 3:6) are not only places where grain is processed, but where rulers are chosen. Since it is the responsibility of the monarch to provide food for the people, the question: "Who will feed Israel?" is decided at the location where food is processed.

Bathsheba waits to promote the candidacy of Solomon until David's administration has run its course. Likewise, Ruth waits to promote the candidacy of David until Boaz eats and drinks (Ruth 3:3-7). The role of women in promoting the candidacy of monarchs in Judah is significant.

Climax: A Liminal Woman Seeks a Child (Ruth 3:9-13)

Ruth dresses not to be seductive, but so that she can act officially as the representative of the household of Elimelech (Ruth 4:3). In the world of the Bible, clothes are not a personal accessory, they are a uniform indicating social status. Ruth goes to the threshing floor and uncovers the feet of Boaz. In the story which follows, she pulls the sandal off the foot of her legal guardian. In both passages, the word foot is a euphemism for a man's penis. By placing herself in the physical position for intercourse with Boaz, she propositions him for marriage. By removing the sandal of her legal guardian, she sues him for divorce. The intercourse here is ritual, not consummated.

Denouement: A Liminal Woman Becomes Mother of a Household (Ruth 3:14-17)

Boaz accepts the proposal of Ruth and sends her home with his grain.[13] The grain which is his return of the land to the household of Elimelech will be matched soon by the semen which will be his return of children to the household. The association between the seed which will give birth to a child, and the seed which will produce a harvest is further strengthened when Boaz pours barley into Ruth's apron making her look like a woman who is pregnant. The grain is a down payment on both the land and the children which will restore the honor of the household of Naomi and Elimelech.

Ruth functions at the threshing floor like Tamar functions at the sanctuary of Timnah in the Book of Genesis (Gen 38). Both use alternative means to access the power of their legal guardians. There are strong parallels between this story of Ruth and the stories of Tamar. Both Elimelech and Judah move their households to strange lands. The mothers of the households and two of their sons die in both stories. Both Ruth and Tamar are liminal women who leave the households of their fathers and go above and beyond the call of duty to preserve the households of their husbands from extinction.

Like the ancestor stories of Moses in the book of Exodus (Exod 1:21-2:25), the Book of Ruth also functions as an apology for the household of David. Like Moses who was accused of being an Egyptian and not a Hebrew, David was accused of being a Moabite. Following the standard apologetic technique, the Book of Ruth admits the accusation and then carefully reinterprets the criticism as a compliment. Though Ruth was from Moab and, therefore, a foreign woman, it is precisely the widow, the orphan

and the stranger whom the Lord favors and through whom the
Lord delivers Israel.

A Story of Ruth (Ruth 4:1-22)

The Book of Ruth concludes with a second story of Ruth
(Ruth 4:1-22) to argue that the Lord returns to Judah when David
becomes its monarch. When a poor woman like Naomi recovers
her land, and a barren woman like Ruth gives birth to a child, the
land is alive and the Lord is present. This story of Ruth (Ruth 4:1-
22) is also an ancestor story. It answers the question so painfully
raised in the parable of the persevering widow by asserting that
in the Israel of David, widows are blessed, not cursed (Ruth 4:14-
16).

Crisis: A Legal Guardian Exercises His Authority Over the Land (Ruth 4:1-4)

When the father of a household died without designating
an heir, the tribe appointed a legal guardian to look after the
household. The tribe could not interfere in the internal affairs of
a household unless the father of the household died with no heir
(Deut 25:5). Most English translations render the word for this
legal guardian or executor (Hebrew: *yabam*; *go'el*; Latin: *levir*) as
brother-in-law or redeemer. Provisions for the appointment of
legal guardians are found throughout the ancient Near East. For
example, the Hittite Code, which represents a legal tradition in the
Empire of Hatti between 1450-1200 BCE, establishes similar
provisions for the appointment of a legal guardian as those found
in the Bible (Gen 38:1-30; Lev 25:25-38; Deut 25:5-10; Jer 32:6-
44). The social institutions and legal vocabulary in these traditions are comparable but not identical. In some cases, the
guardian is delegated to take over only the land of the household
(Hebrew: *go'el*), whereas in others he must father an heir with the

widow as well (Hebrew: *yabam*). Guardians represent the larger interests of the tribe in preventing a leaderless household in one of its villages from losing the ability to feed and protect its members. The second story of Ruth opens when Boaz asks the legal guardian of the household of Elimelech if he can afford to exercise his option to rent and farm its land. With the resources of his own household, the legal guardian was expected to feed and protect the household for which he was legal guardian. The legal guardian of the household of Elimelech publicly affirms his ability to work the land.

Climax: A Legal Guardian Waives His Authority to Parent a Child (Ruth 4:5-12)

Boaz then challenges the legal guardian of the household of Elimelech to assume responsibility for both the land and the children of the household. Although the liabilities of a household without a father were generally greater than its assets, a legal guardian did enjoy the usufruct of the property and the people of the household as long as there was no heir. He could keep any profit realized while he was guardian. While rebuilding the ability of the household to work its land and tend its herds for which it was responsible to the village, the guardian was also to have intercourse with the widow until she had a son. He did not marry the mother of the household (Lev 18:16; 20:21), he simply carried out the physical and economic commitments which her husband had failed to complete before his death. The guardian was authorized to care for her only until she had an heir, and the household could once again care for its own land and children.

For financial reasons, the legal guardian of the household of Elimelech waives his right to father a child with Ruth, and, consequently, to rent and to farm her land as well. Ruth divorces him, and accepts Boaz as her new legal guardian. She abrogates the covenant which obliges one next of kin to restore the household of Elimelech and negotiates a new covenant with another.

In a covenant in Gen 12:1-7, the Lord deeds Abraham and Sarah land in Syria-Palestine, which they claim by surveying it and constructing altars at each of its corners. The altars at Bethel (Gen 12:7), Ai (Gen 12:8) and Hebron (Gen 13:18) form the triangle of the first land which the Lord deeds to the household of Abraham and Sarah. To increase the speed of their surveys, buyers wear sandals. Since they walk off their land in sandals, their sandals become the moveable title to that land, just as the altars are the fixed titles. One of the most interesting aspects of this story of Ruth is the social institution of land tenure and the way in which land owners use their sandals as titles to their land. Sandals are worn during the Passover meal in preparation for surveying the land which is being deeded to the Jews by the Lord during the meal (Exod 12:11). Only the landless who believe in the Lord's promise to make them landowners can celebrate Passover.

Landowners remove their sandals upon entering a house to avoid competition. In a home, everyone is equal. For the same reasons that sandals are not worn in the house, sandals are removed by mourners. Death like one's home is the great democracy which does not distinguish between the landed and the landless (Ezek 24:17-23). Finally, sandals are not worn in the sanctuaries, because the Lord is the only landlord in ancient Israel. The Lord alone holds title to all the land. Households in ancient Israel own land only by proxy. To wear sandals into the presence of the Lord would be tantamount to challenging the Lord's ownership.

To tie or lose the thongs of the sandals is the gesture which slaves or the landless use to show respect for land owners (Mt 3:11; Mk 1:7; Lk 3:16; Jn 1:27; Acts 13:25). When Ruth removes the sandal of her legal guardian (Ruth 4:7), however, she divests him of two rights. The first is called *temurah* (Job 15:31; 20:18; 28:17; Lev 27:10,33), and the second is called *ge'ullah* (Mic 2:2; Isa 5:8). *Temurah* refers to economic power. When Ruth removes the sandal of her legal guardian, his household no longer owns the land of the household of Elimelech. He can no longer walk the land which for which the sandals are his title. *Ge'ullah* refers to political power. When Ruth removes the sandal of her legal guardian, he forfeits all the rights and privileges which he enjoyed as the legal guardian of the household of Elimelech.[14] He may no longer have intercourse with the mother of the household of Elimelech in order to sire an heir for him. A legal guardian is expected to have intercourse with the widow and care for her until she has an heir old enough to administer the land which is her annuity. In this gesture, the sandal is symbolic of the widow's vagina, the foot of the legal guardian symbolic of his penis.[15] Removing the sandal thus terminates the social status of the legal guardian.

Denouement: A Child is Born (Ruth 4:13-22)

According to the standard protocol of the legal guardian, the child should be the son of Chilion, the deceased husband of Ruth. Nonetheless, the women of Bethlehem celebrate the birth of the child, singing: "Praise the Lord...a son has been born to Naomi" (Ruth 4:14-17). Like the words "go back ...each of you to your mother's house" (Ruth 1:8), these words are unexpected. The use of such emphatically women's words may be characteristic of the liminal condition of widows who are operating without any relationship to the households of a father, a husband or a son.[16] It is unlikely that the women, or even the storytellers, name Naomi as the mother of the child in order to erase the memory of Ruth as a sexually forward Gentile woman.[17] The traditions consistently celebrate both Naomi and Ruth as widows, who use their status as liminal women to restore the honor of their common household. These women act together, and they act honorably. The dyadic or collective world of the Bible allows the names of Ruth and Naomi to be interchanged without prejudice to either of them. As liminal women they are entitled to act aggressively to restore the honor of their households.

The story celebrates the support which Ruth offers Boaz as a young landowner to ransom the household of Elimelech. With the help of Ruth, Boaz fearlessly challenges the elders to take possession of Ruth and the land of Elimelech. Ultimately, the story celebrates the ambition of a David whose ambition and fearlessness led him to take control of Israel. The Book of Ruth clearly celebrates the efficiency and success with which David ransoms Israel from the sentence of death imposed on it by the Philistines. Monarchs consider the institutions of the more egalitarian villages to be too slow, too inefficient, too limited in their effects to save the nation. Boaz is the ideal monarch, whose decisive actions bring a dying land to life. The Book of Ruth does not consider ambition, decisiveness, or initiative characteristic of selfish and greedy monarchs, but rather of widows like Naomi and strangers like Ruth whose complete trust is in the Lord. David was not the ruthless descendant of the monarchs of Egypt and Mesopotamia but rather the grandson of widows and strangers.

Audiences in different periods of ancient Israel have heard the traditions which make up the Book of Ruth in the Bible today differently. In the villages of early Israel, households in jeopardy of loosing their land and children asked: "Who will enjoy the blessings of land and children?" In these traditions they heard that land and children belong to persevering widows like Naomi, to fearless strangers like Ruth and to decisive chiefs like Boaz. By challenging the powerful who curse Israel with famine, epidemic, poverty and widowhood, these traditions championed the quiet rights of the powerless celebrating their harvests of barley and wheat. Jews today continue this tradition of harvest storytelling. The Song of Songs is read on Passover in March, the Book of Ruth is read during the celebration of Weeks (Hebrew: *shavuot*) or Pentecost (Jer 36:28-9; Ezek 3:1-3) in April, and the book of Qoheleth is read during the celebration of Booths (Hebrew: *succoth*) in September.[18]

The household of David heard the traditions in the book of Ruth as supporting its right to rule Israel as a state. They showed how the Lord saved Israel with the help of Ruth, a foreign woman who was the grandmother of David. This telling of the traditions developed after 1000 BCE.

When Ezra and the household of David were repatriated to Judah by the Persians after 537 BCE, the Jews who had not been deported heard the traditions in the Book of Ruth as a challenge to the right of the household of David to rule Judah. In the reconstruction of the postexilic community, marriage with women who were not members of the household of David was prohibited. For the people of the land, the Book of Ruth shows that Ruth, though not a member of the household of David, was more faithful to the covenant between the Lord and Israel than those who were.

The Book of Ruth captured the hearts not only of the people on the margins of ancient Israel, but the Jews to whom Jesus preached as well. The New Testament fondly remembered him not as a conquering hero claiming colonies for an emperor or riding triumphant into the cities of his enemies. The lame, the blind, the lepers, the widows, the fishermen, the shepherds, the prostitutes, the tax collectors remembered him as they remembered Naomi. "Foxes have holes, and birds of the air have nests; but the son of man has nowhere to lay his head" (Mt 8:20). Like Naomi and Ruth, Jesus also demonstrated that "...the meek ...shall inherit the earth" (Mt 5:5).

Don C. Benjamin, O.Carm.

Endnotes

1. For H. Gunkel (Ruth, in *Reden und Aufsatze*, [Göttingen 1913] 85) the book of Ruth is a novella. For E. Wurthwein (*Die Funf Megilloth* [Handbuch zum Alten Testament 18; 2nd ed., 1969] 3-4) it is an "idyl...a striving for an ideal and innocent condition...and for patriarchal conditions, such as the appearance of a few, simple, mostly model-type characters." For J. M. Sasson (*Ruth: a new translation with a philological commentary and a formalist-folklorist interpretation.* [Sheffield: *Journal for the Study of the Old Testament*, 1989]) it is a folktale, but "...Ruth is obviously neither a folktale nor a fairy tale of nineteenth-century Russia [like those studied by V. Propp, *Morphology of the Folktale*, 2nd ed., revised and edited with a preface by L. A. Wagner; new introduction by A. Dundes. (Austin TX: 1968)]." For E. F. Campbell ("The Hebrew Short Story: a study of Ruth" in *A Light Unto My Path: Old Testament studies in honor of J. M. Myers*, H. Bream et al., eds. [Philadelphia, 1974]) and P. A. Viviano (The Deuteronomistic History in *The Catholic Study Bible*, D. Senior et al., eds. [New York: Oxford University, 1990] 141-6) it is a short story. R. E. Murphy (*Wisdom Literature: Job, Proverbs, Ruth, Canticles, Ecclesiastes, and Esther* [Forms of Old Testament Literature; Grand Rapids: Eerdmans 1981] 86) agrees that Ruth is a Hebrew historical short story as proposed by E. F. Campbell. Campbell (Anchor Bible 7; [New York: Doubleday, 1975] 5-6) points out the characteristics that make up this genre: (1) the work is composed in a distinctive literary style; (2) an interest in typical people is combined with an interest in mundane affairs; (3) the purposes are several: both entertaining and instructive; and (4) an impression of the artistry and creativity of the author is made upon the reader. Campbell regards the Hebrew short story as probably a new form, a new literary creation, and he dates the work to 950-700 B.C."

2. Gunkel (1913:65-92) proposed using change of scene to structure the Book of Ruth. Murphy (1981:85) agrees: "This structure is determined largely by the change of scenes and the course of action within the story. In addition, a significant use of catchwords hold the units together: *sub* (return) in 1:1-22; *lqt* (glean) in 2:1-17; *g'l* (redeem) in 3:6-15; *qnh* (acquire) and *g'l* (redeem) in 4:1-12." S. Bertman (Symmetrical Design in the Book of Ruth, [*Journal of Biblical Literature* 84; 1965] 165-8) considers its structure to be chiastic.

3. A. J. Levine ("Ruth," in *The Women's Bible Commentary* [C.A. Newsom and S. H. Ringe, eds. [Louisville: Westminster/ John Knox 1992] 79) writes: "...[a]lthough reminiscent of Israel's settling in Egypt (Genesis 46), this move is problematic: Moab is associated with hostility (Numbers 22-24; Judg 3:12-30; but cf. 1 Sam 22:3-4) and with sexual perversity (Gen 19:30-38). Its food is used not for supplying hungry Israelites but for feasting before local gods (Num. 25:1-5). Deuteronomy 23:3-6 (cf. Neh. 13:1) excludes both Moabites and Ammonites from the 'assembly of God,' and the context of this legislation reinforces the association of Moab with improper sexuality. Elimelech consequently may be seen as disloyal to his land and his God."

4. Murphy (1981:89) follows Gunkel (1913:67) here: "...Naomi at first refuses to accept the sacrifice of her daughters-in-law, but eventually permits Ruth to accompany her. As ...[Gunkel] remarks, generosity is arrayed against generosity. Orpah serves as a counterpoint to Ruth, to make Ruth's unusual generosity stand out."

5. The LXX and Vulgate label the Book of Ruth an historical book and place it between the Books of Judges and Samuel-Kings. The MT considers it a writing and places it between Proverbs and the Song of Songs. Not all writings are wisdom traditions which Murphy ("Religious Dimensions of Israelite Wisdom" in *Ancient Israelite Religion: essays in honor of Frank Moore Cross*, Patrick D. Miller, Jr., Paul D. Hanson, and S. Dean McBride, eds. [Philadelphia: Fortress, 1987]

449), and others identify as Proverbs, Job, Ecclesiastes, Sirach, and the Wisdom of Solomon. Like these wisdom traditions, however, divine activity in the book of Ruth is mediated. The name Yahweh appears primarily in the blessings of Naomi and Boaz. Nonetheless, Naomi, Ruth, and Boaz fulfill these blessings by the way they act. There is no direct intervention of Yahweh in the book of Ruth, but Yahweh is mediated by those who live faithful lives. This "...loyal response to the covenant God" (e.g. Deut 6:2, 13, 24) and "...observance of the Torah" (e.g. Ps 119:63; Eccl 12:13) are two understandings of "...fear of the Lord," which, for Murphy defines wisdom as a source of the religion of ancient Israel.

6. Wisdom in the Bible is not just Israel's accommodation to Egypt and Mesopotamia, but an integral part of its own faith and world view. Murphy (1987:449-458) studies the phrase fear of the Lord demonstrating that the wisdom traditions in Proverbs, Job, Ecclesiastes and Ben Sirach are as important and as authentic a source of the religion of ancient Israel as the "Yahwistic" traditions in the books of Genesis, Exodus and Deuteronomy. See also, R. E. Murphy, "Wisdom—Theses and Hypotheses" in *Israelite Wisdom: theological and literary essays in honor of Samuel Terrien*, John G. Gammie et al., eds. (New York: Scholars Press, 1978) 35-8.

7. For Levine (1992:81) "...[t]his scene offers a reverse of the typical meeting found elsewhere in the Bible, between men and women who will eventually marry (cf. Genesis 24; 29; Exod 2:15-22), with Ruth in the man's role: she is the one who leaves home, seeks her fortune, encounters hardships, and has water drawn for her."

8. For Levine (1992:81) "Boaz does not want the Moabite woman to be sexually harassed, but his language could suggest that he himself is attracted to the woman."

9. So Levine 1992:81.

10. K. Whitelam, The Defense of David, *Journal for the Study of the Old Testament* 29 (1984) 61-87.

11. J. W. Flanagan, Chiefs in Israel, *Journal for the Study of the Old Testament* 20 (1981) 47-73.

12. J. W. Flanagan, The Relocation of the Davidic Capital, *Journal of the American Academy of Religion* 47 (1979) 223-44.

13. For Levine (1992:83) "Ruth's comment [to Naomi: 'He gave me these six measures of barley, for he said, "Do not go back to your mother-in-law empty-handed"' (Ruth 3:17)] may be double entendre. She symbolically carries what Naomi most wants: Boaz's seed. By handing Naomi the grain, Ruth anticipates the handing of the child Obed to her mother-in-law. Through Ruth's efforts, Naomi will no longer be 'empty-handed'."

14. J. M. Sasson, The Issue of *ge'ullah* in the Book of Ruth, *Journal for the Study of the Old Testament* 5 (1978) 52-68.

15. T. H. Gaster, *Myth, Legend, and Custom in the Old Testament* (New York: Harper & Row, 1975) 2, 449-50.

16. It has also been suggested that Moab was a matrilocal rather than a patrilocal society. Therefore, Naomi correctly directs her daughters back to the households of their mothers. As yet, there is not enough social scientific evidence to support this conclusion.

17. For Levine (1992:84) "Ruth—whose language and actions sought to incorporate Naomi into her new family—is erased from the text. Her mother-in-law nurses the child, the local women name him, and they even proclaim, 'A Son has been born to Naomi' (4:7). This removes the child from any Moabite stigma. Confirming this pure pedigree is the genealogy with which the book concludes."

18. For A. Berlin (Big Theme, Little Book, *Bible Review* [August 1996] 40-48) the association of the Book of Ruth with *Shavuot* "...commemorates the giving of the Torah.... the usual explanation (that *Shavuot* celebrate the spring grain harvest, which forms the setting for the book) and various

lesser-known explanations (that David, a great-grandson of Ruth, died on *Shavuot* or that Ruth's loyalty to Naomi symbolizes Israel's loyalty to the Torah) touch only upon superficial connections or are clearly midrashic efforts to forge a connection.... The Book of Ruth...is about exile and return, land and people. Like Abraham, and like the family of Jacob...the family of Elimelech was forced by famine to leave its home in the land of Israel and to preserve itself in a foreign land. When the famine abates, Naomi returns to Bethlehem. ...the importance of returning is emphasized in chapter 1 by the repetition of the root *shuv*, 'return,' twelve times as Naomi bids her daughters-in-law return to their families in Maob and as she returns to Judah...."

The Feasts of Saints Elijah and Elisha in the Carmelite Rite: A Liturgico-Musical Study

The Carmelites distinguished themselves from other medieval religious orders by being named for a place rather than for a founder and by a unique mixture of eastern and western elements in their liturgical tradition. As part of this tradition they eventually venerated the prophets Elijah and Elisha as saints with liturgical feasts. This paper discusses the veneration of these two Old Testament figures, an intriguing phenomenon in western liturgical rites, and places this veneration within the context of the Carmelite Order's overall liturgical tradition.

The men who later became the first Carmelites arrived on Mount Carmel as part of the Crusader movement.[1] They settled there probably at the very end of the twelfth century since virtually no mention of them is made prior to the Carmelite formula of life at the beginning of the thirteenth.[2] Elias Friedman described the original Carmelites as Latin hermits to avoid confusion with Greek Orthodox and other hermits who had settled on Mount Carmel at one time or another.[3] The Carmelite rule, given by Albert, Patriarch of Jerusalem, between 1206 and 1214,[4] was addressed to "B" and the other hermits under obedience to him, who live near the spring on Mount Carmel";[5] later texts amplified the locale to "iuxta fontem Eliae" rather than simply "iuxta fontem," identifying the site with the spring of Elijah.[6] Such an addition reflects an already obvious association between the site of Mount Carmel and the activity of the prophet Elijah, amply described in First and Second Kings.[7]

Increasing Saracen raids prompted the Carmelites to begin migrating westward around 1238;[8] this process led to a rapid internationalization of the Order, which numbered ten provinces by 1281.[9] Constitution 13 of the Fourth Lateran Council of 1215 forbade the foundation of new orders lest there be too much diversity among them.[10] This decree forced the Carmelites to appeal to several popes for recognition, which in turn led to a series of bulls officially approving their status as a religious order.[11] As part of this process, however, they adopted most of the characteristics of the mendicant orders, including the common refectory and recitation of the divine office in choir, thus effectively changing their mode of life from eremitic to mendicant. This process was completed by the promulgation of a revised rule by Pope Innocent IV on October 1, 1247,[12] which effectively translated the original Albertine formula of life into a mendicant framework; it enabled the Carmelites to function in medieval European society, but it changed many of the aspects of life which had been part of their original self-understanding on Mount Carmel.

The transition of the Order to a mendicant framework and the displacement of the Carmelites to western Europe with their eventual removal from Mount Carmel itself in 1291,[13] forced them to view their origins in a different light and gradually enabled them to celebrate Elijah and Elisha liturgically along with the other saints of the Order. Their physical removal from Mount Carmel and its environs heightened the Carmelites' appreciation of its spiritual value in their lives. Thus, the Constitutions of the Chapter of Bordeaux in 1281 speak of its value in an exhortation to neophytes:

> We declare, bearing testimony to the truth, that
> from the time when the prophets Elijah and Elisha
> dwelt devoutly on Mount Carmel, holy Fathers

both of the Old and the New Testament, whom the contemplation of heavenly things drew to the solitude of the same mountain, have without doubt led praiseworthy lives there by the fountain of Elijah in holy penitence unceasingly and successfully maintained.

It was these same successors whom Albert the patriarch of Jerusalem in the time of Innocent III united into a community, writing a rule for them which Pope Honorius, the successor of the same Innocent, and many of their successors, approving this Order, most devoutly confirmed by their charters. In the profession of this rule, we, their followers, serve the Lord in diverse parts of the world, even to the present day.[14]

This citation is significant for its spiritualization of the place of Mount Carmel and for the explicit references to Elijah and his disciple Elisha. It identifies the Carmelites with the prophets Elijah and Elisha as well as with the site itself. It traces the order back to the prophets Elijah and Elisha. While the mantle of Elijah has often been associated with the cloak of the Carmelite habit in the traditional lore of the Order, it is part of a larger tradition: both St. Anthony and St. Jerome make the association explicit between Elijah and those who follow the eremitic way of life.[15]

Chapter 7 of the Rule enjoined each Carmelite to remain in his own cell or nearby, pondering the law of the Lord day and night and keeping watch at his prayers, unless attending to some other duty.[16] The "contemplation of heavenly things" linked the Carmelites, the prophets and countless other devout people in a spiritual bond. The translation of the Carmelites into a mendicant framework, where both the canonical hours and apostolic activity intruded into the life of solitary prayer, may have encouraged them to focus on Elijah and Elisha as symbols of the life of prayer which they had originally maintained on Mount Carmel. They personified the approach to spirituality stipulated in Chapter 15 of the Albertine formula of life, which charged the Carmelites to "put on holiness as your breastplate," reminded them that "faith must be your shield" and enjoined them to place on their heads "the helmet of salvation,"[17] citing Eph. 6:14, 16 and 17.

The assumption of Elijah, aptly described in Second Kings, ironically proved a stumbling block to his liturgical celebration, since it implied that he did not die: without a *dies natalis* he had no date of death, hence no birth into eternal life. Thus, while the cult of Elisha entered the Order within the 15th century, that of Elijah came much later, probably not for universal observance until the liturgical reform of the Order in 1585.[18] The Ordinal compiled by the Carmelite Sibert de Beka and promulgated by the General Chapter of London in 1312 prescribed the *incipit* or beginning words of each prayer, reading, chant text and psalm to be used in the divine office as well as each prayer and chant to be used in celebrating Mass for every day of the year. It thus established a uniform liturgical tradition in the Carmelite Order[19] which regulated the texts while allowing each convent to choose its own musical setting; it, of course, makes no mention of Elijah or Elisha, since their cult entered the rite much later.

The Carmelite General Chapter of 1399 prescribed the observance of the feast of St. Elisha as a duplex feast, or rank of high solemnity, on June 14th, using the office of a confessor or holy man until a proper one could be developed.[20] The chapter of 1411 reiterated this prescription. This explains why no chants for this feast are found in the fourteenth-century Carmelite antiphonaries of Pisa,[21] Florence[22] or Krakow, nor in the fifteenth-century antiphonaries of Mainz,[23] nor in a fifteenth-century German Carmelite breviary,[24] also from Mainz. There would be no need for these manuscripts to contain the office if all the chants were derived from the common of the saints.

A Carmelite breviary printed in Venice in 1495[25] provides the earliest instance of the complete office of St. Elisha. Although the breviary includes no music, one can presume that this was the standard office, and probably the first one for this saint in the

years preceding the Council of Trent. Later Tridentine sources use
a different set of texts, indicating that there was no continuity
between the medieval and Tridentine versions. In a somewhat
comparable situation, Benedict Zimmerman's edition of the Ordinal of Sibert de Beka includes the rhymed office[26] for the assumption of Elijah by Robert Bale as an appendix to the original work.
It dates from the late fifteenth or early sixteenth century;[27] here
Elijah is specifically referred to as leader and founder ("principis
et fundatoris") of the Carmelite Order. This office for St. Elijah is
the only pre-Tridentine extant office, but unlike its Elishan
counterpart it is probably a single example by an individual
author rather than a universally observed feast.

Tridentine Carmelite manuscripts contain offices for both
Sts. Elijah and Elisha. The earliest of these sources is Florence,
Carmine, Ms. S, a liturgical supplement written by Fr. Archangelus
Paulius, novice master and then prior of the Carmine in the year
1627.[28] All the Tridentine sources are conservative in nature,
since the story of Elijah's life is contained in the Scriptures and
since the texts in any case had to be approved by the Holy See as
part of the Tridentine liturgical reform. Besides being found on f.
13v - 22 of Florence, Carmine, Ms. S, the office occurs in the
manuscripts, Rome, San Martino ai Monti, Codex F, an early
eighteenth-century Carmelite antiphonal, pp. 53-115, and Rome,
Collegio Sant'Alberto [formerly Santa Maria in Traspontina],
Codex N, also an early eighteenth-century antiphonal; in the last
case, Elijah is referred to as "our father and leader" ("ducis P[atris]
N[ostri]"). The manuscript Stuttgart, Würtembergische
Landesbibliothek, cod. bibl. fol. 62,[29] a fifteenth-century ritual,
includes some office chants for St. Elijah, done by a later, possibly
eighteenth-century, hand. Another manuscript, Avila, Archivo
del Monasterio de la Encarnación, ms. 5,[30] is a processional from
1593 containing several chants for St. Elijah, although not the
office; here he is referred to both as "nuestro Santisimo Padre
Elias" ("our most holy father Elias") and "nuestro Glorioso Padre
Elias" ("our glorious father Elias"). This last manuscript is particularly interesting, since it is a relatively early source and

evidence that the same liturgical tradition and influence applied to both men and women within the Order.

The texts for the offices of Sts. Elijah and Elisha, with their appropriate scriptural references, are included in the Appendix. While their story is well documented in First and Second Kings, the adaptation of the texts for liturgical use is restricted to the Carmelite rite. Although some chants based on the books of Kings are used for the office in ordinary time, none of these is used for the feast. As a result, the texts are absolutely unique to the Carmelite liturgy.

The first antiphon of first Vespers for St. Elijah is "Zelo zelatus sum pro domino deo exercituum," "with zeal I have been zealous for the Lord God of hosts," 1 Kgs 19:10 and 19:14, words which are etched on the self-understanding of every Carmelite. The zeal for God characterizes the life and ministry of the prophet and is pursued without compromise. The first antiphon for Lauds, a reconstruction of the Scriptural text, states that "Elias dum zelat zelum legis receptus est in celum," "Elijah while he was zealous with zeal for the law was received into heaven," reiterating the zeal for God characterizing the life of the prophet, and associating that zeal with his assumption into heaven. The only non-biblical text, the invitatory antiphon, "Regem Prophetarum Dominum, Venite adoremus," "Come let us adore the Lord the King of the prophets," is common to both the offices of Sts. Elijah and Elisha.

A perusal of the Appendix indicates that the chants for Elijah's office are organized with a view to highlight key aspects of his life according to the compiler's judgment, with the striking "Zelo zelatus" text at the very beginning, the first antiphon for first Vespers. What might seem a random selection of chants in fact promotes a structured liturgical reflection on the highlights of Elijah's ministry as well as on the impact of his work (especially in the Benedictus antiphon, taken from James 5).

The structure of the third Matins responsory indicates how the biblical text was adapted for liturgical use. In this passage Elijah revives the dead son of the widow of Zarephath:

1 Kgs 17:22b   The life breath returned within him and he revived.
(Reversa est anima pueri intra eum et revixit)

1 Kgs 17:23a   Taking the child, Elijah brought him down into the
house from the upper room [saying]
(Tulit Elias puerum et deposuit eum in inferiorem
domum dicens)

1 Kgs 17:23b   and [he] gave him to his mother. See! [Elijah said
to her,] your son is alive.[31]
(et tradidit matri sue et ait illi. En vivit filius tuus.)

The great responsory consists of two parts, the responsory and the verse, followed by a restatement of the second half of the responsory, known as the *repetenda* because it is repeated. Here the responsory's first half is 17: 22b, the *repetenda* is 17:23b and the verse is 17:23a, followed by the *repetenda*, then the "Gloria patri" ("Glory be to the Father") and the *repetenda* again. By moving 17:23b ahead of 17:23a to the *repetenda* position the compiler states the announcement that the son is indeed alive a total of three times, clearly highlighting the significance of the miracle. By such a process the musical rendering of the text gives it a liturgical life of its own.

Example 1 shows this responsory, "Reversa est anima," as it occurs in the manuscript, Rome, San Martino ai Monti, Codex F. The responsory has a range from *d* to *d* and ends on *d* at the end of "filius tuus," indicating that it is in the first mode. The verse begins on *a* and follows a pattern of notes which is customary for all first mode responsory verses, ending on *f* at the end of "dicens". This responsory verse formula, known as a "tone," was generally used for first mode responsory verses in the medieval period and was required to be used by the liturgical regulations of the Council of Trent.[32] Its presence here suggests that this responsory was in fact written in the eighteenth century (the era of the manuscript) rather than being copied from an older (i.e., medieval) version of the piece.

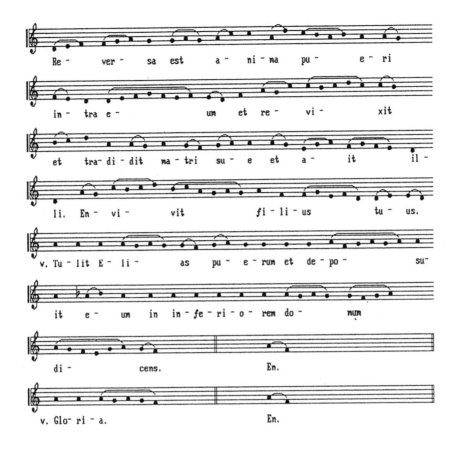

Example 1.   The responsory "Reversa est anima" from the office
              of St. Elijah in the manuscript Rome, San Martino
              ai Monti, Codex F.

The responsory itself is carefully constructed in order to highlight the importance of the scriptural word. Here the high notes signify the most important parts of the text. Thus the responsory begins on *d* and builds to a climax at the word *anima*, soul, or, in this case, life breath, is sustained at the words *et revixit et tradidit*, he revived and he brought [him], and is emphasized again at the words *En vivit*, [your son] is alive. In other words, all the references to the life itself being restored are musically reinforced by the high range of notes. The recurrence of the *repetenda* is thus all the more forceful since the music itself highlights the significance of the text and the miracle of life being restored to the boy. Thus both liturgically and musically this Elijah text takes on new life in its chanted version.

As was the case in the medieval Carmelite office tradition, all the Tridentine sources which contain the feast of St. Elijah maintain textual uniformity while allowing for musical diversity. Table 1 shows the modal organization of these pieces in each of the four sources, giving an idea of the great variety prevailing among them. The following *sigla* are used to identify the manuscripts: F1, Rome, Convento San Martino ai Monti, Codex F; F2, Rome, Collegio Sant'Alberto, formerly from Santa Maria in Traspontina, Codex N; F3, Florence, Carmine, Ms. S; and F4, Stuttgart, Würtembergische Landesbibliothek, Cod. Bibl. fol. 62.

Table 1

Modal Ordering of Chants for the Feast of St. Elijah

Chant	Incipit	F1	F2	F3	F4
1V a1	Zelo zelatus sum	7	1	1	7
a2	Usquequo	3	2	3	7
a3	Si homo Dei sum	1	3	7	1
a4	Non ego turbavi	3	4	4	6
a5	Occidisti in super	5	5	7	6
R	Respexit Elias ad	3	3	5	-
M	Ecce ego mittam	7	7	1	6
Inv	Regem prophetarum	1		1	
N1a1	Factum est autem	1			
a2	Dixit mulier ad	2			
a3	Ait Elias ad	4			
R1	Recede hinc et	8			
R2	Abijt mulier et	5			
R3	Reversa est anima	1			
N2a1	Factum est verbum	8			
a2	Ait Elias ad Achab	4			
a3	Manus Domini facta	7			
R1	Ait Abdias ad Eliam	7			
R2	Cum venisset Elias	3			
R3	Expandit se atque	2			
N3a1	Dixit Elias	3			
a2	Cum iam tempus	8			
a3	Orante Elia cecidit	7			
R1	Ait Elias nuntijs	1			
R2	Ascendit quinqua.	7			
R3	Factum est dum	1			
L a1	Elias dum zelat	1	6	4	8
a2	Factum est autem	6	1	6	3
a3	Tulit Elias pallium	3	8	3	7
a4	Cum Elias et	3	3	2	3
a5	Ascendit Elias per	3	1	5	5
B	Elias homo erat	8	1	7	-
2V M	Tulit Elias pallium	3	7	1	8
Oct B	Proiecit se Elias	7	-	1	-
Oct M	Elias Dei propheta	8	8	8	8

Of these four sources, only F1 includes the Matins chants for the feast. This modal chart graphically demonstrates that there is no musical correspondence from one set of chants to the other as far as Vespers and Lauds chants are concerned, and one can safely presume that the same would hold true for the Matins chants if there was more than one source for them. All the chants conform to the somewhat restrictive prescriptions of the Council of Trent. They are musically valuable and the variety of interpretations for each piece adds to the richness of the Tridentine celebrations for the feast of St. Elijah.

A cursory view of the Appendix shows that the office of St. Elisha recounts in musical and liturgical form the significant aspects of his ministry in a manner similar to that for St. Elijah. The first Vespers chants deal with Elisha's call, something which did not specifically occur in Elijah's case: in 1 Kgs 17:1 Elijah is simply presented as "Elijah the Tishbite, from Tishbe in Gilead." Elisha, by contrast, exercised his ministry in relationship to Elijah, so that the first antiphon of first Vespers for Elisha's office begins with God's command to Elijah to anoint Elisha as his own successor (1 Kgs 19:16b). Since the call to ministry is a legitimizing factor for every prophet[33] the beginnings of Elisha's ministry are appropriately featured at the outset of his office.

Table 2 demonstrates the modal ordering of chants for the feast of St. Elisha according to the following *sigla*: F1, Rome, Convento San Martino ai Monti, Codex E; F2, Rome, Collegio Sant'Alberto, formerly from Santa Maria in Traspontina, Codex N; F3, Florence, Carmine, Ms. S; and F4, Stuttgart, Würtembergische Landesbibliothek, Cod. Bibl. fol. 62.

Table 2

Modal Ordering of Chants for the Feast of St. Elisha

Chant	Incipit	F1	F2	F3	F4
V a1	Eliseum filium	1	1	6	8
a2	Profectus Elias	2	1	1	1
a3	Cumque venisset	3	8	8	3
a4	Eliseus relictis	4	4	4	4
a5	Eliseus ait osculer	5	7	7	7
M	Reversus autem ab	1	3	1	6
Inv	Regem Prophetarum	8		4	
N1a1	Ait Iosaphat Rex	2			
a2	Est hic Eliseus	2			
a3	Dixit autem Eliseus	8			
R1	Cum venisset Elias	7			
R2	Cum transissent	1			
R3	Dixerunt filij	1			
N2a1	Cum caneret Psaltes	7			
a2	Alveus iste	8			
a3	Parumque est hoc	1			
R1	Egressus Eliseus	2			
R2	Dixit vir Dei	8			
R3	Misit Rex Syrie	5			
N3a1	Mulier infundebat	8			
a2	Vade inquit Eliseus	8			
a3	Incubuit Eliseus	4			
R1	Dixit Eliseus ad	7			
R2	Eliseus ait	8			
R3	Factum est dum	7	1	1	2
L a1	Postula quod vis	7	7	1	1
a2	Dixitque Eliseus	1	8	8	1
a3	Rem difficilem	7	8	3	3
a4	Eliseus autem	3	1	5	4
a5	Percussitque aquas	5	7	7	8
B	Videntes autem	7	7	6	-
2V M	Eliseus autem	1	4	6	4
Oct B	Dixit Eliseus	1	-	7	-
M	Clamaverunt filij	7	1	7	1

This textual identity with musical independence in the Tridentine era is consistent with the medieval Carmelite chant tradition, distinguishing it from the Dominican liturgy, for instance, where both text and music were identical from one source to another.[34]

The Vespers chants for Elijah in F2 and Elisha in F1 follow a modal order, the antiphons being in modes 1 through 5 respectively. This is another characteristic of the medieval rhymed office tradition, a practice carried over here although the office itself is not rhymed. The responsories, however, are in no particular modal order. Where a given chant is in the same mode from one source to the other, the music still is not the same between the two versions, so that any similarities from one office to another or from one source to another are coincidental rather than deliberate.

The responsories in the St. Elisha office are divided so as to emphasize a particular textual point in the *repetenda*, as was the case in the office of St. Elijah. The responsory verses follow the appropriate musical formula prescribed for each mode, as was the case in our Example 1, with the single exception of the responsory "Factum est dum tolleret," the ninth responsory for the office of St. Elisha in F3. The ninth Matins responsory generally serves as the first Vespers responsory as well, thereby giving it special importance. The text deals with the crucial event of the assumption of Elijah and, being the first and the last responsory in the Elisha office, puts the entire ministry of the disciple Elisha within this context. Thus the text is highly significant:

2 Kgs 2:1   Factum est dum tolleret Dominus
             Eliam per turbinem in caelum.
             When the Lord was about to take Elijah
             up to heaven in a whirlwind.

2 Kgs 2:12a Eliseus clamabat dicens Pater mi Pater mi
             currus Israel et auriga eius.
             Elisha ... cried out, "My father! My father!
             Israel's chariot and drivers!"

2 Kgs 2:11   Cumque pergerent et incedentes sermocinarentur
                ecce currus igneus et equi ignei diviserunt utrumque
                et ascendit Elias per turbinem in caelum.
                As they walked on conversing,
                a flaming chariot and flaming horses came between
                them, and Elijah went up to heaven in a whirlwind.

Here too the dramatic words of the *repetenda* were sung a total of
three times, so that they give dramatic effect to Elisha's plight on
being left alone to carry on Elijah's work after his assumption.
Both the beginning of the responsory and the verse emphasize the
significance of Elijah's assumption for Elisha's ministry.

This responsory is the only instance in the offices of either
Elijah or Elisha where the responsory verse does not follow an
established tone, but is newly composed, at least in the Florentine
Carmelite version of the office. This means that Archangelus
Paulius either composed the music for this responsory in the
manner of a medieval rhymed office or copied it from an existing
medieval source which is now lost.

Example 2 shows this responsory as it occurs in Florence,
Carmine, Ms. S. As in Example 1, the range from *d* to *d* and the
ending of the responsory on *d* clearly establish this as a first mode
piece. While one would expect the melody of the verse to be more
or less the same as that in Example 1, as medieval custom
dictated and the Council of Trent legislated, a simple perusal of
the verse melody demonstrates that it is entirely different. The
melody in the verse of Example 2 begins and ends on *d*, the final
(last note) of the mode itself. The melodic range goes from *d* to *d*
in the verse as well as in the responsory, reinforcing its first mode
nature. This is consistent with responsory verses in medieval
rhymed offices, but highly unusual in an office from this period.[35]

While this particular responsory is as fascinating stylisti-
cally as it is important theologically, the majority of pieces within
this office reflect a Tridentine approach in which all the verses
conform to the established tone. At the same time, however, the
chant melodies are preserved correctly in accordance with the

Example 2.   The responsory "Factum est dum tolleret" from the office of St. Elisha in the manuscript Florence, Carmine, Ms. S.

best traditions of medieval chant, not truncated or distorted as would later be the case with official Vatican editions.[36]

The celebration of feasts for Sts. Elijah and Elisha represents a conscious initiative on the part of the Carmelite Order to give liturgical expression to the prophetic dimension of their charism. The liturgical texts reflect the importance of the life of prayer to Elijah the prophet and to his disciple Elisha, an intimacy with God which lies at the heart of the Carmelite vocation. The importance of Elijah's life-giving activity and fierce zeal for the things of God, continued in the ministry of his disciple Elisha, provided a useful model of integrity for the Carmelites, which they celebrated with great liturgical fidelity. The music for the office chants of these two distinctively Carmelite saints reflects a respect for the decrees of the Council of Trent combined with a careful effort to preserve the musical settings intact. At the same time, the musical independence of one source from another, both within each feast and between them, meant that each Carmelite house wherein the manuscript was compiled assumed responsibility for its music; it thus represented a conscious effort on the part of each convent to provide an appropriate musical setting to best illustrate the chant texts for these two offices. Such musical independence coupled with textual uniformity maintained a distinctively Carmelite approach to the liturgy which had characterized the Carmelite rite from its inception. At the same time, the different versions of these two offices demonstrate considerable liturgical creativity in the manner in which the Carmelites assembled the chants into a unified office. As a result, these liturgical sources serve as permanent monuments to a vibrant musical and liturgical Carmelite tradition in the Tridentine period; thus these offices of Sts. Elijah and Elisha fittingly reflect the Carmelites' devotion to the prophet Elijah and his disciple and their union with them in maintaining throughout their lives a jealous zeal for the Lord God of hosts.

James Boyce, O.Carm.

Appendix
Office Texts for Saints Elias and Eliseus

Office of St. Elias

V a1	Zelo zelatus sum pro domino deo exercituum quia dereliquerunt pactum tuum filij Israel.	1 Kgs 19:10
	P. Dixit dominus.	1 Kgs 19:14
a2	Usquequo claudicatis in duas partes si dominus est deus sequimini eum.	
	P. Confitebor tibi.	1 Kgs 18:21
a3	Si homo dei sum descendat ignis de celo et devoret te et quinquaginta tuos.	
	P. Beatus vir.	2 Kgs 1:10
a4	Non ego turbavi Israel sed tu et domus patris tui qui dereliquistis mandata domini.	
	P. Lauda pueri.	1 Kgs 18:18
a5	Occidisti in super et possedisti	1 Kgs 21:19
	ecce ego inducam super te malum et demetam posteriora tua.	1 Kgs 21:21
	P. Lauda Jerusalem.	
R	Respexit elias ad caput suum sub cinericium panem qui surgens comedit et bibit.	1 Kgs 19:6
	Et ambulavit in fortitudine cibi illius usque ad montem dei horeb.	1 Kgs 19:8
	v. Angelus Domini dixit illi surge comede	1 Kgs 19:7
	grandis enim tibi restat via qui consurrexisset comedit.	1 Kgs 19:8
	P. Et ambulavit. v. Gloria patri P. Et ambulavit.	

M	Ecce ego mittam vobis Eliam prophetam	
	antequam veniat dies domini	
	magnus et horribilis	Mal 4:5
	et convertet cor patrum ad filios	
	et cor filiorum ad patres eorum.	Mal 4:6
	P. Magnificat.	
Inv.	Regem Prophetarum Dominum.	
	Venite adoremus.	
	P. Venite.	
N1a1	Factum est autem ut egrotaret	
	filium mulieris matris familias	
	et erat languor fortissimus.	1 Kgs 17:17
a2	Dixit mulier ad Eliam	
	quid mihi et tibi vir Dei?	
	Ingressus es ad me et [ut]	
	rememorarentur iniquitates mee	
	et interficeres filium meum.	1 Kgs 17:18
a3	Ait Elias ad viduam	
	da mihi filium tuum	
	et clamavit ad Dominum	
	et revixit puer.	1 Kgs 17:19
N1R1	Recede hinc et vade contra Orientem	
	dixit Dominus ad Eliam.	1 Kgs 16:3a
	Qui abijt et fecit	
	iuxta verbum Domini.	
	v. Abscondere in torrente Charith	1 Kgs 16:3b
	et ibi de torrente bibes	
	corvisque precepi	
	ut pascant te ibi.	
	Qui.	
R2	Abijt mulier et fecit	
	iuxta verbum Prophete.	
	Et comedit ipse	
	et illa et domus eius.	1 Kgs 17:15
	v. Ex illa die hydria farine	
	non defecit et lecytus olei	
	non est imminutus	
	iuxta verbum Elie.	1 Kgs 17:16
	Et.	
R3	Reversa est anima pueri	
	intra eum et revixit	1 Kgs 17:22
	et tradidit matri sue	
	et ait illi.	

En vivit filius tuus.　　　　　　　　　　　　1 Kgs 17:23b
v.　　　Tulit Elias puerum
　　　　et deposuit eum in
　　　　inferiorem domum dicens.　　　　　1 Kgs 17:23a
En.
v.　　　Gloria patri.
En.

N2a1　Factum est verbum Domini ad Eliam
　　　dicens vade et ostende te Achab
　　　ut dem pluviam super faciem terre.　　1 Kgs 18:1

a2　　Ait Elias ad Achab
　　　ascende comede et bibe
　　　quia sonus multe pluvie est.　　　　　1 Kgs 18:41

a3　　Manus Domini facta est
　　　super Eliam accintisque lumbis
　　　currebat ante Achab donec
　　　veniret in Iezrahel.　　　　　　　　　1 Kgs 18:46

R1　　Ait Abdias ad Eliam
　　　cum recessero a te
　　　spiritus Domini asportabit te
　　　in locum quem ego ignoro　　　　　　1 Kgs 18:12
　　　et tu dices.
　　　Dic Domino tuo adest Elias.　　　　　1 Kgs 18:14
　　　v.　　　Dixit Elias
　　　　　　vivit Dominus exercituum
　　　　　　ante cuius vultum sto
　　　　　　quia hodie apparebo ei.　　　　1 Kgs 18:15
　　　Dic.

N2R2　Cum venisset Elias ad portam civitatis
　　　apparuit ei mulier vidua
　　　colligens ligna et vocavit eam
　　　dixitque ei.
　　　Da michi paululum aque
　　　in vase ut bibam.　　　　　　　　　　1 Kgs 17:10
　　　v.　　　Cumque illa pergeret ut afferet
　　　　　　clamavit post tergum eius dicens
　　　　　　affer mihi obsecro
　　　　　　et bucellam panis in manu tua.　1 Kgs 17:11
　　　Da.

R3　　Expandit se atque mensus est
　　　Elias super puerum tribus vicibus
　　　et clamavit ad Dominum.　　　　　　　1 Kgs 17:21a
　　　Et exaudivit Dominus vocem Elie.　　1 Kgs 17:22

v.   Domine Deus meus
revertatur obsecro anima pueri huius
in viscera eius.   1 Kgs 17:21b
Et.
v.   Gloria patri.
Et.

N3a1   Dixit Elias prophetis Baal
eligite vobis bovem unum
et invocate nomina deorum vestrorum   1 Kgs 18:25
qui clamabant et non erat
qui responderet eis.   1 Kgs 18:26

a2   Cum iam tempus esset
ut offeretur holocaustum
accedens Elias oravit ad Dominum.   1 Kgs 18:36

a3   Orante Elia cecidit ignis Domini
et voravit holocaustum et ligna
et lapides pulverem quoque
et aquam que erat in aqueductu lambens. 1 Kgs 18:38

R1   Ait Elias nuncijs regis Samarie
numquid non est Deus in Israel ut eatis
ad Beelzebub?   2 Kgs 1:3
Quam ob rem hec dicit Dominus.
De lectulo super quem ascendisti
non descendes sed morte morieris.   2 Kgs 1:4
v.   Reversi nuncij ad Ochoziam
dixerunt   2 Kgs 1:5
vir occurrit nobis
dicens ite et revertimini ad regem
et dicetis ei.   2 Kgs 1:6
De.

N3R2   Ascendit quinquagenarius et quinquaginta
qui erant sub eo ad Eliam
sedentem in vertice montis.   2 Kgs 1:9
Et descendit ignis de celo
et devoravit eos.   2 Kgs 1:10b
v.   Dixit Elias si homo Dei sum
descendat ignis de celo
et devoret te et quinquaginta tuos. 2 Kgs 1:10a
Et.

R3   Factum est dum tolleret Dominus
Eliam per turbinem in celum.
Eliseus clamabat dicens
Pater mi pater mi
currus Israel et auriga eius.   2 Kgs 2:12

v.   Cumque pergerent et incedentes
sermocinarentur ecce currus
igneus et equi ignei diviserunt
utrumque et ascendit Elias
per turbinem in celum.   2 Kgs 2:11
Eliseus.
v.   Gloria patri.
Eliseus.

L a1   Elias dum zelat zelum legis
receptus est in celum.
P.   Dominus regnavit.

  a2   Factum est autem cum levare
vellet dominus Eliam
per turbinem in celum
ibant Elias et Eliseus de galgalis.   2 Kgs 2:1
P.   Jubilate.

  a3   Tulit Elias pallium suum
et percussit aquas
et diviserunt et transierunt
ambo per sic(c)um.   2 Kgs 2:8
P.   Deus deus meus.

  a4   Cum Elias et Eliseus pergerent
et intercedentes sermoncinarentur
ecce currus igneus et equi ignei
diviserunt utrumque.   2 Kgs 2:11
P.   Benedicite.

  a5   Ascendit Elias per turbinem
in celum Eliseus autem videbat
et clamabat pater mi pater mi
currus Israel et auriga eius.   2 Kgs 2:11b-12
P.   Laudate dominum deum.

B   Elias homo erat similis nobis
passibilis et oratione oravit
ut non plueret super terram
et non pluit annos tres et menses sex
et rursum oravit et celum dedit pluviam
et terra dedit fructum suum.   Jas 5:17-18
P.   Benedictus.

2V M Tulit Elias pallium suum
et involvit illus et
percussit aquas Jordanis
que diviserunt in utramque partem
et transierunt ipse et Eliseus per siccum 2 Kgs 1:8

qui incidentes ecce currus igneus et
equi ignei diviserunt utrumque et
ascendit Elias per turbinem in celum   2 Kgs 1:11
Eliseus autem non vidit eum amplius.   2 Kgs 1:12
P.   Magnificat.

Oct B   Proiecit se Elias et obdormivit
in umbra iuniperi
et ecce Angelus Domini tetigit eum
et dixit illi   1 Kgs 19:5
surge et comede grandis enim tibi
restat via.   1 Kgs 19:7

Oct M   Elias dei propheta comedit
sub cineritium panem   1 Kgs 19:6
et ambulavit in fortitudine cibi illius
quadraginta diebus et quadraginta noctibus
usque ad montem dei horeb.   1 Kgs 19:8
P.   Magnificat.

Office of St. Eliseus

V a1	Eliseum filium saphat qui est de Abelmeula unges prophetam pro te dixit Dominus Elie.	1Kgs 19:16b
a2	Profectus Elias reperit Eliseum filium Saphat arantem in duodecim iugis boum.	1 Kgs 19:19a
a3	Cumque venisset Elias ad eum misit pallium suum super illum.	1 Kgs 19:19c
a4	Eliseus relictis bobus cucurrit post Eliam et ministrabat ei.	1 Kgs 19:20a + 21c
a5	Eliseus ait osculer oro patrem meum et matrem meam et sic sequar te.	1 Kgs 19:20b
M	Reversus autem ab Elia Eliseus tulit par boum et mactavit illud et in aratro boum coxit carnes et dedit populo et comederunt consurgensque abijt et secutus est Eliam et ministrabat ei.	1 Kgs 19:21
Inv	Regem Prophetarum Dominum Venite adoremus. P. Venite	
N1a1	Ait Iosaphat Rex estne hic Propheta Domini ut deprecemur Dominum per eum.	2 Kgs 3:11a
a2	Est hic Eliseus filius Saphat qui fundebat aquam super manus Elie.	2 Kgs 13:11c
a3	Dixit autem Eliseus ad regem Israel quid mihi et tibi est?	

	Vade ad Prophetas patris tui et matris tue.	2 Kgs 3:13a

N1R1   Cum venisset Elias ad Eliseum
       misit pallium suum super illum
       Qui statim relictis bobus
       cucurrit post Eliam
       et ministrabat ei.   1 Kgs 19:10b-
                                                 20a + 21c

       v.   Osculer oro
               patrem meum et matrem meam   1 Kgs 19:20b
               et sic sequar te.
       Qui.

R2   Cum transissent Elias et Eliseus
       Iordanem per siccum
       dixit Eliseus
       Obsecro ut fiat in me
       duplex spiritus tuus.   2 Kgs 2:9a, c
       v.   Elias dixit ad Eliseum
               postula quod vis
               ut faciam tibi
               antequam tollar a te.   2 Kgs 2:9b
       Obsecro.

R3   Dixerunt filij Prophetarum ad Eliseum
       eamus usque ad Iordanem
       et tollant singuli de sylva
       materias singulas
       Aedificemus nobis ibi locum
       ad habitandum.   2 Kgs 6:1a-2
       v.   Ecce locus in quo habitamus
               coram te angustus est nobis.   2 Kgs 6:1b
       Aedifice.
       v.   Gloria patri. Aedifi.

N2a1   Cum caneret Psaltes facta est
       super Eliseum manus Domini
       et prophetavit.   2 Kgs 3:15

a2   Alveus iste replebitur aquis
       et bibetis vos et familie vestre
       et iumenta vestra.   2 Kgs 3:17

a3   Parumque est hoc
       in conspectu Domini
       insuper tradet etiam Moab
       in manus vestras.   2 Kgs 3:18

R1 Egressus Eliseus ad fontem aquarum
misit in illum sal et ait
hec dicit Dominus sanavi aquas has   2 Kgs 2:21a
Et non erit altra in eis
mors neque sterilitas.   2 Kgs 2:21b
    v.   Sanate sunt ergo aque
        usque in diem hanc
        iuxta verbum Elisei.   2 Kgs 2:22
    Et.

N2R2 Dixit vir Dei sanctus
ad Sunamitidem
In tempore isto et in hac eadem hora
si vita comes fuerit
habebis in utero filium.   2 Kgs 4:16a,b
    v.   Noli queso domine
        mi vir Dei mentiri ancille tue.   2 Kgs 4:16c
        Qui dixit ad eam.   2 Kgs 4:16a
    In.

R3 Misit Rex Syrie exercitus
ut caperent Eliseum
Percussitque eos Dominus
ne viderunt iuxta verbum Elisei.   2 Kgs 6:18b
    v.   Eliseus oravit ad Dominum
        dicens percute obsecro gentem   2 Kgs 6:18a
        hanc cecitate.
        Percus.
    v.   Gloria patri. Percus.

N3a1 Mulier infundebat oleum in vasa
Cumque plena fuissent vasa
stetit oleum.   2 Kgs 4:5b,6a, 6b

a2 Vade inquit Eliseus
vende oleum et redde creditori tuo.   2 Kgs 4:7b

a3 Incubuit Eliseus super puerum
et oscitavit puer septies
aperuitque oculos
et reddidit matri sue.   2 Kgs 4:34-35

R1 Dixit Eliseus ad Naaman
vade et lavare septies in Iordane
et recipiet sanitatem caro tua.   2 Kgs 5:10
Et abiij.
Et mundatus est.   2 Kgs 5:14b

v.	Descendit Naaman et lavit in Iordane septies iuxta sermonem viri Dei. Et.	2 Kgs 5:14a

| R2 | Eliseus ait ad Reges Iuda et Israel
facite alveum torrentis huius
fossas et fossas. Tradet
[missing] | 2 Kgs 3:13

2 Kgs 3:16 |

| R3 | Factum est dum tolleret Dominus
Eliam per turbinem in caelum.
Eliseus clamabat dicens
Pater mi Pater mi currus Israel
et auriga eius. | |

v.	Cumque pergerent et incedentes sermocinarentur ecce currus igneus et equi ignei diviserunt utrumque et ascendit Elias per turbinem in caelum. Elis.	2 Kgs 2:11b
v.	Gloria patri. Elise.	

| L a1 | Postula quod vis
ut faciam tibi antequam
tollar a te
Elias dixit ad Eliseum. | 2 Kgs 2:9a,b |

| a2 | Dixitque Eliseus obsecro
ut fiat in me duplex
spiritus tuus. | 2 Kgs 2:9c |

| a3 | Rem difficilem postulasti
attamen si videris me
quando tollar a te
erit tibi quod petisti. | 2 Kgs 2:10 |

| a4 | Eliseus autem videbat
et clamabat
pater mi pater mi
currus Israel et auriga eius. | 2 Kgs 2:12 |

| a5 | Percussitque aquas
et divise sunt huc
atque illuc
et transijt Eliseus. | 2 Kgs 2:14b |

| B | Videntes autem filij prophetarum
qui erant in Iericho | |

       econtra dixerunt requievit spiritus
       Elie super Eliseum.
       Et venientes in occursum eius
       adoraverunt eum proni in terra.   2 Kgs 2:15

2V M   Eliseus autem egrotabat
       infirmitate qua et mortuus est
       descenditque ad eum Ioas Rex Israel
       et flebat coram eo dicebatque
       pater mi pater mi currus Israel
       et auriga eius.   2 Kgs 13:14

Oct B   Dixit Eliseus ad senes
       nunquid scitis quod miserit
       filius homicide
       hic ut precidatur caput meum
       Videte ergo cum venerit nuncius
       claudite ostium et non
       sinatis eum introire.   2 Kgs 6:32b-33

M   Clamaverunt filij Prophetarum
       mors in olla vir Dei
       At ille afferte inquit farinam
       Cumque tulissent misit in ollam
       et non fuit amplius
       quidquam amaritudinis in olla.   2 Kgs 4:40-41

Endnotes

1. For a thorough discussion of the Crusades and the religious establishments in the Latin Kingdom, cf. Steven Runciman, *A History of the Crusades* (3 vols.; New York: Cambridge University Press, 1951-54).

2. This is the view of Fr. Elias Friedman in *The Latin Hermits of Mount Carmel, A study in Carmelite origins* (Roma: Institutum Historicum Teresianum, 1979) 171. Fr. Joachim Smet suggests another viewpoint: the hermits who established themselves on Mount Carmel were ones who regrouped themselves after the battle of Hattin in 1187: Joachim Smet, *The Carmelites*, Vol. I (Rome: Carmelite Institute, 1975) 5-6. All that is known for certain is that it would have been impossible for hermits to exist in parts of the Holy Land not securely held by the Crusaders after 1187. The paucity of documents leaves open a wide path for historical speculation.

3. The Greek Orthodox had settled on Mount Carmel in the middle of the twelfth century at a site known as the cave of Elijah; the Latin hermits, by contrast, lived in the wadi 'ain es-Siah, two miles south of the promontory; cf. Friedman, *Latin Hermits*, 171.

4. For a discussion of Albert of Jerusalem, cf. A. Staring, "Alberto, patriarca di Gerusalemme, santo," in *Biblioteca Sanctorum*, I, cols. 686-90. For a discussion of the rule itself, cf. Hugh Clarke and Bede Edwards, *The Rule of Saint Albert* (Aylesford and Kensington, 1973), and Carlo Cicconetti, *La Regola del Carmelo* (Roma: Institutum Carmelitanum, 1973).

5. Clarke and Edwards, *The Rule of Saint Albert*, 79.

6. Clarke and Edwards, *The Rule of Saint Albert*, 78, f. 2.

7. Elijah appears in 1 Kgs 17, and his deeds are further recounted in chapters 18-21; the first two chapters of 2 Kgs also concern Elijah, concluding with his assumption into heaven in 2 Kgs 2:11. The specific association of Elijah with

Mount Carmel derives from 1 Kgs 18:19, 1 Kgs 18:42, and elsewhere. Cf. *The New American Bible.*

8. Bede Edwards cites 1238 as the beginning of this westward migration, based on evidence of the thirteenth-century Dominican, Vincent of Beauvais: cf. Clarke and Edwards, *The Rule of Saint Albert,* 21. The Carmelites were brought to England by Richard De Grey of Codnor in 1242, according to the Franciscan Thomas of Eccleston; cf. Keith J. Egan, "An Essay toward a Historiography of the Origin of the Carmelite Province in England," *Carmelus* 19 (1972) 67-100.

9. The ten provinces listed in the constitutions of the General Chapter of London of 1281 are, in order of foundation, the Holy Land, Sicily, England, Provence, Tuscany, Lombardy, France, Germany, Aquitaine and Spain; cf. Ludovicus Saggi, "Constitutiones Capituli Londinensis Anni 1281," *Analecta Ordinis Carmelitarum* 15 (1950) 244.

10. *Conciliorum Oecumenicorum Decreta,* ed. Centro di Documentazione, Istituto per le Scienze Religiose (Bologna: Josepho, Alberigo et al, 1962), 218.

11. For a discussion of this documentation, cf. Carlo Cicconetti, *La Regola del Carmelo* (Roma: Institutum Carmelitanum, 1973), and my thesis, *Cantica Carmelitana: The Chants of the Carmelite Office* (New York University, 1984), Vol. I, especially pp. 11-43. I also discuss this process in "From Rule to Rubric: The Impact of Carmelite Liturgical Legislation upon the Order's Office Tradition," *Ephemerides Liturgicae,* 108 (1994) 262-298.

12. Cf. M.-H. Laurent, ed., "La lettre 'Quae honorem Conditoris' (1er octobre, 1247): Note de diplomatique pontificale," *Ephemerides Carmeliticae,* 2 (1948), 5-16 and also the work of Cicconetti.

13. Joachim Smet, *The Carmelites,* Vol. I, 30.

14. Cited from the translation of Joachim Smet in *The Carmelites,* Vol. I, 16-17. The Latin text may be found in Ludovicus M.

Saggi, "Constitutiones capituli Burdigalensis anni 1294," *Analecta Ordinis Carmelitarum*, 18 (1953) 131.

15. Cf. Joachim Smet, *The Carmelites*, Vol. I, 7-8, citing Athanasius, *Vita Antonii*, 7; *Patrologia Graeca* 26, 854 and [Jerome's] *Epistula 58 ad Paulinum*; *Patrologia Latina*, 22, 583.

16. Clarke and Edwards, 82-83.

17. Cf. Clarke and Edwards, 88-89.

18. Fr. Paschalis Kallenberg, "Le culte liturgique d'Élie dans l'ordre du Carmel," *Élie le prophète*, II, *Études Carmélitaines* 35 (1956) 134-150. Although vestiges of devotion to Elijah can be found within the Carmelite Order before this time, 1585 seems to be the first time it was universally legislated to be celebrated. Kallenberg also points out that the Chapter of 1645 still found it necessary to mandate the celebration of the feast in all the convents of the Order; cf. p. 143 of his article for this discussion.

19. R. P. Benedict Zimmerman, *Ordinaire de l'Ordre de Notre-Dame du Mont-Carmel par Sibert de Beka (vers 1312) publié d'après le manuscrit original et collationné sur divers manuscrits et imprimés* (Paris: Alphonse Picard et Fils, 1910).

20. "Primo ordinaverunt, quod de Sancto Heliseo Propheta Montis Carmeli fiat omni anno 18 Kalend. Julii, scilicet die 14. a Mensis Junii Festum duplex vel maius, et fiat Officium de uno Confessore quousque habebitur Officium proprium." (*Acta Capitulorum Generalium Ordinis Fratrum B. V. Mariae de Monte Carmelo*, Vol. I (Romae: Apud Curiam Generalitiam, 1912) 124.)

21. Cf. Paschalis Kallenberg, *Fontes Liturgiae Carmelitanae, Investigatio in Decreta, Codices et Proprium Sanctorum* (Romae: Institutum Carmelitanum, 1962) 244-247 for a discussion of these two antiphonals, originally from the Carmine of Pisa, housed at the time of Kallenberg's writing in Castello, Convento Santa Lucia, hence his sigla of Castello, Conv. S. Lucia, ms. D and codex sine signatura respectively,

and since that time once again returned to the Carmine of Pisa. Kallenberg was not sure whether these two antiphonals were actually Carmelite or not. In my article, "Two Antiphonals of Pisa: Their Place in the Carmelite Liturgy," *Manuscripta* 31 (1987) 147-165, I established that they are authentically Carmelite manuscripts.

22. The Carmelite codices of Florence, now housed in the San Marco Museum and the Carmine of Florence, are described in Kallenberg, *Fontes Liturgiae Carmelitanae*, 247-256 as well as in my articles, "Medieval Carmelite Office Manuscripts, A Liturgical Inventory," *Carmelus* 33 (1986) 17-34, and "The Carmelite Choirbooks of Florence and the Liturgical Tradition of the Carmelite Order," *Carmelus* 35 (1988) 67-93.

23. These Mainz Carmelite codices are described in Kallenberg, *Fontes Liturgiae Carmelitanae*, pp. 256-59 and in my articles, "Medieval Carmelite Office Manuscripts, A Liturgical Inventory," *Carmelus* 33 (1986) 17-34, and "Die Mainzer Karmeliterchorbücher und die Liturgische Tradition des Karmeliterordens," *Archiv für mittelrheinische Kirchengeschichte*, 39 (1987) 267-303.

24. This breviary is now New Haven, Yale University Library, ms. 41.

25. This printed breviary is described briefly in Kallenberg, *Fontes Liturgiae Carmelitanae*, 262.

26. A rhymed office was a significant literary and musical entity in the Middle Ages. All the chants within the office had a poetic rhythm as well as a definite rhyme scheme. The music for these offices was generally much more ornate than more normal Gregorian chants, yielding a highly individual artistic entity. The feast of the Three Marys featured a rhymed office within the Carmelite tradition; cf. my edition of this office from the Carmelite manuscripts Mainz, Dom-und Diözesanmuseum, Codex E and Florence, Carmine, Ms. O, "The Office of the Three Marys in the

Carmelite Liturgy," *Journal of the Plainsong and Mediaeval Music Society* 12 (1989) 1-38.

27. The "Historia Raptus sacratissimi Heliae Prophetae primi principis et fundatoris Ordinis fratrum Carmelitarum, incolae paradisi, edita per theologiae lectorem Fratrem Robertum Bale priorem conventus nostri Burnhamiae" is found on f. 34 of Cambridge University ms. 7, the texts of which are found on p. 341 of Zimmerman's study. This office dates from the end of the fifteenth or from the very beginning of the sixteenth century, since Robert Bale died in 1503; cf. P. Kallenberg, "Le culte liturgique d'Élie dans l'ordre du Carmel," p. 137 for this discussion. Kallenberg also discusses the question of whether the Franciscans celebrated the feast of the assumption of Elijah or of their own St. Francis; cf. p. 136, including footnote 3.

28. The date of 1627 is given on p. 60v of the manuscript itself in an inscription which states that Fr. Archangelus Paulius composed all the offices in the manuscript except that of St. Albert. Another notation on p. 69v of the manuscript, after the office of St. Andrew Corsini, bears the date 1648; this is then a subsequent addition to the manuscript.

29. This manuscript is discussed by Kallenberg on pp. 259-260 of *Fontes Liturgiae Carmelitanae*.

30. This manuscript is described in "El Archivo Musical y el Museo de Instrumentos del Convento de la Encarnación," in Antonio Baciero, *El Organo de Camara del Convento de la Encarnación de Avila* (Consejo General de Castilla y Leon, Ediciones Poniente, 1982). The manucript is described on p. 135 of Baciero's work.

31. The English translation is taken from *The New American Bible*, 1970.

32. P. Raphael Molitor discusses the liturgical legislation of the Council of Trent and its ramifications for chant in *Die Nach-Tridentinische Choral-Reform zu Rom, Ein Beitrag zur Musikgeschichte des XVI. und XVII. Jahrhunderts*, 2 Bande (Verlag von F. E. C. Leuckart in Leipzig, 1901 & 1902).

Robert F. Hayburn discusses this material in *Papal Legislation on Sacred Music, 95 A.D. to 1977 A.D.* (Collegeville, MN: The Liturgical Press, 1979) especially pp. 25-115.

33. The literary significance of the prophetic call narrative has received considerable attention: cf. Burke O. Long, "Prophetic Call Traditions and Reports of Visions," *Zeitschrift für die alttestamentliche Wissenschaft* 84 (1972) 494-500; Normal Habel, "The Form and Significance of the Call Narratives," *Zeitschrift für die alttestamentliche Wissenschaft* 77 (1965), 297-323; Rolf Knierim, "The Vocation of Isaiah," *Vetus Testamentum* 18 (1968), 47-68; William Holladay, *Jeremiah, Spokesman Out of Time* (Philadelphia, Pa.: United Church Press, 1974) for a sampling of studies on this question.

34. For a discussion of the overall characteristics of Carmelite chant, cf. my dissertation, *Cantica Carmelitana: The Chants of the Carmelite Office*, Vol. I (Ph.D. New York University, 1984); also cf. my articles, "The Medieval Carmelite Office Tradition," *Acta Musicologica*, 62 (1990) 119-151 and "The Liturgy of the Carmelites," *Carmelus* 43 (1996), 5-41. Characteristics of Dominican chant are discussed by William R. Bonniwell, O.P., in his book, *A History of the Dominican Liturgy, 1215-1945* (New York: Joseph F. Wagner, 1945). The Dominican Master General, Humbert of Romans, promulgated a complete edition of the Dominican service books, now in Rome, Santa Sabina, Biblioteca della Curia Generalizia dei Domenicani, XIV, lit. 1; the manuscript London, British Library, Additional Ms. 23935 is a portable copy of these service books which was used by the Master General in visitation of the houses to correct the chant books and thereby ensure the musical as well as textual uniformity of the rite.

35. The stylistic characteristics of medieval rhymed office responsory verses are discussed in my article, "Rhymed Office Responsory Verses: Stylistic Characteristics and Musical Significance," forthcoming in *Cantus Planus*.

36. For a discussion of Vatican editions after the Council of Trent and of the post-Tridentine decline of chant, cf. Dom Giulio Cattin, *Music of the Middle Ages* 1 (Cambridge University Press, 1984) especially pp. 94-100.

Grace and Religious Experience: The Everyday Mysticism of Karl Rahner

For wisdom is more mobile than any motion;
because of her pureness she pervades
and penetrates all things.

In every generation she passes into holy souls
and makes them friends of God, and prophets.

For God loves nothing so much as the person
who lives with wisdom.

For she is an initiate in the knowledge of God,
and an associate in his works.

For she teaches self-control and prudence,
justice and courage;
nothing in life is more profitable for mortals than these.

Who has learned your counsel, unless you have given wisdom
and sent your holy spirit from on high?

And thus the paths of those on earth were set right,
and people were taught what pleases you,
and were saved by wisdom.[1]

The preceding verses from the book of Wisdom depict Lady Wisdom in her universal, revelatory and salvific presence. Who is this Lady Wisdom? Citing C. Larcher, Roland Murphy writes:

> The divine Wisdom celebrated in our book [Wisdom] is a harmonious union of the divine presence which creates, preserves, and governs the world, and the presence of grace which reaches all humanity through history, reveals the plans and wishes of the Lord, constantly solicits souls of good will, enlightens and assists them, introduces them to a world of friendship with God and assures them finally of immortality.[2]

After presenting an exposition of the many traits of personified Wisdom in his book, *The Tree of Life*, Murphy concludes that "Lady Wisdom is a divine communication; God's communication, extension of self, to human beings."[3]

Although Karl Rahner never invokes the biblical symbol of Lady Wisdom to underwrite his theology of universal grace and his theology of religious experience and everyday mysticism which flow from it, he well could have. It is not the task of this article to provide Wisdom foundations for Rahner's theology of universal grace. Roland Murphy has already done that.[4] Rather, I wish merely to present Rahner's theology of grace, religious experience and everyday mysticism because of the close affinity this theology has with the theology of Lady Wisdom, about which Roland Murphy has written prolifically. This affinity is seen in that both Lady Wisdom and grace, as understood by Rahner, are the universal, revelatory and salvific presence and self-communication of God.

As will be seen, Rahner refers to the experience of the divine or the Holy Spirit as "the mysticism of everyday life" or "a mysticism of ordinary life."[5] In order to understand Rahner's everyday mysticism, one must first understand its foundations in his philosophical and theological anthropology. Therefore, I first deal with Rahner's anthropology, especially his theology of grace. I limit myself to those points pertinent to the topic at hand.

Rahner's Theology of Grace: Thomas and Created Grace

To appreciate better Rahner's theology of grace, we might first recall the understanding of grace dominant since the time of Thomas Aquinas. In reaction to the understanding of grace found in both the East and the West as God's love itself or the Holy Spirit poured forth into the soul (Rom 5:5), hence *un*created grace, Thomas spoke of grace as a *created* gift of God, not God's gift of God's Self, the Holy Spirit. Hence Thomas defines grace as "a certain *partaking* of the divine nature which exceeds every other nature,"[6] or a "certain participated likeness of the divine nature."[7] As a sharing in the divine nature, such grace is sanctifying, i.e., it makes one pleasing to God (*gratia gratum faciens*).[8]

Thomas' concern for grace precisely as *created* grace, and not God's own gift of God's Self or Holy Spirit, was to insure against Peter Lombard, for whom grace was the Holy Spirit or the love of God, that indeed human acts which would be salutary or meritorious (i.e., lead one to one's goal, the beatific vision) and would be *human* acts (i.e., acts of the person himself/herself and not the acts of the Holy Spirit).[9] Thus what is required is a transformation in the soul itself which is accomplished through created grace.[10]

This view of grace as created and sanctifying has been the dominant view of grace in the West since Thomas Aquinas[11] and is reflected both in catechisms[12] and theological manuals.[13] Although understood by Thomas to be an accident of quality;[14] nonetheless, sanctifying grace even in Thomas is understood in a somewhat quantitative way. It has levels or degrees. There can be more or less of it, and one can grow (or decrease) in it especially through the reception of the sacraments.[15]

In this view of grace as sanctifying grace, the rhetoric about grace tended to be very impersonal, objective, and "reified," for grace was some thing, a divine-like quality and permanent disposition or *habitus* inherent in the soul.[16] In Rahnerian terms, our language about grace was ontic or metaphysical and not ontological or existential.[17] Such impersonal, ontic rhetoric did not lend itself easily to sermons, homilies or retreat conferences.

Another difficulty which Rahner has with post-Tridentine theology, at least in its Molinist strain and in its reified understanding of created grace, is its position that, with the exception of the mystics, grace does not enter into human consciousness or experience.[18] As will be seen below, in dealing with his notion of revelation and everyday mysticism, Rahner objects to this position.[19] But there are even more serious difficulties with the understanding of grace as created, sanctifying grace. Denis Petau, S.J. (d. 1652), was the first to challenge the somewhat novel Thomistic-scholastic understanding of grace as created grace. But Petau was without influence. At the end of the nineteenth century Matthias Scheeben in *The Mysteries of Christianity* returned to the biblical and Greek patristic understanding of grace as uncreated grace, i.e., the presence of God precisely as Father, Son, and Spirit to the person.[20] It is this understanding of grace which will be the primordial understanding of grace for Karl Rahner.

Grace as Uncreated Grace

In a key essay written in 1939 entitled "Some Implications of the Scholastic Concept of Uncreated Grace,"[21] Rahner challenges the primary understanding of grace as created grace.[22] While Rahner was not the first or only theologian of his time to make such a challenge,[23] one could argue, on the basis of Rahner's overall influence, that contemporary theology's emphasis upon grace as uncreated grace is due very much to Karl Rahner.[24] For Rahner, grace in the first instance is not some thing, a created, quantified reality, but some one, namely, the Holy Spirit Herself, God's gift of God's self or love, with which gift come also the Father and the Son. As such the primary meaning of grace is *un*created grace. In Rahner, all of these terms refer to the same divine reality: uncreated grace, Holy Spirit, self-gift or self-communication, the love of God and hence the indwelling Trinity.[25] In speaking about grace in this way, Rahner returns to the biblical and patristic understanding of grace.[26] Hence he has also helped shift the rhetoric about grace back to one which is more personal and covenantal. Grace involves a personal encounter between God and humans, an encounter which can be experienced,[27] as will be seen in more detail below. As the self-communication or self-gift of God, grace, as Lady Wisdom, tells us that our God is a God-for-us.

Rahner's Supernatural Existential

Thus far we have considered Rahner's understanding of grace as uncreated grace or Holy Spirit which can be experienced by us. The second significant aspect of his theology of grace pertinent to the theme of everyday mysticism is his notion of the supernatural existential, a term very much associated with Karl Rahner. The supernatural existential has to do with the extent to which uncreated grace is available, i.e., to whom it is given and how. It is perhaps with his concept of the supernatural existential that Rahner has made the greatest contribution to the contemporary theology of grace, a contribution which was registered at the Second Vatican Council.[28]

By the term supernatural existential,[29] Rahner means that God's self-communication through uncreated grace or the Holy Spirit is given to every human being. For Rahner, the human being is "the event of God's free and forgiving self-communication."[30] If you have a human being, you have God's self-gift of the Holy Spirit to that human being. Hence the only humans who *de facto* exist in the one and only economy of salvation, in which all are created, through and unto Christ, are *graced* human beings. Thus Rahner states:

> . . . we must first of all consider that the thesis
> proposed here about the innermost and ultimate
> characteristic of our basic statement that man is
> the event of God's self-communication does not
> refer to a statement which is valid only for this or
> that group of people as distinguished from others,
> for example, only for the baptized or the justified
> as distinguished from pagans or sinners. Without
> prejudice to the fact that it speaks of a free and
> unmerited grace, of a miracle of God's free love for
> spiritual creatures, the statement that man as
> subject is the event of God's self-communication is
> a statement which refers to absolutely all men,
> and which expresses an existential of every per-
> son.[31]

Although this position of the universality of grace has
some implicit roots in some early Eastern Fathers, it certainly was
never explicitly stated or developed in either the East or the West.
And in the West it was for all practical purposes denied with its
doctrine of original sin, the lack of grace. Humans were not
created graced but un-graced or dis-graced, and the only way to
become graced was through faith-baptism(with some exceptions
as baptism of blood and desire). For Rahner, we are created also
graced (supernatural existential) and not just dis-graced; we are
both Adamic and Christic in our very creation.[32]

Transcendental and Categorical Revelation[33]

One of the consequences of Rahner's supernatural existential is his theology of revelation as transcendental and categorical or historical. If grace (God's self-gift) is universal (supernatural existential), and grace is ontological (i.e., involving personal encounter) and not merely ontic, then there must be also a

type of universal revelation. Hence Rahner speaks of transcendental revelation. In the first instance for Rahner, revelation, as transcendental revelation, is not words or propositions or statements. It is not the Bible. It is pre-words, pre-conceptual, pre-thematic. In the words of Polanyi, it is an "unknown known" or "tacit knowing."[34] Rahner states:

> . . . the supernaturally elevated, unreflexive but really present, and transcendental experience of man's movement and orientation towards immediacy and closeness of God, that is, the experience as such prior to being made thematic reflexively and historically, must be characterized as real revelation. . . . This transcendental knowledge. . . must be distinguished from verbal propositional revelation as such. But it deserves nevertheless to be characterized as God's self-revelation.[35]

Revelation in the first instance is God's own presence or self-gift to all humans in so far as this presence or self-gift affects human consciousness and experience but not yet in a conceptually articulated or thematized way. It is uncreated grace itself or the supernatural existential looked at cognitively,[36] i.e., uncreated grace as experienced, or it is the "divinized transcendentality of man."[37] As Rahner states:

> This transcendental moment in revelation is a modification of our transcendental consciousness produced permanently by God in grace. . . . And as an element in our transcendentality, which is constituted by God's self-communication, it is already revelation in the proper sense.[38]

Since this transcendental revelation is universal, the history of the world "is also and at the same time the history of revelation,"[39] and "the history of revelation in the human race is coextensive with the whole history of the world's freedom."[40] This transcendental revelation is not only the original mode of revelation but also "the mode upon which all other revelation is based."[41]

But this transcendental revelation never exists in and by itself. It must always be mediated, since humans are not pure spirits but "spirit in the world," inserted into the here and now of creation and history.[42] We are not only reference to Mystery, the transcendental dimension of our being; we are also reference to history, the categorical dimension of our being. Therefore, our being as spirit, our transcendence, is always lived out, executed, realized and experienced in the world and in history. Both aspects (the transcendental and categorical) are always at play in all human experience and activity. On the one hand we are reaching for and tasting the divine as spirit, especially as graced spirit, or graced transcendence, but this experience of the divine is always executed by means of our reference to the world. Hence transcendence (i.e., our being beyond ourselves and in the realm of the divine) is always historically mediated, and hence history is ultimately the history of human transcendentality.[43] Rahner states:

> What we are calling transcendental knowledge or experience of God is an *a posteriori* knowledge insofar as man's transcendental experience of his free subjectivity takes place only in his encounter with the world and especially with other people. To that extent the scholastic tradition is correct when it emphasizes against ontologism that man's only knowledge of God is an *a posteriori* knowledge from the world. . . . Hence our transcendental knowledge or experience has to be called *a posteriori* insofar as every transcendental experience is mediated by a categorical encounter.... This is also true of the knowledge of God.[44]

Therefore, our experience of the divine within, or, to say the same thing, our experience of ourselves transcending ourselves, is always executed in intra-worldly ways, because we are in the world. Our immediate experience of God is always a "mediated immediacy."[45] This historical mediation of the transcendental experience of the divine (transcendental revelation) is called by Rahner categorical revelation, one form of which is propositional revelation.[46] Rahner points out that the transcendental and categorical aspects of revelation or the experience of the divine always go together. There is not one without the other.[47] ". . . there is never transcendence which is not accompanied by some degree of reflection, however limited, because every transcendental experience must be mediated objectively."[48] However, this historical mediation of our graced transcendentality, i.e., of God's self-presence in transcendental revelation, need not be explicitly religious or expressed in explicitly religious symbols, cult, propositions and institutions.[49] God can be experienced, though not necessarily named, in any truly human experience. Hence Rahner says: ". . . there is for Christianity no separate and sacral realm where alone God is to be found. Even though a categorical objectivity is in the first instance and explicitly profane, it can be adequate for the mediation of our supernaturally elevated experience which we are rightly calling revelation."[50]

This is why the whole world is a "quasi-sacrament,"[51] i.e., that which mediates or brings the divine to us. For Rahner, any intra-worldly reality or experience can be a moment of grace, a revelatory moment, because our experience of the divine within, of transcendental revelation, is always brought about or mediated through our being-in-the-world, through worldly experience. For Rahner the seven sacraments are only the explicit, official, ecclesial celebration of sacramental reality which is going on all around us.[52]

It is important to note that for Rahner these worldly sacraments, or even the seven Church sacraments, do not really bring grace to us from outside as it were. Since God through uncreated grace or the Holy Spirit is always already present to every human being, the sacraments mediate grace not by bringing it to but out of us. Hence Rahner states:

> The sacraments accordingly are not really to be understood as successive individual incursions of God into a secular world, but as 'outbursts' . . . of the innermost, ever present gracious endowment of the world with God himself into history.[53]

Let us now summarize what has been said thus far. For Rahner, God has given God's self (Holy Spirit—uncreated grace) to everyone. This uncreated grace is experienced by everyone in some way, to some extent. And this uncreated grace (Holy Spirit) is always experienced in and because of intra-worldly events, worldly sacraments or Church sacraments, which put us in touch with the divine within us, and by putting us in touch with the divine, they, as it were, "pull the divine out of us." They may even bring the divine into thematic, conceptually articulated experience. When they do, human beings begin talking about the gods, the divine. Such god-talk *(theo-logos)* is the conceptualized, verbalized or thematic form of categorical revelation.

Rahner's Everyday Mysticism[54]

The theological and philosophical anthropology presented above provides the foundations for Rahner's "everyday mysticism."[55] For Rahner, mystics are not rare birds, the elite, and mysticism (experienced reference to Mystery)[56] is not some rare gift or rare experience.[57] Rahner notes that, for the Exercises, Ignatius "presupposes as both possible and actual an experience of God which . . . is not identical with a verbalized, conceptual knowledge of God. In the Exercises Ignatius wants to lead one to nothing else besides this experience."[58] In speaking of the importance of the classical Spanish mystics as teachers of the personal experience of God, who are particularly adept at making this experience intelligible, Rahner states:

> If these older mystics are to be able to help us in this task, we must of course assume . . . that in every human being . . . there is something like an anonymous, unthematic, perhaps repressed, basic experience of being oriented to God, which is constitutive of man in his concrete make-up (of nature and grace), which can be repressed but not destroyed, which is 'mystical' or . . . has its climax in what the older teachers call infused contemplation.[59]

Rahner points out that in everyday life to a great extent this experience of the divine "remains anonymous, implicit, unthematic, like the widely and diffusely spread light of a sun which we do not directly see, while we turn only to the individual objects visible in this light in our sense-experience,"[60] hence, the existence of anonymous mystics.

Above all, for Rahner mystical experience, the experience of the divine, is not something aworldly or ahistorical. It has nothing to do with a *fuga mundi* mentality, as if God can be experienced outside of history or in cloisters only. For Rahner God can be experienced only in human experience, and, as seen above, human experience is always historical and worldly or categorical. As Egan states: ". . . Rahner's is no theology or mysticism of pure interiority. The human person is basically mystic-in-the-world."[61]

As was seen above in dealing with the notion of categorical revelation, it is the concrete experiences of our life which bring the anonymous, implicit, unthematic and transcendental experiences of the divine into explicit consciousness. "Everyday reality then becomes itself a pointer to this transcendental experience of the Spirit, which is always present silently and apparently facelessly."[62]

Here Rahner is inspired by the Ignatian mysticism of "finding God in all things."[63] Regarding this mysticism of the ordinary, Egan states: "This mysticism of everyday things encompasses even the most humble aspects of daily life: work, sleep, eating, drinking, laughter, seeing, sitting, getting about, standing, and the like."[64]

Thus for Rahner contemplation or mysticism is as universal as transcendental revelation. Everybody, therefore, in virtue of being human has some experience of the divine, has some experience of ultimacy and ultimate concern, of the restless heart made restless because of the experience of the always already present God, even though one may not articulate this experience with the Word God. Hence Rahner states:

> If we want to describe as 'mysticism' this experience of transcendence in which man in the midst of ordinary life is always beyond himself and beyond the particular object with which he is concerned, we might say that mysticism always occurs, concealed and namelessly, in the midst of ordinary life and is the condition of the possibility for the most down-to-earth and most secular experiences of ordinary life.[65]

For Rahner what is more important is not the articulation of the experience of the divine in words but in practice, in our lives, above all in our love for others and for all of God's creation. A person in his/her words may profess to be an atheist but in his/her actions professes to be a believer. Hence, one can be an anonymous Christian mystic.[66] Our experience of the divine, therefore, does not always necessarily take the form of a knowing which is consciously articulated in words, much less religious words. In fact, as we know from the great mystics, their experience of the divine is beyond words. Hence the meaning of the word *mysticism*, from *muein*, to keep silence. The distinction between an atheist and a mystic may be hairline.[67]

For Rahner, therefore, the experience of the divine, of the Spirit, hence spirituality, is something very ordinary not extraordinary. The extraordinary, the divine, is found precisely in the ordinary, the everyday. And that is what Rahner means by everyday mysticism, the experience of the divine which we have constantly going on beneath our noses and usually are not expressly aware of it, i.e., we do not name it. But it is there.

Four Types of Everyday Mysticism[68]

First there is the Ignatian mysticism of Joy in the World.[69] These are the positive experiences of our life, the happy, joyful experiences in which we have the underlying experience that reality is good, meaningful and trustworthy. This is the experience which comes in being able to appreciate the good and beautiful things in life which "promise and point to eternal light and everlasting life."[70] One need only think of experiences such as human love, the birth of a baby, birthday parties, celebrations of any type, recreation, the enjoyment of friends. In all of these we experience ourselves beyond ourselves, caught up by the basic goodness and beauty of life. These are the experiences which "genuinely re-create us, fill us with joy and peace. They produce the fruits of the Holy Spirit in our lives."[71] As Rahner says: "the good things in life are not only for the rascals."[72]

One must not forget that for Rahner, as for Ignatius, this mysticism of joy in the world first presumes indifference, or detachment "from every determinate thing which man is tempted to regard as the point in which God meets him."[73] There is, even in this mysticism, a prior moment of *fuga saeculi*, to be alone in God far from the world, a prior commitment to God in so far as God is always beyond the world.[74] As Rahner points out, "Ignatius approaches the world from God. Not the other way about."[75]

Second there is the experience of immense longing, of disquietude, of restlessness, of profound emptiness, despite all that we possess or have attained. This is a quite common form of everyday mysticism. This is the experience of the restless heart, restless because it already tastes the divine but has not yet fully become one with God. It is the very experience of God that is the cause of our longing and turns us into lonely hunters after the divine.[76]

Third, in line with so much of the mystical tradition, Rahner stresses the *via negativa*, the way of negation.[77] It is especially here that we experience our self-surrender, our transcendence, our moving beyond ourselves and touching the divine.[78] It is the negative experiences of life which can expose us to our infinite emptiness, openness to God. Hence Rahner says: "whenever space is really left by parting, by death, by renunciation, by apparent emptiness, provided the emptiness . . . is not filled by the world, or activity, or chatter, or . . . deadly grief . . . there God is."[79] And again: "When we have let ourselves go and no longer belong to ourselves, when everything (including ourselves) has moved away from us as if into an infinite distance, then we begin to live in the world of God himself, the world of the God of grace and of eternal life."[80]

Here Rahner reflects the classic apophatic mysticism, the mysticism of negation, which calls for the need to be silent and empty so as to let God fill the void. Here the harsh and negative experiences of human existence become the primary possible moments of the experience of grace or pointers to the transcendental experience of the Holy Spirit, who is always present silently. They throw us into dark nights of faith and abandonment to God. Regarding these negative experiences Rahner says:

> . . . a pointer of this kind is perceived most clearly where the definable limits of our everyday realities break down and are dissolved, where the decline of these realities is perceived, when lights shining over the tiny islands of our ordinary life are extinguished and the question becomes inescapable, whether the night that surrounds us is the void of absurdity and death that engulfs us or the blessed

holy night already shining within us is the promise
of eternal day.[81]

In Egan's words: "The best moment is when everything
that props up our life fails. Then we are forced to ask if the
inescapable darkness engulfing us is absolute meaninglessness
or a blessed, holy night."[82]

The primary mystical experience of everyday life for Rahner,
therefore, is the courageous, total acceptance of life and of oneself
when everything tangible seems to be collapsing. "Anyone who
does so accepts implicitly the holy Mystery who fills the emptiness
both of oneself and of life."[83] Here Rahner is in line with mystics
such as John of the Cross, Teresa of Avila and Thérèse of Lisieux.

Finally there is a mysticism of "contrast experiences"[84] or
what I would call a protest or prophetic mysticism. Contrast
experiences are the experiences which we have when we experience that things should not be the way they are. And in these
experiences, we protest. For example, we are shocked by tragedies
such as Auschwitz, Bosnia, Northern Ireland, Oklahoma City, the
senseless killing of innocent victims, especially children. Why are
we shocked and why do we protest? We are shocked and we
protest because this is not the way things are supposed to be. Why
not? Because we always already experience the way things should
be. We experience the realm of the divine. And because of that
antecedent experience, we protest the experience of evil in our
world.

One can see then how banal, ordinary, down-to-earth and
everyday, how "worldly" are the spirituality and mysticism of Karl
Rahner. As Egan says: "For Rahner there is nothing profane about
the depths of ordinary life. Wherever there is radical self-forget-
ting for the sake of the other, an absolute letting go, an absolute
yielding of everything, surrender to the Mystery that embraces all
life, there is the Spirit of the crucified and risen Christ, the
mysticism of every day life."[85]

For Rahner God is always already with us, to be found in
and by means of the ordinary events of our everyday life. God is

always already at home, closer to myself than I am to myself as Augustine says. The question is "are we at home, are we in our depths," which for Rahner demands taking the ordinary of our everyday life very seriously? To the extent that we are in our depths and allow these depths to be drawn out by the everyday events of our life, to that extent we experience God. Mystics in the more usual sense of that term, John of the Cross, Teresa of Avila, Thérèse of Lisieux, are people who are always at home. We, on the other hand, tend to be out of the house quite a bit, distant from ourselves and hence from God (not God from us). This raises the question of the distinction in Rahner between his everyday mysticism and what he calls mysticism "in the strict sense."

Everyday Mysticism and Mysticism in the Strict Sense

As both Egan and Wiseman point out, Rahner distinguishes mysticism in the strict sense from his everyday mysticism.[86] But the distinction is one of degree not of kind. Rahner states: "Mystical experience is not specifically different from the ordinary life of grace (as such);"[87] and again, ". . . mysticism can be conceived of only within the normal framework of grace and faith."[88] Rahner insists that mystical experience in the strict sense, i.e., infused contemplation as experienced for example by the great Spanish mystics, must not be understood to be an experience which transcends and supersedes the supernatural experience of the Spirit in faith. Thus Rahner states that it is the task of Christian theology

> to render intelligible the fact that the real basic phenomenon of mystical experience of transcendence is present as innermost sustaining ground (even though unnoticed) in the simple act itself of Christian living in faith, hope, and love, that such . . . implicit transcendence into the nameless mystery known as God is present by grace in this

very believing, hoping, and loving; it seems to us that mysticism in its explicit sense and as expressly practiced may signify a higher degree of the Christian ascent to perfection from the standpoint of an objectively reflecting psychology, not from a properly theological standpoint, and that mysticism in an explicit experience has therefore . . . a paradigmatic character, an exemplary function, to make clear to the Christian what really happens and is meant when his faith tells him that God's self-communication is given to him in grace and accepted in freedom whenever he believes, hopes and loves.[89]

In Rahner's view, therefore, mystical experiences in the strict sense are merely "extremely intense instances of a basically universal experience of God. . . ."[90] For mystics in the strict sense, the ever-present, implicit experience of the divine found in everyday, ordinary mysticism becomes more explicit. But it is the life of faith, hope and love that constitute the heart of both mysticisms, mysticism in the strict sense and everyday mysticism, as well as the Christian life as such.[91]

What constitutes mystical experience in the strict sense as distinct from the Christian normal experience of the Spirit is due solely to the natural sphere, to the natural ability to "return to one's self."[92] As Egan explains Rahner, this extremely intense experience of God is due not to God or grace but to "natural psychology and to the natural abilities of the human person for concentration, meditation, submersion, self-emptying, and other contemplative techniques. . . ,"[93] with the result that this experience is to a greater or less extent a non-conceptual experience of transcendence, an experience mediated without imagery or categories.[94]

Conclusion

The Christian journey is the mystical journey because it is the life of faith, hope and love. Hence the often cited statement of Rahner: "the devout Christian of the future will either be a 'mystic', one who has experienced something, or he will cease to be anything at all."[95]It is the journey of reappropriating the depths of our own being. The Spirit is the divine energy and impulse which drives and enables us to undertake this task of appropriation. In the appropriation we ourselves become more and more Christ-like, and the goal of that journey is to be brought back to God/Father. And so our Christian life, our Christian journey, and our Christian mysticism end up not only being quite everyday and worldly, but also, as it should be, quite Trinitarian. It involves a deeper immersion into the very Trinitarian life of God.

How Christian is this mysticism! It takes dead seriously the world, the flesh, and history, just as did God in the Incarnation. Perhaps too often we run to the mountain tops to find God in prayer, forgetting that our God, revealed in Jesus, came down the mountain to be with us in history. It is there that our God can be experienced. In the words of John's Gospel: "and the Word became flesh and lived among us." (Jn 1:14)

Donald Buggert, O.Carm.

Endnotes

1. Wis 7:24, 27c-28; 8:4, 7b; 9:17-18.
2. Roland E. Murphy, "Israel's Wisdom: A Biblical Model of Salvation," *Studia Missionalia* 30 (1981) 29, citing C. Larcher, *Études sur le livre de la Sagesse* (Paris: Gabalda, 1969) 413.
3. *The Tree of Life: An Exploration of Biblical Wisdom Literature* (New York: Doubleday, 1990) 147.
4. See Murphy, "Israel's Wisdom."
5. Karl Rahner, "Experience of the Holy Spirit," *Theological Investigations* vol. 18, Edward Quinn, trans. (New York: Crossroad, 1983) 203, 205. Henceforth references to *Theological Investigations: TI*.
6. ST, I-II, q. 112, a. 1.
7. ST, I-II, q. 110, aa. 3 and 4; III, q. 62, aa. 1 and 2. Thomas often cites 2 Pet 1:4 to substantiate his position of grace as sharing or partaking in the divine nature.
8. ST, I-II, q. 110, a. 1, a. 2 ad 2, a. 3. The term sanctifying grace is not actually found in Thomas. As Haight indicates, in Thomas Aquinas created grace, elevating grace and habitual grace refer to the same reality. See Roger Haight, *The Language and Experience of Grace* (New York: Paulist Press, 1979) 62.
9. E. M. Burke, "Grace," in *The New Catholic Encyclopedia*, 6, 662, 668. See also Henri Rondet, *The Grace of Christ*, Tad W. Guzie, trans. (New York: Newman Press, 1967) 198.
10. ST, II-II, q. 23, a. 2. Thomas is insistent upon the necessity for human acts themselves to be meritorious because, for Thomas, grace is necessary not in the first place because we are sinners but because we are finite creatures who nevertheless have a goal, namely, the beatific vision, which, as the vision of the divine essence itself, is beyond the possibilities of our human nature as such. Thus the need for a new nature which will elevate human nature to an order above human nature, the divine or supernatural order. As thus

elevated, the soul is now commensurate to its goal, the beatific vision. This grace is the created or sanctifying grace spoken of above and its ultimate task is to elevate human nature to the supernatural order. Hence it is called by Thomas *gratia elevans*. With such grace the soul is now empowered to act graciously or divinely and thus able to attain (i.e., merit) its goal, God. ST, I, q. 95, a. 4 ad 1; I-II, q. 109, aa. 1, 2, 5, and 9 and q. 112, a. 1.

11. Haight, *The Experience and Language of Grace*, 69; see also Burke, Grace, 662.

12. See e.g., Peter Gasparri, *The Catholic Catechism*, Hugh Pope, trans., (New York: P.J. Kenedy & Sons, 1932) 33; *The Baltimore Catechism No. I* (Rockford, IL: Tan Books and Publishers, 1977) 15. The *Catechism of the Catholic Church* in its treatment of grace first deals with created, sanctifying grace but states that "Grace is first and foremost the gift of the Spirit who justifies and sanctifies us." (Washington, D.C.: United States Catholic Conference, 1994) 485.

13. See e.g., S. González, "De Gratia," in *Sacrae Theologiae Summa*, vol. 3 (Madrid: Biblioteca de Autores Cristianos, 1953) 594. "Gratia sanctificans est donum creatum, physice permanens, realiter a caritate distinctum."

14. ST, I-II, q. 110, a. 2.

15. See e.g., ST, I-II, q. 112, a. 4; q. 114, a. 8; II-II, q. 62, a. 3. The Council of Trent likewise taught in chapter ten of its *Decree on Justification* that "when faith works along with their works..., the justified increase in the very justice which they have received through the grace of Christ and are justified the more." John F. Clarkson, et al., *The Church Teaches* (St. Louis, MO: B. Herder, 1962) 236. The *Catechism of the Catholic Church*, 487, likewise speaks of the increase of grace. "Moved by the Holy Spirit and by charity, we can then merit for ourselves and for others the graces needed for our sanctification, for the increase of grace and charity, and for the attainment of eternal life."

16. See Haight, *The Experience and Language of Grace*, 71.

17. See Rahner, "Concerning the Relationship Between Nature and Grace," *TI*, vol. 1, Cornelius Ernst, trans. (Baltimore: Helicon, 1961) 316. The distinction between the ontic/metaphysical-ontological/existential runs throughout Rahner. Ontic or metaphysical categories are categories which are applicable to any and all beings. Ontological or existential categories are applicable only to personal beings or beings of self-consciousness. See e.g., Karl Rahner, "Current Problems in Christology," *TI*, vol. 1, 168-169; *Foundations of Christian Faith*, William V. Dych, trans. (New York: Seabury Press, 1978) 302-303. Henceforth cited as *Foundations*.

18. See "Concerning the Relationship Between Nature and Grace," *TI*, vol. 1, 316; "Nature and Grace," *TI*, vol. 4, Kevin Smyth, trans. (Baltimore: Helicon) 165-188, *passim*.

19. Thus, for example, Rahner writes: "The statement, 'man is the event of God's absolute self-communication,' does not refer to some reified objectivity 'in man'. Such a statement is not a categorical and ontic statement, but an ontological statement. It expresses in words the subject as such, and therefore the subject in the depths of his subjectivity, and hence in the depths of his transcendental experience." *Foundations*, 126. See above, n. 17, for the meaning of "ontic" and "ontological."

20. See Burke, "Grace," 665.

21. *TI*, vol. 1, 329-346.

22. It is beyond the scope of this article to detail Rahner's arguments for his position that grace in its most primordial meaning and reality is uncreated grace. In summary, Rahner appeals to the biblical and Greek patristic understanding of grace as the gift of God Him/Herself, i.e., the Holy Spirit. He then offers a highly speculative argument (pp. 325-334) to the effect that if grace is, as Thomas argues, the anticipation of the beatific vision (*inchoatio gloriae*) and if the beatific vision consists in God's self-gift to the person, then grace

itself must in the first instance consist in God's self-gift or uncreated grace.

23. Reference was made above to Scheeben; others such as Galtier, de la Taille and Dumont made similar challenges.

24. Not without reason has Rahner been called "the most brilliant theologian since Thomas Aquinas." See Thomas Sheehan in *New York Review* (February 4, 1982) 13.

25. Rahner, Experience of the Spirit and Existential Commitment, *TI*, vol. 16, David Morland, trans. (New York: Seabury Press, 1979) 38-39; "Experience of the Holy Spirit," *TI*, vol. 18, 198. Obviously as uncreated, grace cannot have degrees; one cannot grow in it, although one can grow in one's response to or appropriation of it.

26. Since his 1939 article, Rahner has consistently maintained his position on the primary understanding of grace as uncreated grace. See e.g., his *Foundations*, 116-126; "Nature and Grace," *TI*, vol. 4, 165-188; "Grace-Theological," and "Grace-Structure of De Gratia," in *Encyclopedia of Theology*, Karl Rahner, ed., (New York: Seabury, 1975) 587-598.

27. "Concerning the Relationship Between Nature and Grace," *TI*, vol. 1, 316; Grace-Theological, *Encyclopedia of Theology*, 588-595, *passim*.

28. See *The Pastoral Constitution on the Church in the Modern World (Gaudium et Spes)* # 22; *The Dogmatic Constitution on the Church (Lumen Gentium)* # 16; *Decree on the Church's Missionary Activity (Ad Gentes)* # 7.

29. Rahner's use of the term existential is influenced by Martin Heidegger. An existential is a characteristic or structure of de facto historical existence, e.g., that humans are bodily and hence in space, time, history. The latter (our being-in-the world) is a natural existential, i.e., it belongs to us *qua* human. Rahner claims there is also a supernatural existential, i.e., it does not belong to us *qua* human but as a divine gift beyond what is absolutely requisite as human, hence a supernatural gift, the gift of uncreated grace itself.

30. Karl Rahner, *Foundations*, 116. There is without doubt development in Rahner's thinking concerning the supernatural existential. In an early essay first published in *Orientierung* 15 (1950) and again in *Theological Investigations* vol. I, 297-317, entitled "Concerning the Relationship Between Nature and Grace," Rahner presents his early or initial understanding of the supernatural existential as a created grace which accounts for the yearning within human beings for divine fulfillment through uncreated grace and glory and which demands such fulfillment. This early understanding of the supernatural existential was developed by Rahner to mediate between Henri deLubac's position concerning a natural desire for God demanding fulfillment in grace and the condemnation of this position in 1950 by *Humani Generis*. Many authors in dealing with Rahner's supernatural existential limit their treatment to this early 1950 article and thus present it as merely a created grace which calls out for the uncreated grace of God's self-communication. As Rahner develops his own theology, it becomes clear that the supernatural existential is no longer a yearning and demand for uncreated grace but is uncreated grace itself. See also the sub-sectional heading on p. 126 of *Foundations*: "The Offer of Self-Communication as 'Supernatural Existential'."

31. *Foundations*, 127. See also e.g., "Observations on the Problem of the 'Anonymous Christian,'" *TI*, vol. 14, David Bourke, trans. (New York: Seabury) 288.

32. *Foundations*, 113-114. See also "Original Sin," in *Sacramentum Mundi* vol. 4, K. Rahner et al., ed., (New York: Herder and Herder, 1969) 329-331; "Salvation," in *Sacramentum Mundi*, vol. 5, 437; "Justified and Sinner at the Same Time," *TI*, vol. 6, Karl-H. and Boniface Kruger, trans. (New York: Seabury Press, 1974) 218-249. It is beyond the scope of this article to present Rahner's arguments for the supernatural existential. Sufficient to say that he is influenced by his Scotistic Christology according to

which the de facto economy of creation is Christological. Everything is created in, through and unto Christ, the definitive and irreversible moment and goal of God's self-communication. See Rahner, "Christology Within an Evolutionary View of the World," *TI*, vol. 5, Karl-H. Kruger, trans. (Baltimore: Helicon Press, 1966) 157-192. Since the only economy is the Christic economy, the only grace is the grace of Christ. Hence, Rahner's supernatural existential, with its roots in Rahner's Christocentrism, underlies also another notion unique to Rahner, the Anonymous Christian. Everyone is graced with the grace of Christ. Some know it and some do not! For the notion of Anonymous Christian, see pertinent articles in vols. 5, 6, 12, 16 and 18 of *TI*.

33. See *Foundations*, 138-175; "Revelation," in *Encyclopedia of Theology* 1460-1468.

34. Michael Polanyi, *The Tacit Dimension* (Garden City, N.Y.: Doubleday, 1967).

35. *Foundations*, 149; see "Revelation," 1463.

36. "Revelation," 1462.

37. *Foundations*, 138, 171-172.

38. Ibid., 149.

39. Ibid., 144.

40. Ibid., 145.

41. Ibid., 150; "Revelation," 1463.

42. For Rahner's basic philosophical anthropology, see *Foundations*, 31-43.

43. *Foundations*, 52, 140-141. For Rahner our experience of our own self-transcendence is itself the experience of God, hence of grace or the Holy Spirit. "...in the actual order of reality, experience of transcendence (which is experience of God) is always also experience of grace, since the radicalness of the experience of transcendence and its dynamism are sustained in the innermost core of our existence by God's self-communication making all this possible, by the self-communication of God as goal and as strength of the movement towards him that we describe as grace, as the

Holy Spirit.... The experience of transcendence permitting God to be present...is in fact always experience of the Holy Spirit...." "Experience of the Holy Spirit," *TI*, vol. 18, 198. See also "Experience of Transcendence from the Standpoint of Catholic Dogmatics," *TI*, vol. 18, 182-183, 187.

44. *Foundations*, 52.

45. Ibid., 83-84.

46. One form of propositional revelation is that found within the Old and New Testaments, which Rahner refers to as "public, official, particular and ecclesially constituted revelation," the criterion for which is Jesus Christ. See *Foundations*, 155, 157-158, 173-175.

47. Ibid., 140-142, 144, 150, 172-173. See also "The Experience of God Today," *TI*, vol. 11, David Bourke, trans. (New York: Seabury Press, 1974) 151-152.

48. *Foundations*, 144, 172-173.

49. Ibid., 143-144, 151, 173. See also "Experience of the Spirit and Existential Commitment," *TI*, vol. 16, 28-29.

50. *Foundations*, 152.

51. See "Current Questions in Christology," *TI*, vol. 1, 167.

52. See Rahner, "On the Theology of Worship," *TI*, vol. 19, Edward Quinn, trans. (New York: Crossroad, 1983) 141-149.

53. Ibid., 143.

54. Rahner's theology of everyday mysticism does not exhaust his mystical theology. He has several writings dealing with aspects of mystical theology or with mystics such as Ignatius of Loyola, Teresa of Avila and John of the Cross. Moreover, in the assessment of Harvey Egan, Rahner's theology as a whole is a mystical theology. See "The Devout Christian of the Future Will... be a 'Mystic'. Mysticism and Karl Rahner's Theology," in *Theology and Discovery: Essays in Honor of Karl Rahner*, William J. Kelly, ed., (Milwaukee: Marquette University, 1980), esp. 140-148. A similar assessment is made by J. B. Metz who claims that Rahner's theology is "a type of existential biography," "the mystical biography of

religious experience, of the history of a life before the veiled face of God...." Karl Rahner Ein Theologisches Leben: Theologie als mystische Biographie eines Christenmenschen heute, *Stimmen der Zeit* 192 (1974) 308.

55. As will be seen below, Rahner distinguishes everyday mysticism from mysticism as it is more commonly understood or mysticism in the strict sense. What constitutes the essence of both mysticisms is the experience (implicit or explicit, articulated or not articulated) of one's own self-transcendence or self-surrender to God in faith, hope and love. See Rahner, "Experience of Transcendence from the Standpoint of Christian Dogmatics," *TI*, vol. 18, 173-188 *passim*; "Experience of the Holy Spirit," *TI*, vol. 18, 197-198; "Experience of the Spirit and Existential Commitment," *TI*, vol. 16, 27- 29.

56. This is Egan's description of Rahner's understanding of mysticism. See "The Devout Christian of the Future," 149.

57. See Rahner, "The Experience of God Today," *TI*, vol. 11, 153; "Experience of the Holy Spirit," *TI*, vol. 18, 193. In his insistence upon the possibility open to all of an immediate experience of God, Rahner exhibits his truly pastoral concern. He states: "I am convinced that such an immediacy between God and the human person...is of greater significance today than ever before. All the societal supports of religion are collapsing and dying out in this secularized and pluralistic society. If, nonetheless, there is to be real Christian spirituality, it cannot be kept alive and healthy by external helps, not even those which the Church offers, ... but only through an ultimate, immediate encounter of the individual with God." See The Immediate Experience of God in the *Spiritual Exercises* of Saint Ignatius of Loyola, in *Karl Rahner in Dialogue*, Paul Imhof and Hubert Biallowons, eds., Harvey D. Egan, trans., (N.Y.: Crossroad, 1986) 176. A similar point is made in "Christian Living Formerly and Today," *TI*, vol. 7, David Bourke, trans., (New York: Seabury, 1977) 15.

58. "The Immediate Experience of God . . . ," in *Karl Rahner in Dialogue*, 175. Regarding this experience of the divine, both Harvey Egan and James Wiseman note the influence upon Rahner of the Ignatian *Exercises*. See Egan, "Karl Rahner: Theologian of the *Spiritual Exercises*," *Thought* 67 (1992) 258; James Wiseman, "I Have Experienced God: Religious experience in the Theology of Karl Rahner," *American Benedictine Review* 44 (March 1993) 25-27.

59. Karl Rahner, *Opportunities for Faith*, Edward Quinn, trans. (New York: Seabury, 1974) 125. Wiseman contends that it was Rahner's conviction that the mystics had truly experienced God that led Rahner to examine the conditions for the possibility of such experience and hence to develop his transcendental method of doing theology. See Wiseman, "I Have Experienced God: Religious Experience in the Theology of Karl Rahner," 28.

60. "Experience of the Holy Spirit," *TI*, vol. 18, 199. Note the Platonism of Karl Rahner!

61. "The Devout Christian of the Future," 154.

62. "Experience of the Holy Spirit," *TI*, vol. 18, 199.

63. See Karl Rahner, "The Ignatian Mysticism of Joy in the World," *TI*, vol. 3, Karl-H. and Boniface Kruger, trans. (Baltimore: Helicon, 1967) 277-293.

64. Egan, "The Mysticism of Everyday Life," 9. See Karl Rahner, Everyday Things, in *Belief Today*, Ray and Rosaleen Ockenden, trans. (New York: Sheed and Ward, 1967) 13-36.

65. "Experience of the Holy Spirit," *TI*, vol. 18, 197. Rahner's everyday mysticism with its insistence upon the experience of grace in everyday life is a reaction to the Molinist position mentioned above that the experience of grace is beyond normal human experience and is restricted to those favored with mystical graces. Rahner states: "A true theology of grace, faith, possession of the Spirit, the indwelling of God, etc., deals with realities which cannot be merely understood as objective gifts, existing beyond the consciousness, as a modern Molinist misinterpretation would suggest." See

"Mystical Experience and Mystical Theology," *TI*, vol. 17, Margaret Kohl, trans. (New York: Crossroad, 1981) 93. For the same point, see also "Experience of the Spirit and Existential Commitment," *TI*, vol. 16, 38-39.

66. Rahner, "Experience of Transcendence from the Standpoint of Christian Dogmatics," *TI*, vol. 18, 181-183. See also Rahner, "Anonymous and Explicit Faith," *TI*, vol. 16, 55-59.

67. For a very enlightening treatment of the relation between atheism and contemplation see Michael J. Buckley, "Atheism and Contemplation," *Theological Studies* 40 (1979) 680-699.

68. I am guided here by Harvey Egan, "The Mysticism of Everyday Life," *Studies in Formative Spirituality* 10 (1989) 9-19. For examples of everyday human experiences which are experiences of grace or the Holy Spirit, see "Reflections on the Experience of Grace," *TI*, vol. 3, 86-90; "The Experience of God Today," *TI*, vol. 11, 157-158, and "Experience of the Holy Spirit," *TI*, vol. 18, 200-203.

69. See Rahner, "The Ignatian Mysticism of Joy in the World," *TI*, vol. 3, 277-293 and "Everyday Things," 13-36.

70. Rahner, Experiencing the Spirit, *The Practice of Faith. A Handbook of Contemporary Spirituality*, Karl Lehmann and Albert Raffelt, eds., (New York: Crossroad, 1983) 81.

71. Egan, "The Mysticism of Everyday Life," 11.

72. *Karl Rahner—I Remember. An Autobiographical Interview with Meinold Krauss*, Harvey D. Egan, trans. (New York: Crossroad, 1985) 84.

73. "The Ignatian Mysticism of Joy in the World, *TI*, vol. 3, 290.

74. Ibid., 281-293.

75. Ibid., 290. In this regard Ignatius and John of the Cross seem to be quite similar.

76. Egan, "The Mysticism of Everyday Life," 10.

77. Rahner, "Experience of the Holy Spirit," *TI*, vol. 18, 199-200.

78. Rahner, "Reflections on the Experience of Grace," *TI*, vol. 3, 87-88; Experiencing the Spirit, *The Practice of Faith*, 81.

79. *Biblical Homilies*, Desmond Forristal and Richard Strachan, trans. (New York: Herder and Herder, 1966) 77.
80. "Reflections on the Experience of Grace," *TI*, vol. 3, 89.
81. "Experience of the Holy Spirit," *TI*, vol. 18, 200.
82. "The Mysticism of Everyday Life," 11-12. Examples of such experiences include sacrificing something without receiving any thanks, loneliness, suffering, ingratitude on the part of others, the specter of death, not receiving recognition, following one's conscience without experiencing any satisfaction or being able to explain one's decision of conscience to others, loving God without enthusiastic feeling or when we seem to be calling out into emptiness and our cry seems to fall on deaf ears and everything seems to become apparently senseless. See above n. 68 for sources.
83. Ibid., 17.
84. Ibid., 12-13. As Egan points out (p. 25), Rahner himself does not use the term "contrast experience."
85. Ibid., 23.
86. Egan, "The Devout Christian of the Future Will," 148-154; Wiseman, "I Have Experienced God," 44-47. Wiseman (p. 44) points out that Rahner's understanding of mysticism did undergo development. In his early writings Rahner understood mysticism only in the narrow or strict sense, that is "as a phenomenon relatively rare among Christians and marked by visions, ecstasies, a tendency toward otherworldliness, 'revelations of the Spirit,' and contemplation (especially the 'infused contemplation' that later became a privileged category for scholars describing the mysticism of the classical Spanish mystics Teresa of Avila and John of the Cross)." This mysticism in the strict sense seemed to Rahner to have little to do with the life of ordinary Christians.
87. Rahner, "Mysticism," *Encyclopedia of Theology*, 1010-1011.
88. Rahner, "Mystical Experience and Mystical Theology," *TI*, vol. 17, 94. Rahner's argument here is theological and not empirical. He states: " . . . it is not possible for a real theology

of grace to insert, between faith and the experience of grace on the one hand and glory on the other, an intermediate state which on the one hand transcends the giving of grace to the Christian in the real sense of the word and on the other is not a (transient) participation in the beatific vision of God. Man's deification and possession of uncreated grace cannot . . . be surpassed by anything that is not glory. See Mysticism, *Encyclopedia of Theology*, 1010. See also "Mystical Experience and Mystical Theology," *TI*, vol. 17, 93-94.

89. Rahner, "Experience of Transcendence from the Standpoint of Christian Dogmatics," *TI*, vol. 18, 176. See also pp. 174-75 on the paradigmatic function of mysticism in the strict sense. Mystical experience in the strict sense is "a paradigmatic elucidation of what happens in faith, hope, and love on the Christian path to the perfection of salvation...." As Evelyn Underhill puts it in her classic work on mysticism, "the mystics are the pioneers of the spiritual world." *Mysticism* (New York: New American Library, 1955) 4.

90. Egan, "The Devout Christian of the Future," 150.

91. "Mystical Experience and Mystical Theology," *TI*, vol. 17, 96.

92. Ibid., 95.

93. Egan, "The Devout Christian of the Future," 150. Hence Rahner states: "For mystical theology it is essential to make clear at this point that mystic experiences sustained by the Spirit, which make God's spirit accessible, do not differ from normal Christian existence because they are of a higher nature simply by virtue of being *mystical* experiences of the Spirit. They are different because their natural substratum (for example an experience of suspension of the faculties) is as such different from the psychological circumstances of everyday life." See "Mystical Experience and Mystical Theology," *TI*, vol. 17, 97-98.

94. Rahner, Mysticism, *Encyclopedia of Theology*, 1011; *The Dynamic Element in the Church*, W. J. O'Hara, trans. (New York: Herder and Herder, 1964) 147.

95. "Christian Living Formerly and Today," *TI*, vol. 7, 15.

With Mary His Mother:
A Theologian Reflects on Recent
Scripture Studies

Theology concerned with the mystery of Mary has profited enormously from New Testament studies in the three decades since the Second Vatican Council. Even before the Council closed an extraordinary meeting of minds between systematic theologians and biblical experts had taken place in the spring of 1965. This was the international Mariological Congress (in the series that began in 1950, continuing in 1954 and 1958). This meeting was held at Santo Domingo in the Dominican Republic. Organized by the International Pontifical Marian Academy, under the dynamic leadership of Charles Balic the Croatian-born Franciscan, the congress brought together scholars from many countries to consider the relationships between Scripture study and theology about the Blessed Virgin. A number of the speakers were *periti* at the still ongoing Council.

The conciliar constitutions, *Sacrosanctum concilium* (December 4, 1963) and *Lumen gentium* as well as *Unitatis redintegratio* (both November 21, 1964) had already been published, so that the congress speakers could call on them, especially the Marian eighth chapter of *Lumen gentium*, "The Blessed Virgin Mary, Mother of God, in the Mystery of Christ and the Church," for which *Sacrosanctum concilium* had provided a preview the year previous by describing the holy Virgin "as inseparably joined to the saving work of Christ," so that the Church holds up and admires in her "the most excellent fruit of the redemption." "In her as in a faultless model the Church joyfully contemplates what the Church herself wholly desires and aspires to be." Documents from the fourth session (fall of 1965) were not yet available; most of these would contain contextual allusions to the Blessed Virgin, and the dogmatic constitution on divine revelation (*Dei verbum*, November 18, 1965) would have special relevance to the Santo Domingo subjects.

An impressive array of participants were at Santo Domingo. There had been an abortive attempt in the early sixties, concomitant with the Council itself, to discredit responsible exegesis by Catholic scholars and to stifle scriptural scholarship, even after *Divino afflante spiritu* (1943). That danger was surmounted, as much by the tone of the Council as by its formal statements. Some papers at the spring 1965 gathering were specifically on the relationships between the two disciplines of systematics and exegesis. P. Benoit, O.P., and Gérard Philips represented the respective positions, and from the United States Eugene Maly and Eamon R. Carroll, O.Carm., did the same. Numerous scholars presented papers: A. Feuillet, R. Laurentin, H. Cazelles, B. Rigaux, F. Mussner, and many others. William J. Cole, S.M., of the University of Dayton, spoke on "Scripture and the Understanding of Mary among American Protestants," a topic to be brilliantly exemplified in the 1978 book *Mary in the New Testament*.

Soon after the Council Catholic authors like R. Laurentin and R. LeDeaut, and Lutherans like W. Quanbeck and O. Cullmann considered the Council's use of Scripture with respect to our Lady. A common negative criticism was that the Council gave a too favorable interpretation to the so-called "difficult sayings" (Mk 3:31: "Then his mother and his brothers came; and standing outside, they sent to him and called him" [cf. the parallels in Mt 12:46 and Lk 8:19]; and Lk 11:27: "While he was saying this, a woman in the crowd raised her voice and said to him, 'Blessed is the womb that bore you and the breasts that nursed you!')." A built-in conciliar *cautela* is easily overlooked by critics, perhaps because almost all vernacular translations by-pass a distinction intended by conciliar protocol, i.e., that the Latin control documents use the abbreviation "cf." (confer) to convey an allusion to, but not a decision about the exact sense of a text. Seventeen of the nineteen biblical references in chapter eight of *Lumen gentium* are prefaced by the monitory "cf." Illustrative is the footnote for no. 55 to Isaiah, Micah and Matthew: the "cf." governs Isaiah and Micah, but is omitted for Matthew. The references to the public life of Jesus (no. 58) in Mk 3:35 and Lk 11:27 are prefaced by "cf." and so is the Vulgate translation *gratia plena* for Lk 1:28 (no. 56).

There are sharp differences of interpretation about Mary's place in the New Testament: one school argues for a substantial "historicity." The French exegete Rene Laurentin is the most prominent protagonist of this position. His early masterpiece, *Structure et Théologie de Luc I-II* (Paris, 1957) still wins praise even from those who disagree with the views he has espoused in subsequent books and articles such as, most recently, "La foi de Marie dans l'epreuve," in *Études Mariales* for the 1995 meeting of the French Mariological Society. Other books by Laurentin include *Jésus au temple—mystère de Pâques et foi de Marie en Luc 2,48-50* (Paris, 1966) and *Les Évangiles de l'Enfance du Christ* (2nd ed., Paris, 1982) which has also appeared in English: *The Truth of Christmas. Beyond the Myths* (Petersham, MA, 1986). Partisans of historical-critical method, such as Raymond E. Brown, take strong exception to Laurentin's approach; both authors do not hesitate to name their antagonists. At times the theologian onlooker might hope for more light than heat in the debate. Some years ago a gentlemanly interchange occurred in print between R. E. Brown and the English exegete John McHugh, author of *The Mother of Jesus in the New Testament* (Garden City, NY, 1975). Their views were juxtaposed in the final number of *The Ampleforth Review* (1980), under the title "Exegesis and Dogma: A Review of Two Marian Studies." Brown has written of Mary and the Scriptures on various occasions, e.g., the updated edition of

The Birth of the Messiah (Garden City, NY, 1994), *The Death of the Messiah* (Garden City, NY, 1995), and earlier in the Anchor Bible Commentaries, *The Gospel According to John I-XII* (Garden City, NY, 1966) and *The Gospel According to John XIII-XXI* (Garden City, NY, 1970). The advice of the Servite scholar Neal Flanagan (d. 1985) is apposite. Conceding the symbolic character of Mary's biblical presence he added sagely: "Primarily symbolic though they be, these paintings of Mary must flow from historical memories that established her as a primary Christian model...the frustrating difficulty is that we can no longer reach back through the symbol to the historical elements that made the symbol plausible." Relative to the sometimes acrimonious debate among exegetes, he added gently: "I do expect all of us, no matter what opinion we have at the moment, to listen to others with openness and respect. Only thus can theology and mariology advance."[1]

It has been noted by Catholic and Protestant scholars alike that the Gospels have more about the Virgin Mary than about any other woman, and that more is known about her than about most of the apostles.[2] Whether the biblical references to Mary be interpreted biographically or symbolically, or both, there is no denying her presence as part of the Jesus-story. Neither the earliest nor the latest mentions of Mary give her name. In St. Paul's letter to the Galatians she appears as guarantor of her Son's humanity (Gal 4:4: "born of a woman") and in the Johannine Gospel she is simply "the mother of Jesus." Admittedly the entries about her are few; yet, they place her at critical junctures of her Son's life and ministry: birth and infancy, childhood, start of public life (Cana), with family and disciples (e.g., Luke 8), on Calvary, and in Acts 1:14 and 2:1 awaiting with the apostles the outpouring of the Pentecostal Spirit.

The infancy narratives have attracted the greatest interest in biblical investigations, with the Magnificat exercising an enduring fascination.[3] For the single appearance of Mary common to the three synoptics—"the coming of the mother and the brethren," also called "the true kinsmen" (Mt 12:46-50; Mk 3:31-35; Lk 8:19-21)—a fair amount of debate has arisen: did Mary share the family failure to understand (Mark?), or does Jesus include her among his "true family" (Luke?). Chapter eleven of Luke has as well the oblique reference to Mary and her Son's enigmatic response to the salute of the anonymous enthusiastic woman of the crowd. The Second Vatican Council gave positive interpretations to both Lukan stories.[4]

The Mariological Society of America had been founded in 1950, and from the start it brought together systematicians and exegetes. The annual conventions have featured Scripture scholars such as Barnabas Ahern, Christian Ceroke, James Reese, Eugene Maly, Carroll Stuhlmueller, Reginald H. Fuller, and their talks have been published in *Marian Studies*. At the 1967 convention of the Mariological Society, Richard Kugelman, C.P., onetime president of the Catholic Biblical Association, presented a survey of recent scriptural studies on the Virgin Mary. Subsequently he was part of the team of writers that produced the American Bishops' joint pastoral: *Behold Your Mother: Woman of Faith* (November 21, 1973). In 1968 the present writer included a section on Scripture in his "Survey of Recent Mariology." This section has continued to appear regularly including the forty-seventh annual convention, held at Villanova University, Philadelphia, May, 1996.[5]

The specialist journals of Mariology, *Marianum* (Rome) and *Ephemerides Mariologicae* (Madrid), and the proceedings of the Mariological Societies of various countries, especially France and Spain, to a lesser extent Germany and of late also Italy, frequently carry articles on Mary and the New Testament.[6] *Études Mariales* has published H. Cazelles, veteran expert, e.g., on the biblical faith of Mary.[7] The Spanish *Ephemerides Mariologicae* devoted a double number to the theology and spirituality of the Magnificat, with R. Schnackenburg among the authors. The entire volume for 1993 was on Mary in the New Testament.[8]

It would go beyond the assigned limits of this *Festschrift* essay in tribute to my own former teacher and Carmelite confrere, Roland Murphy, to attempt an adequate roster of scriptural publications on the Blessed Virgin that have proven helpful to my theological studies, but I do offer a truncated list based on my surveys since 1967. Ignatius de la Potterie, S.J., has written extensively on our Lady, and some of his work, such as *Mary in the Mystery of the Covenant*, translated by Bertrand Buby (Staten Island, 1992), has appeared in English. André Feuillet has also written frequently on our Lady. One of his titles in English is: *Jesus and his Mother: the Role of the Virgin Mary in Salvation History and the Place of Woman in the Church* (French original 1974; English 1984, Still River, MA). In an article on the wedding feast at Cana, A. Feuillet noted as a striking historical verification, how just two days before the wedding, which is set on the "third day" (Jn 2:1), two followers of John the Baptist became disciples of Jesus: "They spent the day with him; it was about the tenth hour" (Jn 1:39). M. J. Lagrange saw similar realism there.[9] Feuillet notes how Jesus, though a guest, usurped the groom's role of serving the best wine, since as messianic bridegroom he is the new host. Mary his Mother plays the role of new Eve in the scene, her Son the new Adam. One may hope for in-depth studies of the groom-bride relationship of Christ to his Church, reaching back to the bond between God and Israel.

I find very stimulating the many contributions of the Italian Servite Aristide Serra, though the Australian exegete Francis J. Moloney, S.D.B., finds that Serra exaggerates the Marian import of some of his conclusions.[10] Serra's writings appear regularly in the Roman periodical *Marianum* and *Theotokos*. His doctoral thesis at the Biblical Institute (1976) was on the contribution of ancient Jewish literature to the exegesis of John 2:1-11 and John 19:25-27. In 1982 he published *Sapienza e contemplazione di Maria secondo Lc 2,19.51b* with four chapters dedicated to the Magnificat, a paschal hymn of triumph. At her son's birth Mary received the shepherds, treasured their words and pondered them in her heart. After Easter, in Acts, the Mother of the Risen Jesus, the Christ, continues to be attentive to the pastors: now the shepherds are the apostles. Serra devoted a chapter of that book to the sign of the swaddling clothes, considered also by J. A. Grassi in the 1988 title *Mary, Mother and*

Disciple (Collegeville, MN). Both Serra and Grassi reflect on associated elements—as manger and bread (name of Bethlehem, and eucharistic overtones). Serra has also gathered in book form a series of previously published articles.[11]

Francis J. Moloney wrote the book *Mary: Woman and Mother* (Collegeville, MN, 1989) and has a section on Mary in *Woman: First among the Faithful* (Notre Dame, IN, 1986) To the sixth international conference on biblical studies at Oxford, April, 1978, he presented his study: "From Cana to Cana (Jn 2:1-4:54) and the Fourth Evangelist's Concept of Correct (and Incorrect) Faith."[12] Bertrand A. Buby, S.M., of the University of Dayton, has in progress the trilogy *Mary of Galilee*, of which two titles have appeared: *Mary in the New Testament* (Staten Island, 1994) and *Woman of Israel: Daughter of Zion* (Staten Island, 1995). The third volume will be about Mary in the apocrypha and sub-apostolic authors. A previous book by Buby was *Mary the Faithful Disciple* (Mahwah, NJ, 1985).

Bruce Malina, John Pilch, and Jerome Neyrey have looked into the contemporary circumstances of Palestinian life to see how Jesus and Mary lived. Neyrey writes: "Although Mary is unique in the Mediterranean world as a virgin Mother, the presentation of her virginity and her maternity fully reflect the general cultural evaluation of females in Mediterranean culture."[13] Acts 1:14 ("With one heart all these joined constantly in prayer, together with some women, including Mary the Mother of Jesus, and with his brothers") (Jerusalem Bible) has not been much studied. In an address on Mary in the communion of saints which R. Laurentin gave in England, April, 1973, he was able to find only a single recent article by Cardinal Bea in 1950. As it happened, just then the Dominican journal *Sacra Doctrina* published an article by Benedetto Prete, "Il sommario di Atti 1,13-14 e suo apporto per la conoscenza della Chiesa delle origini."[14] Prete chose a middle position between exaggerating Mary's role (making her queen) and saying no more than that this is just the last New Testament mention of her (G. Staehlin). She is the "mother of Jesus," Jesus of whom the preceding verses have been speaking—who after his passion appeared to his disciples "speaking to them about the reign of God," and commanding them to wait "for the fulfillment of my Father's promise." The Marian chapter of the Council saw a parallel between the role of the Spirit at the Annunciation and in Acts. "With one heart" echoes Sinai (Exodus 19): for the "whole group of believers was united heart and soul...." Recent ecumenical conversations about the role of the holy Virgin have turned increasingly to the neglected credal "communion of saints." The place of Mary at Pentecost speaks to that concern and can be carried forward to her share in the worship of the entire heavenly Church described in the Apocalypse.[15]

Under the auspices of the Lutheran-Roman Catholic Dialogue, *Mary in the New Testament* was co-published by the Paulist Press and the Lutheran Fortress Press in 1978. By now, 1996, the Dialogue has been going on some thirty years in the United States and produced a remarkable series of "consensus statements" on central issues, such as the Nicene creed, baptism, ministry, etc. The seventh statement appeared in 1983, *Justification by Faith*, and was followed in 1992 by *The One Mediator, the Saints, and Mary*. *Scriptura sola* is moderated but remains an ecumenical hurdle. The 1978 book sought a consensus. The editors were two Catholics, R. E. Brown and J. Fitzmyer, and two Lutherans, J. Reumann and K. Donfried, part of a group of twelve representing different Churches, Episcopal and Reformed as well. One participant was the renowned British-born Anglican Reginald Horace Fuller. Their goal was "to see whether as a group of scholars from different Church backgrounds, we could agree upon a presentation of the New Testament data about Mary." Limiting themselves to the Scriptures, employing historical-critical methodology, deliberately making no judgment on subsequent doctrine and devotion, they agreed that the New Testament regards Mary the Virgin as the disciple par excellence. "From the New Testament pictures of her we learned afresh something of what faith and discipleship ought to mean within the family of God." Among the provocative insights of the book was its appeal to "canonical criticism," by force of which what is said in one book admitted into the canon assists the understanding of other books as well, quite applicable to the New Testament portrait of the Blessed Virgin. This hermeneutical tool shows a similarity to the analogy of faith, spoken of by the first Vatican Council, and important for the proper appreciation of doctrines of the faith. The indispensable, if easily abused, theological interpretative argument of fittingness also comes to mind.

Mary in the New Testament has had an enthusiastic reception with many reprintings and translations. Reviewers have also been favorable, though with understandable reservations. For example, Joseph Weber of Wesley Theological in Washington, D.C., while rejoicing that the positive contributions of the study admirably illustrate common ecumenical scholarship, illuminate aspects of the role of Mary in salvation that are often overlooked, and focus attention on Christ who leads his people to a fuller understanding of the truth, notes at the same time that "the negative contribution of the Mary study is that it drives another coffin nail into the simplistic notion that all controverted issues can be settled by the Bible alone." Jerome Quinn (d. 1988), member of the Lutheran-Roman Catholic consultations, and Donald Senior made somewhat similar comments.[16] Quinn especially asked that the voice of the Christian East be heard, so that the ecumenical discussion might move from the neutral ground of history ("Mary is mother of Jesus") to the theological affirmation of Ephesus "*theotokos*, the mother of God."

There has been no equally significant follow-up book to the 1978 book *Mary in the New Testament: A Collaborative Assessment by Protestant and Roman Catholic Scholars*, though an increasing number of authors of Anglican and Protestant, and occasionally of Orthodox, backgrounds have written on the Virgin Mary in the New Testament. Joseph C. McLelland of McGill University of Montreal wrote an enthusiastic foreword to the book by the Canadian Montfort Father, Jean-Pierre Prévost: *Mother of Jesus*, beginning with the words: "Something new is happening in Catholic attitudes to Mary, something which we Protestants need to hear." Dr. McLelland commends the Prévost book "to all, particularly those Protestants who still suffer from the 'silent conspiracy' among us which caused us to drop Mary from our theological concerns. We have missed so much!" Readers of Prévost will appreciate his biblically-rooted appeal to other Christians, also his advice to fellow Catholics, especially movements with the "commendable goal of restoring Marian devotion, yet ignoring the council's directions and subsequent teachings, such as Pope Paul VI's and the present Holy Father's." To those who nourish themselves almost exclusively on private revelation he puts the question: "should Marian teaching be limited to these kinds of experience?"[17]

Given the wide range of exegetical approaches and the even broader spectrum of Christian outlooks, there is a great variety of treatments of Mary in the Gospels. Here such labels as conservative and liberal are often misleading. Fundamentalists join Catholics (and the Calvinist Karl Barth) to defend vigorously the conception of Jesus from the Virgin Mary (popularly called the virgin birth), yet give a very literal reading to the brothers and sisters of the Gospels, even though the early Reformers, Luther and Calvin, and later John Wesley all held the life-long virginity of the Mother of Jesus. It hardly needs saying that the role of blessed Mary has not been of compelling concern for biblical experts who are not Catholics. The Reformation prohibition of the invocation of Mary and the saints, as also the rejection of vowed religious life, were factors little conducive to interest in the Virgin Mary, either devotionally or doctrinally. The Presbyterian systematician of Union Theological Seminary (Richmond, VA), Donald A. Dawe, who has served as president of the American Ecumenical Society of the Blessed Virgin Mary, expressed this well in the title of his paper, "From dysfunction to disbelief."[18] Enlightenment challenges to and denials of the virginal conception of Jesus led to a new interpretation of even the ancient title Virgin Mary. As the old and new quests for the historical Jesus waxed and waned, so also the quest for an historical Mary became rather a quest for the kerygmatic Mary. For many Protestants,

Mary's presence at Bethlehem and Calvary (Luke and John) was an emotional one, her limited motherly function. Nor was there any special significance attached to her presence in the Upper Room before Pentecost.

From the standpoint of theology touching the mystery of Mary some recent second thoughts may be noted about the relationship between scriptural historical criticism and subsequent reflection about the holy Virgin. John Reumann raised this question in his article entitled: "After historical criticism, what? Trends in biblical interpretation and ecumenical interfaith dialogues." The following year Reumann co-authored with J. Fitzmyer, S.J., the article: "Scripture as Norm for our common faith."[19] The importance, even the poignancy, of such inquiries is evident to readers of the recent agreed statements from the Lutheran-Roman Catholic consultations: *Justification by Faith* (1983); *The One Mediator, The Saints, and Mary* (1992), and the latest (the ninth) *The Word of God: Scripture and Tradition* (1995). *Sola scriptura* proves still an ecumenical hurdle, no less in the register of historical-critical exegesis.

New Testament studies with a feminist outlook are being published in ever-increasing numbers, frequently with a self-described hermeneutic of suspicion that chokes rather than promotes dialogue with those who disagree with the authors' versions of political, *lege* theological correctness. Mary of the Gospels fares well or poorly depending on the outlook of the author; for some, she takes second place to the women at the tomb of the Risen Lord, especially Mary of Magdala. Respecting the insights of R. E. Brown's *The Birth of the Messiah* and a similar sensitivity to women's issues in the collaborative *Mary in the New Testament*, Janice Capel Anderson of the University of Idaho expanded their emphasis on Mary as "the first Christian believer, disciple, and model of faith for men and women."[20] She writes out of the conviction "that a feminist rhetorical literary analysis provides a new perspective on the Matthaean and Lukan birth narratives." Although both Matthew and Luke associate female gender with birth and nurture, under the control of patriarchal social, political, religious, and economic arrangements, there are tensions in both narratives, for Mary differs from all previous scriptural models.

Matthew's genealogy is patrilineal; Jesus the Christ is son of Abraham and son of David. Yet, five women appear in the patriarchal pattern; four rather unlikely choices, Tamar, Rahab, Ruth, Bathsheba, then Mary. Commentators do not agree on the reason for their presence: sinners, since Jesus came as Savior; the Gentile world; instruments of God's plan to continue the messianic line? Anderson takes the positive tack—God has power over life and death, control of the womb, leading to the virginal conception and thereby giving an affirmative value to the antecedent women. She writes: "The women foreshadow Mary and prepare the implied reader for a woman's irregular production of the Messiah outside of ordinary patriarchal norms yet within God's overarching plans and an overall patriarchal framework." In Luke a similar pattern unfolds; he both celebrates and domesticates female difference. "The very 'otherness' of Mary and of Jesus' conception make Mary and Elizabeth foils for one another...."

Underplaying the hermeneutic of suspicion, though not rejecting feminist concerns, the Protestant Scripture scholar, Beverly Roberts Gaventa of Princeton University, has just published the remarkable book: *Mary: Glimpses of the Mother of Jesus* (University of South Carolina Press, Columbia, SC, 1995), a title in the series *Studies on Personalities of the New Testament.* Without eschewing either the historical-critical approach or the theology of the later Christian Church, she chooses instead the way of literary analysis. Instead of looking behind the gospel texts (historical-critical method) and instead of looking beyond the early writings to convictions about Mary that developed in the subsequent community, Dr. Gaventa takes up the narratives as we find them in the final stage of Gospel composition. She considers the stories in themselves and explores the varying characterizations of Mary in four sources: Matthew, Luke-Acts, John, and the second-century Protevangelium of James. I limit my present remarks to her insights on the first three. Mary appears with her own individuality yet caught up in a common dynamic of scandal, rooted in the scandal of the incarnation. She writes of glimpses, given the fragmentary nature of the Gospel references. As the narratives develop, the character of Mary emerges, always serving the goal of understanding Jesus, a goal that is of course admittedly also theological.

The Mary of Matthew is both threatened and threatening, in the strange genealogy, and within the mystery of her Son's conception and birth, with Joseph's perplexity and Herod's murderous designs. God's intervention saves both child and mother. For Matthew, Mary's exclusive role is mother. As with the women in the genealogy God has decided to use her for the salvation of all people.

The chapter on Luke-Acts sees Mary as disciple, as prophet (Magnificat), and as mother (direct and obvious yet very complex). Mary is no passive figure, unless this means no more than that God is in control. Her presence brings together significant segments of the narrative, giving shape to what would otherwise be a mere series of events. Mary is the slave of the Lord—and slave is the best possible translation in full scriptural setting. She is Mother of Jesus and herself first of the saved: she knows the salvation of God not only through herself but for herself.

For John, Dr. Gaventa comments on the dialogue at the Cana wedding and the scandalous Calvary scene. Through Mary, the Word became flesh and thereby gave offense to the world. On the cross Jesus finally surrendered all earthly relationships to return to the Father. Disciples of Jesus "must not take offense but take on the offensiveness of Jesus." In summary, the author writes of Mary's vulnerability, her pondering (initiating Christian reflection), and her silent witnessing (living out a simple yet eloquent form of faithfulness).

Eamon R. Carroll, O.Carm.

Endnotes

1. N. Flanagan's address appeared in *Marianum* 48 (1986), also in *Listening: Journal of Religion and Culture* 22 (Autumn, 1987).
2. The Lutheran scholar Philip H. Pfatteicher writes: "The New Testament shows Mary present at all the important events of her Son's life...," in *Proclamation: Aids for Interpreting the Lessons of the Church Year. The Lesser Festivals*, vol. 1 (Philadelphia, 1975). Hans Urs von Balthasar in *You Crown the Year with Your Goodness* (San Francisco, 1992).
3. Samuel Terrien, *The Magnificat: Musicians as Biblical Interpreters* (Mahwah, NJ, 1995) provides musical illustrations of the Magnificat with recommendations of phonographic recordings.
4. *Lumen gentium*, 58.
5. My "A Survey of Recent Mariology" began to appear in the proceedings of the Mariological Society of America, *Marian Studies*, in 1967 (vol. 18) and has continued annually with the exception of 1972 (vol. 23) which was given over to a report of the international Mariological congress held at Zagreb, August, 1971. As of this writing, the 1995 Survey has been published in *Marian Studies* 46 (1995) and the 1996 Survey (Philadelphia convention, May, 1996) is in press. A section "Mary in Scripture" forms part of the ten-year run-down which I wrote for *Theological Studies* 37 (June, 1976): "Theology on the Virgin Mary: 1966-1975."
6. Journals devoted to theology about the Virgin Mary are principally: *Marianum*, from the Servite pontifical faculty of that name, twice a year, Viale Trenta Aprile, 6, 00153 Rome, Italy; *Ephemerides Mariologicae*, edited by the Claretians, four times a year, Buen Suceso, 22, 28008 Madrid, Spain; and the newcomer, now into its fourth year, *Theotokos: Ricerche Interdisciplinari di Mariologia*, organ of the Italian Mariological Society, twice a year, Centro Mariano

Monfortano, Via Prenestina 1391, Colle Prenestino (Rome, Italy). *Études Mariales: Bulletin de la Société Française d'Études Mariales* can be had from Sécretariat: N.-D. de Pontmain, 2 Place de la Basilique 53220 Pontmain, France.

7. H. Cazelles wrote of Abraham, Isaiah and Mary in a volume of *Études Mariales*, devoted to "the faith of Mary, Mother of the Redeemer," 51 (1994).

8. *Ephemerides Mariologicae* 43 (1993): January-March on Matthew; April-June on Luke-Acts; July-September on the Gospel of John and the Apocalypse.

9. A. Feuillet, "Les espousailles du Messie: La Mère de Jesus et l'Église dans le quatrième Évangile," *Revue thomiste* 86 (1986) 536-575.

10. F. J. Moloney, "The Johannine Passion and the Christian Community," in *Salesianum* 57 (1995) 41-44.

11. *E c'era la madre di Gesù: saggi di esegesi biblico-mariana (1978-1988)* (Rome-Milan, 1989).

12. F. J. Moloney's paper, read at Oxford, April, 1978, has been published in the proceedings of the Oxford conference, and again in *Salesianum* 40 (1978) 817-843.

13. *Biblical Theology Bulletin* 20 (Summer, 1990). Neyrey's article is "Maid and Mother in Art and Literature."

14. *Sacra Doctrina* 18 (January-June, 1973), a double-number (quaderno 69-70) titled "Maria di Nazareth nella Chiesa." Prete's article: pages 65-124.

15. For comment on Mary in the communion of saints, see Eamon R. Carroll, "Ecumenical Roundtables at International Mariological Congresses," in *Mater fidei et fidelium* (Theodore Koehler *Festschrift*) as the combined volumes 15=23 (1985-1991) of *Marian Library Studies* (Dayton, OH), also E. R. Carroll, "Mary in Ecumenical Perspective" *The Sword* 55 (1995) 47-62, a lecture at Seton Hall University, So. Orange, NJ, November 14, 1995.

16. The contrasting reviews by Joseph Weber and Donald Senior appeared in *Ecumenical Trends* 8 (November, 1979).

J. Quinn's review appeared in *Biblical Theology Bulletin* 10 (July, 1980) 134-136.

17. Jean-Pierre Prévost, *Mother of Jesus* (Novalis, Ottawa, Ontario, 1988). Appeared also as *La mère de Jesus*, but the French does not have the McLelland foreword. The materials for further study/reflection that follow the chapters are English language in one case, French in the other.

18. Donald A. Dawe's paper was given as a talk to the Ecumenical Society of the Blessed Virgin Mary; full title is: "From Dysfunction to Disbelief: The Virgin Mary in Reformed Theology," among other places in A. Stacpoole, ed., *Mary's Place in Christian Dialogue* (Middlegreen, Slough, England, 1982, and Wilton, CT, 1983).

19. The Reumann article, "After Historical Criticism, What?..." appeared in *Journal of Ecumenical Studies* 29 (Winter, 1992); the Fitzmyer-Reumann article appeared in *Journal of Ecumenical Studies* 30 (Winter, 1993).

20. The Anderson article was in *Journal of Religion* (April, 1987).

Elijah and Elisha:
A Psychologist's Perspective

Introduction

The first thing the Rule of Saint Albert tells us is that Carmel is evangelical. The Rule appears to be a collection of phrases, almost all of which were taken from the Scriptures. To read it is to be nourished by the Word of God. The first document of the Order calls us to be steeped in the Scriptures as part of our daily living. *Lectio divina*, in its renewed form,[1] provides a means for living out this fundamental part of the Carmelite charism. It calls us to pray with the texts and to see them as both a window into the past to see what happened to our forebears and a mirror into the present with which to see what is happening to us today.

In this paper, I would like to look at two major figures in the Scriptures and in our Carmelite tradition: Elijah and Elisha. Like all of us, I approach these Old Testament prophets with the lens of a twentieth century person and, in particular, with the lens of one who has been trained as a psychologist. I would like to hold up the mirror of my experience to see how these two zealots for God open up the journey into God we latter-day Carmelites share with them. What does their experience as described in the Old Testament tell us about our experience? How do we see our experience of God reflected in theirs? What twentieth century psychological insights help us appreciate more deeply their experience of being zealous for God?

235

Elijah

Elijah, the Tishbite, suddenly appears out of nowhere, informing Ahab that a punishing drought is about to lay waste Israel (1 Kings 17:1). Thus begins the Elijah cycle that reveals a man zealous for the Lord God of Hosts. Elijah's focus is the primacy of God. Yahweh's power is manifested through Elijah who brings about the drought in response to Ahab's resistance. Yahweh orders him to flee to the desert where he is nourished and cared for in preparation for continued exploits in the name of Yahweh.

Immediately upon his return he feeds a hungry widow with jars of meal and oil and then raises her dead son back to life (1 Kings 17:7-24). It is significant that the biblical writers locate these two miracle stories right after his retreat into the desert. For Elijah's retreat is not a vacation, but a time of spiritual empowerment that he immediately makes available to those on the periphery of society: the widow and the fatherless son.

Next, Elijah sets to challenging Ahab and the prophets of Baal as to the primacy of the God of Israel (1 Kings 18:16-40). Once again, Yahweh uses Elijah to communicate divine power by bringing down fire on the sacrificial bull. The prophets of Baal are then executed. Upon hearing of these events, Jezebel calls for Elijah's death (1 Kings 19:1-2). Hearing his death sentence, the shaken Elijah quickly flees Israel and heads to Mount Horeb where Moses originally encountered God. Drained from his desert trek and defeated in his prophetic task, Elijah enters the cave on Horeb. He asks to die! He feels spiritually dead and defeated; he has failed.

Among those who struggle daily with difficult social problems and with discovering meaning in their lives there is a growing phenomenon known as burnout or mid-life crisis. Whether it is religious and priests who deal daily with the numbing problems of the people in inner-city parishes, or medical personnel who minister to persons with AIDS confronting death, the temptation is the same as Elijah's: this is my burden alone. With

Elijah we think that saving society is something I must accomplish by myself. This thinking is an enormous energy drain that leads to depression, "burn out," and a soul-shaking crisis.

Carl Jung[2] was the first modern psychologist to document the individuation process whereby mid-life adults re-integrate and re-evaluate the sources of meaning in their lives. It is decidedly an interior journey versus the more exterior preoccupations of one's younger years. Daniel Levinson[3] explored in greater depth the experience of men as adults, noting the reality of various crises occurring throughout the adult life cycle. What is important to note is the depth of this experience in the lives of many people, especially during their middle years. Circumstances, events, successes and failures precipitate this crisis of reflection and re-assessment of one's goals and dreams.

Elijah's experience on Horeb fits this perspective. He was not some robotic prophet, always sure of Yahweh's presence and support, supremely confident in his own power, vision, and energy. No, in this crisis he confronts his messiah complex, his childish hope of success, his selfish dreams of fame. Further, he had to acknowledge his egocentric claims on society's approval. Elijah had failed, and like prophets before and after him, he sought death, perhaps longing never to have been born.

In the cave on Horeb, Elijah, stripped of his pretension, of his false self, meets Yahweh. Yahweh asks: "Why are you here, Elijah?" Then he commands him to arise and climb to the top of Horeb. Elijah looked for Yahweh in the mighty wind that split the rocks, in the earthquake that shook the earth, and then in the fire. But Yahweh surprised him. Yahweh was in none of these. The Divine Presence came in a breeze so mild, so gentle, that Elijah covered his face in fear. There the voice charged him with continuing the heroic mission: return to Israel and carry on the prophetic ministry of faith and justice. But this time he would let go of his society-sensitive ego and his need for approval from others.

Reborn and renewed by his encounter with himself and by Yahweh's gentle presence to his real self, Elijah returns to Israel

with new fire. He supports the exploited (1 Kings 21). He challenges the wicked (2 Kings 1). He chooses a disciple (1 Kings
19:19). Then he disappears into the heavens in a chariot of fire,
vanishing as quickly as he appeared (2 Kings 2).

Elisha

Elisha is an important figure in our Carmelite heritage. We
know about him from the Bible and from *The Book of the First
Monks*, one of the early reflections on our charism. Elisha was the
foremost disciple of Elijah, called from the plough when Elijah
returned from Horeb. According to tradition, he was seen as a
prodigy from his birth when one of the golden calves in the temple
bellowed, showing that he would destroy such idols. He received
the spirit of prophecy from God (2 Kings 3:15); he struck the
Syrian army blind (2 Kings 6:18); he relieved siege and famine (2
Kings 7); he called people to true worship (2 Kings 10). As he was
buried in Samaria, his bones raised a man to life (2 Kings 13:21).
Jung's theories regarding archetypes suggest that Elisha fits
surprisingly into the shaman or healer archetype.[4] It is surprising
because Elisha took up the mantle of Elijah, whose stories were
charged with fire and conflict. Elisha, on the other hand, has
stories that have images of water and tales of healing. He is a
person who cures illness, restores wholeness, and heals wounds.

Like many of us, Elisha did not accept his vocation
because of some life-threatening situation, health crisis, or crisis
of faith. Unlike his mentor, Elijah, who faced the danger of death
on Horeb and overcame it, Elisha became Elijah's disciple in a
simple way. Nevertheless, it is implied that he inherited in his own
person the shamanic healing experience of his master. Elisha's
identification with his mentor was total. As a sign of his complete
discipleship, Elisha kissed his parents good-bye and slew his
oxen.

The mantle motif occurred in a dramatic farewell scene at
the Jordan River (2 Kings 2). Elisha, insisting that he inherit a
double portion of his master's spirit, followed the departing Elijah

across the Jordan. Suddenly a chariot of fire appeared and swept Elijah up to heaven in a whirlwind; Elisha never saw him again. But he wisely seized his mentor's cloak—the shaman's mantle that would hereafter confer Elijah's power on the wearer—and with it struck the waters of the Jordan. The waters divided and Elisha crossed over dry-shod once again into the promised land.

Immediately, the people of Jericho asked the prophet to heal their city's water supply. Whereas Elijah experienced miraculous signs involving earth, wind, and fire (1 Kings 19:10-14), Elisha became adept at conjuring up wonders with the fourth natural element, water. He requested a bowl and salt—like a magical potion—and healed Jericho's spring water for all time (2 Kings 2:19-22). This first miracle story is a psychologically significant one: the healer, once summoned and energized, curses the wound in the earth that brought death and miscarriage and brings new life for the whole people.

So Elisha is off to a good start. His first foray into ministry is energetic, enthusiastic, and successful. But the ensuing Elisha narrative delivers a typical biblical description of the shadow side of God's prophets. Full of himself and puffed up with power, he began his climb up the road to Bethel in the hill country of Ephraim (2 Kings 2:23-25), and he promptly stumbled into tragedy and evil. On his path, gangs of little boys taunt him. Angry, Elisha allowed his healing power to turn demonic. He went over to what today we would call "the dark side of the Force." Cursing these youngsters with his shamanic power, Elisha summoned his spirit-animals from the woods. Two she-bears roared out of the forest and mauled these boys.

This action was an abuse of his power. He used his power to harm rather than to heal. He used it for revenge. The she-bear story reminds us that it is all too easy to consider one's spiritual powers as personal possessions to be used however one pleases. But they are not so. This power is given for the healing of people and not for convenience of the healer.

After his close encounter with evil, more water miracles flowed from Elisha. First, during a war against Moab, the allied kings of Israel, Judah, and Edom pleaded with the prophet to find their troops water; a reluctant Elisha produced the needed pool (2 Kings 3:12-20). Second, at Gilgal, he purified some poisoned soup on behalf of his fellow prophets (2 Kings 4:38-41) and later floated an iron ax-head that one of these same prophets dropped into the Jordan (2 Kings 6:1-7). Elisha's third and greatest water miracle healed, not one of his own colleagues or even an Israelite, but the enemy Syrian general Naaman, stricken with leprosy, whom Elisha ordered to wash seven times in the Jordan (2 Kings 5:1-14).

The meaning of this well known gesture is clear: the healer is called beyond the limits of his own petty self-interest and beyond his political beliefs and religious ideologies as well. The healer ultimately is the archetype by whom people reconcile themselves to their former enemies by experiencing with them a common need for healing and life.

None of these tests could match Elisha's greatest challenge: the son of the great lady of Shunem lying stone-cold dead on his bed (2 Kings 4). Perhaps he turned to his mentor, Elijah, who had once raised a dead youth to life (1 Kings 17). As the prophet came in person to the deathly room, he lay down upon the child, pressing mouth to mouth, eyes to eyes, and hands to hands. Elisha seven times breathed into the boy the breath of life. When the child's eyes blinked open, the prophet returned the boy to his mother. This was Elisha's greatest moment and a healing moment for himself as well. Only a short while earlier he had used his powers in an evil way to injure little boys. Now he used those same powers as a healer to raise a son to new life.

One may rightly wonder why the biblical tradition would portray such a supposed healer as Elisha as the instigator of the Jehu uprising that wiped out the entire Ahab regime (2 Kings 9-10). It is not the usual image of the healer. The answer lies in the mythology of the Shaman archetype itself. Masculine healing is not especially nurturing, gentle, or nice. On the contrary, the male healer often must act as a warrior wielding a blade, typically harsh, cold, and antagonistic to evil spirits and all life-threatening enemies. He is the surgeon, willing to slice into a frail body and coldly cut out a cancerous growth to save the whole person. He is the psychotherapist who insists that we face our most painful memories in order to heal them. The Elijah/Elisha cycle can be interpreted through this lens. The prophets saved individuals with their power. They saved Israel with a painful operation that sliced out the cancer of Ahab's regime.

This biblical story reminds us of an important facet of the Carmelite charism. As Carmelites, we have accepted the mantle of Elijah in the spirit of Elisha, and therefore we are called to be healers. We must acknowledge that we have the healer in us, that we must at times call upon it if we are to bring about wholeness in our world. Sometimes that healer is one who burns the field so that new crops can grow, who amputates a limb to save the body. This healer knows well his own wounds and his own vulnerabilities, who humbly admits his need for help. He cooperates with his spiritual friends in a mutually healing therapeutic alliance.

This healer is the recovering alcoholic who becomes a source of compassion and encouragement for other alcoholics. This healer is the hopeful person with AIDS who teaches those around him gratitude for life. This healer is the cancer patient whose fight for life ennobles all who encounter him.

The lives of Elijah and Elisha as handed down through our tradition offer much rich, human experience for our reflection. It is the experience of triumph and tragedy, of grace and evil—experiences that are truly human even for people in the service of God. Our psychological perspective can help to uncover and to propose the possibilities of what that experience might have been like. Such a perspective enables us to see parts of ourselves in their experience and to draw strength from those who have gone before us marked with the sign of faith, marked with that desire for God which consumed both of these proto-Carmelites. Such a perspective is helpful to the extent that it encourages us to experience more deeply our own responsibility to embrace our humanity as the only way to the holiness of God. Indeed, Elijah and Elisha would challenge us to discover the living God in the context of our lives and our times. It is in our personal and social histories that the voice whispers gently: "...why are you here?"

Quinn R. Conners, O.Carm.

Endnotes

1. Carlos Mesters, *The Carmelite Rule and the Reading of the Bible: Reflections on lectio divina* (Middle Park, Vic., Australia, 1991) 11-30.
2. J. Cambell, ed., *The Portable Jung* (New York: Penquin, 1971) 3-69; 456-479.
3. D. J. Levinson, *The seasons of a man's life* (New York: Knopf, 1978) 1-68.
4. P. M. Arnold, *Wildmen, warriors, and kings: Masculine spirituality and the Bible* (New York, 1992) 134-144.

One Irishman and a Revolution

There are frequent times when the life of a single individual intersects with the large movements of history and becomes entangled with events beyond anyone's control or understanding. Such was the story of an Irish Carmelite in the mid-nineteenth century who was caught up in the earthshaking movement called the *Risorgimento*: the struggle to unite Italy.

In his excellent work on the Carmelites of Ireland, Peter O'Dwyer refers to a mysterious Irish friar named W. Aloysius Kelleher,[1] who was living in several Carmelite houses in central Italy. The first mention we have of him appears in January, 1841, when he was ordered to return to Ireland for reassignment by his Vicar Provincial. He did not go. Subsequently, he was moved from one Italian house to another, apparently because of quarrels with local Carmelites. There is no mention of him after 1847, when he was transferred to Ancona.[2]

The world of the 1840's was not a time friendly to religious orders or to established religion. The Irish and Italian provinces, like the entire Carmelite Order, were badly depleted in numbers and influence because of the French Revolution and the subsequent secularization of houses by unfriendly governments. The Italian houses where Kelleher lived and worked belonged to the Province of Romagna and the Marches, located in the eastern portion of the Papal States, where the Pope was prince, as well as prelate.

243

The election of Pius IX in 1846 began with a burst of enthusiasm for a "reforming Pope" who wanted to transform his state into a model of enlightened government. Unfortunately for Pius, the fires of Italian nationalism would prove to be hotter then he could survive. He endured a revolution against him in 1848-9, and was restored to power by the French army. Military campaigns in 1860 and 1870 resulted in the piecemeal loss of his provinces. Before he died in 1878, the entire papal realm had been incorporated into the Kingdom of Italy.

It is not known how Aloysius Kelleher first came to Italy, but he may have arrived as early as 1836 and formally requested to be affiliated with the house at Jesi. This affiliation was granted, but Kelleher seems to have been a difficult person, causing much discord in the community.[3] He was ordered to return to Ireland in January, 1841, but did not go. Another obedience in April transferred him to the house in Lugo (not Lucca). The prior of Jesi, Carmelo Chiodi, was moved to Senigallia at the same time. In June of the same year, Kelleher was transferred from Lugo to Forli.[4]

Whatever the outcome of these frequent transfers, there is little mention of dissension for the next several years. It appears, however, that the Irish friar continued to follow a restless existence. A letter from Kelleher in January, 1847, requests faculties to hear the confessions of Irish sailors in Ancona, the largest port in the Papal States.[5] He received a formal transfer to the Ancona house in September, 1847. There is no further mention of him in Carmelite sources.[6]

By 1847, Ancona and the other cities of the Papal States were imbibing the heady wine of overdue political reform and liberalization. Pius IX had reached the peak of his popularity, as he tried to push his state rapidly into a more open and free society. Because his reform decrees followed one another so quickly, there was much confusion and disruption surrounding the lines of authority and responsibility. Administrators and police officers frequently did not know exactly what was expected of them, and the atmosphere of doubt and confusion sometimes led to chaotic, and even criminal, situations.

But more serious than this confusion was a growing spirit of revenge, especially in Ancona, where political factionalism had a long and bloody history. For most of the early 19th century, papal police officials and administrators had strengthened their power against potential rebels by recruiting and arming conservative citizens to intimidate and spy on their fellow villagers. These citizen militias were variously known as sanfedists or centurions; after 1832, they were given a para-military command structure and black uniforms, and were known as Pontifical Volunteers. The Volunteers were widely hated because of their reputation as bullies and exploiters, and they proved to be a considerable embarrassment to more than a few conscientious officials.

Pius IX abolished the Volunteers in 1847 and substituted a National Guard recruited from a broader segment of the population. He hoped that this new militia would command more popular support as they helped maintain order amid increasing turmoil. Unfortunately, the disbanded Volunteers became the targets of their old political rivals, especially of the more radical republican or nationalist partisans. In Ancona, as in other cities like Bologna, Lugo, and Faenza, bitter factional battles erupted as violent and resentful insurgents set out to even old scores. The weakened government forces were often unable to keep peace in the streets.

Although the vast majority of citizens supported the Pope's reform efforts, there was a small faction of political organizers and nationalists who quietly planned the demise of the papal regime. The most disciplined of these was the Young Italy organization, led by Giuseppe Mazzini. Their principal strategy called for vocal and enthusiastic support of all of the Pope's reforms, while at the same time calling for even more, and using the cheering crowds to actually increase the disruptive pressures on the already confused government.

Mazzini's great opportunity came at the end of 1848, the Year of Revolutions. Revolts had broken out all over Europe, and new leaders had come to power in France, Austria, and many other states. The Kingdom of Piedmont, led by King Charles Albert, had invaded the Austrian provinces of northern Italy, calling for a crusade of all patriotic Italians to drive Austria back over the Alps. Although he achieved some stunning successes, Charles Albert was eventually defeated by the well disciplined Austrian regulars, and his failure aroused disappointment and anger among many Italians.

Although Pius IX had strongly supported Italian unity, he refused to join the war, and suffered a sharp reverse to his own popularity as a result. When his own prime minister was assassinated in November, Pius realized that he could no longer continue his headlong rush toward reform in such a turbulent situation. He still commanded wide support and sympathy among his people, but drew the hasty conclusion that his reforms had been a total failure. He fled from Rome and sought refuge in the Kingdom of Naples, calling for troops from other states to restore him to his throne.

The government in Rome felt betrayed and abandoned by the Pope, but tried to carry on in his absence, in spite of growing chaos in the streets. By the early months of 1849, Mazzini gained control of the provisional government, intending to make it the center of republican nationalism for all of Italy. As Charles Albert had done before him, Mazzini called on Italian patriots to support his Roman Republic against foreign intervention. Perhaps his strongest backing came from Giuseppe Garibaldi and his romantic band of adventurers, who became the heart and soul of Rome's defense.

Austria, Spain, and Naples all pledged troops to restore the Pope to power, but the most significant help came from France. The fall of the French monarchy in 1848 had led to the formation of the conservative Second Republic, whose president was none other than Louis Napoleon Bonaparte. This nephew of Napoleon I had long planned to restore his uncle's empire in

France, and would do so in 1852, after scrapping the republican constitution. History knows him better as Emperor Napoleon III.

In his efforts to build his power base among French voters, Louis Napoleon saw helping the Pope as a golden opportunity to woo the most devout Catholics to his side. But the Bonapartes were also an Italian-speaking family from Corsica; Louis Napoleon had spoken strongly and frequently of his support for a strong and united Italy. He was aware of the inherent contradiction of his Italian policy, but he hoped that few others would notice.

The first French troops landed outside of Rome in April, 1849. Mazzini had no illusions about the military survival of his Roman Republic, unless he could gain diplomatic sympathy and protection from Britain and other major powers. He was keenly aware that many neutral leaders saw him as an anti-clerical agitator, and that public opinion identified revolution with the atrocities of the Reign of Terror. Mazzini belabored his dedication to worthy republican principles and the protection of human rights. He insisted that he was not against the free exercise of religion, only the power of the Pope as a secular tyrant. As he prepared his Republic to defend itself, he needed unity and sacrifice from all dedicated citizens. The last thing he needed was chaos in the provinces.

Unfortunately, chaos was the order of the day in several areas of the Marches and Romagna. In Ancona, as in other towns like Senigallia and Imola, bands of thugs murdered officials and other citizens under the guise of rooting out the old Pontifical Volunteers and die-hard supporters of the Pope. In fact, there was little political consistency in these crimes. Dangerous and violent men killed and looted with impunity, simply because there was no one strong enough to stop them.

In the city of Ancona, there was a secret society called the Infernal League (also the Bloody League) which paid lip service to liberty and to the Republic to cover the most common of crimes. Several policemen, customs officials and civil servants belonged to the League, lending protection to the others. League members murdered officers, aristocrats, and clergy who tried to oppose them, and thoroughly intimidated others in positions of leadership.

Mazzini realized that mob rule in even a few of his cities damaged his noble image as a defender of human rights. He sent two deputies, Bernabei and Dall'Ongaro, to stabilize the situation in Ancona. The two emissaries were intensely loyal to Mazzini, but their political strength in Ancona was nil. Their imagination never extended beyond a form of glorified bribery: they hired members of the League, at 5 paoli per day, to act as auxiliary customs inspectors.[7] The crimes continued unabated.

Finally, things came to a head with a crime that could not be ignored. Aloysius Kelleher, who had lived in Ancona since 1847, lost no opportunity to badger and quarrel with the local anti-clericals. According to another priest, Don Achille Perini, he had been outspoken in his criticism of the anarchy, and had gotten into frequent arguments with local people. Especially after the disastrous battle of Novara (March 23), Kelleher proclaimed loudly that the Austrians would win the war in the north, and that Charles Albert and the Italians had no hope.[8] He acted on the principle that the only way to oppose bullies was to hit back.

On April 18, Kelleher went to hire a carriage to take two English captains to Loreto the following day, which was Holy Thursday that year. In the Calamo district, he found coachman Giovanni Gobbi who quoted him a rate of 15 scudi for the day. Kelleher called the price outrageous and booked seats instead on the Postal Coach, which left at 5 a.m. The coach returned a half-hour behind schedule that evening, and Kelleher got off alone. As he made his way homeward, he was cornered in a quiet street by several armed men. One of them shot him at close range with a pistol, then another shot him again. There were 2 or 3 others waiting with weapons, but Kelleher fell dead on the steps of the criminal court building. Among those who recovered the body was a League member, policeman Antonio Biagini, who continued verbal abuse over the dead man.[9]

Whether the feisty Irishman had approved or not, he was a British subject. His murder provoked a strong protest from the British consul, Mr. Moore, and the presence of a British corvette in Ancona harbor. If Mazzini's Roman Republic was incapable of protecting the lives of foreign nationals, the Royal Navy would evacuate British citizens and diplomats altogether. Even though Mazzini was now working night and day to prepare for the imminent siege of Rome, he sent another special emissary to save Ancona.

The new man was Felice Orsini, armed with sweeping powers and an inflexible will. He was a relatively young man with a high forehead, neatly trimmed hair and beard, and piercing black eyes. Orsini was not one of Mazzini's inner circle, but he was the perfect choice for this daunting task. He was highly intelligent, and had no illusions about what he had to do.[10]

Orsini arrived at Ancona two days after Kelleher's murder. There were few armed men at his disposal: no more than two hundred carabinieri, soldiers and customs officers, and many of these were badly dispirited. Only two officers seemed trustworthy, the colonel of the carabinieri and the fortress commander. But Orsini questioned them extensively about the names and addresses of the League's known ringleaders and explained his plan to them in detail. He then declared a state of siege and acted quickly and decisively.[11]

At 2 a.m. on April 27, he sent mixed patrols of his men to block the principal street intersections, then surrounded several houses and arrested 20 of the League's best known leaders. More arrests followed the next day, and the prisoners were locked in the harbor fortress instead of the city jail. Protests against Orsini followed, as crowds of partisans tried to release the prisoners, but the League had been virtually paralyzed from the first hour. The prisoners were later moved by sea and sent to a remote fortress in the mountains. With the worst thugs out of action, Orsini persuaded the National Guard to help him maintain order, and the state of siege was suspended after only three days.[12]

Orsini's success at restoring order to Ancona earned him the gratitude of Mazzini and another assignment of the same type. During May, as the French tightened their siege lines around Rome's ancient walls, Orsini was sent to the province of Ascoli Piceno to suppress an armed rebellion. Although he still had a mere handful of troops at his disposal, he effectively overpowered several hill towns where the peasants were fighting to restore Pius IX. The Pope's government later charged Orsini with serious crimes, including theft and extortion at the expense of local citizens. He had long since fled the Papal States, of course, and was not present for his trial. He was still condemned *in absentia.*[13]

The members of the Infernal League were also brought to trial after the Restoration. Following their arrest, they had been moved from one prison to another. From Foligno, they were transferred to Spoleto, and then to Narni, where they were locked in the local military barracks. Garibaldi's men released all of them during their epic flight from Rome, and most scattered to other parts of Italy. Of the forty defendants named in the indictment, only eight were in custody for the trial in 1851. In addition to Kelleher's murder, the charges included the killing of four others and the wounding of eight. Four of the accused were policemen, while most of the others were artisans and working class people.[14]

Five men were accused of murdering Kelleher, including Gobbi, the coachman. Also in custody were Vincenzo Rocchi, a 27-year old cook known as "the Moor," and Pietro Cioccolanti, an unemployed man of 24. Charged, but not present, were Odoardo Serafini, called "the Tiger," and Giorgio Fabretti, a landowner who had fled to Athens. Evidence was presented to indicate that Rocchi had fired the first shot, and Cioccolanti the second. Both were found guilty of Kelleher's murder (and three others) and condemned to death by firing squad. The evidence against Gobbi was weak, and he was released to police surveillance.[15]

Of all the participants in the Kelleher case, perhaps the most interesting subsequent adventure belongs to Felice Orsini. Mazzini's trouble shooter found his way to exile in France, where he continued to work passionately for Italian unity. He was deeply distressed that Emperor Napoleon III had not acted on his pledge to help the Italians. On the evening of January 14, 1858, he and several companions intercepted the imperial carriage in front of the Paris Opera. They threw three powerful bombs, which killed the horses and shattered the coach, but did not harm the Emperor or his wife. There were eight other people killed, however, and well over a hundred wounded.

Orsini was arrested, and from his prison cell, he wrote a letter to Napoleon, exhorting him to take up the cause of Italian freedom. He addressed another letter to the young people of Italy, in which, ironically, he condemned political assassination. Naturally, Napoleon III was badly shocked by the attempt on his life, but he was also quite impressed at Orsini's courage and dedication to his cause. Orsini might also have touched a deeply held conviction from the Emperor's youth, when he and his brother were exiles themselves. The brothers had participated in the revolution against Pope Gregory XVI in 1831, and only escaped capture because of the kindness of the Bishop of Imola...a man who later became Pius IX.

Now another committed zealot had taken resolute action for the same cause, and Napoleon himself was seen as the enemy. Orsini went to the guillotine on March 13, but the following year, Napoleon III led France to war against Austria. That Italian War of 1859 broke the back of Austrian domination, and allowed Piedmont to annex Lombardy and other northern provinces. The unification of Italy was definitively set in motion, and would continue until 1870, with the capture of Rome and the final collapse of the Papal States.

Aloysius Kelleher, O.Carm., did nothing to cause these events, of course, but his death gives him a strange connection to one of the most significant movements of the ninteenth century.

This short tale is lovingly dedicated to another determined Irishman, who has made his own century much better than he found it.

Leopold G. Glueckert, O.Carm.

Endnotes

1. The name is variously spelled in Italian, English, and Latin. Aloysius is often written Luigi or Louis. Kelleher is also written as O'Kelleher, Okeller, or Keller.
2. Peter O'Dwyer, *The Irish Carmelites* (Dublin: Carmelite Publications, 1988) 209.
3. *Archives of the Order, Rome*, II, CO, 56.
4. Ibid.
5. *Archives of the Irish College, Rome, Cullen Letters.* No. 1308.
6. *Archives of the Order, Rome.* II, CO, 1 (66) register.
7. Carlo Tivaroni, *L'Italia durante il Dominio Austriaco* (Torino: L.Roux, 1893) 2:279.
8. Roman State Archives, *Tribunal of the Holy Consulta*, busta 402, file 22.
9. Ibid.
10. Giuseppe Leti, *Carboneria e massoneria nel risorgimento italiano* (Genova: Libreria Editrice Moderna, 1925) 264.
11. Giorgio Manzini, *Avventure e Morte di Felice Orsini* (Milano: Camunia, 1991) 106ff.
12. Ibid.
13. Roman State Archives, *Tribunal of the Holy Consulta*, busta 416, file 927.
14. Roman State Archives, *Tribunal of the Holy Consulta*, busta 402, file 22.
15. Ibid.

Hebrew Biblical Anthropology and Modern Environmental Concerns

Hebrew Scripture is a library of ancient theologies, wherein one can listen to the perennial human struggle to comprehend the mysteries of God and life on earth. This unique and "inspired" literature often uses myths that echo the searching questions and theological insights of other ancient peoples: Canaanites, Egyptians, Babylonians, and others who at one point or another influenced the Hebrew people. The authors of the Bible borrowed some literary forms and creatively developed their own. Encased in this library of poetry, song, story, prayer, history, law and many other kinds of literature is an enormous treasure of Hebrew faith and wisdom. This resource has provided the foundation for Christian thought and belief and has been a key factor in shaping many world cultures. Even today, its perceptions, beliefs, and values bear application to the struggles facing the contemporary world.

The application of the Scriptures to today's problems must not be done arbitrarily or capriciously. Hebrew Scripture is a complex collection, which was gathered, edited, and interpreted throughout many centuries of Israel's on-going history.[1] Each piece has its own original context and meaning, a historical sense, which modern biblical criticism has endeavored to unearth. This historical sense, however, does not exhaust the meaning of scriptural texts. Scripture is a living word that has been constantly interpreted and applied to many historical and cultural situations throughout history. The tradition of both Jewish and Christian interpretation indicates that these texts were introduced to new communities, and that many other levels of meaning were subsequently uncovered.[2] As long as one recognizes the intricate complexity of Scripture and endeavors to be true to the original context and meaning, it would seem legitimate to apply cautiously these Scriptures to the events and issues of our own day.

In this article I will examine some perspectives of the Hebrew Scriptures on human life and will then suggest some connections that might be made between these ancient beliefs and modern environmental concerns.

The Origins of Human Life

When we open the Bible, we immediately come upon an account of the origin of human life. The "in the beginning" account in Genesis 1 is actually a very sophisticated post-exilic story written around the 6th century B.C.E. Composed by the so-called "Priestly author" and echoing a Babylonian myth called *Enuma Elish*, this story is a cosmic and liturgical account of creation which paints the whole process on a large canvas.[3] Here humans are created as the last and climactic creature on the sixth and final day of a long week of creating. After commanding the earth to bring forth cattle, creeping things and wild animals, God gathers his heavenly consorts and says: "Let us make humankind in our image." The Priestly writer then tells us: "God created humankind in his image; in the divine image he created them; male and female he created them" (Gen 1:27). Then this cosmic Creator of good things blessed the god-like creatures, told them to multiply and subdue the earth, and gave them dominion over the fish, the birds, and all living things on earth. The Creator was pleased with creation and took a well-earned rest on the Sabbath.

We are perhaps more familiar with the account of the origin of human life that appears in Genesis 2. This is an earlier myth and seems to have been composed around the 9th century B.C.E. The story begins on a barren stretch of soil, with a stream welling up out of the earth and watering the ground. The Creator, a more rural and homey figure than the cosmic God of the first story, fashions a human being out of mud, and then makes the figure into a living being by giving it the breath of life. Then this potter-like God plants a garden and places the mud person in it, asking him to cultivate and care for it. The Lord God also sets down the first law: "You are free to eat from any of the trees of the garden except the tree of knowledge of good and bad." This God is portrayed as caring and thoughtful, a divinity concerned about the loneliness of the new creature. God makes a stab at finding a suitable companion for the first human by making animals and birds out of the same mud. When God's first efforts miss the mark, the man is put to sleep, and, after removing one of his ribs, God finally gets it right. A woman is formed to be the suitable companion and spouse for the first man.

This Yahwist creation tradition continues with the account of how the woman was deceived by the serpent to eat the fruit of the forbidden tree. She believes the serpent rather than her Creator about what will happen should the fruit be eaten; she eats the fruit, and then offers some to her mate who eats as well. In this story, which finds some parallels in the Babylonian Gilgamesh poem, the first humans lose their innocence. The woman must now experience pain in childbirth and mastery by her mate. The man must sweat and toil amidst the difficulties of nature, and then return to the earth from which he was made. The Creator then clothes his creatures in leather garments and banishes them from the garden.

The stories continue for seven more chapters, mythically describing the first murder whereby Cain kills his brother Abel, and then tell of the growth of the human family and the appearance of Noah.[4] Chapter six opens with further echoes of pagan myths, as the mysterious sons of heaven come to earth and take as many wives as they wish from the beautiful daughters of the tribes on earth. The Lord is outraged at human wickedness, regrets having made living creatures and decides to start all over again. God instructs Noah to build an ark and to take his family and two of every living creature aboard. A great flood destroys all life on land, but when the waters recede, Noah is able to take his family and his entire entourage from the ark to begin creation once again.

God then makes a covenant with Noah, his descendants, and every living creature that was in the ark. The Creator vows never again to devastate the earth and says: "This is the sign that I am giving for all ages to come, of the covenant between you and me and every living creature with you: I set my bow in the clouds to serve as a sign of the covenant between me and the earth" (Gen 9:12-13). The story then continues to describe the beginning of new clans and nations. When humans begin to build a tower to the heavens, God punishes them by confusing their languages and scattering them all over the earth. The story then reports of the birth of the great patriarch, Abram.

The Hebrew library contains a number of other creation theologies on human life. Among them, The Book of Job explores the question of "why bad things happen to good people," and ends with some profound observations by the Creator. The Psalms cover a whole range of human feelings with regard to life on earth. Proverbs proffers many insights from the sages on human living and gives voice to Lady Wisdom. Qoheleth, the preacher, expounds on his somewhat skeptical views of life, and then gives his own fatalistic advice for enjoying the gifts of this mysterious God before we face death. The Song of Songs celebrates the sensuality and joy of human love in the context of God's beautiful creation. Throughout this Hebrew library we learn of the nobility and depravity of human beings. Let us look more closely at the library to see what it tells us about humanity.

The Hebrew Portrayal of Human Life

The Hebrews seemed to derive their anthropology from below, that is, from their experiences of everyday life. Life experience told them that people could display great virtue, and yet were also capable of horrible evil. There is both a light and dark side to human nature, and throughout the Hebrew Scriptures these contrasts are explored. The description of human beings can range from image of God to the lowly worm. They are portrayed as having royal dominion, and at the same time as being the authors of wanton destruction and injustice. Humans can join the stars in praising the Creator, and yet betray their sacred trust with God in many grievous ways. They can sing of love and moan in desperate abandonment. In what follows we will explore some of these elements of Hebrew anthropology to see what implications they might have with regard environmental concerns.

Made in the Image of God

The depiction of human beings as made in the image and likeness of God is perhaps the most widely known and discussed element of Hebrew anthropology. This image has had a profound influence on the Judeo-Christian moral teaching about the sacredness of human life. It has also been used at times by one race or nation to claim superiority over others. One thinks of how the Conquistadors of the 16th century declared the indigenous people of the New World to be sub-human and considered them created to be enslaved and deprived of their rich resources. Slavery and even the Holocaust were often justified by saying that certain peoples were not fully human, not truly created in the image of God.

Surprisingly, this notion that humans are images of God is not common in the Hebrew Scriptures outside of the Priestly passages in Genesis (1:26-27; 5:3; 9:6). It is echoed only one other time in Psalm 8 where the human being is described as crowned with glory, "a little lower than God," and having dominion over creation.[5] The actual meaning of this belief has received a great deal of attention from scholars over the centuries, and views have ranged from humans resembling God by virtue of their reason, freedom, spiritual make-up, or even gender.[6]

The Hebrew word used for image (*selem*) is a concrete word, which elsewhere in Scripture is used to refer to a statue or an icon. This biblical language echoes Egyptian texts which describe the Pharaoh as the image of the deity.[7] Von Rad has suggested that biblical use of this term might also have been influenced by the custom in which great kings and pharaohs placed images of themselves throughout their empires in order to symbolize their presence and authority. Anderson suggests that the image conveys the notion that humans gain their worth and dignity from being crowned as in the manner of queens and kings, and assigned to represent God in creation. Hence, we might say that humans in the Genesis 2 creation story are created to function as commissioned viceroys of the Creator.[8]

Authentic kings and queens in the Hebrew Scriptures are expected to represent God's powerful leadership justly and honorably. The rulers were fully responsible for the welfare of the people and country entrusted to them.[9] In the Psalms the good king is described as one who "trusts in the Lord;" one who loves beauty and brings justice and peace to the afflicted and the poor (Psalms 21; 45; 72). Deuteronomy says that the king should not acquire many things for himself and that he should not be one who is "exalting himself above other members of the community" (17:20).[10] Whenever the rulers are not capable of guaranteeing the welfare of those entrusted to them, they are no longer authentic leaders and must forfeit dominion.[11] It is for this reason that the prophetic literature so often condemned royal abuses of justice and benevolence and predicted that tyrannical oppressors would be struck down by the Lord (Isa 14:10).

As images of God then, humans were created to act nobly in the place of the Creator. They were commissioned to stand for

God and represent the caring and creative will of God.[12] Since Yahweh was a God of constant love, compassionate care, and saving power, this too was to be the role of humans toward all of creation. Individually and corporately, humans of all nations, races, and religions possess this same unique dignity and mirror God's presence in the world.[13] It seems clear that this leaves no room for lording over or mastering humans or other living things.[14]

The notion that persons are images of God also seems to indicate that God created humans beings to be companions for the Creator. God created someone who could relate to and communicate with God as a friend; one who could be articulate in the praise and worship of the deity.[15] The I of God made a thou who could name the animals, act freely, and act responsibly in partnership with God in the creative process. This companion of God would also be empowered to multiply and to produce other images of God through procreation.[16] All humans, regardless of race, religion, nationality, or world-view would thus be children of God, and by this very fact, they would possess a unique dignity.

Humbler Images

Elsewhere in the Hebrew Scriptures, humans are described in a more earthy fashion, with all their limitations, weaknesses and sins. The human person is at times described as a fool, a worm, a sinner. They are creatures of the dust, whose lives are a brief moment, and who often can make little or no sense of the meaning of life.

The most familiar image of the human being appears in Genesis 2. This is the mud-man, a creature made from the earth, bearing for a brief moment the breath of life. The word *Adamah* in Hebrew means earth, and thus Adam is an earth man, who is forever linked to the other creatures of the earth, and like them is destined to die and return to the soil from which he was made. This is an ancient anthropology with roots in Babylonian and

Egyptian literature. It shows how the human race belongs both to the gods and the earth. Humans take their origins from the Creator, and yet the elements of the human body are the same as those of the earth from which they are derived.[17] This is a more humble (*humus*-earth) image of the human, and as we shall see in what follows, it helps puts the notion of dominion into proper perspective.

It is the breath of life (Gen 2:7) that makes the human a living being. Scholars are quick to point out this image does not refer to the traditional notion that a soul is given to a body. As Westermann points out: "The Bible does not say that a human being is made up of body and soul, or of body, soul, and spirit. God's creation is this man in the totality of his being. Therefore God is concerned not only with the soul, but equally with the body. A higher regard for the spiritual ideal than for the corporeal or material has no basis in the creation faith of Genesis."[18] There is no question here of a dichotomy between the material and spiritual, of the spiritual being higher than the material, or of the soul being superior to the flesh.

The creation theology of Genesis 1 also links humans and animals in that both are described as living beings and are blessed with the capacity to multiply. Psalm 104:27-30 goes even further and proclaims that all living beings are provided for by God and share the breath of life (*ruah*). This breath of life, which God shares with all, sustains and constantly renews creation:

> These all look to you
> to give them their food in due season;
> when you give to them, they gather it up;
> when you open your hand, they are filled with good things.
> When you hide your face, they are dismayed;
> when you take away their breath, they die
> and return to their dust.
> When you send forth your spirit, they are created;
> and you renew the face of the ground. [19]

Dominion

The notion of humans having dominion over "all the living things that move on the earth" has been a subject of extensive debate, especially since the much-discussed article by Lynn White, where the author charged that this notion led to a Western dualism of humans over nature and resulted in extensive exploitation of the environment.[20] This so-called White-thesis is broadly recognized as an over-simplified account of the development of the modern environmental crisis. Nonetheless, it started a debate which has forced many scholars to look more closely at the real meaning of dominion in Genesis.

The original meaning of dominion does not seem to carry any connotation of exploitation or abuse. As mentioned earlier, this royal prerogative that humans share with God, as divine representatives, is that of being co-creators who act out of justice and care.[21] Humans are created to share a personal relationship with God, and, by reason of this relationship, are called to represent the Creator in sustaining order, peace and harmony on the earth. Such healing and peace-making was God's way of dealing with ancient Israel, and it is God's law that those made in the divine image do the same. As Bernard Anderson puts it: "Thus the special status of human kind as the image of God is a call to responsibility, not only in relation to other humans, but also to all of nature. Human dominion is not to be exercised wantonly but wisely and benevolently so that it may be, in some degree, the sign of God's rule over the creation."[22] One can see this notion of stewardship reflected in the laws of Deuteronomy which forbid the careless and wanton destruction of nature (Deut 22:6; 25:4; 20:19ff.). This theme also comes through clearly in God's command to Adam to be the caretaker of God's garden by working and protecting the garden (Gen 2:25). Israel's creation theology never indicates that the earth was created to be exploited by humans. Rather, humans are commissioned to sustain creation with the Lord's ultimate purpose in mind, and in this way creation will give glory to the Creator.[23]

Neither does the notion to subdue the earth (Gen 1:28) imply either a command or permission to exploit or misuse nature. Instead, this notion seems to consist in a blessing.[24] For the Israelites, it seemed to indicate a divine commissioning to deal properly with nature in a way that would help bring forth food and resources. Most certainly, the Creator's commissioning does not justify the exploitation of the earth's resources or the enslavement of other humans.[25] In fact, in the Book of Job, the Lord makes it clear that humans have neither knowledge or power over God's creatures (Job 38:9-39:12).

Claus Westermann maintains that dominion here refers to responsible care that a leader would be expected to exercise over those in his care. He writes: "'Dominion' is not meant here in the sense of arbitrary employment of power. That would be a fateful misunderstanding of this commission for dominion. It is meant rather in the sense of the other classic form of dominion, that of kingship. It means the full responsibility of the ruler for the welfare of the people and country entrusted to him."[26]

It seems clear, then, there is no textual basis in the Hebrew Scripture for the exploitation of creation. Any form of such violence toward creation would be viewed by the ancient Israelite as contempt for God's commission. Such desire to gain mastery over nature was not a value for ancient Israelites. Nature was indeed viewed as beyond their control, and in fact they often felt subjugated and even punished by nature. Indeed, the earth was the Lord's, and the Hebrews seemed to see themselves as creatures who were called to care for the earth in God's name.[27] In contrast to the Sumerian myths where the God Enki creates human beings to be surrogate laborers for the gods who are unwilling to do the arduous tasks on earth, the Hebrew God commissions humans to share in the on-going process of creating.[28]

There is no evidence that subsequent Christian teachings on creation, which developed out of Hebrew creation theology, took the notion of dominion to mean domination. The early Christians, the Desert Fathers, Celtic saints, Francis or medieval theologians did not use this notion for permission to exploit the environment.[29] If fact, the divine image and dominion notions were often used as a basis for defending human dignity against discrimination and social injustice. If anything, these beliefs denoted a calling to deal with all of creation sensitively and responsibly.

Exploitative interpretations of dominion would seem to be largely a modern phenomenon, prevalent since the discovery of the New World, the oncoming of the Enlightenment, and the development of modern science and technology. The ecological crisis should be more attributed to these movements, as well as attributed to such modern developments as colonialism, secularization, nationalism, industrialization, fascism, and communism. Seldom were these movements driven by interpretations of the Hebrew Scriptures! And, if creation theology was used as justification for mastering the world, it has been done only by distorting the original meaning of the Hebrew texts.

Human Limitations

Though humans are described in Hebrew theology as images of God, "a little lower than God," and as creatures having dominion, the Hebrew Scriptures often view the limitations and failings of humans. Qoheleth, for instance, laments that we humans are quite powerless:

> Indeed, they do not know what is to be, for who can tell them how it will be?
> No one has power over the wind to restrain the wind, or power over the day of death.... (Eccl 8:7-8)

The Preacher here characterizes the human search for meaning as futile. He challenges the traditional views that the good get rewarded and the bad punished, and he denies that there is any apparent divine justice or providence. There is, therefore, no future upon which humans can depend, no real hope for purpose or meaning. One cannot have much confidence in the next generation for they don't learn from those who came before them. He detests the fruits of his labors because he must leave them to someone who will come after him, and "who knows whether he will be a wise man or a fool" (Eccl 2:19).[30] All humans can ultimately look forward to is death; so, Qoheleth maintains that we have no other choice than to seize the day and enjoy the gifts that God has given us. The Preacher does in fact choose to obey the commands of God, but with little apparent reason other than a certain fear of God.[31]

Other sections of the Hebrew library also deal with human limitations. Sirach points out that we often feel insignificant as individuals among countless people that simply do not know us. We at times feel lost in a boundless creation in which we are unable to comprehend the foundations of things or the ways of God.[32] Proverbs tell us that, in our confusion, it is only God who can direct our steps and establish our purpose (Prov 16:9; 19:21). The psalmist at times seems overwhelmed at how weighty and vast are the thoughts of God, thoughts so countless as to be compared to sand (Ps 139:17-18). Though humans are crowned with glory and honor, the psalmist wonders why God could possibly be mindful of us (Ps 8:5-6). We are weak and vulnerable, and the lives of some are "but a breath," while others live out a mere "a delusion" (Psalm 62). Psalm 103:15-17 reflects on how life is transitory; the only constant is the love of God:

> As for mortals, their days are like grass;
> they flourish like a flower of the field;
> for the wind passes over it, and it is gone,
> and its place knows it no more.
> But the steadfast love of the Lord is from everlasting to
> everlasting.

The Book of Job explores human shortcomings in some depth. Like Qoheleth, Job challenges the traditional wisdom that the good receive rewards, and the evil are punished. In this dramatic story, a good man's life is reduced to rubble, and rather than being patient, as Job is often characterized, he rebels and challenges God for such injustice. The Lord comes out of the whirlwind and puts Job through an extremely intimidating interrogation (Job 38:2-41). Where was he when the foundations of the earth were laid, or when the stars and heavenly beings shouted out for joy? Where was he when the sea rushed from the womb of the earth and was wrapped in garments of clouds and swaddling clothes of darkness? Where was he when the dawn of morning, the snow, hail, rain, and thunder came forth for the first time? What does Job know of deserts and grasslands, or the habits of lions or ravens?

Job comes to realize how insignificant a role humans play in creation.[33] He learns that humans cannot challenge or debate with God, and finds out that "human standards are not adequate to deal with the mysteries of creation."[34] All that one can do in the face of life mysteries is abandon one's self to the Lord. In this story humans seem puny and helpless. They are at times comparable to maggots and worms (Job 25:5-6). Here they certainly are not the marvels of creation as they often seem to be in Genesis or the Psalms![35]

Humans as the Source of Sin

The ancient Israelites were clear in their belief that the source of evil in the world was the abuse of human freedom, rather than the cruelty or capriciousness of the gods, as pagan mythology would often have it. Disobedience, pride, jealousy, greed, and lust lay at the base of sin. This is clearly demonstrated in the garden story in Genesis 2 in the account of the forbidden fruit. Though Genesis does not speak of a fall, or degradation of the person into an inferior state of being (as in Augustine's notion of original sin), it does concern itself with the origin of human limitations such as death, pain, toil and sin.[36] As we read through the Hebrew Scriptures, although humans never cease to be images of God, they do bring upon themselves shame, guilt, pain, enslavement, violence, oppression and corruption as a result of their limitations and sinfulness. Their greed and selfishness often move them to oppress others and to take more than their share of God's gifts, thereby depriving others of sustenance.[37]

This human capacity to sin is often explored in the Psalms. The psalmist points out how transgression speaks deeply within the heart of the wicked because of their lack of fear of God and their self-flattery. The wicked are filled with deceit, and they are preoccupied with plotting evil (Ps 6). Sin affects humans down to their very bones, and weighs heavily on them as a burden (Ps 38). Personal sin is described by Amos in terms of afflicting the righteous, taking bribes, and pushing aside the needy (Am 4:12-13). Sirach speaks of anger toward neighbor, acts of insolence, arrogance, and injustice (Sir 10:6-7). Hosea sees that sinful self-destruction can come from lack of knowledge: "My people are destroyed for lack of knowledge" (Hos 4). A particularly serious crime is the ignorance that our Creator is the one responsible for what we have. Sin here consists in forgetting that God is our maker.[38] The prophet cries out: "Israel has forgotten his Maker" (Hos 8:14). Earlier the Lord had complained of Israel: "She did not know that it was I who gave her the grain, the wine, and the oil, and lavished on her silver and gold..." (Hos 2:8).

Throughout the Hebrew Scriptures, Israel is portrayed as a sinful nation that has been unfaithful to God's covenant and God's law. Sinfulness involves the disturbance of the natural order and harmony that the Creator has placed in the universe. Idolatry, disobedience, and corruption so often infected God's people and alienated them from their Creator.[39] Yet God's constant love and forgiveness repeatedly calls them back and restores them to peace and harmony that is the will of the Creator.[40] The Psalmist recalls how both his community as well as their ancestors have repeatedly sinned. He speaks to the Lord about how his ancient ancestors in Egypt "did not consider your wonderful works; they did not remember the abundance of your steadfast love, but rebelled against the Most High" (Ps 106:7). Yet constantly God saves Israel, not because of their merits but out of pure love and graciousness.

On a More Positive Note

The Song of Songs untypically sets aside the traditional negative views of the human person. In this magnificently sensual poetry, one does not find Eden's shame about nakedness, nor the fear of the Creator. In the Song of Songs, we have lovers who are comfortable with nature and see it "as musical accompaniment to the inner stirrings of the human heart."[41] Woman here is not a helper, nor is she portrayed as a seducer, as we see in other portions of the Hebrew Scriptures. The woman here is an open-hearted and tender lover; one who views human sexual love as something "beautiful and desirable in itself," and not merely as a way to "increase and multiply."[42] Both lovers liken each other to many of the most beautiful sights of nature and rejoice in their love for each other. They celebrate the sexual oneness that is given them in Gen 2:24-25:

> Therefore a man leaves his father and his mother
> and clings to his wife, and they become one flesh.
> And the man and his wife were both naked, and
> were not ashamed."

In this magnificent love poetry, there is no mention of the dark side of humanity that is often emphasized in the Hebrew Scriptures. There is gender equality with no sense of dominance or submission. Once again creation is viewed as becoming whole again, and human love mirrors the divine love that brought it forth.[43] As Roland Murphy comments: "The experience of love not only draws upon the textures of nature for its metaphors, it opens the eyes of the lovers themselves to the beauty of the world around them...a vision of God's creation become whole again."[44]

Hebrew Anthropology and the Environment

Our survey of the Hebrew understanding of humanity allows for many applications to the environmental issues of today; I will signal just a few. First, human persons have been made in the image and likeness of God, meaning that they are to be representatives of God. They stand in for a creative God, whose constant love and healing power is present in the world. Made in the image of such a God, human beings carry the responsibility of being trustees, caretakers, and sustainers of the earth and its resources. As Pope John Paul II puts it: "God entrusted the whole of creation to the man and woman, and only then–as we read–could he rest."[45]

God's creation is good, in that each and every element of it has a purpose and contributes to the success of the whole. Each species needs to be preserved so that it can carry out its own unique function in the web of life. Each area of creation needs to be respected as having value in itself, and not just for its use to humans. We are commissioned by God to preserve and sustain the web of life, to maintain the beauty and the bounty of the earth's resources.[46] We are blessed with resources that we need, but they must be used without jeopardizing future generations.[47]

As people who come from the earth and return to it, we need to be part of and not greater than. We are made from the same elements of the earth, and share the same breath of life as other living creatures. We are connected integrally with our environment, and there is a mutual interdependence among ourselves and all the living things. Therefore, dominion in no way justifies abuse or exploitation of our environment. We are care-takers, trustees of many precious gifts, and this sacred trust is to be carried out conscientiously and responsibly. If we do have a nobility among living things, this obliges us to act toward our environment with compassion, love and justice. As Bernard Anderson puts it: "Humans, for their part, are called to an ecological task: to be faithful manager's of God's estate.... Human responsibility, however, is grounded in God's covenant, which is universal and ecological. Its sign is the rainbow after the storm: a phenomenon of the natural order known to all human beings."[48]

It is clear from the Hebrew Scriptures that although humans have a unique dignity they also are limited. Even with all our technological and scientific advances, there is much about the workings of the environment that we do not understand and perhaps never will. Astrophysics, micro-biology, and many other sciences have often offered more questions than answers. Such limitations indicate that we proceed cautiously with our commitment to progress. So much that was deemed advancement and development in the past has seriously damaged our environment. Now that we understand this, future decisions need to be made with more long-term considerations.

The sciences will continue to uncover more of the what of reality, but will always fall short on the how and the why of things. As great scientists like Einstein and Hawking have recognized, even with our great advances in knowledge, we stand before a Mystery beyond our comprehension. For people of faith, only God is the source of the ultimate meaning of creation. Religious beliefs and values, therefore, must play a vital role in any decisions that we make regarding our environment. A purely secular approach to ecological matters is too often driven by utilitarian or even greedy motives. Without a religious perspective, we can easily lose touch with the sacred dimension of the world.

Sins Against the Earth

Of course, human sinfulness becomes abundantly apparent as we begin to learn of the untold damage that has been inflicted upon God's creation. Human ignorance, greed, and deceit have from the beginning been destructive to the earth. Humans have consistently disturbed the harmony and integrity of the world around them, but much of the serious damage has been done in modern times. In the last 200 years we have done extraordinary damage to the earth and its resources. With the advent of modern technology we are now more capable than ever of doing irreparable damage to our eco-systems. Our air, water, and soil have been severely damaged. The world's resources, given us to share, are now inequitably distributed, are often shamefully wasted, and are being rapidly exhausted. We have disturbed the natural harmony of many eco-systems, destroyed countless species, and brought many others to the brink of extinction. We have seriously damaged the delicate layers in the outer atmosphere which affect our weather and filter out deadly ultraviolet rays. We have morally offended the earth as well as many of its occupants by forcing large populations into refugee areas, where they proceed to devastate the small areas that they are forced to inhabit.

The Sacredness of the Earth

The Hebrew creation theology can bring us back to the giftedness of nature, to the sacredness of life. The Hebrew Scriptures present the earth as belonging to the Lord and also as a gift entrusted to humans that may sustain it, care for it, and help bring it to its ultimate fulfillment. Creation is the temple of God, the house of the Lord, where each person is privileged to live for a few brief years, making what contributions he or she can to the enrichment of the earth. From this perspective, we are clearly caretakers of a sacred gift on loan, that needs to be cherished, cared for, and then passed on to future generations. One thinks of Chief Seattle's well-known answer to the President of the United States when the latter asked to purchase the Northwest. The Chief was obviously perplexed and wrote: "The land does not belong to us. We belong to the land." And, of course, Chief Seattle believed that it all belonged to the Great Spirit.

The Hebrew notion that God dwells in nature is obviously valuable for anyone concerned about the environment. Nature is a sanctuary where we have access to the Creator's beauty and power. This notion is captured marvelously in the following reflection from Appalachia: "...the mountain forests are sacred cathedrals, the holy dwellings of abundant life-forms which all need each other, including us humans, with all revealing God's awesome majesty and tender embrace."[49]

To harm nature is an offense against the Creator; environmental issues rightly become moral issues. Pollution of the air with deadly gasses, dumping toxic waste materials in the oceans, the slashing and burning of our rain forests can be seen as offenses against the Creator, against humanity, and against the earth.

New Perspectives

The creation theology of the Hebrew Scriptures can provide us with new perspectives in regard to the environment. First of all, we see that creation is much more than human life. We are not the center of it all. There is a vastness in creation which transcends human life, and which seems quite capable of going on without us. As the one free creature on earth, we can choose to destroy or sustain the place we have been given for the short period of our lives. People of faith take seriously their responsibilities to sustain the earth. The love they have for their God, their children, and future generations moves them to act with care and respect for the earth.

Brennan R. Hill

Endnotes

1. Joseph Blenkinsopp, *A History of Prophecy in Israel* (Philadelphia: Westminster, 1983) 93 ff.
2. Roland E. Murphy, *Wisdom Literature* (Grand Rapids: Eerdmans, 1981) 104.
3. Richard J. Clifford, *Creation Accounts in the Ancient Near East and in the Bible* (The Catholic Biblical Quarterly Monograph Series, 26, 1994) 82 ff. See also Lawrence Boadt, *Reading the Old Testament* (New York: Paulist, 1984) 116; Bernhard Anderson, *Creation Versus Chaos* (New York: Association, 1967) 29. Bruce Vawter, *On Genesis: A New Reading* (Garden City, NY: Doubleday, 1977) 38ff.
4. See Claus Westermann, *Elements of Old Testament Theology* (Atlanta: John Knox, 1982) 87ff.
5. Bernhard W. Anderson, *From Creation to New Creation* (Minneapolis: Fortress, 1994) 15.
6. See Norbert Lohfink, *Theology of the Pentateuch* (Minneapolis: Fortress, 1989) 3ff. The image of God notion is applied in the New Testament to Jesus Christ. See J. McCarthy, "Le Christ cosmique et l'âge de écologie," *Nouvelle revue théologique* (Jan.-Fév., 1994) 116/n. 1, 37-47.
7. Lohfink, *Theology of the Pentateuch*, 4ff.
8. Anderson, *From Creation to New Creation*, 15.
9. Ibid., 130.
10. Wesley Granberg-Michaelson, ed., *Tending the Garden* (Grand Rapids: Eerdmans, 1987) 53ff.
11. Westermann, *Elements of Old Testament Theology*, 98. See also Vawter, *On Genesis: A New Reading*, 58ff.
12. See G. von Rad, *Genesis* (Philadelphia: Old Testament Library, 1972) 60. Von Rad indicates that ancient kings would erect images of themselves in the provinces of their empires to indicate their dominion. There is also evidence that Egyptian Pharaohs saw themselves as the living images of the god Re. See Anderson, *From Creation to New Creation*,

127. See also Claus Westermann, *Genesis* (Grand Rapids: Eerdmans, 1986) 11.

13. Westermann, *Elements of Old Testament Theology*, 97. See Vawter, *On Genesis: A New Reading*, 57.

14. Ronald Simkins, *Creator and Creation* (Peabody, MA: Hendrickson, 1994) 39.

15. Claus Westermann, *Roots of Wisdom* (Louisville: Westminster John Knox, 1995) 18; also his *Creation* (Philadelphia: Fortress, 1974) 55ff. See also Anderson, *From Creation to New Creation*, 33ff.

16. Westermann, *Creation*, 56ff. See also William Dyrness, "Stewardship of the Earth in the Old Testament," in Wesley Granberg-Michaelson, *Tending the Garden*, 39ff; and Westermann, *Elements of Old Testament Theology*, 97ff.

17. Westermann, *Genesis*, 18. See also his *Creation*, 77.

18. Westermann, *Genesis*, 18-19.

19. Ibid., 10.

20. Lynn White Jr., "The Historical Roots of Our Ecologic Crisis," *Science* 155 (1967) 1203-7.

21. Sean McDonagh, *The Greening of the Church* (Maryknoll, NY: Orbis, 1990) 124ff. See also Vawter, *On Genesis*, 59.

22. Anderson, *From Creation to New Creation*, 130. See Westermann, *Creation*, 50ff.

23. Ibid., 130.

24. Lohfink, *Theology of the Pentateuch*, 7ff.

25. Westermann, 54. See also Lohfink, *Theology of the Pentateuch*, 9ff.

26. Westermann, *Elements of Old Testament Theology*, 98. See also Vawter, *On Genesis: A New Reading*, 58 ff.

27. Simkins, *Creator and Creation*, 33 ff.

28. See Clifford, *Creation Accounts*, 42.

29. See Jeremy Cohen, "Be Fertile and Increase: Fill the Earth and Master It," *The Ancient and Medieval Career of a Biblical Text* (Ithaca, NY: Cornell University, 1989) 5.

30. Dianne Bergant, *Job. Ecclesiastes* (Wilmington, DE: Michael Glazier, 1982) 232ff.

31. See Roland E. Murphy, Ecclesiastes (WBC 23A; Waco TX: Word, 1992) 4ff. See also Murphy's *Wisdom Literature*, 126ff; *Responses to 101 Questions on the Psalms and Other Writings* (New York: Paulist, 1994) 71ff; *Seven Books of Wisdom* (Milwaukee: Bruce, 1960) 94ff. See also Bergant, *Job. Ecclesiastes*, 229ff.

32. See Claus Westermann, *Roots of Wisdom* (Louisville: Westminster John Knox, 1995) 125ff. and Bruce Vawter, *Job and Jonah* (New York: Paulist, 1983) 79ff. See also James Crenshaw, *Gerhard Von Rad* (Waco: Word, 1978) 147ff.

33. Kenneth G. Hoglund et al. (eds.), *The Listening Heart: Essays in Wisdom and Psalms in Honor of Roland E. Murphy, 0.Carm.*, The Journal for the Study of the Old Testament, Supplement, Series 59, 1987) 224. See also Roland Murphy, *The Psalms. Job* (Philadelphia: Fortress, 1977) 70ff; and his *Wisdom Literature*, 21ff; *Responses to 101 Questions on the Psalms and Other Writings*, 51ff. See also Claus Westermann, *The Structure of the Book of Job* (Philadelphia: Fortress, 1981) 108ff.

34 See Vawter, *Job and Jonah*, 79 ff.

35. Murphy, *Responses to 101 Questions on the Psalms and Other Writings*, 52.

36. Westermann, *Genesis*, 28.

37. Walter Brueggemann, *Abiding Astonishment: Psalms. Modernity and the Making of History* (Louisville: Westminster John Knox, 1991) 48ff.

38. Abraham J. Heschel, *The Prophets* (New York: Harper and Row, 1962) 45ff. See also Anderson, *Creation versus Chaos*, 59.

39. Anderson, *From Creation to New Creation*, 36.

40. Ibid., 30.

41. Murphy, *Song of Songs*, 68.

42. Ibid., 69. See Murphy, *101 Questions*, 65ff. and his *Song of Songs* (Minneapolis: Fortress, 1992) 100ff. and *Wisdom Literature*, 99ff.

43. Murphy, *Song of Songs*, 103ff.

44. Ibid., 103.

45. John Paul II, *The Ecological Crisis: A Common Responsibility* (Washington, D.C.: USCC, 1990) 1; see also Catholic Committee of Appalachia, *At Home in the Web of Life* (Webster Springs, WV: 1996) 12ff.

46. See United States Catholic Conference, *Renewing the Earth* (Washington, DC: USCC 1991) 2.

47. James Nash, *Loving Nature* (Nashville: Abington, 1991) 64.

48. Anderson, *Creation and New Creation*, 150.

49. Catholic Committee on Appalachia, *At Home in the Web of Life*, 5.

The Emphasis on the Word of God in Carmel During Recent Years

The theme of the XII Council of Provinces in Salamanca in September 1991 was: *Carmelite Charism: Journey into God, Following the Word. St. John of the Cross: Memory Alive for Today.* The occasion of the meeting in Spain was the fourth centenary of the death of St. John of the Cross. In a final message to the Family of Carmel, the participants discussed one result of their fraternal and prayerful experience:

> In our time here we have felt like pilgrims who, after a long journey, finally reach home. The preceding eleven Council of Provinces, dealing with the various aspects of our life and spirituality, have led us towards the center of our charism: the mystical life and the Word. It is here, in this center, that we must dwell as Carmelites, and it is from here that the light of our charism must shine out in the world.

During my twelve years as General, and in my previous experience as Provincial, I saw a tremendous new interest in the Word of God among our members. There is a stronger awareness that the Word of God lies at the very heart of our Carmelite charism.

There are many reasons for this phenomenon but the impact of the Second Vatican Council has been the foremost cause. The dogmatic constitution on Divine Revelation (*Dei Verbum*) and the document on the Church (*Lumen Gentium*) are considered the two fundamental documents produced by the Council. All the other documents depend on faith in God's Word. The decree on the Appropriate Renewal of Religious Life (*Perfectae Caritatis*) likewise encouraged the study of the Scriptures. This document stated that the ultimate norm of renewal for religious must be the following of Jesus Christ as set down in the pages of the gospel. Since the time of the Council individual Carmelites, communities, and provinces have realized how fundamental the Scriptures are in our Christian and religious life.

On the international level of the Order, there are only a few Carmelites who are well known for their significant contributions in the field of Scripture and who are also highly respected for the encouragement that they have given to our members to deepen an interest in the Word of God. One of these individuals is Roland Murphy. For over fifty years as professor, lecturer, and writer, he has been a living witness that "the word is very near to you; it is in your mouth and in your heart for you to observe" (Deut 30:14).

In this essay honoring Roland on his eightieth birthday, I would like to share some observations in three areas from my own international experience: (1) recent documents of the Order that have encouraged an interest in the Word of God, (2) attempts to incorporate *lectio divina* into our life in the context of a better understanding of the Rule, and (3) a seminar on Elijah the Prophet held in 1991 that brought some of our Scripture scholars and theologians into more direct personal contact with Roland.

Recent Documents of the Order

Since the Second Vatican Council closed on December 8, 1965, the Order has had six General Chapters, four General Congregations, and thirteen Councils of Provinces. One of the key purposes of all these meetings was to review on a regular basis the life of the Order and to keep our members moving forward in the direction called for by the Council. Each of these international meetings has looked to some extent at our *identity* as Carmelites— brothers of Our Lady who listen to the Word of God and who put themselves at the service of humanity in its quest for holiness and justice. The meetings have ordinarily issued a message or a document that has emphasized certain gospel values important for our Carmelite way of life. There was a hope that these values would be like nuclei, having the potential to explode and release vast energy within the Carmelite Family. The Word of God was one such nucleus, and international interest in it has truly been like an explosion that has occasioned a new prophetic, fraternal, and contemplative enthusiasm among our members in recent years.

I refer to two documents from these meetings. The first is the message of the V Council of Provinces that was held on Mount Carmel (Israel) in October, 1979, entitled: *A Return to the Sources* (an examination of the biblical significance of Mary and Elijah). Because of the site for the meeting, this Council of Provinces was permeated with the characteristics of a pilgrimage, and it became for the participants an unforgettable experience. It offered the opportunity to have close contact with places that are identified with the three most important figures in our tradition and spirituality: Jesus, Mary and Elijah. The message for the Order, composed at the end of this Council of Provinces, spoke of the three sources of inspiration for our Carmelite Family: (a) the words and example of Jesus Christ as they are found in the gospels which are fundamental documents to learn to walk in his footsteps and to serve him with a pure heart, (b) Mary, the Mother of Jesus, who exemplifies the ability to listen to the Word of God, to treasure it in one's heart, and to practice it in one's life, and (c) Elijah, the "man of God" in the midst of the people, whose entire life was dominated by the living God with whom he spoke in faithful friendship, even as he remained sensitive to the needs of the people in their religious and social situations.

The second document is the message of the XII Council of Provinces in Salamanca during September 1991. This message encouraged all members of Carmel to strive to read the Bible with a new perspective, not simply remaining with the text as such but experiencing the written Word of God as if it is a mirror in which our own lives are reflected, or as if it is a lamp that allows us to see the person of the Living Word who is present to us in the circumstances of daily life. There was a conviction among the Council's participants that, if we read or meditated upon the Word of God in the silence of our rooms, or if we listened and shared about it in community meetings, it would truly come alive in our hearts and be present on our lips. It would teach us to look at the world with the eyes of God, leading us to be true contemplatives who radiate God's presence and love for humanity in the style of St. John of the Cross.

The Practice of *Lectio Divina*

During recent years it has been a very encouraging sign to attend a General or a Provincial Chapter and see the participants setting aside time for *lectio divina* in small groups. This practice has become fairly common in chapters, and it was especially noticeable to me in meetings when members of the Carmelite Family from different countries and cultures came together. Within the past six years congresses were held in Rio De Janeiro, Manila and Mutare (Zimbabwe) to study the inculturation of the charism and spirituality of Carmel in a South American, Asian or African setting. The participants—friars, sisters, laity—were eager to practice daily *lectio divina,* and it proved to be an excellent aid for creating an environment of acceptance and understanding.

Such phenomena did not happen twenty years ago, not only because international congresses of the Carmelite Family were rare, but also because the practice of *lectio divina* in common was more rare. Due to the work and the encouragement of Scripture scholars in the Order like Roland Murphy, Carlos Mesters (Brazil), and Kees Waaijman (Holland), this practice has become more frequent, and our members are becoming more at ease in their use and appreciation of this form of prayer and sharing.

It is truly surprising that *lectio divina* was out of date among us for so many years, but perhaps we as Carmelites reflected an attitude that unfortunately was quite prevalent in the entire Roman Catholic Church. Perhaps we should have known better, since our Rule gives significant emphasis to the Word of God. Albert cited and evoked both the Old and the New Testament without distinction when he responded to the hermits' request. It would be difficult to know exactly how many times the Rule uses the Bible, but some believe that it is more than one hundred times. As Carlos Mesters has commented: "It appears that the Rule is a collection of phrases taken from the Word of God to express the thought of the *propositum* put forward by the first Carmelites to Albert."

Even though the Rule is a very short document, it recommends in eight different places that Carmelites read or share about the Word of God: (1) listen to the Sacred Scriptures during meals in the refectory (chapter IV), (2) meditate upon the law of the Lord day and night (VII), (3) pray the psalms during the Hours (VIII), (4) take part in the Eucharist (IX), (5) be fortified by holy thoughts which come from prayerful reading of the Scriptures (XIV), (6) the Word must dwell in your mouth and in your heart (XIV), (7) work at all times in accordance with the Word of God (XIV), and (8) read frequently the letters of St. Paul (XV).

It is interesting to see how the pedagogy for assimilating the Word of God that is sketched faintly in the Rule is a reflection of the age-old practice of *lectio divina* with its traditional four steps: reading (*lectio*), meditating (*meditatio*), prayer (*oratio*), and contemplation (*contemplatio*): a) first of all, the Word has to be heard or read ... in the refectory, in the Eucharist, in the canonical hours (*lectio*), b) afterwards, the Word which has been heard has to be pondered and meditated upon ... by day and by night, without ceasing, above all in one's cell (*meditatio*), c) the Word, once heard and pondered, has to be enveloped in prayer ... keeping vigil and fortified by holy thoughts (*oratio*), d) and finally, the Word of God is to invade one's mind, one's heart and one's actions so that the world in which a Carmelite lives is seen through the eyes of God, and everything is done in the name of the Lord (*contemplatio*).

The Seminar on Elijah the Prophet

During the General Chapter of 1989, I had the opportunity to talk with Murray Phelan, who was then Provincial of the American Province of the Most Pure Heart of Mary, about the possibility of a seminar at Whitefriars Hall, Washington, on the theme of Elijah the Prophet. Would the Province be willing to subsidize a seminar, giving younger scholars in the Order who were interested in Scripture or Elijan spirituality the opportunity to be in contact and to share personally with Roland Murphy? Murray responded enthusiastically to this proposal.

During Easter week, April 3-9, 1991, this seminar on Elijah the Prophet took place at Whitefriars Hall, Washington. Twelve Carmelites from around the world, including Roland, participated in the discussions. In a book entitled, *A Journey with Elijah*, Paul Chandler (Australia) edited the eleven talks that were given, and he presented a report of the work that was done at the seminar to the General Council. The articles give excellent insights into the biblical figure of Elijah, and he is proposed to Carmelites as a model for the spiritual journey. It is interesting to note that Roland, at the end of his own article during the seminar, encouraged members of the Order who profess to live in the spirit of Elijah to use *lectio divina* as a means to return to our roots so that our Carmelite religious heritage and tradition might be better understood and followed. All of us as Carmelites are sincerely grateful to Roland for his participation in this seminar and for his commitment to the Word of God in his personal and professional life. We hope that he will continue to share his expertise and love of the Scriptures for many years to come.

John Malley, O.Carm.

Pater et Dux:
Elijah in Medieval Mythology

Lo, I will send you the prophet Elijah before the
great and terrible day of the Lord comes. He will
turn the hearts of parents to their children and
the hearts of children to their parents, so that I
will not come and strike the land with a curse.

Malachi 4:5

The hero of my tale, whom I love with all the
power of my soul, whom I have tried to portray
in all his beauty, who has been, is, and will be
beautiful, is Truth.

Leo Tolstoi, *Sevastapol*, 1855

Elijah's return is God's concluding promise in the canon
of the covenant with Israel and so, with one eye ever wakeful,
generations of those who esteem God's pledge have looked for the
Tishbite to emerge suddenly from the fog of this terrestrial life and
kindle the blaze that will herald the new heavens and the new
earth. Rabbis and monks alike have searched for the portents of
his advent and even occasionally consulted one another in
anxious inquiry. Tables have been set and wine poured in his
honor while numberless persons have come claiming to be he.
Prophet in Israel, he has slipped the bonds of Judaism to enthrall
the faithful of disparate creeds. Thirty times the New Testament

calls out his name! Elijah long ago became a mythic figure; the devotion of Jews, Christians, Muslims, and Druze show that his specter can provoke the human heart to tremble in anticipation.

Such a personality was destined to become mythic. Stories could not but abound, his spirit could not but be confused with a host of demi-urges that haunt the mountains, wastes, rivers, and dells to which the various faiths brought his name. Truth could not contain him any more than history has been able to define him. Leave it to a tawdry band of mendicants to kidnap the hero, dress him in their own garb, and claim him for their very own–or even more audacious, claim themselves to be his legacy. Whatever dissimulation those friars brewed in their pot of legends and sermons, our hero Elijah manages to come forth as resplendent as ever, his truth intact.

A deception of which we Carmelites are guilty is our belief that the relationship between Elijah and the Carmelites is somehow unique to the band of hermits that first gathered on Elijah's mountain at the eastern end of the Mediterranean Sea. This prevarication is due not to any malice but rather to historical naiveté and bold presumption that we alone are worthy of such a master.

There is an unfortunate conceit among many Carmelites that Elijah is a figure whom our medieval forebears somehow rescued from obscurity when they claimed him as their *pater et dux*. This is all but a reversal of the actual historical situation. Far from a Carmelite revival of his fortunes, Elijah was a remarkably popular figure in medieval mythology, one whose popularity may well have rescued the early Carmelites from oblivion, if not actually from extinction. The assumption that Elijah was waiting for the first Carmelites to bring him out of retirement is an easy one to make. The Carmelite connection with Elijah was both early and natural. The original hermits gathered on Elijah's mountain by a well reputed to be his. Although the Carmelite Rule never mentions him, the *Rubrica Prima*, which dates perhaps from as early as the period of moving from Palestine to Europe (1238-1247), draws a definite connection between the Carmelites and

Elijah.[1] It would seem to those who are unfamiliar with medieval culture that Elijah was one of those marvels whom returning crusaders, in this case Carmelites, brought to Europe.

It is curious that the early Carmelites never thought much about preserving any of the details of their founding. The foundation stories should have been in living memory when the Carmelites first came into contact with the other mendicants. The lack of a charismatic founder such as Francis or Dominic was an inconvenience, not only when they arrived in Europe, but also when they sauntered into the local town of Acre where both Franciscans and Dominicans had settled well before the middle of the thirteenth century.[2] Why did the hermits turn to Elijah to explain their origins rather than recall the man, or men, who had first gathered them in the wadi some twenty or thirty years previously?

I cannot adequately explain why those early Carmelites chose to weave a story about Elijah, but I can comment on their decision. It was far more than a design of a story to replace a vacant memory, if indeed (and improbably) the historical memory had been lost when they first adopted Elijah. In claiming Elijah as their founder, the first generations of Carmelites were not hiding their obscurity by tracing their lineage, but rather they were boastfully attributing to themselves a pedigree of unparalleled elegance among the religious families of the day. The claim is so flamboyant that we moderns must be very careful in our interpretation of the actions of those early Carmelites who claimed descent from Elijah.

The principal danger to be avoided is an anachronistic attribution of an historical understanding to this claim. The author(s) of the Elian foundation of the Order were pre-historic; that is to say, they were writing in a culture that was more interested in meaning than in historical fact. It was unimportant to them who the actual founder of their order was; what mattered to them was the purpose and mission for which their order was founded. They were concerned more about the possibilities for the future than the details of the past. In this they were not unique. Franciscans and Dominicans did not limit their founders to

historic realities but so overlaid them with hagiographical traditions that they (especially Francis) are all but unrecoverable
historically.

What was the significance of the prophet Elijah for the
early Carmelites who adopted him as their founder, relinquishing
the memory of those first hermits who lived in the wadi-'ain es-
Shiah? In this tribute to Father Roland Murphy I hope to offer
some insights about how their choice of Elijah reflects how they
wanted to be perceived. To do this I provide a brief survey of how
Elijah surfaces in medieval culture. I draw from that survey how
Elijah was understood by Latin Christians in the Middle Ages, and
finally I contextualize the Carmelite claims of Elian lineage in this
popular understanding. In the end I hope that we will understand
the dreams that the first Carmelites had for themselves and for
generations of Carmelites who came after them.

The prominence of Elijah in medieval culture can be
traced back to antiquity, to his popularity in the inter-testamental
period of biblical literature. Various cultures and histories contain the legends of those archetypal figures who are expected to
return at critical moments for the deliverance of their people.[3]
Elijah was such a figure. Even in the cycle of his stories which
found their way into the scriptural canon he had an eerie ability
to appear out of nowhere and to vanish into the ether when his
tasks were completed. His final departure in the whirlwind left his
mortality unresolved, and opened the possibility that he might
return unexpectedly at any time. The legend grew and persisted
that he would return in Israel's moment of urgency. Malachi
prophesied his return, and Israel kept its ear alert to hear the
rushing wind of his resurgence. This expectancy increased as
invader after invader ravaged Israel's land. A popular expectation
was that Elijah's return would mark the advent of the Messiah,
the one to set Israel free. Hearts of patriotism and of faith waited
for the day of deliverance. The gospels convey this very expectation "Some say John the Baptist, others Elijah...." "The scribes
claim that Elijah must come first." "If you are prepared to accept
it, he is Elijah, the one who is to come." "Elijah has appeared and

has restored all things." Over and over again, on Tabor and Calvary, in the teaching and in the questioning, we sense the expectation that Elijah is to appear.

Who was this Elijah who was anticipated by the crowds that flocked to see John or to hear Jesus? He had evolved far beyond the limits of First and Second Kings. He was a miracle worker[4] and a model of efficacious prayer.[5] Some expected an ascetic like John who lived in the desert, clothed in camel skin, and living on an austere diet. Others thought that the better fed and more affable Jesus might be he. The expectation was widespread but consensus was lacking and so the questions were posed to John and to Jesus: "are you he who is to come, or shall we look for another?"[6]

As the Christian community acknowledged Jesus as the Messiah, John the Baptizer was accorded the role of Elijah. That should have been the end of Elijah's story. Not so. He began yet again to take on a new character, one which suited the temperament of the maturing Church. As Christianity developed from small communities of the devout and to a movement that began to influence–and threaten–the Roman world, its story provided an alternative to the various religions and philosophies of the empire. Elijah developed from the example of efficacious prayer in the epistle of James, to a model of mystical prayer among those early Christian apologists who interpreted Christian experience for a Church that now found itself in a Hellenistic world. And so Origen writes of Elijah:

> And Elijah, who shut up heaven for the wicked for three and a half years, later opened it. This, too, is always accomplished for everyone who through prayer receives the rain of the soul, since the heavens were previously deprived of it because of his sin. [7]

Origen applied a distinctly non-historical hermeneutic and made the tale tell something far different that its original theme. He not only used the story to teach mysticism, he drew out from the text a mystical significance. Uncovering the mystical meaning(s) of the text would become the normative hermeneutic for Christian thinkers over the next thirteen centuries. Origen did not invent this hermeneutic but appropriated it for Christian Scriptures from his teacher, Philo of Alexandria, a Hellenized Jew and neo-platonist who taught that every material reality had a corresponding and higher, spiritual meaning.[8] In neo-platonic thought the mystical significance of a text was more central to the truth than the literal meaning. The primacy of the spiritual meanings of the scriptural text would be asserted throughout late antiquity and the Middle Ages. The Elian texts proved to be particularly attractive to those who searched the Scriptures for mystical and ascetical guidance.

Since the fifteenth century, and most particularly in the post-Enlightenment world, scholarship has focused on critical studies of ancient texts, both the sacred and secular. We are anxious to understand the text according to the historical situation in which it was produced. Nothing could have less interested the ancient and medieval mind. In a neo-platonic world, to focus on the literal was to retreat into the darkest corner of the cave. To what were the images of the story analogous? What were the allegories within the story? What were the moral truths? Images, symbols, and attributes, conscious and even better unconscious (for it was in the unconscious that the divine was revealing itself) were what was needed to discover the truest meaning of the revealed text.[9]

In this spirit, the Christian community that witnessed the transition from classical antiquity to the medieval period refashioned Elijah to express the values of a faith that wished to transform the indulgence of old Rome to the ascetical purity of the new Jerusalem. The sporadic periods of persecution had made the Church wary of Rome but the cessation of the persecution under Constantine caused greater anxiety yet. History has shown that the best way to destroy the Church is not to persecute it but to accommodate it. It did not take the early Church long to see the hazards nestled within imperial patronage. Whetted by the blood of the martyrs, the more devout in the Church were determined to resist the dilution of the faith that the recognition of Christianity provided. If the empire would not offer red martyrdom, the Church itself would propose white martyrdom, i.e., monasticism, as a voluntary alternative to those who were determined to remain intrepid. Monasticism proposed asceticism as an alternative to the luxury of the Roman way of life. Elijah was a most convenient model of this spiritual valor because the scriptural texts allowed for an interpretation which projected a Christian ascetic ideal on this ancient prophet.

Christian monasticism, at least in its earliest phase, involved the rejection of urban society and its materialistic lifestyle. Roman life was essentially urban life. While the upper classes had their villas in the country or by the sea, they spent the majority of their time in city houses. They gathered in the markets and the theaters and in the baths to gossip, to arrange business matters and to discuss politics. Monks fled the cities to live in the desert, away from the vanity of such lives, so that they could grapple with the Word of God. Basil of Caesarea (+379) saw Elijah as a man who fled the tumult of human society, finding his true happiness only in the desert. His spirit steadfastly set on searching for truth, Basil informs us, Elijah renounced the mercenary interchange of urban life in order that he might see God in solitude.[10] Basil goes on to tell us that Elijah not only chose solitude, he chose, like John the Baptist, to live without home or servant, without livestock, roof, bed or even bread. So, declared Basil, live all holy persons.[11]

Monks also left the cities to live in the wilderness because they rejected the sensuality of Roman life with its the rich foods and fine wines. They understood that a sensual life blinded one to things of the spirit. Jerome (+420), like Basil, admired Elijah because he was one who saw God, and Jerome connects this vision with the prophet's asceticism: "Elijah, after the preparation of a forty days' fast saw God on Mount Horeb...."[12] Seeing God was not the only privilege of Elijah: he also "entered on immortality before he approached death."[13] This privilege of escaping death was not even given to Moses, and the text makes it clear why Elijah was given this favor that was denied to Moses: Moses had been married whereas Elijah was a virgin. The silence of the scriptural text on this question was no barrier for Jerome's doctrine of the prophet's virginity, but then both text and historical fact were beyond Jerome's point. Nothing in the text rules out the prophet's virginity, no wife for Elijah was ever mentioned; so Jerome presents him as a model for those who consecrate themselves to chastity in the midst of a world given to sensuality.

The fourth century Church presented Elijah as a man of virginity, of fasting, of prayer and of solitude. He withdrew from worldly concerns and lived in poverty. His reward was to see God and to avoid death. In interpreting his life in this way, the Church fathers of the fourth century anachronistically imposed the monastic ideal on the ancient prophet. Their methodology did not reflect a historical-critical hermeneutic of the stories of the ancient prophet; instead, they took the details of his life and reinterpreted them to meet the needs of the Church and to present evangelical ideals to their society. Basil and Jerome were both monks themselves, but their audience was far wider than the monastic world. The Elijah presented in their writings was meant not simply to encourage those who had taken up the monastic vocation, but to inspire the post-persecution generation of Christians to look beyond their self-indulgence and follow a dream of an ascetical Christianity that would replace the indulgence of the now baptized but not yet fully converted Roman society.

Elijah's asceticism became part of the lore of the Church and was often repeated in a variety of patristic sources. Paulinus of Nola (+431) commented, albeit in passing, on the prophet Elijah withdrawing from the world.[14] Chrysostom, (+407) expanding on Jerome's insight, declared that Elijah, because of his virginity, was equal to the angels.[15] Actually, Chrysostom praised not only Elijah but Elisha and John the Baptizer as "these brothers in their love for virginity." The idea that Elijah had companions in his virginity was not new with Chrysostom; Jerome had written that not only was Elijah a virgin, but so too was Elisha and "many sons of the prophets."[16] Such claims helped to develop the idea that Elijah was the founder of the monastic ideal. Jerome referred to these sons of the prophets, i.e., the disciples of Elijah and Elisha, as the "monks of the Old Testament."[17]

To hold Elijah as a paragon for monks was a significant step in providing a scriptural justification for monastic life, but to say that his values, particularly ascetical chastity, were shared by his disciples was a yet more significant move towards making Elijah the inventor of monastic life. John Cassian (+c.435) took that step and posthumously invested the Tishbite with the monastic cowl. Following Origen, Cassian saw Elijah as a mystic, but by Cassian's day no one expected the average Christian to have a mystical life. Monasticism was the way of life for those called to mystical prayer.

> Some direct all their efforts toward the secrets of the desert and purity of heart. In the past there was Elias and Elisaeus. In our own day there are the blessed Antony and those others who follow the same purpose, and we know that in the quiet of their solitude they enjoy the closest union with God.[18]

John Cassian presented Elijah as the proto-monk–the model on whom later monastics would base their vocation. Along with Elisha and with John the Baptist, Elijah prefigures the new type of disciple, the monk, for whom ordinary Christian life offers insufficient challenge.

> And so it was that, as I have said, there arose out of the discipline of the early days another way of seeking perfection. Adherents of this are rightly called anchorites, that is, people who go aside into a retreat. It is not enough for them to have successfully trampled down the snares of the

devil among men, they long to join in open combat and in clear battle against the demons. They are not afraid to push into the great hiding places of the desert. They are surely the imitators of John the Baptist, who remained in the desert throughout the whole of his life. They do like Elias and like Elisaeus, about whom the apostle had this to say: 'They wandered around dressed in the skins of the sheep or goats. They were persecuted and poor–they of whom the world was unworthy. They went to live in lonely places, on mountains, in caves, in the hollows of the earth' (Heb 11:37-38).[19]

The conferences of John Cassian were foundational in creating the monastic culture of the Middle Ages. Long before the Carolingian Reformation imposed Benedict's Rule on the monks of the western Church, one of the unifying factors in western monasticism was the universal familiarity with Cassian's conferences. Cassian was standard reading in refectories. Scriptoria copied and disseminated his books, and abbots relied on his insights as they guided their monks. Cassian had created the monastic ideology of the western Church, and through his conferences the monks of the west came to appreciate Elijah as their model and guide. When he bursts out again into the larger world, it will be through the agency of monastic preachers and writers.[20]

Elijah's re-emergence was occasioned by the apocalyptic panic that swept Europe in the tenth, eleventh, and twelfth centuries. Originally the emphasis of this frenzy was the Anti-Christ, a figure made popular by Adso, the tenth-century abbot of Moutier-en-Der (+992), who wrote a popular treatise on the final challenge to Christianity before the Lord's return at the end of the world. He charged the medieval period with expectation that the moment of crisis was at hand and prophesied that a Frankish ruler would first restore the Roman Empire and then lay down his crown in Jerusalem. Immediately upon this abdication, the Anti-Christ would rise, but the world would be prepared for the conflict by the teaching and preaching of Enoch and Elijah. Anti-Christ would slay these prophets after three and a half years, initiating a great persecution against the Church.[21] Adso's treatise provided the foundation for the *Ludus Antichristi* which enjoyed wide-spread popularity as church drama.

Many apocalyptic preachers picked up Adso's theme which did much to spread the fame of Elijah, but none was more important than the twelfth-century Cistercian abbot Joachim of Fiore (+1202). Joachim was not shy in expressing his belief that the established monastic communities, including the one in which he held office, had devolved into moribund institutions and that the Holy Spirit was about to renew the face of the earth using two new communities: a community of preachers in the spirit of Elijah and a community of hermits in the spirit of Moses. Within a decade of Joachim's death, Francis of Assisi began his mission and many who knew the prophecies of Joachim identified Francis with Elijah.

At this point a brief digression may assist in understanding the place of Elijah in medieval culture. The identification of Francis with Elijah is not only historically significant, but it helps one to better appreciate the immense popularity Elijah enjoyed in the thirteenth century. The fame that Francis enjoys in the twentieth century, Elijah enjoyed in the thirteenth. Christians of all stripes know, and to varying degrees venerate, Francis. The historical Francis has been so overlaid with legend and piety as to be all but superseded by the mythical Francis, even among his Franciscan heirs. Zeferelli's artistic genius and Donovan's musical talent pay homage to Francis in the transhistorical *Brother Sun, Sister Moon*, a film which shapes the ideal which so many want for Francis. Elijah was such a figure in the thirteenth century. The comparison between the modern popularity of Saint Francis and the renown of Elijah in the Middle Ages are not to be taken lightly. There was an explicit identification of Francis with Elijah. When Francis, at his death, was reported being seen ascending as a bright star into the heavens, Giotto interpreted this legend by painting Francis rising to heaven in a fiery chariot. This painting is part of the iconography commissioned for the basilica erected over the saint's tomb, giving a very definite sanction to the identification of Francis with Elijah. This theme has often been repeated in Franciscan art. Indeed the identification of Francis with Elijah solidified the familiarity of the medieval audience with the prophet at a time when the Carmelites decided to kidnap the Tishbite for their own purposes.

The symbols of Elijah's life: the raven bringing him food, the fire falling from heaven to consume the sacrifice, the fiery chariot, the mantle falling on Elisha are all stories and images with which medieval people were very familiar. At the end of the twelfth century, about fifty years before the Carmelites made their first appearance in Europe, a monastic scriptorium, probably in Bavaria, produced a book called the *Biblia Pauperum*. This book, presumably for preachers, has illustrations from thirty-four episodes in the Savior's mission, ranging from the annunciation to the last judgment. These thirty-four episodes are each accompanied by two episodes from the Old Testament which parallel the life and mission of Jesus. Elijah and/or his disciple Elisha are the focus of eight of these sixty-eight parallels.[22] This book served as the model for other books that popularized the parallels between New and Old Testament themes; it also served to inspire a variety of expressions in the visual arts, notably in stained glass and church sculpture. Elijah appears time and again in medieval churches, often clad in monastic garb, being fed by the ravens, raising to life the son of the widow of Sarepta, and calling down fire upon his sacrifice. He was a central figure in medieval consciousness and his frequent appearance in monastic garb reenforced the legend that he was the institutor of monastic life.

An outstanding testament to the popularity of Elijah surviving the Middle Ages and enduring well into the Renaissance is the splendid marble inlay of the cathedral floor in Siena. Fifty-six panels tell the story. Thirteen of these fifty-six are from the Elijah cycle.[23] Furthermore, these thirteen are located in the most prominent place in the cathedral, immediately before the entrance to the choir at the crossing of the nave and the transept. The Elijah story is familiar not only to Carmelites, but to a much larger audience, indeed to an audience that may never have heard of the Carmelites but knows well the prophet from Tishbe.

The thirteenth century was a critical time for the Carmelite Order. It was not until the very end of the century that it was certain that the papacy was not going to suppress the Carmelites as it had so many other groups after the Second Council of Lyons. Furthermore, the proliferation of mendicant communities created an often fierce competition for patronage, alms and personnel. We do not know why the early Carmelites abandoned the memory of their historical founders, but it should not be a surprise that they clung to Elijah's mantle. Beneath that mantle they could claim to be the original monastic movement, predating not only the other mendicants but even Benedict. The predictions of Joachim of Fiore empowered Elijah to offer not only a past but a future to the sons who adopted him. The Carmelites do not seem to have exploited these prophecies, but their claim upon Elijah was enough to trigger connections in the popular mind.

The myth of the Elian foundation of their order was a success as the Carmelites survived threatened suppressions. The order was never as large or powerful as the Franciscans and Dominicans. In all probability, despite the popularity of Elijah, the faithful seem to have been rather nonplused at the stories the Whitefriars told. Obviously the Carmelites touted their heritage, but seemingly few outsiders got too worked up about it. Chaucer ridiculed it in the Summoner's tale, but then Chaucer was a revisionist born out of due time. Possibly the most important believers of the legend were the Carmelites themselves. At the end of the fourteenth century, approximately the same time Chaucer was writing, a Carmelite wrote *The Institute of the First Monks*. It was a valiant call for reform and renewal in the Order. All the old Elijah stories were paraded out and interpreted in ways to challenge the friars to return the traditional values for which the Church Fathers had praised Elijah: withdrawal from worldly affairs, solitude, fasting, chastity, and the hope of seeing God. *The Institute of the First Monks* has had a powerful influence on Carmel. It helped shape the vision of Saint Teresa and through her to renew the Carmelite Order at a particularly climactic time.

Of course, moderns know that Elijah did not found the Carmelite Order. Nor was he a monk, nor necessarily a virgin. There is little scriptural warrant to say that he experienced deep contemplation in the wadi Cherith. His reason for withdrawing from society was not a yearning for God but a fear for his life. But we must be careful about ridiculing past generations for making him into their own image and likeness for we imaginatively appropriate the Elijah stories according to our contemporary categories. Naboth's vineyard provides us with an opportunity to see Elijah as a prophet of social justice. The experience of God in the still breeze of Horeb lets us attribute to Elijah the highest proficiency in mental prayer. His confrontation with the prophets of Baal allows us to describe Elijah as one who confronted the crass materialism and religious ritualism of his day. Our myths might be more closely tied to the texts than the medieval stories, but they say more about us and our aspirations than they say about Elijah. Elijah might be a far less known figure today than he was in medieval society, but at least for Carmelites he still has the ability to capture a truth that surpasses historical fact.

Patrick McMahon, O.Carm.

Endnotes

1. A. Staring, *Medieval Carmelite Heritage* (Rome: Institutum Carmelitanum, 1989) 34. The earliest extant version of the *Rubrica Prima*, however, is that which prefaces the 1281 Constitutions.
2. Joachim Smet, *The Carmelites: A History of the Brothers of Our Lady of Mount Carmel*, 4 vols. (Darien, IL: private printing, 1976-1988) 1 (new edition) 4. The Dominican presence in Acre was strong enough for them to maintain a *studium* there by the middle of the thirteenth century. Jonathan Riley-Smith, *The Crusades: A Short History* (New Haven: Yale University, 1987) 51.
3. From antiquity through the medieval period, the historical figure who attains mythic identity was often portrayed as one who would return to restore a people to past grandeur. Barbarossa slumbered in the Kyffhäuser until it was time to restore the Reich. This was no idle legend; in the early 16th century pseudo-Fredericks appeared and secured significant followings. Geoffrey Barraclough, *The Origins of Modern Germany* (London: W.W. Norton, 1984) 362. Similar legends and hopes surrounded Charlemagne. These myths can be traced back from the Middle Ages into late antiquity and indeed back into the ancient world, but it is beyond the scope of this paper to sketch that history.
4. Donald Senior, "Aspects of New Testament Thought: The Miracles of Jesus," *The New Jerome Biblical Commentary*, Raymond E. Brown, Joseph A. Fitzmyer, Roland E. Murphy, eds. (Englewood Cliffs, NJ: Prentice Hall, 1990) 1370.
5. Thomas W. Leahy, "The Epistle of James," *The New Jerome Biblical Commentary*, 916.
6. "This striking phrase created by Matthew turns the debate into one on the nature of Jesus' messiahship, but originally it may have been over whether he was a divine messenger

like Elijah." Benedict T. Viviano, "The Gospel According to Matthew," *The New Jerome Biblical Commentary*, 652.

7. Origen, "On Prayer," *Origen: An Exhortation to Martyrdom, Prayer, First Principles: Book IV Prologue to the Commentary on the Song of Songs, Homily XXVII on Numbers*, Rowan A. Greer, trans.; Classics of Western Spirituality (New York: Paulist, 1979) 108.

8. Beryl Smalley, *The Study of the Bible in the Middle Ages*, (Notre Dame IN: Notre Dame Press, 1964) 3. Smalley traces this hermeneutic through Philo to Greek literature.

9. See Frederick B. Artz, *The Mind of the Middle Ages: A.D. 200-1500, An Historical Survey* Chicago: University of Chicago Press, 1980). Artz has several sections explaining the hermeneutic approaches of the ancient and medieval periods; see especially pp. 376-383.

10. Basil of Caesarea, "Commentary on the Prophet Isaiah," *S.P.N. Basilii, Caesarae Cappadociae Archiepiscopi, Opera Omnia Quae Exstant*, edited by Monachorum ordinis sancti Benedicti e congregatione S. Mauri (Paris: J.-P. Migne, 1857) Tomus II, 130.

11. Ibid., 315.

12. Jerome, "Against Jovinianus, Book II," *St. Jerome: Letters and Select Works*, vol. VI of *A Select Library of the Nicene and Post-Nicene Fathers of the Christian Church*, Second Series. Philip Schaff and Henry Wace, eds. (Grand Rapids: Eerdmans) 399.

13. Ibid.

14. Paulinus of Nola, "Poem 16," *The Poems of St. Paulinus of Nola*, P.G. Walsh, ed. *Ancient Christian Writers: The Works of the Fathers in Translation* (New York: Newman, 1975).

15. John Chrysostom, "De Virginitate," *Sancti Joannis Chrysostomi, Archiepiscopi Constantinopolitani, Opera Omnia*, edited by Monachorum ordinis sancti Benedicti e congregatione S. Mauri (Paris, 1842) II, 592.

16. Jerome, "Letter 22 (to Eustochium)," *The Letters of St. Jerome*, Charles C. Mierow, trans. (Westminster MD: Newman, 1963) I, 153.

17. *Les Carmélites du Monastère Saint Élie, Le Saint Prophète Élisée*, Spiritualité Orientale, 59, (Bégrolles-en-Mauges, Maine-&-Loire: Abbaye de Bellefontaine, 1993) 24.

18. John Cassian, "Conference Fourteen," *John Cassian: Conferences*, Colm Luibheid, trans.; Classics of Western Spirituality (New York: Paulist, 1985) 157.

19. Ibid., 187.

20. The focus of this article is only on the place of Elijah in the west, particularly in monastic culture. He enjoyed popularity in the Eastern Church throughout the Middle Ages and figures such as John Damascene wrote about him as a monastic prototype.

21. Adso of Montier-en-Der, "Letter on the Origin and Time of the Antichrist," *Apocalptic Spirituality: Treatises and Letters of Lacatantius, Adso of Montier-en-Der, Joachim of Fiore, The Franciscan Spirituals, Savanarola*, Bernard McGinn, trans.; Classics of Western Spirituality (New York: Paulist, 1979) 94.

22. Robert A. Koch, "Elijah the Prophet, Founder of the Carmelite Order," *Speculum* 34 (1959) 551.

23. Unfortunately, several of these are nineteenth century replacements for the renaissance originals.

The Liberation Reading
of the Bible
in the Base Ecclesial Communities
in Brazil

Editors' note: This article was translated from Portuguese into English with the assistance of Luisa Maria Varela Almendra, a student at the Pontifical Biblical Institute in Rome.

The liberation interpretation of the Bible is a wellspring from which the people who live in base communities draw. They receive from the Bible strength and light that guides their lives, and through the Bible they come to a new experience of God and a new vision of the transforming and liberating action of the Gospel in their lives. I begin this article by describing a few significant realities which are drawn from daily life in Brazil, and then I will present some observations to clarify the meaning of these realities for the popular reading of the Bible that occurs within base communities.

I. Three Experiences that Illustrate the Situation in Which We Find Ourselves

A. Colombia

It happened during the first meeting of a Bible course. There were twenty-five people in the course and on the wall was written the phrase GOD IS LOVE. The priest who was teaching the course asked: "Who wrote that?" A lady answered: "I did!" The priest continued: "Why did you write that?" She replied: "I found the wall a bit empty." "Why did you choose this particular phrase?" he inquired. She answered: "I considered it very nice." "Where did you come up with this phrase?" She answered: "It was I who created it! This is what we must live as Christians!"

"Let us open our Bibles to 1 John 4:8," the priest continued. It took some time before everyone found the text. "Read it," he asked the woman. Taking up her Bible she proclaimed: "Whoever fails to love does not know God because GOD IS LOVE." This was the first time she had ever opened the Bible, and she remained surprised that, without having ever read this text, she had written the phrase on the wall. Not having studied the Word of God she had learned that it was already in her life. Overwhelmed by the experience, she had difficulty sleeping that night during which she found many other phrases that she knew. By the next day her Bible was stuffed with pieces of paper marking particular passages.

This simple event is meant to illustrate that the interpretation of the Bible occurs within Christian communities.

1. The Bible is accepted by the faithful as the Word of God. This faith already exists before they come to the Bible and on this faith they hang all that a teacher may have to say. Without the underpinning of faith, the process of biblical interpretation would be different.

2. It is by a process of ongoing discovery that people learn that the Word of God is not only in the Bible, but also in daily life. The purpose of reading the Bible is not only to interpret it, but also

to interpret daily life in light of the Bible. Then the community discovers that God continues to speak today through historical events.

3. The Bible comes not through the door of authority but through the door of personal and communal experience. It presents itself not as a book that imposes thoughts from above, but as the Good News that reveals the liberating presence of God in the life and the daily struggles of humanity. The Bible affirms human experience and action. It gives hope.

4. Until recent times the Bible was kept at a distance. Now it is near! And as the Word comes near, so also God comes near! What was mysterious and inaccessible has become part of the common life of the poor. Perhaps it is difficult for us to appreciate the new experience that the Bible offers to the poor.

B. The City of Nova Iguaçu in the State of Rio de Janeiro, Brazil

The title recalls a biblical meeting that was held in Brazil for Afro-Brazilians. It began by listening to the personal histories of two senior individuals, histories of suffering and discrimination. As they told their stories we recalled the history of black people in Brazil, a history of slavery and oppression. Then they asked how the traditional history of Brazil recounted their past. In the end they had two histories close in content, two histories of oppression and struggle for freedom. This was the first part.

In the second part, the group decided to consider the history of Israel and, in particular, the period spent by the Israelites in captivity in Babylon. The hope was that this event would illuminate their present captivity in Brazil in the twentieth century. Their study produced many discoveries. They identified strongly with the Suffering Servant of Lord about whom the prophet Isaiah had spoken (Isa 42:1-4; 49:1-6; 50:4-11; 52:13-53:12). As they read these texts they came to see their situation through other eyes.

My observations:

1. When people in base communities read the Bible, they bring with them their own history and the problems of their arduous life. The Bible becomes a mirror, a symbol (cf. Heb 11:19) of what they live each day. They discover a direct relationship between the Bible and their life following a method of reading the Bible similar to that done by the church fathers.

2. To develop this relationship between the Bible and life, it is important:

   a) to have in mind questions that emerge from the reality of life today and to avoid artificial questions that have nothing to do with the life of the people;

   b) to realize that we travel the same paths, yesterday and today;

   c) to view the Bible as connected with the real situation of the readers.

Reading the Bible in this way will provoke an interchangeable illumination between the Bible and life. The meaning of the Bible is revealed and is enriched when the Bible is read in light of what one lives and endures in life.

3. Through this new relationship between Bible and life, the poor come to the most important discovery: If God was with us in the past, then God is with us now in our struggle for freedom. Our outcry is heard.

C. The City of Cabedelo in the State of Paraiba, Brazil

The final celebration of this biblical meeting began with a reading of the story of the disciples of Emmaus. When we came to the passage: "... our own hope had been..." (Lk 24:13-24) we felt the urge to answer the pressing question: the cross killed the hope of the disciples: what is the cross that is killing our hope today?

As we continued reading we heard how Jesus interpreted the Scriptures for the two disciples (Lk 24:25-27). Then we divided into small groups of three: each group representing Christ with the two disciples. Each person was invited to share a moment in his or her life when a brother or a sister, with his or her word, had acted like Christ by making the heart burn.

After ten minutes, the groups gathered to hear how the disciples had arrived at Emmaus and how they had recognized Jesus in the breaking of the bread (Lk 24:28-32). Then in that place we celebrated the "breaking of the bread." After communion we read about the disciples returning to Jerusalem, where the forces of death, that had brought Jesus to the cross, continued to exist. But the two disciples had already gained victory by faith in the resurrection (Lk 24:33-35).

Some observations:

1. This experience reveals that, for proper biblical interpretation, it is very important to create a space of faith and fellowship with songs, prayers, and celebrations. In fact, without a context filled with the Spirit, it is not possible to discover the meaning a text has for us today, because the meaning of the Bible is not only an idea or message to be grasped by the mind, but also a feeling or a consolation that can only be understood with the heart.

2. Little by little a new interpretation and view of the Bible emerges. The Bible is not seen as a foreign book, but as our book, written for us, "those who are at the end of history..." (1 Cor 10:11).

3. Interpretation is an activity that involves not only an intellectual contribution of the biblical scholar, but also a process within the community: discussions in small groups, personal reading, theater, liturgy, prayer, and recreation. Interpretation is primarily an experience of commenting on the Scripture, an activity in which all can participate, each one according to his capacity, including the biblical scholar.

Conclusion:

There are many other examples but these three are sufficient to grasp that a new wind is blowing and that we find ourselves in a new situation. This method has developed over many years. Its seeds were planted in the '40's - '50's when the renewal first began. When we talk about a base "ecclesial" community, we are talking about a small group. In order to describe this method of biblical interpretation, it is necessary to present it systematically. We will see that it has two aspects: (1) the internal dynamics within this process and (2) the new possibility it offers.

II. The Internal Dynamics of the Process of Interpretation

A. Three Factors

Although many factors have contributed to the development of this method for reading the Bible in Brazil, I emphasize only the three most important.

1. The work of Juventude Operária Católica (Young Catholic Workers): a new way to understand revelation.

The method: perceiving, discerning, and acting. The method gradually leads to a new appreciation for perceiving and experiencing the action of God within history. At the outset people begin by trying to interpret what God is saying within their local situation and the problems that confront them. Then, with the help of biblical texts, they attempt to discern their situation. Gradually their talk about God comes not only from the Bible but from their lives, illuminated by the Bible. This provokes a move toward action in a new way.

2. The Second Vatican Council and *Dei Verbum*.

The conciliar document *Dei Verbum* opened the Church to a new way of perceiving God's action in history. God continues to speak today through historical events and persons, and we are able to discover their meaning with the assistance of the written Word of God which is our canon.

3. Military coup and the crisis in the Vanguard.

In Brazil in the early nineties the plight of the people was being totally neglected. By 1994, the military was no longer functioning effectively. The vanguard was in shock. There was a need for careful and patient work among the people, a work that would respect their culture and their way of life. The Church offered the only possibility for accomplishing this work free from political oppression. In 1968 renewal had begun at the very base of society and from there it moved into every community. People began to read the Bible. The most important factor was the action of the Holy Spirit working in and through these events. The Spirit acts in this local situation in Brazil, guiding it along: "Listen to what the Spirit says to the churches!"

B. Three Aspects

In these last few years three aspects within this process of interpretation have emerged. Each one has appeared in a sacred moment, one after the other. They represent the three objectives for interpreting the Bible among the people:

1. To know the Bible—to instruct.

The desire to know the Bible led many individuals to an enthusiastic and frequent reading of the Word of God. The renewal of exegesis, the encyclicals of Leo XIII, Benedict XV, and Pius XII, together with the work of biblical scholars, brought the Bible closer to the people. Moreover, in Brazil, what helped urge Catholics to a greater enthusiasm for the Bible was the missionary impulse of the Pentecostal Churches.

2. To create community—to celebrate.

Once the Word became known, it began to produce its fruits. The first fruit was the creation of community. Biblical study weeks done on a popular level, the diffusion of the Bible in different languages, the celebration of the Word, Bible courses, meetings, classes, Bible groups, the month of the Bible, all produced a new enthusiasm for the Word of God.

3. To serve the people—to transform.

From 1968 onward another stage emerged. The new enthusiasm for the Bible found its objective: the service of the people of God. Given that the poor had neither money nor time to read books about the Bible, they began to read the Bible through their own faith journey, a faith lived in a community well acquainted with suffering and oppression. This was the only experience they knew. In the Bible they discovered something they had not realized prior to this moment: it spoke of a history of oppression similar to their own experience; a history of a struggle for the same values that they hunger for today: land, justice, sharing, fellowship, and one life in common.

C. The Internal Dynamic

These three stages are also the three objectives of this method for interpreting the Bible. Among them exists an internal dynamic that marks the process of popular interpretation: to know the Bible leads one to live in community; to live in community leads one to serve the people; to serve the people provokes a desire for a deeper knowledge of the context from which the Bible emerged. The dynamic relationship among these three components has neither a beginning nor an end. Each component presupposes the others and leads into the others.

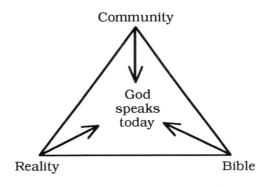

The position from which one begins interpreting the Bible is not important. The process depends on the historical situation, the culture, and the motives of the community. It is only important to understand that one aspect is incomplete without the other two.

In every community there are individuals who identify themselves with one of these three aspects:

- persons who want to know the Bible and are more concerned with study;
- persons who insist on community life and its internal function;
- persons who are concerned with serving the people and making their contribution to politics and popular movements.

These three persons produce a dynamic tension within community that is healthy and generative. For example, in some communities the intensive political experience of the last few years has required a deeper understanding of biblical texts and a more intensive experience of the spirituality of freedom. In other places, the experience of reading the Bible has required action that is more involved with popular movements. In other words, the tensions among these three elements of community life serve to develop a balance which sustains the interpretation of the Bible and prevents one element from dominating the community.

At times the tension can become a negative force and the process closes in on itself and the community begins to exclude others. This method of biblical interpretation among the people is sometimes tense and filled with conflict; it risks shutting out others and regressing to previously held positions.

D. The Danger of Shutting Out Others

When a community arrives at the goal of one of these three aspects (study of the Bible, community, service), some members, because of their fidelity to the Word, want to go farther while others, in the name of the same fidelity, refuse new openness. This division within the community is both a moment of crisis and a moment of grace and the side that desires to push ahead does not always prevail.

1. All pastoral movements turn to the Bible to support their position. Backed with biblical citations some fundamentalists refuse to be open to present historical reality. In some places biblical groups close in on themselves and on the words of the Bible. The biblical scholar can also endanger the free and progressive study of the biblical text with a closed approach to the Bible.

2. Many groups within the charismatic movement in Brazil close in on themselves, and they refuse to be open to the political situation. Though they are open to the service of the poor, their service does not lead to transformation and freedom.

3. The community can focus solely on service based upon a politics of conscience. Fearing that religiosity can be manipulated by the dominant ideology, it concludes that religious piety is not good for social transformation. Such a community is in danger of limiting itself to social and political transformation of the people.

This tendency to limit and close off the life of the community is tragic because none of the three elements referred to above reveals the meaning of the Bible by itself. To overcome this danger it is important to keep dialogue alive, because where the human word moves with freedom and without restrictions, the Word of God gives rise to freedom.

III. The New Possibilities and the Extent to Which "Popular" Biblical Interpretation Can Reach

Within the process of biblical interpretation done by the poor there exists a new possibility that is of importance for the life of the Church. This method is really an old tradition! The following seven points highlight the development of this tradition.

1. The objective of this method of interpretation is no longer to retrieve information about the past, but rather, to clarify the present in the light of the presence of God-with-us, the God of freedom. This involves interpreting life with the help of the Bible. It becomes possible to discover once again in human experience the new vision of revelation described and defined by the conciliar document *Dei Verbum*.

2. The task of interpretation is no longer the sole property of the biblical scholar. To interpret the Bible is an activity in which everybody can participate, including the biblical scholar, who, within this process, plays a vital role. Therefore, it is important for the biblical scholar to read the Bible with the eyes of faith within a vibrant community and to be an effective member of that community, searching the Bible within the community's shared reality. The biblical scholar's active membership in community influences the function of scholarly exegesis which is placed at the service of the community.

3. The social context in which biblical interpretation takes place is among the poor, the excluded, and the marginalized, and it is this context that shapes one's study of the Bible. Many times, because of a lack of social and critical thinking, interpreters become victims to ideological preconceptions, and, without being aware, they use the Bible to legitimize inhuman oppression.

4. A reading that generates a relationship between the Bible and life is ecumenical in nature and results in freedom. The ecumenical reading does not refer only to instances when those of different faiths discuss their different interpretations of a biblical text and come to a shared conclusion. Though this may be a consequence, it is, in fact, much deeper. The ecumenism we share must be based upon the life that God gives us. In Latin America, the life of one part of the population, the poor, is in danger; theirs is not life anymore. The ecumenical reading means interpreting the Bible through our common life and not through our institutions and ideas. At the present moment, in the situation in which Latin Americans find themselves, a reading in favor

of life must ground the yearning for freedom. This is why it is so contentious and a sign of contradiction.

5. This process distinguishes itself from European biblical scholarship. The major problem among us is not that faith is in danger of a growing secularization, but that life is in danger of being destroyed as it becomes more and more inhuman. The Bible is in danger of being used to legitimize this situation in the name of God, just as, in the time of the Kings of Judah and Israel, the tradition was used to legitimate idols. The popular interpretation discovers, reveals, and denounces any manipulation of God's Word.

6. The method and the process used by the poor in their meetings is very simple. They do not employ technical language supported by argumentation and logic. They prefer to tell their stories and to compare their situation with that of the Bible. The process functions through the association of ideas and its first aim is not to make known but to discover.

7. The function and limits of biblical interpretation are apparent: the Bible is not the end in itself, rather, it serves the interpretation of life. By itself the Bible cannot function, it cannot open our eyes, because that which opens our eyes is the breaking of bread, the sign of our community. The Bible must be interpreted within a wider process which does not forget the community and our social reality. The Bible is like the heart: removed from the body of the community and divorced from the life of the people it dies, it brings death!

IV. The Challenges that Reveal the Current Situation

A. The Feminist Reading

The feminist reading asks questions that reveal the masculine interpretation of the Bible in the past. This reading cannot be considered an unimportant phenomenon or an exegetical curiosity on the part of biblical scholars, because it is one of the more important characteristics emerging within the popular reading of the Bible. Its success is bigger than we think. In Brazil, this reading is of great importance because there are many enthusiastic women in biblical groups who support the struggle of the people in many places.

B. Fundamentalism is on the Rise

A two week meeting organized by CESEP in Goiânia (the capital of the state of Goiás) in January, 1991, involved more than six hundred participants including many young people from almost every state in Brazil. During the three years dedicated to the study of the Bible, the line of interpretation was clearly that of freedom. In talking with the participants, however, many times a different approach to the Bible emerged. There was the tendency, mainly among young people, to mix fundamentalism with the theology of liberation. How can this phenomenon be explained? From where does it come? Perhaps it is provoked by a deeper reality that is altering the unconsciousness of humanity. In fact, the danger of fundamentalism exists not only in Christian churches, but also in other religious traditions: Jewish, Muslim and Buddhist.

C. The Quest for a Spirituality within this Method of Interpretation

Now everywhere people are hearing and feeling a desire for a deeper reality, a mystical reality, a spiritual reality. The Word of God offers two valuable aspects: from one side it illuminates and clarifies ideas, revealing false ideologies and communicating a more critical consciousness. From the other side the Word of God brings strength, and in this sense it fills its readers with enthusiasm and it readies them to communicate with courage and happiness, because it offers a creative strength that produces something new and unexpected, and provokes us to love one another. Unfortunately, in pastoral work these two aspects sometimes are divided. On one side, there are charismatic movements and, on other side, there are the movements of liberation. The charismatic movement in Brazil multiplies prayers while missing the critical vision. They share with the fundamentalist interpretation an individualistic approach to the Bible. Such prayer groups need to familiarize themselves with the text and with the social context. Though the movements of liberation in Brazil have a deep critical conscience, sometimes they lack the perseverance of faith when confronting the human situation with their scientific analysis. This will not help transform society. Often they have difficulty understanding the purpose of praying without any immediate result.

D. The Culture of our People and the Old Testament

Upon hearing the Brazilian myth of Tucuman, which explains to the Indians of the Amazon region that the origin of evil in the world is not a woman's sin but a man's sin, someone asked: "Should we not use our myths instead of those of the Hebrew people?" No one answered. The same question was asked during a biblical course in Bolivia in May, 1991. The participants, who were almost all Aymaras (an indigenous people of Bolivia, descendants of the Icans), asked: "Why do we use only the Bible? Our stories are beautiful, less masculine and better known to our people?" In the Asian religions, traditions older than ours, the same questions arose some years ago. What is the value of our story and our culture? Our culture is not that of the Old Testament. However, the Old Testament, the history of the people of Israel, is the canon, the inspired norm, which helps us to interpret our situation and reveals to us a deeper dimension of our culture and history.

E. The Need to Create a Center for Bible Study in Latin America

The method of biblical interpretation within base communities is gradually growing. From the heart of this popular experience has sprouted a new approach to interpretation which is not new; in fact, it is quite old. It must be legitimized by the tradition of the Church and through exegetical scholarship. The reading done by the poor and from their situation has its own exigencies. As Bible reading develops, the need for scholarly knowledge about the Bible grows. There are many teachers who desire to know the languages of the Bible, and the economic, social, political and ideological context in which the Bible was born. They also want to bring to the Bible the questions that anguish people in their faith journey. As the number of priests continues to decrease and as the hope for a change in this situation fades, there is a desperate need for good Bible teachers who are able to respond to the needs of those in biblical formation and to confront the dangerous problem of fundamentalism. The experience of reading the Bible that occurs in the communities of Latin America has already had consequences for the Church and has provoked discussion in many places. There are many other exciting signs of increased Bible reading in Latin America. This is why it is important to create a center for biblical formation that is oriented toward the concrete problems experienced in our communities.

Carlos Mesters, O.Carm.

Prophecy as Charism

This essay from my doctoral dissertation concerns the role of prophecy in decision making. By extension, scholars of the post-Vatican II era have been called to use the charism of prophecy in opening up the riches of Scripture to all believers. Such a scholar has been my brother, Roland, who has stood strong and resolute in exploring the pages of that greatest of all books, the Bible.

Introduction

Increasingly the words prophet and prophetic appear in the literature of various disciplines. Claude Geffre[1] has written of prophetic theology; William Kuhns[2] and Arend van Leeuwen[3] have discussed the implications of prophecy and prophets in technocracy, the former from a philosophical, the latter from a biblical point of view. John C. Bennett[4] has compared prophetic ethics with the concept of grace. Harvey Cox[5] has seen the need of a new perspective in the future which he has deemed prophetic. Sister Marie Augusta Neal[6] has described the presence of prophecy and how it lives and functions from a sociological point of view. These are but a few among many modern writers who view the need of prophecy as an urgent necessity in our time.

It is not clear that these writers share a common meaning of prophecy and prophet. Because of increased usage, the validity of this term, as used by people who share in the Judaeo-Christian tradition, should be understood from the biblical setting in which it originally appeared. It is my intention to discuss the theological meaning of prophecy and to examine its historical presence in the Old Testament, New Testament, and modern times. Before an examination of the concept of prophecy in itself, however, an initial perspective is to be gained through an understanding of charism.

The Meaning of Charism

Charism, a specifically Pauline concept, is defined in its widest sense as "God's call to the individual person in view of a specific service within the community, including the ability to perform this service."[7] A list of these gifts, enumerated by Paul, is found in Rom 12:6-8: "We have gifts that differ according to the grace given to us: prophecy, in proportion to faith; ministry, in ministering; the teacher, in teaching; the exhorter, in exhortation; the giver, in generosity; the leader, in diligence; the compassionate, in cheerfulness."

Hans Küng adds that charisma, call and service are all related. From 1 Cor 12:4-6 ("Now there are varieties of gifts, but the same Spirit; and there are varieties of services, but the same Lord; and there are varieties of activities, but it is the same God who activates all of them in everyone") it is clear that charisms and services are interchangeable. Rom 11:29 ("the gifts and the calling of God are irrevocable") stresses the same idea.

From Scripture it is clear that charisms are granted to individuals and communities:

> 1 Cor 12:7 "To each is given the manifestation of the Spirit for the common good."
>
> 1 Thess 5:12 "Respect those who labor among you, and have charge of you in the Lord and admonish you."

It may also be deduced that charism should be considered as a common phenomenon with diverse expressions and not the prerogative of a special few. Küng elaborates:

> If by charisma we mean this, and do not see it simply as some rare ability to perform something extraordinary and wonderful, we may also translate charisma briefly with 'gift of grace' (the individual has received this gift and this call: even in secular language these two words almost cover each other).[8]

One of the essential qualities of a charism is that it is relational, that is, it is not isolated from or peripheral to the core of the person who receives it. A charism is understood only within a context, namely, the charisma itself, the person receiving it, and the purpose of the charism. Thus the charism of teaching, the teacher, and the importance of the message from the church are clearly interrelated.[9]

Charisms exist for a purpose outside of themselves, even beyond the perimeters of the community in which they are found. They represent the various ways in which the Spirit functions within the community for the community's service to the world. The real value of a charism, Koupal adds, "does not exist in the community as such."[10] Thus charisms are not to be equated with or compared with one another in the sense of one being greater than another. "For charisms do not relate to each other but to the community as a composite whole. Therefore the individual gift does not have value in itself, but in what it serves a community which through the Spirit is itself in service to the divine plan of salvation."[11]

Hans Küng[12] introduces three questions and answers which clarify the role and character of charisms:

1. Is the charism an extraordinary or ordinary phenomenon? While acknowledging the pres-

ence of exceptional charisms, Küng states that "charismata are therefore in no way limited to the extraordinary: they are rather altogether ordinary phenomena in the life of the church. We should strive after the greater charismata. But these greater charismata are precisely not the exceptional ones like speaking with tongues, but the ordinary ones."

2. Is there more than one kind of charism? Paul, in 1 Cor 12:11 ("All these are activated by one and the same Spirit, who allots to each one individually just as the Spirit chooses") affirms a diversity of charismata as given to the faithful through the action of the Holy Spirit.

3. Are these charismata only given to some individuals or to all? Paul, in 1 Cor 12:7, writes: "To each is given the manifestation of the Spirit for the common good." This would substantiate what Cardinal Suenens has said: "Each and every Christian, whether lettered or unlettered, has his charism in his daily life. . . ."[13]

Thus, it is fair to state with Küng that charisms are not primarily extraordinary but common, of many kinds and open to all individuals. Küng then goes on to add: "All this implies that they are not a thing of the past but eminently contemporary and actual; they do not hover on the periphery of the church but are eminently central and essential to it."[14]

William Koupal has written that there has as yet been no in-depth study by theologians of the subject of charisms and finds this to be disturbing at a time when ecclesiology has assumed such importance. Charisms have either been dealt with in isolated fashion or as no longer necessary as they once were for the building up of the church.[15]

Prophecy - A Charism

Within this understanding of charism which is the product of modern-day theological reflection, it is necessary to determine the meaning of prophecy for present times. The appearance of prophecy from the times of Elijah and Jeremiah to the twentieth-century figures to whom the term prophet has been applied will be considered under the headings of Theology, Old Testament, New Testament, and Vatican II documents. The purpose of these divisions is to determine if there is a thread of continuity in the designation of people as prophets and to interpret the appearance of prophetic characteristics as they merge in history and especially for their present implications. The goal is to establish the characteristics proper to the prophetic message. This does not mean that the person of the prophet or the concept of prophetism is being passed over. As stated previously, the person, the charism, and the message cannot be separated, for their interrelation is essential for the appearance and effectiveness of the prophetic word. In addition, this will deal mainly with the history and understanding of prophecy as it is found in the Catholic Church.[16]

Theology of Prophecy

Karl Rahner states that "in contrast to medieval theology, the present-day theology of the schools pays relatively scant attention to prophetism."[17] A summary of Thomas Aquinas' theology of prophecy is presented to indicate the type of thinking that marked medieval thought and to provide a basis for the reflections of Avery Dulles and Hans Küng on this question. By prophecy, Thomas understands: "essentially knowledge, supernaturally given to man, of truths exceeding the present reach of his mind, which God teaches him for the benefit of his community."[18] He describes it as a social charism which is meant for the good of the community, and as a charism of knowledge which involves both words and actions on the part of the recipient. Consequent to this, the will of the person is involved in order that the received message be transmitted to others. When the question is proposed: "Is there prophecy in a charism which merely illuminates human and everyday truths with divine charity?,"[19] Thomas answers affirmatively and designates this as "prophetia intellectualis" under the heading of "prophetica revelatio" but states that it is inferior because it does not contain a vision. He admits that there are inspired persons and refers to them as hagiographers to distinguish them from true prophets, though he admits they approach the status of the latter. Thomas' discussion of this matter is both complex and obscure for he later admits that it is not necessary for the prophet to be aware of his gift. Further, he states that in prophecy there are grades according to which it is more or less perfect. This widely depends on whether the prophet is aware or unaware of the charism and on whether the prophecy is accompanied or unaccompanied by representations. It also depends on the type of vision involved: intellectual, imaginary or sensory.

In commenting on Thomas' treatment of prophecy Avery Dulles[20] notes that Aquinas was concerned largely with prophecy as a supernatural mode of knowledge and as a means by which the deposit of faith was built up in biblical times. He assigns three reasons for the lack of a more modern interpretation by Aquinas: "the sharp dichotomy between the speculative and practical intellect, inadequate realization of the importance of post-biblical history and a spirituality that was geared to man's hope for eternal life hereafter."[21] It was in apparent defense of the meaning of the close of revelation that Thomas made a very careful distinction: the mission of prophecy is two-fold: it is sent to establish the faith and to correct morals; but (today) the faith has already been founded, for the promises were fulfilled by Christ. But for that which is concerned with correcting morals, prophecy never has, never will be lacking.[22]

In commenting on 1 Cor 14:29-30, Laurent Volken admits of the same distinction:

To prophesy did not necessarily mean to reveal; however, to communicate revelations apparently was an act which expressed the highest sense of the prophetic function. The following practice imposed by Paul, proves this: "Let no more than two or three prophets speak, and let the rest judge the worth of what they say. If another sitting by, should happen to receive a revelation, the first ones should then keep quiet."[23]

It may be concluded from Thomas' treatment that prophecy allows for degrees of understanding and application from the circumstances involved, the personality of the participant and the degree of perception.

Prophecy in the Old Testament: Moses to the Classical Prophets

The term under which prophet and prophetic are included is prophetism, broadly defined as "that understanding of history which accepts meaning only in terms of divine concern, divine purpose, divine participation."[24] More specifically, prophetism is defined as:

peculiarly the function of a concentrated succession of men—notably, Amos, Hosea, Isaiah, Micah, Jeremiah, Ezekiel, Second Isaiah—appearing in a brief span of about two centuries, preceded by a hundred years or more and even anticipated by the marvelously vigorous prophet Elijah, and followed and at once recalled by a fading succession of lesser lights.[25]

Both the wide and narrow definitions are acceptable in the sense that the persons designated as prophets in each case are shown in various ways to have a common understanding of God's intervention in history and were at once the instruments and preservers of divine revelation. This also distinguishes them from various other forms of prophecy (e.g., ecstatic and predictive) which were prevalent in the religions of peoples about them. While the prophets shared many of the characteristics of other religious prophets, the differentiating element was their comprehension of history, their particular understanding of God's revelation among humankind.

One difficulty with the definition is that, in referring to the writing prophets, it omits the broader picture of disciples and lesser prophets who were instrumental in the oral transmission of their message. Prophecy was associated not just with the outstanding figures in the Old Testament. The prophets were the recipients of an essential prophetism, "a core tradition of Yahwism maintained in an unbroken but fluid continuum from Moses to Malachi, and the expression of the centrally and characteristically prophetic bent of mind long in advance of and in necessary preparation for the emergence of classical prophetism."[26]

In turn, what the writing prophets clarified and developed became part of the history of the Jewish people even when there was a decline in prophetic figures as in the post-exilic centuries.

Hence, essential to all prophetism in the Old Testament and a point which is beyond dispute among all biblical scholars is that:

> the prophetic (be it invective or judgment, assur-
> ance or promise, cry of anguish or confession,
> symbolic act or relationship, or whatever), the
> characteristically prophetic phenomenon, always
> presupposes (consciously or unconsciously, made
> explicit or taken for granted, immediately relevant
> or only of indirect, ultimate pertinence) the deci-
> sive impingement of Yahweh upon history. Where
> this sense of effective relationship of Yahweh to
> history is absent, prophetism is also absent.[27]

Prophecy in the New Testament: The Apostolic Church

Differences must be noted in the treatment of prophecy between the Old Testament and the New Testament. First, the New Testament tends to describe prophecy in terms of the function it has for the new Christian communities: "Pursue love and strive for the spiritual gifts, and especially that you may prophesy" (1 Cor 14:1). In *The Jerome Biblical Commentary* (first edition), it is stated concerning this verse: "Prophecy, which is a divinely inspired message of exhortation, warning, comfort, or correction, is the best of the charisms because it contributes most to the 'building up' of the church."[28] This represents essentially the understanding of prophecy in the New Testament. Few prophets are named as such and the presumption from the readings is that there are prophets to be found in each community: "Let two or three prophets speak, and let the others weigh what is said.... For you can all prophesy one by one, so that all may learn and all be encouraged" (1 Cor. 14:29,31). Thus, where the name and message of the prophets of the Old Testament were so strongly represented as to be ultimately included in the canon of Scripture, there are no prophetic books of the New Testament, and it is simply assumed that prophecy is one of the gifts of the Spirit given to the early church.

There is an implicit understanding in the New Testament that revelation has culminated in the person of Jesus Christ, that all of the predictions and promises of the Old Testament prophets have been fulfilled in Him. Therefore, while prophets remain, they will appear somewhat differently than the portrayal of those in the Old Testament. In distinguishing prophets respectively from apostles, evangelists, teachers, and ecstatics, Avery Dulles states that prophets

> give more particular admonitions on the basis of what the Spirit teaches them. . .proclaim not the basic news of God's salvific deed in Christ, but its further implications for life and conduct. . . are

concerned with urging, on the basis of an inspired
insight, the course to be taken in the present
concrete situation...speak with full self-possession
in a language that all men can understand.[29]

New Testament prophecy is concerned chiefly with preaching about religious matters, and "unlike its Old Testament counterpart it often connotes not only the communication of God's message to men but also the prediction of the future."[30] These are, however, not qualitative differences. Though there are few details about the life, experiences, and sayings of the New Testament prophets,[31] their function was the same as the Old Testament prophets: "one may conclude that the New Testament concept of prophet carries on that of the Old Testament."[32]

The post-apostolic church witnessed the endurance of prophecy until the rise of Montanism in the latter part of the second century with its undue emphasis on prophetic gifts, ecstatic states, and heretical beliefs.[33] Concurrent with this was the growth of the church as an institution with its attention to law and the magisterium which led to "fuller control of the ministry of the Word. This trend continued in the Middle Ages."[34] From the time of the Reformation, prophecy in the Catholic tradition declined further to the point of its being relegated to the position of an extrinsic sign, i.e., as validating by prediction what someone claiming to speak in God's name was saying. The Protestant emphasis on the Word as against the Catholic emphasis on sacraments contributed to this condition. A perusal of the theological manuals shows that prophecy has never been treated as a separate tract: "parts of it are scattered in fundamental, dogmatic, biblical and mystical theology, as well as elsewhere."[35]

Prophecy in Present Times

The increased usage of the words prophet and prophetic in modern writings has already been noted. *Concilium*, a theological series in the age of renewal, has devoted a volume under the title of church history to the *Prophets in the Church.*[36] Various articles deal with St. Francis of Assisi, St. Ignatius of Loyola and such figures, noting that these saints are considered more as reformers than prophets. Avery Dulles suggests that "the mere mention of Bernard of Clarivaux, Francis of Assisi, and Catherine of Siena should suffice to prove prophetism remained in lively tension with sacerdotalism throughout the Middle Ages."[37] After citing a number of people who ended up as heretics or martyrs, Dulles confirms that the church historically was less than receptive to prophetic figures. However, Dulles looks to a rehabilitation of prophecy in the present day and finds initial encouragement in Vatican II documents. In *The Dogmatic Constitution on the Church,* it is stated: "The holy People of God share also in Christ's prophetic office. It spreads abroad a living witness to Him, especially by means of a life of faith and charity and by offering to God a sacrifice of praise...;"[38] "Again, that the laity, by their very vocation, seek the Kingdom of God by engaging in temporal affairs and by ordering them all to the plan of God;"[39] "And that Christ, the great prophet....continually fulfills His prophetic office until His full glory is reached. He does this, not only through the hierarchy. . ..but also through the laity."[40]

These statements, Dulles admits, reflect only dimly the vigor and strength shown by the Old Testament prophets. While the documents acknowledge the presence of prophecy today, there is no attempt to spell out what prophecy would look like or how living a life of Christian witness is a sharing of the prophetic office of Christ. The *Decree on Ecumenism*[41] and *Pastoral Constitution on the Church in the Modern World,*[42] without any specific mention of prophecy, do provide for two important elements of prophecy: the freedom to criticize within the church,[43] and the presuppositions that the Church is led by the spirit of God and that God shows His presence and purpose in the events of today.[44]

In *Visions and Prophecies,* Karl Rahner concedes that, while prophecy today will tell us nothing essentially new beyond the Scripture perspective and interpretation of the future, it will contain a concrete imperative "for a future which always remains dark and threatening." Further, he sets up criteria by which the good in every prophecy can be shown: if it awakens us to the gravity of decision in courageous faith, if it fills us with confidence in the one Lord of the still secret future, if it brings us to prayer, to conversion of heart, and to faith that nothing shall separate us from the love of God.[45]

This historical presentation of the meaning and history of prophecy does not offer an incisive answer to the problem posed earlier regarding the use of the words prophet and prophetic. Yet, the presence of prophets today is being called for by leaders of the church. Cardinal Suenens has written:

> It was not in past ages alone, not only in the time
> of St. Thomas Aquinas or St. Francis of Assisi that
> the Church was in need of the charisma of teach-
> ers and prophets and other ministries: she needs
> them today as well and needs them in her ordinary
> everyday life.[46]

It is my contention that the variety of prophet and prophetic in modern times is contained within the biblical understanding of what prophets are. That there are certain characteristics or qualities shared by the prophets despite the difference of personalities, times, circumstances, and problems involved. That the possession of these qualities indicate the true prophet or, at least, the dimension[47] out of which such figures work.

One biblical scholar who has concerned himself with this problem is W. Sibley Towner. Concerned with the loose use of these words, he elicited from various church groups the names of people considered as prophetic voices today: Malcolm X, Saul Alinsky, James Groppi, Daniel Berrigan, Pope John XXIII, The Beatles, Norman Thomas, and Eugene McCarthy. He further admitted that they exhibit some common characteristics: "They have style; they have a message which they present with passion, they run against the stream at some risk to themselves."[48]

Concerning these spokespersons the question arises: "whose words are they speaking?" This represents the crucial point in Towner's mind for the correct use of the word prophet in designating modern figures: "We are concerned with the application of the biblical title prophet to contemporary spokesmen because the implication of that title is, the words these men are speaking are as the word of God for us.[49]

Towner suggests the following question be asked when the designation of prophet is given to a modern figure:

> Are you using this term in any way similar to the way in which the religious tradition uses it? If so, what is the precise nature of that continuity which you see between the biblical prophets and the speaking and acting of a man today which warrants your designation of the latter as a prophet? Are you claiming such authority for his 'prophetic' words that those words should become guidelines for our own speaking and acting?[50]

Underlying the use of the word prophet as applied to divergent modern figures and the questions of Towner is the presumption that an analogy exists between the term prophet as understood in the Old Testament and the manner in which it is employed today. Because this is a question of a hermeneutical analogy between an Old Testament concept and a present day concept, Towner argues that it is the province of the biblical scholar to set up the historical side of this analogy so that it may act as a standard or norm by which modern users may judge their understanding of the term. The meaning of the word and its use in tradition are to be kept clear so that there is no doubt as to what is meant when applied to a quality of a person.

Before listing the identifying characteristics of Old Testament prophetism, Towner states:

> I proceed upon the assumption that valid analogies between biblical situations and modern ones can be drawn; that biblical and traditional language can appropriately be used at such points; that certain persons might therefore legitimately be called prophets today.[51]

He considers this exercise to be essential for the preservation of the word as it is used in political and social-ethic discussions today. These identifying characteristics are described in terms of style, rhetoric, constituencies and message:[52]

Style:	While the prophets proposed their message with a certain flamboyancy and, at times, ecstatic behavior, it is relevant only to the importance and seriousness of their message.
Rhetoric:	The prophets drew upon the cultural background and familiar ways of speaking to express themselves, always, however, realizing that it was not their word as such, but that of God.
Constituencies:	The prophets spoke to and for the particular groups that were their responsibility.
Message:	Towner describes this as the most characteristic of the Old Testament prophets. He lists four consistent themes which prevailed through prophetic thought and writing:

a. the call for justice for the politically weak, the powerless, the economically outcast.

  b. the indictment of corruption in circles of power.

  c. the purification of the religious establishment.

  d. the hope for redemption and peace.

Further, all these themes are based on a religious understanding which is asserted or grounded on the fact "that God is, that he is good, that he loves all his people, that he redeems all of his world, that he has a kingdom to which these kingdoms are being and will be conformed, that he summons us into that future."[53]

Agreeing with Towner, I do not feel that style, rhetoric and constituencies are as important as the message of the prophets. These three categories relate more to the cultural and historical circumstances of their prophetic action. The need today is to find in the prophetic message those qualities which identified a person as speaking for God or, more basically, the dimension from which prophets were able to arise.

David J. Murphy, O.Carm.

Endnotes

1. Claude Geffre, *A Prophetic Theology*, Concilium 96 (1974) 7-16.
2. William Kuhns, *The Post Industrial Prophets* (New York: Weybright & Talley, 1971).
3. Arend van Leeuwen, *Prophecy in a Technocratic Era* (New York: Scribner, 1968).
4. John C. Bennett, *The Radical Imperative* (Philadelphia: Westminster Press, 1975) 82.
5. Harvey Cox, "Tradition and the Future," I & II, *Christianity & Crisis* 27 (1967-68) 218-20, 227-231.
6. Marie Augusta Neal, "How Prophecy Lives," *Sociological Analysis* 33 (1972-73) 125-141.
7. Hans Küng, *The Charismatic Structure of the Church*, Concilium 4 (1965) 41-61.
8. Ibid., 59.
9. Ibid.
10. William Koupal, "Charism: A Relational Concept," *Worship* 42 (1968) 543.
11. Ibid.
12. Hans Küng, 50-58
13. Hans Küng, Yves Congar, D. O'Hanlon, eds. *Council Speeches of Vatican II* (New York: Paulist, 1964) 31.
14. Hans Küng, 58.
15. William Koupal, 539.
16. The stronger presence and persistence of prophecy is acknowledged in Protestant sects. However, the emphasis in my larger study on Catholic executives precludes a detailed study of the historical reasons.
17. Karl Rahner, *Sacramentum Mundi*, 5 (New York: Herder & Herder, 1970) 112.
18. Paul Synave and Pierre Benoit, *Prophecy and Tradition* (New York: Desclée 1961) 61.
19. Ibid., 67.

20. Avery Dulles, *The Survival of Dogma* (New York: Doubleday 1971) 128.

21. B. D. Napier, "Prophet, Prophetism," *The Interpreter's Dictionary of the Bible* 3 (New York: Abington, 1962) 896.

22. Thomas Aquinas, *Summa Theologiae*, 2-2, 172, 4.

23. Laurent Volken, *Visions, Revelations and the Church* (New York: P. J. Kenedy, 1961) 36.

24. Napier, 896.

25. Ibid., 905.

26. Ibid.

27. Ibid.

28. *The Jerome Biblical Commentary*, R. Brown, J. Fitzmyer, R. Murphy, eds. (Englewood Cliffs, N. J.: Prentice-Hall, 1968) 2:272.

29. Dulles, 126.

30. *The Jerome Biblical Commentary*, 2:325.

31. *The Fathers of the Church: The Apostolic Fathers*, F. Glimm, J. Marique, G. Walsh, trans. (New York: Cima, 1947) 171-184. The Didache mentions only that prophets are to be received by communities and how true prophets may be distinguished from false.

32. *New Catholic Encyclopedia* (New York: McGraw-Hill, 1967) 11:867.

33. Ronald Knox, *Enthusiasm* (Oxford: University Press, 1950). Under the heading of enthusiasm, Knox describes the excesses that have occurred in misunderstandings of the work of the Spirit throughout the centuries. The Montanist challenge is described on pp. 24-49.

34. Dulles, 128.

35. *New Catholic Encyclopedia*, 11:861.

36. "Prophets in the Church," Concilium 37 (New York: Paulist Press, 1968).

37. Dulles, 128.

38. *The Documents of Vatican II*, Walter Abbott and Joseph Gallagher, eds. (New York: Guild Press, 1966) 29.

39. Ibid., 57.

40. Ibid., 61.
41. Ibid., 341-66.
42. Ibid., 199-308.
43. Ibid., 349-50.
44. Ibid., 209.
45. Karl Rahner, *Visions and Prophecies* (New York: Herder & Herder, 1963) 106.
46. Küng, Congar, O'Hanlon, 32.
47. The concept of dimension is introduced here for the first time. The definition of dimension used in this essay is: one of the constitutive elements of a thing having its own particular set of circumstances or environmental factors within which promise of something exists or reference by which something is viewed.
48. W. Sibley Towner, "On Calling People 'Prophets' in 1970," *Interpretation* 24:494.
49. Ibid., 494.
50. Ibid., 495.
51. Ibid., 496.
52. The descriptions that follow represent the main thrust of each characteristic (Towner, pp. 497-509). The presentation of these characteristics are in summary form. Other authors present somewhat different prophetic traits, cf. Daniel D. Williams, "Priest, Prophets, and the Establishment," *Zygon* 2 (1967) 309-330; Howard L. Parsons, "The Prophetic Mission of Karl Marx," *Journal of Religion* 44 (1964) 52-72. Towner's perspective is that of the biblicist and the most valid as a true analogue.
53. Towner, 509.

Saint Thérèse of Lisieux
and Scripture

Sacred Scripture as the Word of God has always maintained a foundational, normative and formational role in the Church and for Christians. The Catholic Church's relationship to God's Word has a rich history reaching back to the spiritual and symbolic interpretations of early Christian writers and to the more contemporary scholarly exegesis based upon literary, textual and historical criticism and analysis. The church's magisterium moved gradually into a full acceptance of the role of biblical criticism and by the mid-twentieth century officially recognized the new efforts in reading and understanding the Scriptures. Vatican II's Constitution on Divine Revelation accentuated with new vigor the role of Scripture in the life of the Church. *Dei Verbum* recognized that Scripture serves the Christian community in authentic discipleship of Jesus Christ. More specifically, the Council noted that "prayer should accompany the reading of sacred Scripture, so that a dialogue takes place" between God and us.[1] The Holy Spirit attends God's Word and inspires the life of grace in the midst of the community of disciples of Jesus Christ.

More recently the Pontifical Biblical Commission offered an important statement on *The Interpretation of the Bible in the Church.*[2] The document, which appeared in November, 1993, proposes a nuanced set of observations regarding the use of Scripture in view of contemporary biblical scholarship. The document includes a section on actualization, which is a new concept coming from the Pontifical Biblical Commission. Actualization, which builds upon the *literal* sense of a passage, i.e., the sense intended by the human author, simply underscores that the scriptural text needs to be read again in "the light of new circumstances and applied to the contemporary situation of the people of God."[3] The document of the Biblical Commission states that "actualization is possible because the richness of meaning contained in the biblical text gives it a value for all time and cultures (cf. Isa 40:8; 66:18-21; Mt 28:19-20)."[4] In other words, one is to hear the Word of God within the context of one's concrete situation, to identify how the Word of God serves to comfort or to challenge one's life and to draw from the biblical text whatever will advance one's journey of faith according to God's saving will in Christ.[5] "Actualizing God's Word" includes *lectio divina* as well as personal and communal discernment before the biblical Word.

Vatican II's focus upon the centrality of Scripture in the life of the faithful as well as the recent endorsement of actualization by the Pontifical Biblical Commission affirm Thérèse of Lisieux's relationship to the Word of God within the context of her own time. Her autobiography, *The Story of A Soul*, indicates the central role of Scripture in nourishing her faith life in the midst of aridity. She wrote: "...it is especially the *Gospels* which sustain me during my hours of prayer, for in them I find what is necessary for my poor little soul. I am constantly discovering in them new lights, hidden and mysterious meanings."[6] Anyone familiar with her autobiography and her letters recognizes that Scripture permeates her writings. Not only does she offer many direct quotes but many indirect ones as well. For the sake of statistics Pascal-Marie Jerumanis has counted 420 direct or indirect references to the Old Testament and 658 such citations from the New Testament in the writings of Saint Thérèse.[7] More importantly, however, Scripture was her direct contact with God and God's Word. As von Balthasar noted in his study of Thérèse: "She plays about with the words of Scripture like a child who knows that they all belong to her, so that she can select the ones she pleases. There is a sort of naiveté about her conviction that Scripture is there for her service."[8]

Of course in the Carmelite tradition Saint Thérèse is not alone in reflecting a lively engagement with the Word of God. Teresa of Avila, John of the Cross, John of Saint Samson and other Carmelite spiritual writers through the ages have taken Scripture as a guide and a norm in discerning an authentic following of Jesus Christ. Scripture generates a world of encounter with Christ.

This study reflects on Thérèse's use of Scripture. It focuses upon three aspects of her relationship to God's Word. First, the essay offers a review of those resources which enabled Thérèse to encounter the scriptural Word. Secondly, the study will demonstrate ways in which Scripture served Thérèse's own faith. Thirdly, this article indicates some of the ways that Thérèse used Scripture in providing guidance and direction to others. A conclusion offers a summary of the study and provides some evaluation of the role of Scripture in Thérèse's life.

Thérèse's Scriptural Resources

A careful study of Thérèse's use of scriptural texts appeared in 1979, the work of Sr. Cecile, a nun from the Carmel of Lisieux and Sr. Geneviève, O.P., of the monastery of Clairfontaine.[9] The book, contains an engaging introduction by Carmelite Bishop Guy Gaucher, O.C.D., in which he notes Thérèse's concern for accuracy in translating the biblical Word. Thérèse was disturbed by varieties in translation and perhaps this prompted her to say that had she been a priest she would have learned Hebrew and Greek in order to have a better grasp of the root meaning of scriptural words.

In the latter half of the nineteenth century a Carmelite monastery did not have the benefit of biblical commentaries and scholarly publications. In fact, very few nuns had a copy of the complete Bible in their cells; only the New Testament seemed to be in general usage. This situation raises the question of the resources available to Thérèse for her own appropriation of the scriptural Word.

Each nun had one hour every day for reading, study or personal prayer. This hour could be given to scriptural reading and reflection. Any member of the community could obtain permission to have a copy of the complete Bible or could borrow one from the library. Thomas Bird, who has written about Thérèse's use of Scripture,[10] once wrote to the Carmel of Lisieux in order to ascertain whether Thérèse might have had a copy of the complete Bible at her disposal. The brief reply from the Carmel indicated that such was probably the case. The note added that Thérèse frequently used her personal hour to dwell with the scriptural Word. I think that further verification of Thérèse's access to a complete Bible comes through in the plays she wrote in which scriptural passages frequently appear and sometimes as many as four to five verses of a chapter are quoted.

The liturgy offered her a primary context for encountering the Word of God. The readings from Scripture at the Eucharist as well as the Psalms recited each day from the breviary offered her access to the revelation of God's love and mercy. While the breviary was in Latin, translations of the Psalms were available. It is important above all to note that Thérèse had an engaging relationship with God's Word. Scripture helped to shape her self-awareness and her faith responses in personal and communal life. As Thérèse wrote in a letter to Céline on July 7, 1894, beginning with a quote from Jn 14:23: "'If anyone loves me, he will keep my word, and my Father will love him, and we will come to him, and we will make in him our abode.' To keep the word of Jesus, that is the sole condition of our happiness, the proof of our love for him...."[11] As a youngster at Les Buissonnets, the family home in Lisieux, Thérèse became familiar with the volumes on the liturgical year by Dom Guéranger. These books (nine of eleven volumes were published in Thérèse's time) brought the Scriptures to bear on the liturgical seasons and feasts. Besides her reading of John of the Cross and her familiarity with a volume containing the New Testament and the Psalms entitled *Manuel du Chrétien*, Thérèse had memorized the *Imitation of Christ*, which was laden with scriptural passages. She had read l'abbé Blaise Arminjon's *Fin du Monde Present et Mystères de la vie Future*,[12] which also was replete with quotations from Scripture. There exists a note-book in which Céline had copied passages mainly from the Old Testament to present as a gift to Thérèse. Finally, a translation of the Old Testament from the Latin Vulgate by Le Maistre de Saci (Paris: 1844) was also available to her. But it lacked Tobit, Judith, Wisdom, Ecclesiastes, Baruch and Maccabees.

Contrary to much of the conventional opinion, I suggest that Thérèse had a rather liberal access to scriptural readings. She internalized and made her own what she read and also she went to the sacred text to find verification for her own religious experience. The following three sections will review how Scripture engaged Thérèse's life both in relationship to herself and in her relationship to others.

Scripture as Guide

Scripture entered into her personal life primarily in two ways: 1. There are passages which *guided or informed* her understanding of the life of faith, hope and charity and 2. There are passages which *affirmed or confirmed* Thérèse's own convic-tions about who God is and her relationship to God in Jesus Christ. For example, the so-called "little way" of the spiritual life in Thérèse springs from biblical sources. The distinction between scriptural passages which *guided* her and those which *confirmed* her experience cannot be rigidly conceived because there exists such an integral relationship between the Word of God and her faith development. She consistently verifies or challenges her life situation in view of the biblical Word.

Thérèse in her *Story of a Soul* (manuscript C) notes that people in the world generally look for wisdom in people who are older. After all, they have the wisdom of experience. Thérèse is quick to point out that wisdom can also be found among the young. She uses Scripture as her point of reference and tells the story of King David, who claimed that he was despised in his youth, yet proclaims in Ps 118:100: "I understand," and further in verse 105: "Your word is a lamp to my feet, and a light to my path." Thérèse views her own experience within the context of this story when she writes to Mother Marie de Gonzague: "Why weren't you put off by my youth and inexperience? I suppose you remembered that God does sometimes see fit to bestow wisdom on the least of us, and that Jesus did once...thank his heavenly Father for keeping his secrets hidden from the prudent, and revealing them to little children."[13] Thus Thérèse is confident enough to recognize that her experience of God's Word rings true and offers some wisdom.

It is important to note that Thérèse had difficulty internal-izing some aspects of the French religious culture of her time as practiced in the convents of religious. She could not measure up to some of the more rigorous forms of mortification, e.g., wearing an iron cross with sharp edges. The prevailing image of God as judge, while certainly having a place in Scripture, seemed to Thérèse more in tune with a law of fear[14] than with the new covenant law of love. She wished to celebrate the God of mercy and of love. As she wrote in her autobiography (manuscript A): "To me the Lord has always been 'merciful and good, slow to anger and abounding in steadfast love.'"[15] She transcended the limits of her milieu by focusing upon love as central to the experience of God in Jesus Christ and by developing her so-called "little way" as both foundational in relationship to God and as a more palpable and engaging form of response to God's call.

Because she felt unable to do "great things" for God, whether in the form of mortifications or heroic deeds, she found the image of the child suitable for herself. Obviously it was not to escape from the discipline involved in discipleship of Jesus Christ that she chose the symbol of the child, but rather to underscore that holiness of life springs from the gracious gift of God's action in our lives. More specifically, she was taken with the image of the child who runs to her parents' arms after having committed her last blunder. In like manner the image of the little flower portrays the same sense of being small and rather hidden, but she notes that the little flower gives glory to God by its very material presence in nature. Again Thérèse writes (manuscript A): "The flower about to tell her story [namely, Thérèse herself] rejoices at having to publish the totally gratuitous gifts of Jesus. She knows that nothing in herself was capable of attracting the divine glances, and His mercy alone brought about everything that is good in her."[16]

She was guided in her portrayal of the child and littleness by a number of passages in Scripture. Surprisingly, Matthew 18:3-4 which speaks of becoming a child in order to enter the kingdom of heaven is never directly quoted in the Thérèsian corpus. Rather she chooses to work from the Old Testament. Three quotations in particular appealed to her: "Whoever is a little one, let him come to me" (Prov 9:4); "For the lowly may be pardoned out of mercy, but the mighty shall be mightily put to the test" (Wis 6:6) and: "As nurslings you shall be carried in her arms, and fondled in her lap; As a mother comforts her son so will I comfort you" (Isa 66:12-13). Some of the Psalms also fed her imagination: "The declaration of your words gives light and understanding to little ones" (Ps 119:130) and "The Lord is the keeper of little ones" (Ps 116:6). These passages gave shape and direction to the "little way." Thérèse's way is fundamentally a way of commitment, fortitude, fidelity, creativity and profound love.

At times Thérèse's writing style can obscure the bedrock of personal religious experience upon which her images depend. Thus one needs to be attentive to what Thérèse is communicating through her literary devices. For example, the "little way," grounded in Scripture, is reflected in the following passage (manuscript B): "O Jesus, Your *little bird* is happy to be *weak and little*. What would become of it if it were big? Never would it have the boldness to appear in Your presence, *to fall asleep* in front of You. Yes, this is still one of the weaknesses of the little bird: when it wants to fix its gaze upon the Divine Sun, and when the clouds prevent it from seeing a single ray of that Sun, in spite of itself, its little eyes close, its little head is hidden beneath its wing, and the poor little thing falls asleep, believing all the time that it is fixing its gaze upon its Dear Star. When it awakens, it doesn't feel desolate; its little heart is at peace and it begins once again its work of *love*."[17] Even though the passage reflects Thérèse's sense of being little, it does not evade what Thérèse sees as the focus of discipleship: "its work of *love*."

Love of course is the central image which guided the religious life of Thérèse. Perhaps one of the best known passages in *The Story of a Soul* occurs in manuscript B where she reveals her engagement with 1 Corinthians 12-13. She went to this epistle of Paul "to find some kind of answer" to her heart's desire to live out so many vocations: "the warrior, the priest, the apostle, the doctor, the martyr." She read in chapter 12 that just as the body has many parts which work for the good of the body, so too the church is composed of many members, each having a different role. She was not yet satisfied, so she kept reading into chapter 13 and of course discovered that the most perfect gifts are nothing without love. "Charity gave me the key to my vocation," she wrote.[18] She understood that the Church had a *heart* (this element is missing in 1 Corinthians 12) and she wrote: "I understood it was Love alone that made the Church's members act, that if Love ever became extinct, apostles would not preach the Gospel and martyrs would not shed their blood. I understood that LOVE COMPRISED ALL VOCATIONS, THAT LOVE WAS EVERYTHING...." and then her famous sentence... "my vocation, at last I have found it...MY VOCATION IS LOVE".[19]

Not only was love or charity the unifying element in focusing her desires, but it was the scriptural word that so often mediated the specifics of her personal discipleship of Jesus Christ. For example, her suffering could not be understood except in relationship to Christ. Besides the Child Jesus, Thérèse adopted "the Holy Face" as part of her religious name because she could identify with the suffering of Jesus. Isaiah 53 spoke to her of the mature Christ, self-emptying on behalf of a sinful people.

She wished to identify with Christ in all of her suffering and so to allow her suffering to enter into the mystery of the redeeming Christ.

Scripture helped her to express in writing her spiritual journey. Borrowing the Pauline phrase, "I have been crucified with Christ; and it is no longer I who live, but it is Christ who lives in me," Thérèse wrote: "I would repeat the Words of love as they touched and embraced my soul." Indeed, Scripture ran through her mind and heart to help in forming her very being in love.

Scripture as Confirmation

Thérèse not only sought guidance from the Scriptures; she also examined God's Word for *confirmation* of her insights and convictions. Several examples can bear out this process of correlation which is not unique to her, but evidence of her openness to being formed by God's Word in the ordinary and in the everyday.

In the beginning of *The Story of a Soul* Thérèse makes clear that her life is a story of God's grace and mercy. She sees her life reflected in the imagery of Psalm 22/23. She wrote: "The fire of sufferings, outward and inward, has brought me to maturity; I am like a flower that can lift its head, refreshed, after the storm has passed by. I can read my own experience in the words of the twenty-second Psalm: 'The Lord is my shepherd; how can I lack anything? He gives me a resting place where there is green pasture, leads me out to the cool water's brink, refreshed and content. As in honor pledged, by sure paths he leads me....' To me the Lord has always been 'pitying and gracious, patient and rich in mercy'."[20]

When Thérèse knew that her sister Pauline was to enter Carmel, she was filled with delight and gratitude. She found that Psalm 118 expressed her sentiment well: "...give thanks to the Lord; the Lord is gracious, his mercy endures forever."[21]

In her autobiography Thérèse provides a descriptive account of the experience which led to her conviction that Jesus would be her spiritual director. She got to know Almire Pichon, S.J., who had served as spiritual director to her sister Marie. In fact, it was at Marie's profession when Father Pichon was present (1888: Thérèse had entered the Carmel on April 9, Marie's profession took place on May 22) that Thérèse chose to make a general confession. In that sacramental encounter Father Pichon assured Thérèse that she had never committed a mortal sin. She found his words, as she put it, "consoling." And Pichon added: "...may Our Lord always be your superior and novice master." Thérèse accepted this advice and added a further observation: "Jesus was also my Director."[22]

Thérèse's direct dependence upon Pichon ended after one year. She wrote: "Upon entering Carmel, I met one who was to serve in this capacity [spiritual director] but hardly had I been numbered among his children when he left for exile. [Pichon went to Canada as a preacher, leaving France in November, 1888.] Thus I came to know him only to be deprived of him. Reduced to receiving one letter a year from him to my twelve, my heart quickly turned to the Director of directors, and it was He who taught me that science hidden from the wise and prudent and revealed to *little ones*."[23] It is interesting to note that her decision to have Jesus as her spiritual director is linked to a scriptural resource, namely, Matthew 11:25: "...although you have hidden these things from the wise and learned, you have revealed them to the childlike."

In her autobiography (manuscript C) Thérèse states that in the gospels she always came upon new lights, hidden meanings in passages that previously meant very little to her. One is reminded of T.S. Eliot's lines in "Little Gidding" of the *Four Quartets* where Eliot notes that our explorations in the end come to rest where they began but matured now by insight and discovery.[24] Thérèse daily explored the Scriptures and often made new discoveries. For example, she claimed to understand what is meant by the text, "The kingdom of God is within you" (Lk 17:21) when she wrote: "For myself, I never heard the sound of his voice, but I know that he dwells within me all the time, guiding me and inspiring me whenever I do or say anything."[25]

The Song of Songs resonated with her experience; recall that the spousal figure was a centering image for Thérèse. She was familiar with the Canticle's place in the writings of John of the Cross. While modern biblical scholarship recognizes that the Song of Songs is an expression of human love, contemporary hermeneutics would acknowledge that a text takes on a life of its own within a community. One can appreciate that there exists an analogy between human and divine love. The Christian community has viewed the Canticle as an expression of the love between Christ and the community or Christ and the Christian. The Jewish community similarly saw in the Song a story of the relationship between the Lord and Israel. Both John of the Cross and Thérèse of Lisieux saw the Canticle in this relational sense. In a letter to Mother Agnes (Pauline), Thérèse used the Song of Songs as a vehicle to express her relationship to Christ: "Jesus does well to hide Himself, to talk to me only from time to time, and 'through the lattices' (Song 2:9), for I feel I should be unable to bear anymore, my heart would break, being powerless to contain so much joy...."[26]

Thérèse's correspondence with Céline continually goes to Scripture as a way of identifying faith experience in relationship to Jesus Christ and to draw light, consolation and strength for the journey in discipleship.

As we move to consider Thérèse's relationship to others by guiding them in letters and counsel, we find that again it is Scripture that very often forms the medium of her communication.

Scripture and Counsel in St. Thérèse

Thérèse's novice mistress, Sr. Marie of the Angels and of the Sacred Heart, testified in 1915 at the beatification/canonization process when she remarked that Thérèse had the gospels at her disposal and went to them for insight and consolation. "She had a rare understanding of the Holy Scriptures," stated Sr. Marie. "You can see evidence of this by the way she handled Scripture in *The Story of a Soul*."[27] This sense of engagement with the Word of God informed her work as an assistant novice mistress and also appears in her letters as she offers encouragement and affirmation to others.

Sr. Marie of the Trinity, Thérèse's favorite novice, underscored Thérèse's love for Scripture when she gave testimony at the beatification process. She claimed that Thérèse often cited Scripture when giving instruction to the novices: "...you might say her conversations were a commentary on the Bible."[28]

Céline often received consolation and encouragement from Thérèse with references to Scripture. In a letter to Céline in July, 1894 (LT 165), Thérèse notes again that life involves suffering. But Jesus too had trials. And Thérèse writes: "Many serve Jesus when he is consoling them, but few consent to keep company with Jesus sleeping on the waves, or suffering in the garden of agony... Who will be willing to serve Jesus for himself?...Ah! we shall be the ones....Céline and Thérèse will unite always more and more; in them will be accomplished this prayer of Jesus: 'Father, that they may be one as we are one'."[29]

On July 1, 1896, Léonie wrote a letter to Thérèse in which she confesses that, while Thérèse is prepared to appear before God, she has nothing to present to God except empty hands. Eleven days later Thérèse responds: "At the time of the law of fear, before the coming of our Lord, the Prophet Isaias already said, speaking in the name of the King of heaven: 'Can a mother forget her child?...Well, even if a mother were to forget her child, I myself will never forget you.'[Isa 49:16] What a delightful promise! Ah! we who are living in the law of love, how can we not profit by the loving advances our Spouse is making to us.... It is not little sacrifices you lack, dear Léonie, is not your life made up of them?"[30] In other words, Thérèse is trying to comfort Léonie with the assurance that her little sacrifices have a role to play in God's providence.

Thérèse bonded quickly with the two "spiritual brothers" assigned to her. Scripture was a frequent source of her counsel to them. Maurice Barthelemy-Bellière was a seminarian when the correspondence began. He confessed to Thérèse that his own vocation was wavering when he left the seminary to take up military service required by law. Writing to Bellière upon his return to the seminary, Thérèse was sensitive to his personal situation: "Now that the storm has passed I thank God for having made you pass through it, for we read in our holy books these beautiful words: 'what does he know who has not been tempted?' (Sir 34:10)."[31]

It has been the opinion of the team that put out the critical edition of Thérèse's plays, *Théâtre au Carmel: Récréations Pieuses*, that Thérèse did not try to offer any instruction or teaching to her sisters. "Rien n'est plus etranger à soeur Thérèse que de vouloir profiter d'une tribune privilégiée pour 'faire la lecon' a ses soeurs."[32] (In other words, Thérèse would never use any forum to try to teach her sisters in the community.) This scholarly team was led by Bishop Guy Gaucher, O.C.D., and Sr. Cecile from the Carmel of Lisieux and included in its membership Conrad de Meester, O.C.D., Pierre Descouvement and Bernard Bro, O.P. However, I believe that Thérèse did offer some direction to her community, however implicitly or even unconsciously, because of her fundamental conviction about truth. Truth is meant to be communicated. Furthermore, Scripture was an aid to her in communicating truth. For example, when she wrote "The Triumph of Humility" (RP 7), the community had just recently completed a stressful election of Mother Marie de Gonzague as prioress. She replaced Mother Agnes (Pauline) who had served as prioress for only three years. The election lasted through seven ballots. Thérèse began the "Triumph of Humility" on a Johannine theme of love and unity. She wrote: "What joy to have all of us together.... Have you ever seen anything in the world as charming as our union of hearts...?"[33] Given the circumstances of the election of the prioress that line seemed far more a hope than a reality. Was Thérèse calling the attention of the community to the need for deeper communal conversion? Is she influenced here by the gospel value of unity in love? Moreover, in three of the eight plays there occurs a process of conversion within each play from an initial attitude of fear of God to one of love: RP 1: "The Mission of Joan of Arc"; RP2: "Angels at the Christmas Crib" and RP 4: "Jesus at Bethany." In all three plays Thérèse draws upon biblical sources that point to a God of love and mercy. She had always been consistent in using this particular image of God, even though it was not the centerpiece of nineteenth century French piety.

A great deal more could be said about Thérèse's favorite passages, her rather uncritical use of scriptural sources, her selectivity in the use of Scripture. However, given the particular geography of exploration I have chosen in reviewing her use of Scripture, I will now draw some conclusions.

Conclusions

Thérèse's love for Scripture was based upon the conviction that one encounters God in the Word. Thus, she engaged the Scriptures for guidance, for consolation, for instruction, and in forging her own religious identity. Scripture helped her to deal with her aridity, her suffering, and all of her relationships.

Thérèse was a student of the Scriptures with the means available to her. She did not have access to commentaries or learned monographs. So she learned how John of the Cross and Teresa of Avila used God's Word; other texts such as the *Imitation of Christ* and Arminjon's book on the life of the blessed provided her with further insights into the meaning of scriptural texts. For example, the place of the Song of Songs in the writing of John of the Cross spoke to her heart.

Thérèse read the Scriptures with the lenses of her own epoch, i.e., nineteenth century French spirituality. Thus, she has a strong sense of a futurist eschatology (this world is a vale of tears to be endured with love), she leaned toward perfectionism and

revealed a touch of the reparative style of spirituality characteristic of her time. But she also found that Scripture taught her
some ways to transcend the limitations of her time: she emphasized a relationship to the humanity of Christ (the Child Jesus and
the Holy Face) rather than to the Kingship of Christ; she overcame
the joyless emphasis of a reparative style of spirituality by
emphasizing confidence and trust in God, both characteristics
based upon her knowledge of Scripture; she portrayed a God of
love and mercy over a God of justice, i.e., a God who punishes or
rewards us according to our deeds. Furthermore, through Scripture she seized upon the *leitmotif* of Christian spirituality through
the ages, namely, the centrality of love and brought out its
meaning in ways that ordinary people could grasp and follow.

Scripture, therefore, so engaged her life that Thérèse
reveals that association on almost every page of her autobiography and her letters. While the rule and the constitutions of the
Carmelite Order as well as the writings of Carmelite saints and
others were part of her religious heritage, it was God's Word that
energized her spirit of childlike simplicity and self-emptying love.

John Russell, O.Carm.

Endnotes

1. *Vatican Council II*, vol. I, rev. ed. (Grand Rapids, MI: Eerdmans, 1992) no. 25, 764.
2. Pontifical Biblical Commission, "The Interpretation of the Bible in the Church," 23:29 (*Origins*, January 6, 1994) 497-524.
3. Ibid., 520.
4. Ibid.
5. Ibid., 521.
6. *The Story of a Soul*, John Clarke, trans. (Washington, D.C.: Institute of Carmelite Studies, 1975) 179.
7. Pascal-Marie Jerumanis, "Pour Pénétrer dans La Parole de Dieu," in *Thérèse de L'Enfant Jesus, Docteur de L'Amour* (Venasque: Editions du Carmel, 1990) 33.
8. Hans Urs von Balthasar, *Thérèse of Lisieux: The Story of a Mission*, Donald Nicholl, trans. (New York: Sheed and Ward, 1954) 41.
9. Sr. Cecile, O.C.D. and Sr. Geneviève, O.P., *La Bible Avec Sainte Thérèse of Lisieux* (Paris: Cerf et Desclée de Brouwer, 1979).
10. Thomas Bird, "The Use of Sacred Scripture in the 'Autobiography'," *Sicut Parvuli* 19 (1957) 148-156.
11. *Letters of St. Thérèse of Lisieux*, 2, John Clarke, trans. (Washington, DC: Institute of Carmelite Studies, 1988) 862.
12. Blaise Arminjon, *Fin du Monde Present et Mystères de la vie Future* (Paris: Victor Palme, 1887).
13. *Autobiography of St Thérèse of Lisieux*, Ronald Knox, trans. (New York: P. J. Kenedy and Sons, 1958) 250.
14. *The Story of a Soul*, 195.
15. Ibid., 15.
16. Ibid.
17. Ibid., 199.
18. Ibid., 194.
19. Ibid.

20. *Autobiography of St. Thérèse of Lisieux*, Knox, trans., 35-36.
21. Ibid., 119.
22. *The Story of a Soul*, Clarke, trans., 150.
23. Ibid., 151.
24. T.S. Eliot, *The Complete Poems and Plays: 1909-1950* (New York: Harcourt, Brace and World, 1971) 145.
25. *Autobiography*, Knox, trans., 219.
26. *Letters of St. Thérèse of Lisieux*, 2 (Washington, DC: Institute of Carmelite Studies, 1988) 1101. LT 230.
27. *Procès de Beatification et Canonisation de L'Enfant-Jesus et de la Sainte-Face* 2 (Rome: Teresianum, 1976) 349.
28. Christopher O'Mahony, *St. Thérèse of Lisieux by Those Who Knew Her* (Dublin: Veritas, 1975) 242.
29. *Letters*, 2:862.
30. Ibid., 966.
31. Ibid., 1010.
32. Thérèse de Lisieux, THÉATRE AU CARMEL (Paris: Cerf et Desclée de Brouwer, 1985) 29.
33. Ibid., 247.

Ayguani's Commentary
on Psalm 72

*Roland has had a lifelong affair with Wisdom literature;
indeed one might say that, in terms of scholarly interests, it has
been his only love. Wisdom literature, surely, comprises some of the
most spiritually nourishing, as well as the most poetic books of the
Old Testament, and one should not be surprised to find a Carmelite
drawn to it.*

*Roland's interest produced its first fruit in 1948, when he
published his doctoral dissertation at the Catholic University of
America, **A Study of Psalm 72 (71)**. That is why, as a student of
history, hard pressed to make a contribution to a biblical scholar's
Festschrift, I thought it apt to present him with a translation (not
that Roland needs it) of the commentary by a 14th century confrere
on the topic of his dissertation.*

*Michael Ayguani, of Bologna (+1400), is one of the out-
standing medieval scholastics of the Carmelite Order. After obtaining the doctorate at the University of Paris in 1364, he joined the
newly founded faculty of theology of the University of Bologna.
(Another Carmelite, Peter Thomas, was one of the founders of the
faculty.) During the Western Schism, Michael led the Urbanist
section of the Order until 1386, when he returned to the halls of
Academe.*

*Like other university lecturers in the Middle Ages, Michael
was required to be equally proficient in philosophy, theology and
Sacred Scripture. His works in these fields have remained in*

*manuscript, except for his **Lectura super psalterio**, which, once printed, attained a wide dissemination down to recent times. The Dominican, Heinrich Denifle, biographer of Martin Luther (1905), calls it "one of the most extensive (**grössten**) commentaries on the Psalms which to my knowledge has ever been written." The Anglican priest, J.M. Neale, declares (1869), "To my mind, the Commentary of Michael Ayguan is, on the whole, the best of those that have been contributed to the treasury of the Church." **Pace** modern exegetes.*

Joachim F. Smet, O.Carm.

Psalm LXXI

1   **A psalm on Solomon.**

2   **Give to the king thy judgment and to the king's son thy justice.**

This psalm has the title: *On Solomon.*

According to the opinion of many Jews and also of our doctors, David composed this psalm as a prayer for his son whom he had constituted king, praying God that under his hand Israel would prosper in justice and truth. Therefore, it is titled "by Solomon," not as its author but as the one for whom it was composed. But *Jerome* in his prologue to the psalter expressly states that Solomon composed it, and this is more commonly held. Hence, in explanation of the title it should be known that this psalm is not about the prosperity of the kingdom of the Jews under Solomon but about the prosperity of the Church ruled by Christ in truth and justice, for many things in this psalm cannot be applied to Solomon.[1] For instance, *In his days shall justice*

spring up, and abundance of peace, till the moon be taken away,
&c., for the peace which endured under Solomon did not last until
the moon was taken away, which will occur on the day of
judgment. In fact, at his death, his reign was immediately divided,
as is evident from 3 Kgs 11. Moreover, Solomon did not hold
dominion from sea to sea, nor to the ends of the earth (as is said
here), but he ruled only over Judaea and a few neighboring lands.
But all that is contained in the psalm applies precisely to Christ.
And for Solomon here understand Christ, for Solomon is interpreted "peaceful,"[2] which in all truth applies to Christ, who as a
true mediator brings peace to the world. Wherefore, as soon as he
was born, the angels sang, "Glory to God in the highest and peace
to men upon earth," *Lk 2*; he made our peace with God through
his blood. "For he is our peace, who hath made both one." *Eph 2*.
With those who injured him he remained at peace. "With them
that hated peace I was peaceable." *Ps 119*. Hence, this psalm is
directed to this truly peaceful Solomon. This said, I proceed to the
division of the psalm.

Therefore, this psalm, which is about Christ, is divided
into five parts, because, first of all, it treats about Christ's judicial
power; secondly, about Christ's humble birth: *he shall come
down*; thirdly, about Christ's adorable divinity: *and he shall rule*;
fourthly, about Christ's commendable goodness: *he shall deliver*;
fifthly, about Christ's praiseworthy majesty: *let his name*.

The first part is divided in three, because it treats, first of
all, of Christ's power; secondly, of the authority of his power: *he
shall judge*; thirdly, of his eternity: *and he shall continue*.

The first part is divided into three, because Christ's power
is predicted optatively; secondly, is explained declaratively: *to
judge*; thirdly, how it is received is shown: *let [them] receive*.

As to the first, it should be noted that relative names which
are applied to God are twofold, because some are intrinsic, some
extrinsic. Intrinsic are those which are said of God eternally, like
Father and Son, Breather and Spirit. Extrinsic are those which
involve a relation to a creature, as Lord is said regarding servant,
ruler regarding ruled, conserver regarding conserved, and king

regarding subjects. Since, therefore, relative things act relatively and things destroyed are destroyed, and since a servant did not exist from eternity nor one governed nor conserved nor ruled by another, it follows that God was not Lord from eternity, nor preserver, nor ruler, nor king, but began being such together with the creature, and such relative names could be predicated extrinsically about God. And since such relations are extrinsically applied equally to the three Persons, it follows that all three are equally said to be one Lord, one conserver, one ruler, one king relative to creatures. However, God communicated this regal dignity to Christ when the Word assumed our humanity. Previsioning this, the Psalmist now speaks to God, saying, *Give to the king your judgment, God*, that is, to the man, Christ, who is king, insofar as you, O God, bestow the judiciary power by which he will be able to judge. Since, namely, judging is an outward action and as a consequence pertains to the whole Trinity, however, because only the Son will be seen in his humanity by all, therefore, judgment is especially attributed to the Son. He is also the son of the king, because he is the son of God, about whom is added, *and to the king's son thy justice*. The same idea is repeated with other words, because repetitions of the same idea with the same words or others greatly enhance divine speech, especially those which are in the same kind of speech as the effect to be produced on the mind, as when is said, "O God, my God, why hast thou forsaken me?" *Ps 21*. Or when is said, "O Lord, the God of my salvation." *Ps 87*.

Or, on the other hand, according to the grammarians there is a difference between judgment and justice, because judgment [*iudicium*] comes from law [*ius*], as it were, the statement [*dictio*] of law [*ius*], and it is judgment when a case is being pleaded, but justice when the case is settled. Thus, in the final judgment Christ will judge when he says, "I was thirsty, and you gave me," etc. *Mt 25*; but he will perform justice, when he says, "Come, ye blessed of my Father," etc.

And note that although God is threefold and one is truly our king, because he governs and reigns, yet Christ incarnate is declared to be our king in a special manner. For the *Philosopher*, *Primo Polit.*, says that a king should be of the race of those over whom he rules, for thus there will exist the greatest mutual love between king and subjects.[3] Hence, Christ, in order to be more fittingly our king, wanted to be of our race when he took our nature. And this Scripture sufficiently makes clear, saying, "Thou mayst not make a man of another nation king, that is not thy brother." *Deut 17.* And of this king it is said, "But God is our king before ages: he hath wrought salvation in the midst of the earth," *Ps 73*, that is, Christ, our king, who is king before all ages.

To judge thy people with justice and thy poor with judgment.

Here the judiciary power of Christ is declared, for, because [the Psalmist] first predicted that judiciary power was to be given to Christ, it now declares why, as though it said, Give your judgment to the king, namely, *to judge thy people with justice.*

Note that judgment is twofold, namely, of discernment and of condemnation. Here [the Psalmist] refers to both, speaking of judgment of discernment, namely, that [Christ] should distinguish his people from those who are not his and the poor from the rich—that is, the humble from the proud; this he does in the present, not indeed by place but by virtue of merit. In judgment he will do both, by place and merit, when he separates the sheep from the goats, *Mt 25.* And notice here that *thy people and thy poor* are taken to mean the same. For who are properly called people see above, verse 816.[4] But whoever thus constitutes people is humble and consequently poor in spirit; see above, verses 99 and 128. And so by people and poor the just are indicated. Those, therefore, he will *judge with justice*, declaring sentence upon them, and *with judgment*, distinguishing their merits. Note also that in saying, *thy* singular and *thy* plural, he shows that everything that is the Father's is also the Son's and vice versa.

Whence the Son said to the Father, *Jn 17*, "All my things are thine, and thine are mine."

3   Let the mountains receive peace for the people: and the hills justice.

Here is shown how the power of Christ and Christ himself are understood. First, should be noted what is meant by mountains and what by hills; secondly, what by peace and what by justice. First, by mountains holy angels are signified, who protect us like mountains. Thus, *Gregory* says, "Mountains are the sublime power of the angels who restore us by ministering and helping; who by God's goodness protect us in strife; by whose defense against adversaries we are protected on all sides."[5] About them is said, "Mountains are round about," *Ps 124*, that is, angels, as *Augustine*, explains.[6] And so by hills, which are smaller mountains, are understood the holy apostles and doctors, to whom through the ministry of angels divine mysteries are revealed, *Rev 1*, "and [God] signified, sending by his angel to his servant John." Wherefore, about divine mysteries is said, "They have gone from mountain to hill," [*Jer 50, 6*]. [The psalmist], therefore, says, *Let the mountains receive peace for the people*, because the holy angels received the commission from God of announcing peace to the people, when Christ was born, "And on earth peace to men of good will. *Lk 2.*

And the hills justice. However, by justice here understand the evangelical law which justifies the man who observes it. This because the apostles and other doctors received the commission to preach the gospel to the people, *Mk, last ch.*, "Go ye into the whole world and preach the gospel to every creature." Or again, by mountains understand the apostles, prelates, and others who stand out from the rest in dignity and by their lives are closer to heaven. About these *Ps 120* says, "I have lifted my eyes to the heavens, etc." But by hills understand lesser folk and subjects. For to prelates and superiors especially pertains obtaining peace and unity for their subjects, as is had in [c. 1] *dist. 90 Discordantes.*[7] To subjects, however, humility pertains, by which they obey their superiors. Humility itself is signified by justice, *Mt 3*, "For so it becometh us to fulfill all justice."

Take the psalm, therefore, to say, *Let the mountains receive peace for the people*, that is, let prelates and doctors receive the commission of keeping peace among the people, because the elite in the Church should see to peace with a vigilant spirit, lest acting proudly because of their honors they bring about schisms and the mutuality of unity be disrupted.[8]

And the hills justice, that is, subjects [receive] humility so that they may obey their superiors, putting Christ in their place, so that it may be said of them, "The hills of the world were bowed down." *Hab 3*.

4   He shall judge the poor of the people, and he shall save the children of the poor: and he shall humble the calumniator.

Here the authority of Christ's power is treated. But it should be noted that since poverty is of many kinds, some namely of necessity, some of non-spiritual will, some of spiritual will, only the third is to be understood, because it is such poor that Christ saves, as *Bernard* shows on *Mt 5*, *Blessed are the poor in spirit*,[9] saying, "What is so absurd[10] as that poverty should be blessed? But it is truth that speaks, which can neither mistake nor be mistaken. And so, you witless sons of Adam, do you seek after riches, still desire riches, when the blessedness of the poor is divinely recommended? With what impudence, what state of mind, does a Christian seek after riches, after Christ has declared the poor blessed? But attend carefully that he does not simply call persons poor because they are of the lower class, poor out of dire necessity, not willingly; to these he does not refer here, but to those who can say, 'I will freely sacrifice to thee' [*Ps 53, 8*]. But not all voluntary poor find approval with God. For philosophers are also known to have voluntarily left their all, in order that, freed of worldly cares, they might be more available for the study of truth; they were unwilling to abound in wealth[11] that they might abound in their own opinions. These [Christ] distinguishes, as was stated, by the spirit; that is, by the spiritual will for the sole pleasure of God and the welfare of souls, *for theirs is the kingdom of heaven*, and rightly so, for that miserable host of old was cast out of heaven because it pretended to a high state, presumed to be exalted. Does it not follow that those are blessed who demean themselves in the humility of poverty? And see how wisely Wisdom acted, opposing the first remedy to the first sin, as though she said, 'Do you wish to obtain the kingdom of heaven which the proud angel lost by confiding in his own strength and his own riches? Embrace useful poverty and it (the kingdom) will be yours'."

This is what the psalm says in other words, *he shall judge the poor of the people*, that is, among the people, but it immediately adds how it will judge them: because, that is, *he shall save the children of the poor*. The poor and the children of the poor are the same, as the city of Sion and the daughter of Sion are the same.

There follows, *and he shall humble the calumniator*. Who the calumniator is *Gregory* shows, saying, "We may rightly call all the wicked calumniators, not only those who steal external goods but also those who by their bad morals and the example of their reprobate life try to dissipate our internal goods. For, the former attempt to invade what is outside us, the latter seek to prey upon our interior. The former incessantly rage out of love of material things, the latter out of hatred of virtue. The former envy what we have, the latter that we live. The former attempt to steal external goods because they like them, the latter try to dissipate internal goods because they dislike them. Therefore, as moral life differs from the substance of things, so much the worse is the calumniator who by living evilly influences our minds than one by exercising violence inflicts material damage, etc."[12] From this it is clear that the calumniator is twofold, namely, one, spiritual, who preys on spiritual goods; the other, temporal, who preys on temporal goods. The first is the devil; the second, any tyrant. About both of them [the psalm] explains as follows. First, about the spiritual calumniator, the devil, whom Christ humiliated, when by his passion he deprived him of dominion over the world. Whence the *Master* in the *Gloss* says that the devil, the calumniator, was humiliated by the passion of Christ, when by the calumnies of the Jews he slew him over whom he had no right; hence he rightly lost those over whom he seemed to have some right."[13] He is truly called a calumniator, because he seeks to draw the innocent into guilt, which is to calumniate. Christ humiliated him by his passion, but he did not completely destroy him. Whence is written in another place, *Ps 88*, "Thou hast humbled the proud one, as one that is slain." This may also be understood about temporal calumniators, because Christ humiliated tyrants who persecuted the faithful, as is evident in the case of Nero, who instituted the first persecution against the Church, and of Diocletian, who instituted the second; both were cast out of power. The first killed himself, the second was slain by the senate, and so on about many others.

5   And he shall continue with the sun, and before the moon, throughout all generations.

Here, the eternity of Christ is treated. Note that Christ has two natures, divine and human. According to his divine nature he is simply eternal, but according to his human nature he is not eternal beforehand, but afterwards. Note, moreover, that by the sun is meant all time, but by the moon all temporal things. By the sun, therefore, all times are signified, because according to the course of the sun times change and are distinguished. Such is the meaning.

And he shall continue with the sun, that is, according to his humanity he shall continue as long as he wishes, namely in the Church through the sacrament of his body. *Mt, last verse*: "I am with you all days, even to the consummation of the world." This he says to the confusion of those who say the Church, or the Christian religion, will sometime cease to be. With regard to the divinity, [the psalm] says, *before the moon.* For by the moon, which never remains in the same state, understand every creature, which of itself is changeable. If, therefore, Christ continues before the moon, it follows that he continues before every creature and so is eternal; *Heb 13,* "Christ yesterday and today and the same forever."

Again, by the sun understand God the Father, because like the sun he possesses brightness coeval to him, and so has the Son, who is the brightness and figure of the substance of the Father, *Heb 1.* He continues, therefore, with the sun, because he is coeternal with the Father as to divinity. He continues before the moon, by which is understood the Church, which from the present generation, that is, the mortal one, will pass over to the immortal generation. Therefore, he continues *before the moon,* that is, in the sight of the Church, protecting it until it passes from the mortal to the immortal generation.

6   He shall come down like rain upon the fleece; and as showers falling gently upon the earth.

Continuing, here the incarnation and birth of Christ are treated. [The Psalmist] does two things, because he places first the manner of the nativity, secondly its fruit: *shall spring up* [verse 7]. As to the first, it should be known that this verse is based on history which is found in *Judg 6.* For when the people of Israel because of their sins had been given over as slaves to Midian, an angel of the Lord appeared to Gideon, saying that he would free the people from the hand of Midian. But Gideon, wishing to have some assurance about this, said to the angel, "In this I shall know that the Lord will free the people by my hand: I will place this fleece upon the floor, and if this night dew will descend on the fleece alone, so that all the ground of the floor be dry." And it was so. For rising in the morning, he found the entire fleece moistened, so that he wrung a whole vessel full of dew from the fleece, and all the ground about was dry. Then, to be certain, he asked the opposite sign, namely, that all the ground be wet and only the fleece be dry, which was also done. For during the night the rain fell gently and drop by drop and filled the whole floor. Only the fleece remained dry.

Similar to this history, therefore, the Psalmist shows that the incarnation of Christ is to take place. Here it should be noted that in his incarnation he does not come in great power but with the benignity of the greatest humility, as had been prophesied, *Zach 9*, "Behold, thy king comes to thee meek, etc." Noting this, [the Psalmist] says, *he shall come down like rain upon the fleece*, that is, he will come down gently and imperceptibly upon the virgin, because he will come in the greatest humility and gentleness. And so it is. Christ will come down into the womb of virgin like rain on fleece, who could have come with great power had he wished. He descends gently without a sound into the womb of the virgin, like rain upon fleece. It is an apt simile, as the *Gloss* notes,[14] for wool in receiving and shedding water does not fall apart but remains intact. Thus, in the glorious Virgin Mary virginity remains intact before, after, and during birth.

[The Psalmist] adds yet another simile, saying, *and as showers falling gently upon the earth.* For a drop (*stilla*) is combined with falling (*cado*), *dis. & fit stilicidium, dij.*,[15] that is, water falling gently, drop by drop, which descends very gently like dew. Who, therefore, the *Gloss* adds,[16] after so apt a simile will doubt the virgin birth? And avert to the fact that by this sign Gideon freed his people from the hand of Midian. For Gideon is interpreted "turning in the womb," and refers to Christ, who while existing in the womb of the virgin, by turning embraced the whole world. Midian is interpreted "evil" or "contradiction," and signifies the devil, who in his iniquity contradicts all good things. This simile the Psalmist wishes to use to demonstrate the incarnation of Christ.

This verse is expounded in another way by the *Gloss*,[17] which says, "The example of Gideon mystically signifies that the people of Israel was first moistened by the grace of Christ, while the floor of the Gentiles remained dry; later the Gentiles were rained upon, while the fleece of the Israelites remained dry. By fleece Israel is signified, which was despoiled of its teaching authority, as a sheep is despoiled of its wool. By fleece Israel is signified, because it retained the doctrine which it refused to preach to the Gentiles, as fleece retains rain. Therefore, it is said about Christ that he first *shall come down like rain upon the fleece*, that is, the grace of Christ first descends on the Jewish people, from amongst whom he chose his mother and the apostles, while the floor of the whole world remained dry, as the rain first came down on the fleece of Gideon, but afterwards it will come down *as showers falling gently upon the earth*, that is, upon the Gentiles, while the fleece of the Jews remains dry, as afterwards the floor of Gideon was moistened, while the fleece remained dry. Thus, Christ first came to the Jews, leaving aside the Gentiles; later, to the Gentiles, leaving aside the Jews."

7   In his days shall justice spring up, and abundance of peace, till the moon be taken away.

Here the fruit of Christ's birth is demonstrated. It should be noted that by justice the evangelical law is meant, in which all justice is contained, because the Old Law taught only exterior justice, but here the exterior together with the interior [is taught]. Wherefore, under the name of justice *Psalm 118* says about the New Law, "Thy justice is justice for ever: and thy law is the truth." About this justice is said, *in his days shall justice spring up*, because after his birth Christ himself on the mountain imparted the law of justice to his disciples.

And abundance of peace. Some apply this to temporal peace, which obtained throughout the whole world at the time Christ was born, when there was one monarch in the world. But this does not seem to agree with the following text, *till the moon be taken away*, because that peace did not last long, especially in

Judaea, the Jews themselves rebelling against the Romans, wherefore Jerusalem was destroyed and many cities. But about this text can be said that the Psalmist predicts that two times of Christ will occur, namely, the evangelical justice of the law and abundance of peace, whereof the first will endure till the moon be taken away, not the second. Thus, *till the moon be taken away* refers to justice not to *abundance of peace*.

In another and better way [the text] is applied to the spiritual peace which Christ brings. About this peace, the angel said, when he was born, "And on earth peace to men of good will," because in good men the peace of a better conscience always endures, as is said in *Prov 12*, "Whatsoever shall befall the just man, it shall not make him sad." This [peace] endures till the moon be taken away, because by the moon is meant the Church, for as the moon is illuminated by the sun, so the Church is by Christ. Whence *Gregory*, says, "What is meant by the moon if not the whole Church taken together, according to the testimony of the prophet, who says, *Hab 3*, 'The sun and the moon stood still in their habitation,' because when Our Lord ascended into heaven, Holy Church was forthwith strengthened in her authority to preach, etc."[18] About the Church, therefore, is said, *till the moon be taken away*; that is, let the Church be taken from the mortal state in which it now is and removed to the state of immortality. Whence, another reading has, "till the moon be lifted up"; that is, until the Church is lifted up by the state of resurrection. *Till* is to be taken here as it is above in verse 915.

8   And he shall rule from sea to sea, and from the river unto the ends of the earth.

Continuing, here [the psalm] treats of the adorable divinity of Christ and is divided into four parts: first, the spread of Christ's kingdom; secondly, the conversion of the Gentiles to the faith, *before him* [verse 9]; thirdly, the recognition of Christ's dominion, *the kings of Tharsis* [verse 10]; fourthly, the multiplication of the faithful throughout the earth, *they shall adore* [verse 11].

With regard to the first [part], it should be noted that the kingdom of Christ was spread, firstly, through his power, which was able to subjugate the hearts of infidels by his grace. He had this power from the first instant of his conception in the womb of the virgin. Secondly, it was spread through the preaching of the law and the conferral of the sacraments and began with the baptism of Christ, when he was baptized by John in the river Jordan.

[The Psalmist] notes the first cause of spreading, saying, *and he shall rule from sea to sea.* For by "sea" the Virgin Mary is sometimes understood, whence the name Mary is derived from the sea. Nor is this surprising, for like the sea she is of great purity, spaciousness, and utility. This is evident, firstly, because [the sea] can retain nothing impure; thus, neither did the Virgin contract any impurity of sin. Hence, about her is said, *Rev 4,* "And in the sight of the throne was, as it were, a sea of glass like to crystal." For glass and crystal are clear and cold, which fits the purity of the Virgin. Secondly, it is evident, because all rivers empty into the sea; thus, all graces were gathered in the Blessed Virgin. Whence, *Jerome,* "Others are given partial graces, but the plenitude of grace is infused in Mary, etc."[19] Whence, *Gen 1,* "the gathering of the waters he called seas [Vulgate: maria]. Thirdly, it is evident, because this land (situated above the sea) is not sterile; thus also, the Blessed Virgin grants copious graces to all sinners who approach her with devotion. Whence, *Bernard,* "Mary opens the bosom of her mercy to everyone, in order that all may receive of her plenitude."[20]

Secondly, by "sea" the state of penitence is sometimes understood; sea [*mare*] comes from bitterness [*amaritudine*]. Whence, *Richard, Super psalm 135,* "He who divided the red sea into parts says, 'The waters of the sea are very bitter.' What, therefore, is the sea if not the bitterness of penitence? The sea, therefore, remains undivided when one can sigh only out of fear of damnation. But the sea is divided when the bitterness of the heart sighs from compunction, when namely one sighs the tears of compunction, so that one not only laments the evil which one fears, but also the good which one desires."[21] In this sea of penitence the Egyptians are submerged, because by penitence all sins are cancelled. Whence, *Mic 7*, "He will cast all our sins into the bottom of the sea." Therefore, that is the sense of the psalm, *and he shall rule from sea to sea*, because the dominion of Christ, by which through his grace he rules over the faithful, began in the sea of the glorious Virgin Mary, when, namely, he was conceived in her, and continued through the whole world from sea to sea, that is, to all who are bitter through penitence for their sins.

Secondly, Christ's kingdom was spread through the preaching of the gospel and the conferral of the sacraments, and in this regard [the Psalmist] says, *and from the river unto the ends of the earth.* For this river, according to the *Gloss*,[22] was the Jordan in which Christ was baptized; and upon him the voice of the Father sounded, "This is my beloved Son." From thence, therefore, the doctrine of Christ had its beginning, from thence the sacraments had their beginning, because baptism is the entrance to and foundation of all the sacraments. From thence, that is, from this river flows the doctrine of Christ and the sacraments *unto the ends of the earth*; that is, it was diffused through the whole earth, as is said in *psalm 18*, "Their sound hath gone forth into all the earth, etc.," that is, of the apostles and other preachers.

Or again, note that the whole earth is surrounded by the sea. For the oceanic sea, though it is one sea, is variously called according to its divers parts, like the eastern sea from its eastern part, western from its western part, northern from its northern part, and so on with regard to the others. Therefore, what is *from sea to sea*, if not from one extremity of the earth to the other extremity? Consequently, "into all the earth," because in every part of the earth Christ has someone subject to him by faith. However, because this preaching began at the river Jordan, as has been said, therefore is added, *from the river unto the ends of the earth*, as above.

9   Before him the Ethiopians shall fall down: and his enemies shall lick the ground.

Here the conversion of the Gentiles to the faith of Christ is demonstrated. Note that at the preaching of the apostles some of the Gentiles were converted to Christ, but others remained in their infidelity. Of the first [the Psalmist] says, *before him the Ethiopians shall fall down.* They were converted at the preaching of St. Matthew, the apostle, because coming to that province and raising from the dead the son of the king, he baptized the king himself with his son and consecrated to Christ one of his daughters, a virgin, and he baptized most of the people of that kingdom of Ethiopia. Thus, the Ethiopians, who were first Gentiles, are taken to mean all Gentiles in general, as it is the habit of Scripture to take a part for the whole. Hence, about the converted Gentiles [the Psalmist] says, *before him*, that is, Christ, *the Ethiopians shall fall down*, that is, Gentiles in general. For, according to the grammarians, *dis.*, "fall" (*cado*) joined to "before" (*pro*) becomes "fall before" (*procidere*), *dis.*, that is, "fall before" (*ante cadere*), as when one wishes to adore someone, he prostrates himself, falling down before the other, as is said in *Ps 94*, "Come let us adore and fall down before the Lord.

Concerning those, however, who remained in infidelity, is added, *and his enemies shall lick the ground*, namely, the pertinacious and schismatics who envy the glory of Christ; they *shall lick the ground*, namely like a serpent, about which is written, "earth shalt thou eat" [*Gen 3, 14*]. They *shall lick the ground*, that is, they shall love earthly things, spurning the glory of Christ: *Mic 7*, "They shall lick the dust like serpents."

But in another way [the text] is explained in a good sense, namely, about the Gentiles who were first enemies of Christ through idolatry, but having heard the Gospel preached they bowed down to adore Christ devoutly, as if out of devotion and humility they wished to lick the ground, as was predicted in *Is, ch. 60*, "They shall come to thee who slandered thee and shall worship the steps of thy feet." And so is fulfilled in them what was said in

Is 49, "They shall worship thee with their face toward the earth and they shall lick up the dust of thy feet."

Or in another way this is applied by some to the Jews who obstinately opposed Christ. In the siege of Titus they were so overcome with hunger that they sought to eat the leftovers of food which had been cast on the ground and so they seemed to lick the ground.

10   The kings of Tharsis and the islands shall offer presents: the kings of the Arabians and of Saba shall bring gifts.

Here is set forth the recognition of Christ's dominion, because other kings of the earth came to Christ as soon as he was born, in order to recognize him as a true king and by way of tribute offer him gifts. Hence, this is literally applied to those three kings of whom is said *Mt 2*, "When Jesus was born, &c. Behold, wise men" &c came to adore the Lord with gifts, who literally were from the provinces named here, together with islands, that is, some from far flung parts. Hence, they also said, "We are come with gifts to adore him," so that the psalm foresaw this, saying, *the kings of Tharsis and the islands shall offer presents*, &c For, opening their treasure chests, they offered him gifts of gold, incense, and myrrh. Each one of them offered these three gifts. Hence, they recognized him to be true God, because they offered incense, which is offered in sacrifices to God; true king, because they offered gold, which is offered to kings; and true mortal, because they offered myrrh, with which the bodies of the dead are embalmed. Hence, *Augustine* in his sermon on the Epiphany says that gold is paid to him as to a great king, incense is immolated to him as to the true God, myrrh is given him for health to one about to die to all things.[23] Hence each one offered these gifts, because each one with his gifts prophesied him to be king, God, and man.

This verse can also be applied to other kings and princes of the world, who upon being converted to faith in Christ gave generous gifts for the support of the poor and the construction of churches.[24]

11   And all kings of the earth shall adore him: all nations shall serve him.

Here the multiplication of the family of Christ throughout the world is set forth. It should be noted that this was fulfilled in the time of Constantine, whom all the kings of the earth obeyed like monks, and he commanded churches to be built everywhere in honor of Christ. And so all the kings of the earth adored Christ, because Constantine did so, who was the chief of all kings.

Or it is understood in another way, that here *all* stands for classes of individuals, not for individuals in a class, because there was no class which at least in a part of it did not adore Christ. But what adoration is and how divers kinds must adore in a different way is explained above, verse 320.

12   For he shall deliver the poor from the mighty: and the needy that had no helper.

This is the fourth principal part, in which Christ's commendable goodness is treated. Here it should be noted that two virtues are especially suitable to kings (as *Isidore* says); namely, justice, so that the unjustly oppressed might be liberated, and mercy, by which rewards are conferred on the good.[25] And accordingly, here the goodness of our king is commended; first in the liberation of the oppressed, secondly, in the bestowal of good things, *he shall live* [verse 15].

With regard to the first, it should be known that before the coming of Christ the human race was oppressed in three ways. First, it was subjugated to the devil; secondly, it was stained by sin; thirdly, it was obliged to penalty. Of these three things Christ liberated us. And thus, the first part is divided in three ways, because, first, it is shown that he freed us from the devil; secondly, from sin, *he shall spare* [verse 13]; thirdly from penalty, *from usuries* [verse 14].

First, therefore, before the coming of Christ the devil held us captive. That is why he was called the prince of the world (Jn 12), because no one could completely resist his temptations, as *Gregory* concludes, saying, "From Adam until the coming of the Lord the devil dragged all nations behind him. He circled the world and walked about it, in order to impress the print of his iniquity on the hearts of the nations. For, falling from the heights, he by right possessed the human nations, because he bound them against their will with the bond of his guilt, and he wandered so widely about the earth that by his offence no one was found free in all things. It was his to circle the world as though by his own power, finding no one who could completely resist him."[26] Hence, about him it is said, *Job 42* [=41], "There is no power upon earth that can be compared with him." But from his power Christ freed us, so that he could not do as much to us as he could before. This the *Master, lib. 3, d. 19*, indicates, saying, "By his death Christ conquered the devil, so that when he tempted us in this life, he might not prevail. For although he tempts us after Christ's death, with the methods with which he formerly tempted, he cannot conquer as he previously conquered. For Peter, who before Christ's death, terrified by the voice of the maid servant, denied Christ, after Christ's death, led before kings and chiefs, did not yield. *Mt 26, Acts, 4 & 5, and many places.* Why? Because a stronger one, namely Christ, with power entering the house, that is, our hearts where the devil dwelt, bound the strong one, that is, restrained him from seducing the faithful, etc."[27] And thus it is, that the Psalmist, foreseeing this, says, *For he shall deliver the poor*, I say, namely, the humble and faithful folk, *from the mighty*, that is, the devil, whom not his own strength but the sins of men made strong. This poor person no one but Christ could free, because neither an angel, nor an ordinary just man, nor free will were able to free him, except the lion of the tribe of Judah alone.

And this is why [the Psalmist] adds, *and the needy that had no helper.*

13   He shall spare the poor and needy: and he shall save the souls of the poor.

Here [the Psalmist] shows how Christ freed us from sin, because, namely, he forgave sin. But whose? The poor and needy. Hence, note that he is called poor who has something, though it be little. He is called needy, however, who has nothing. Therefore, for poor understand sinner, who has faith in Christ, but unformed, such as, for instance, one who sins after having received the faith. For they have not enough, because such unformed faith, although not meritorious, nonetheless disposes to repentance, because it disposes one to think on the sin committed. For the needy, however, understand infidels and idolaters, who have no faith in Christ. Christ spares both these types of sinners and forgives their sins: of the poor, by an act of repentance; of the needy, when he supernaturally inspires them to believe.

Or by the poor and needy understand the humble, who presume nothing of themselves, but [trust] only in the grace of God. But here a doubt arises: how does God spare the sinner, when unpunished sin cannot be forgiven? Whence it is written, "I feared all my works, knowing that thou didst not spare the offender," *Job 9*. To this *Gregory,* treating the above mentioned words, responds, saying, "For if the guilty is not spared, who will be snatched from eternal death, since no one is found free of sin? Does [God] spare the penitent and not the guilty? For when we bewail our sins, we are in no way still guilty. How is it that Peter, while denying looks back and recalling the denied Redeemer is prompted to weep? How is it that while attempting to extinguish the name of the Redeemer from the earth, Paul merited to hear his voice? However, in both of them guilt is punished, because of Peter the Gospel says, 'And Peter remembered the word of the Lord and, going out, wept bitterly' *Lk 22*. The same with regard to Paul;

the Truth which called him says, 'For I will show him how great things he must suffer for my name's sake' *Acts 9.* Therefore, the Lord in no way spares the guilty, for he does not leave the sin unpunished: either penitent man punishes it in himself, or God, vindicating himself, strikes man. Therefore, in no way does he spare sin, because by no means relaxes vindication."[28] Thus, therefore, God spares the penitent. "I will spare them, as a man spareth his son" *Mal 2 [= 3].* Foreseeing this, the Psalmist says, *He shall spare the poor,* etc., and there follows, *and he shall save the souls of the poor,* namely, bestowing the grace to perform justice and meritorious works. And note that, according to the *Master* in *Gloss,* a twofold help of grace is here commended.[29] The first consists in the remission of sin, when [the Palmist] says, *He shall spare the poor and needy.* The second consists in the participation in justice, when he adds, "*and he shall save the souls of the poor.*

14   He shall redeem their souls from usuries and iniquity: and their names shall be honourable in his sight.

[The Psalmist] shows here that Christ frees us from punishment. Here, it should be understood for its illustration that usury is of many kinds, namely, usury of guilt, usury of punishment, usury of glory.

The first is usury of guilt, as in the case of guilt, when one makes exaction beyond the principal in matters consumed by use. Of this it is said, "Lord, who shall dwell in thy tabernacle," etc., and there follows, "he that hath not put out his money to usury" *[Ps 14].* From this many things should withhold us. First, fear of the divine majesty. "Fear thy God, that thy brother may live with thee. Thou shalt not give him thy money upon usury" *Lev 23 [=25].* Secondly, love of the divine goodness. "To thy brother thou shalt lend that which he wanteth without usury: that the Lord thy God may bless thee" *Deut 23.* Thirdly, hatred of cunning evil, against which the psalm says, "And usury and deceit have not departed from its streets" *[Ps 54].* The fourth is desire of happiness of heaven, to which no one practicing usury ascends, as is written, "he that hath not put out his money to usury" etc. *[Ps. 14]*. About this kind of usury see above, verse 886.

The second is usury of punishment, namely, when more punishment is exacted than the crimes committed. Of this [usury] the verse, *from usuries*, etc., is understood. For usuries, according to the *Gloss*, are when more is exacted in punishment than was committed in faults.[30] And this "more" has many meanings, namely, with regard to several things. For instance, when a homicide kills only the body of a person but does not harm the soul, that homicide's body and soul are lost in hell. Or it can be understood with regard to duration, because the pleasure of sin is brief and transitory, but the punishment is eternal; or with regard to intention, for greater and intenser by far is the affliction in punishment than was the pleasure in the fault. "Thou hast taken usury and increase" *Ezek 22*.

The third is usury of grace or glory. About it is said, "Why then didst thou not give my money into the bank, that at my coming, I might have exacted it with usury?" *[Lk 19, 23]*. For the Lord practices usury with us, because he lends us the Word of God through his preachers and with words exacts from us works. Hence, expounding these words, *Chrysostom* says that in material and temporal riches, debtors are liable only for what has been lent; for, as much as they received, that much they must give back, nor is more required of them. With regard to divine words, however, we are exhorted not only to preserve but also to multiply them. For whoever receives from a doctor the money of the Word to be believed must pay it back with the interest of works; and also from what he hears, he must strive to understand others which he did not learn from the mouth of the preacher."[31] To the matter at hand, here the usury of the second kind is referred to, because when God frees us from guilt, he also absolves us from the obligation of usury, for one follows from the other. Therefore, [the Psalmist] joins these two together, saying, *He shall redeem their souls from usuries and iniquity*, and there follows, *and their names shall be honourable in his sight*, because, namely, these he gives an honorable place before him in the kingdom. Or according to another text, *And his name is honorable in their sight,* because these, so liberated by Christ, hold the name of Christ in great reverence and honor.

15 And he shall live, and to him shall be given of the gold of Arabia, for him they shall always adore: they shall bless him all the day.

Here, the goodness of Christ is commended because of his granting of gifts. He bestows two gifts, particularly on his own [followers], namely, the knowledge of truth and confirmation in goodness. *There shall be* [verse 16]. As to the first, it should be noted that in Scripture wisdom is designated by gold. About which Solomon says, "A desirable treasure rests in the mouth of the wise."[32] Indeed, he recognizes that gold is wisdom, which he calls a treasure, because as temporal things are bought with gold, so are eternal things with wisdom. For if gold were not meant as wisdom, the angel would in no way say to the church of Laodicea, "I counsel thee to buy of me gold fire tried" [*Rev 3, 18*]. Gold indeed we buy, if we offer obedience before receiving wisdom. To this contract, namely, a certain wise man fittingly urges us, "Desire wisdom, keep the commandments, and the Lord will grant it to you," etc.

By Arabia, which is interpreted humble, understand the virtue of humility. What is it, therefore, to say, *to him shall be given of the gold of Arabia,* if wisdom is given to him, namely, Christ, by which he will humble himself for us unto the death of the cross? For God bestowed on the soul of Christ so much wisdom that he could hold no more, because he knew all that God did, as the *Master* shows, *Bk. III, dist. 13.*[33] He had humility, because he humbled himself, taking the form of servant, etc. For which cause God also hath exalted him, etc. *Phil 2. And he shall live,* that is, although he died for us, nevertheless, he will rise immortal, because Christ, rising again from the dead, Christ dieth now no more. *Rom 6. And to him shall be given of the gold of Arabia* from the fountain of divine wisdom together with the most profound humility. And all this Christ received on our account: wisdom, in order to enlighten us about the mysteries of the faith, himself saying, "I am the light of the world," *Jn 8*; humility, in order to incline us to humility, "Learn of me, because I am meek," etc., *Mt 11*. And therefore, the faithful enlightened by Christ with faith, humble themselves before him, adoring him. This the Psalmist foresaw, saying about the faithful, *for him they shall always adore*; namely, those who are his, that is, of his body which is the Church, shall always adore Christ as true God; and this either by an act or habitually *they shall bless him all the day*, namely, giving thanks for the benefits received from him.

Again, for the gold of Arabia understand secular wisdom, for Arabia is interpreted earthly. And so, there will be given of the gold of Arabia, because the wise of the world will be subjected to it. For this is the explanation of the *Gloss*,[34] which says, *And to him shall be given of the gold of Arabia*, that is, the wise of the world will believe in Christ. For Arabia means nations. By gold, however, which excels among all metals, [is meant] wisdom, which excels among doctrines. Or [the Psalmist] says this because after the resurrection of Christ many princes and potentates, converted to the faith of Christ, gave gold and precious gifts for the construction of churches.[35] And so it is likely that they gave of the gold of Arabia, which is more precious, etc.

16   And there shall be a firmament on the earth on the tops of mountains, above Libanus shall the fruit thereof be exalted: and they of the city shall flourish like the grass of the earth.

Here [the Psalmist] shows that Christ contributed to the confirmation in good. Here it should first be noted that according to some doctors this text is corrupted due to the mistake of the scribe, when it says, *and there shall be a firmament*, because it should say, "and there shall be wheat." This they prove by the fact that the Hebrew reads, "and there will be abundance of wheat." And Jerome's translation reads, "And the wheat will be memorable." And therefore they say that the common translation was corrupted by scribes because of the similarity of the words, rendering firmament for wheat. Hence, the Jews expound this passage, saying that at the coming of the Messiah, to which they falsely look forward, wheat will grow to the height of the cedars of Lebanon and will produce tall and wide kernels, from which, when the wind blows, will fall the finest flour, with which the Jews will be able to satiate themselves at will. But granted that the text should read, "and there shall be wheat," nevertheless, this exposition seems to be rather puerile and untrue. Wheat should be taken to mean the sacrament of the Eucharist, in which Christ, who compares himself to a grain of wheat, is truly present.[36] Then [the passage] would be expounded thus, *and there shall be wheat,* that is, the sacrament of the Eucharist, *on the earth on the tops of mountains,* because bishops and priests, who in the Church of God are like mountains, raise the sacrament above their heads.[37] *Above Libanus shall the fruit thereof be exalted,* because the fruit of this sacrament raises man to the heights of heaven and a life of blessings. *Jn 6:* "If any man eat of this bread, he shall live forever."

And they of the city shall flourish like the grass of the earth, that is, Christians who live by faith and charity in the Church, as in a city, for city means a union of citizens. The Christians of this city, therefore, will flourish, that is, be multiplied, and this like the grass of the earth. Hence, this means that as grass is quickly multiplied, so also Christians in a short time were multiplied throughout the whole earth.

But reading this text as the common translation has it, namely, *and there shall be a firmament on the earth,* etc., it is to be noted that by mountains Sacred Scripture means preachers, as Gregory shows, saying, "In Sacred Scripture by the word, mountains, the eminence of preachers is often meant. Of them, the Psalmist says, *Let the mountains receive peace for the people.*"[38]

Indeed, those chosen to be preachers of the eternal kingdom are deservedly called mountains, because by the loftiness of their life they leave the heights of earth and draw near to heaven.[39] Therefore, *the tops of the mountains* are the supreme preachers of the Scriptures, namely the prophets and apostles, of whose prophecies Christ was incarnated. *Firmament,* because everything predicted by them was sealed and completed by Christ. And this *on the earth,* that is, for those who are on the earth. Hence, therefore, for this Christ came on the earth, in order that what had been predicted might be fulfilled. The *firmament,* therefore, is of the prophets, because it fulfilled what they said.

Above Libanus shall the fruit thereof be exalted. For who is the fruit of Christ if not every just person? About this fruit Jesus said to the apostles, "I have appointed you, that you should go... and your fruit should remain" [*Jn 15,16*]. About this fruit, therefore, [the Psalmist] says *above Libanus shall the fruit thereof be exalted.* This, therefore, he says, because as Lebanon produces large and tall fruit, so Christ lifts up his just higher, when he elevates them to heaven.

And they of the city, that is, the Church, as was said above, *shall flourish like the grass of the earth.* Note that grass is here to be taken for greenness, not for age, as is said about the just in another place. The just shall flourish like the palm tree [*Ps 91*], because they will always have the greenness of glory.

**17   Let his name be blessed forevermore: his name
       continueth before the sun.
       And in him shall all the tribes of the earth be blessed:
       all nations shall magnify him.**

This is the last part, in which [the Psalmist] treats of the majesty of Christ to be praised. In it he proves that the majesty of God is to be revered for many reasons. And first, by reason of his eternity, for *his name continueth before the sun,* therefore, before all creatures. This is deduced as follows. From the beginning, all the kinds of creatures were created together and not successively, "He that liveth forever created all things together," *Eccl 18*. This *Augustine* takes to mean that all things were created together according to matter and form, but Gregory only according to matter, for afterwards by the work of seven days they were distinguished according to their species.[40] From this it follows that no creature existed before the sun, or at least before the matter of the sun. Therefore, all that existed before the sun is eternal. But Christ existed before the sun, because *his name continueth before the sun*, which is true regarding the *suppositum*[41] of Christ.

Again, by *sun* is meant the nature of angels, because just as the sun is more bright than the other stars, so also the nature of angels [outstrips] the rest of creatures, although it does not attain the clarity of divine knowledge, because as *Ecclesiasticus 23* says, "The eyes of the Lord are far brighter than the sun," which is explained as applying to the nature of the angels. When, therefore, nothing was created before the nature of the angels, the conclusion is that one who existed before the sun is eternal. And the Psalmist assigns this reason for praise, saying, *Let his name be blessed*, that is, that he is worthy of praise is proved by reason of eternity, *his name continueth before the sun*.[42]

And in him shall all the tribes of the earth be blessed: all nations shall magnify him.

Here [the Psalmist] shows that Christ is to be praised by reason of his goodness, which, namely, he communicates to all. Note that when he was incarnated in the world, he lived, suffered, and died, not for one people only, such as the Jews, the Saracens, or the Greeks, but for all in general with regard to sufficiency, but for the elect alone with regard to efficacy. Of these, the passion was the cause of salvation, participating in which they obtained the blessing of heaven from Christ himself. And this will occur on the day of judgment, when he will call all the elect gathered together, saying, "Come, ye blessed, possess," etc. *Mt 25*. This is the promise made to Abraham, "In thee shall all the kindred of the earth be blessed," *Gen 12*, as a universal sign, because[43] "all" is to be taken for kinds of individuals, not individuals of [various] kinds, which was fulfilled in Christ, who was of the seed of Abraham. This the Psalmist also now foresees, saying, *And in him shall all the tribes of the earth be blessed.*

Here it should be noted that this name, tribe, is taken from *tris* or *tribus*. And tribe is called progeny from *tris*, because in the beginning the Romans were assigned by Romulus in three ways, namely, senators, soldiers, and plebeians. And so, one is the progeny of senators, another of soldiers, a third of the plebeians. And in this manner, the twelve sons of Jacob comprised the twelve tribes, because from each of them the aforementioned three progenies descended, since each progeny is to be reduced to the three. Because each one belongs either to the progeny of lords, or soldiers, or plebeians, it follows that for all tribes all men are to be understood. Therefore, *all tribes shall be blessed in Christ,* that is, every man. And because the saints blessed by Christ are not ungrateful to him, therefore *all nations* follows; namely, those thus blessed by God *shall magnify him.* For the manner in which Christ is magnified and extolled by us see above, verses 272, 503, and 551.

18   Blessed be the Lord, the God of Israel, who alone doth wonderful things.

Here [the Psalmist] shows that Christ is to be praised by reason of his power, for he alone does wonderful things. For all the works of the Trinity *ad extra* are indivisible and so apply equally to the Son and the Father. Since, therefore, only God does wonderful things with his infinite power, it follows that also Christ alone does wonderful things, since Christ is God. Hence, *Job 5:* "Who doth great things and unsearchable and wonderful things without number." Expounding on this text, *Gregory* says, "Who can sufficiently examine the wonders wrought by God almighty, for he created all things from nothing: the very artefact of the world, arranged by the wonderful strength of power: heaven suspended upon the air, earth poised upon the abyss; for this entire universe is made up of invisible things; for he made man, constructing, if I may say so, another world in miniature; for, constituting him of body and soul, by an unsearchable disposition of power mixed spirit and earth? Of all these things, therefore, in part we know, in part we are, but we neglect to wonder at them, because those things which are wonderful by unknowing investigation by custom become common to human eyes. Thus, it happens that if a dead man is resuscitated, all leap with admiration, and everyday a man who did not exist is born and no one wonders, while it is undoubtedly clear to all that it is a greater feat to create what did not exist than to repair what already was. Because Aaron's lifeless rod flowered, all marvelled. Every day a tree is produced from dry soil, and the potency of dust is turned into wood, and no one wonders. Because five thousand men were sated with five loaves of bread, because food was multiplied in the mouth, everyone wondered. Every day, scattered grains of seed are filled with plenteous ears of corn, and no one wonders. Seeing water turned into wine one time, all wondered. Every day, the humidity of the earth, drawn by a trench to the root of the vine, is turned into wine, and no one wonders. Therefore, all those things which men neglect to admire are wonderful, because from use they grow too apathetic to notice, as we have already said."[44] And in the following chapter [Gregory] adds other apt examples, from which is evident to all the marvelous power of God which works wonders and so is judged worthy of praise.

Attending to all this, the Psalmist now says, *Blessed be the Lord, the God of Israel, who alone doth wonderful things.* And if you say, do not other men sometimes do wonderful things, like Peter, who by the mere shadow of his body cured the sick, by a word alone raised the dead, lifted up the lame, gave sight to the blind, as did others who were also holy? How, therefore, is it said of Christ, *who alone doth wonderful things?* To this the *Gloss* responds that whoever else does wonderful things does them in him,[45] "because all things were made by him," *Jn 1*. Hence *Is 26*: "For thou has wrought all our works for us."

19   **And blessed be the name of his majesty forever: and
the whole earth shall be filled with his majesty. So be
it. So be it.**

20   **The praises of David, the son of Jesse, are ended.**

Here [the Psalmist] shows that the majesty of God is to be
praised because of its immensity. As, namely, the eternity of God
contains all time as present, so also the immensity of God fills all
places and all of Nature together, so that he is present everywhere.
For as the *Master* says, *Bk. 1, dist. 37,* "God, being ever unchang-
ing in himself, is in all of Nature by his presence, potency and
essence; that is, by his essence without definition of himself,
everywhere without circumscription, and in all time without
change, etc."[46] Whence, *Jer 23,* says, "Do I not fill heaven and
earth, saith the Lord?" Whence *Gregory* says, "Indeed the creator
of men does not exist partially because he is everywhere; and he
is then least likely to be found, when he who is everywhere is
sought for in part. For an uncircumscribed spirit contains
everything within itself; by filling everything, it circumscribes
them; by circumscribing them, it fills them; by sustaining them,
it transcends them; by transcending them, it sustains them."[47]

This immensity of God, namely, that he fills everything,
can be proven by natural reason, if one argues as follows: Either
God is essentially everywhere, or nowhere, or somewhere now
somewhere not. If the first, the proposition is proven. If the
second, then God is nowhere, given that he is alone. For who
would dare to say that the divine essence never existed? If the
third—that he is somewhere now somewhere not—it follows that
God is local and that he can be moved from place to place, which
no philosophy holds.

Neither are valid the arguments regarding this proposition made by some who say God was not everywhere from eternity;
therefore, he is not essentially everywhere. The consequence is
evident, because everything that befits God essentially befits him
from eternity, because from eternity his essence was most perfect.

The antecedent is evident, because from eternity [God] was not in Bologna,[48] because Bologna did not exist, nor in some place, because places did not exist. In confirmation [of their argument they say that] God is essentially unchangeable; therefore, he is not everywhere. The consequence is evident, because then it would follow that at the creation of a new place, he would be in a place in which he had not previously been. Whence *Damascene*, bk. l, "Because God is immaterial, he is not in a place."[49]

These [arguments] are not conclusive. Not the first, for when they say that everything that befits God essentially, befits him from eternity, this is to be understood about that which does not connote a creature. For God is essentially the Lord of all, which was not the case from eternity, because God being Lord connotes the servitude of creatures. So I say to the point that God being everywhere connotes a creature, because it connotes a place. To the second, I say in like manner that only that which acquires a new place by circumscription, or a habit, is lost in that way, for only such a thing is changed. God, however, does not acquire a new place circumscriptively or lose a habit, because he is only said to be in a new place, because the place is new; or [is said] to lose a habit because a habit ceases to be a place. With regard to Damascene, I likewise say that he refers to being in a place circumscriptively.

To the point, therefore, because of this divine immensity the Psalmist shows that the majesty of God is to be praised, saying, *and blessed be the name of his majesty forever.* And he adds the reason, saying, *and,* meaning because, *the whole earth shall be filled with his majesty.*

So be it. So be it. And according to the distinction made in the beginning, here ends the second book of the psalter, because wherever there occur the words, so be it, so be it, there is the end of the book.

What is meant by the name, majesty? The *Catholicon* says that majesty comes from major, and majesty is the same as dignity, so called because it is like a greater power.[50]

Endnotes

1. The paragraph this far is taken literally from the gloss of Nicholas de Lyra, O.F.M., *Postillae super psalterium, In Solomonem.* For the reference to Jerome, cf. *Breviarium in psalmos,* Ps. 71; PL 26, 1089.
2. *Glossa Ordinaria,* Ps. 71, *In Salomonem.*
3. Not found in Bk. I of Aristotle's *Politics.* Ayguani may be paraphrasing.
4. The number refers to the marginal number assigned to each verse of the psalms in the printed editions. In some editions, as here, the twenty verses of Psalm 71 are numbered 1164 to 1183.
5. *Moralia,* Bk. 30, ch. 29 [=19]; PL 76, 559.
6. *Enarrationes in psalmos,* Ps. 124; PL 37, 1650.
7. *Corpus iuris canonici,* ed. Richter/Friedberg, I, 913: "Discordantes clericos episcopus vel ratione vel potestate ad concordiam trahat."
8. These lines were written during the Great Schism and in effect are an appeal to the claimants to the papacy to settle their differences.
9. Cf. *Sermones de sanctis,* Sermo 1 in festo omnium sanctorum; PL 183, 456-457.
10. PL 183, 456 has "hidden" (*absconditum*), following upon the previous comment on hidden things.
11. PL 183, 457: *censu.* Ayguanus: *sensu,* which misses the play on words.
12. *Moralia,* Bk. 26, ch. 9 [-14]; PL 76, 300.
13. *Glossa ordinaria super psalterium,* Ps. 71, *humiliabit.* The *Gloss* quotes Augustine. Cf. *Enarrationes in psalmos; PL* 36, 905.
14. *Glossa Ordinaria,* Ps. 71, *Descendet.* The *Glossa* cites Cassiodorus. Cf. *Expositio in psalterium,* Ps. 71; PL 70, 509.
15. Not found. Perhaps a misreading?

16. *Glossa Ordinaria*, Ps. 71, *Descendet* (mystice). The *Gloss* cites Cassiodorus. Cf. *Expositio in psalterium*, Ps. 71; PL 70, 509.
17. Ibid.
18. *Moralia*, Bk. 17, ch. 8 [=16]; PL 76, 21-22.
19. Jerome, *Epistula ad Paulam et Eustochium de Assumptione*; i.e., Paschasius Radbertus, ed. A. Ripberger, 1985; line 227.
20. Bernard, *Opera*, ed. J. Leclercq and H.M. Rochais, 1968, p. 263.
21. Richard of St. Victor, *Mysticae adnotationes in psalmos*; PL 196. 303-304. The passage occurs in the commentary on Psalm 28. Richard commented only certain psalms, and Psalm 135 was not one of them. On the *Mysticae adnotationes* see *Dictionnaire de spiritualité*, XIII, 618-620.
22. *Glossa ordinaria*, Ps. 71, *A flumine*. The *Gloss* cites Augustine. Cf. *Enarrationes in psalmos*, Ps. 71; PL 36, 909.
23. In his sermons on the Epiphany, Augustine regularly applies this symbolism to the gifts of the Magi; cf. PL 38, 2007, 2013, 2014, 2015, 2018.
24. Nicholas de Lyra, *Postillae*, Ps. 71, *Reges Tharsis*; see also ibid., verse 15, *Et dabitur*.
25. Not found in Isidore, *Sententiarum libri*, Bk. III, ch. 49, De justitia principum; PL 83, 720-721. But see ch. 52, De judicibus, "Omnis qui recte judicat stateram in manu gestat et in utroque penso justitiam et misericordiam portat"; ibid., 721.
26. *Moralia*, Bk. 2, ch. 22; PL 75, 575. PL has "human minds" for "human nations" and "willingly" for "against their will."
27. Peter Lombard, *Sententiarum* lib. III, dist. 19; PL 192, 796.
28. *Moralia*, Bk. 9, ch. 27 [=34]; PL 75, 889.
29. *Glossa Ordinaria*, Ps. 71, *Quia liberabit*. Cites Cassiodorus. Cf. *Expositio in psalterium*, Ps. 71; PL 70, 51.
30. *Glossa Ordinaria*, Ps. 71, *Ex usuris*. Cites Augustine. Cf. *Enarrationes in psalmos*, Ps. 71; PL 36, 910.
31. Cf. Chrysostom, *Adversus Judaeos oratio 8*; "Usura autem doctrinae nihil aliud est quam operum exhibitio. Ergo, quoniam nos quoque deposuimus pecuniam in aures vestras,

necesse est ut vos redeatis usuram Domino; hoc est, salutem fratrum vestrorum"; PG, 1, 942.

32. Prov. 21, 20, actually reads, "There is a treasure to be desired, and oil in the dwelling of the just."

33. Peter Lombard, *Sententiarum* lib. III, dist.13; PL 192, 781.

34. The *Glossa ordinaria*, Ps. 71, *Arabia*, has: "Per Arabiam gentes." Nicholas de Lyra, *Postillae*, Ps. 71, *Et dabitur*, has: "Multi principes et potentes ad fidem conversi [sunt]."

35. Nicholas de Lyra, *Postillae*, Ps 71, *Et dabitur*; see also ibid., v. 10, *Reges Tharsis*.

36. The paragraph this far is taken literally from Nicholas de Lyra, *Postillae*, Ps. 71, *Erit firmamentum*. Some editions of Ayguani's *Lectura* correct the text, substituting *frumentum* for *firmamentum*. Auguani's comment reflects the medieval suspicion of Hebrew. The Carmelitana Collection in Washington, D.C., as of this date, May, 1996, has five 17th century editions of Ayguani's commentary.

37. At the consecration of the Eucharist, presumably.

38. See above, verse 3 of this Psalm.

39. *Moralia*, Bk. 9, ch. 2 [=6]; PL 75, 861.

40. Augustine, *Contra adversarium legis et prophetarum*, Bk. 1, ch. 8; PL 42, 609. Gregory, *Moralia*, Bk. 32, ch. 12; PL 76, 644-645.

41. *suppositum*: A term of scholastic philosophy: that which exists of itself.

42. Ayguani's commentary on the verse ends, "A 'ly' stands for 'because' (*Ubi ly, &, stat pro quia*)." This was probably a marginal note in the manuscripts which found its way into the text. In fact, a 'ly' occurs in the next paragraph. See the next note.

43. because: *ly*.

44. *Moralia*, Bk. 6, ch. 6 [=15]; PL 75, 738-739.

45. Nicholas de Lyra, *Postillae*, Ps. 71, *Qui facit*: "Maxima enim mirabilia in mysteria Christi continentur."

46. Peter Lombard, *Sententiarum* lib. I, dist. 37; PL 192, 621.

47. Ayguani cites *Moralia*, Bk. 10, ch. 15. The text is found, ibid., Bk. 16, ch. 30; PL 75, 1140.
48. This example is interesting, because it suggests the university at which Ayguani taught.
49. John Damascene, *De fide orthodoxa*, Bk 1, ch. 13: "Et quidem Deus, ut qui materiae expers sit et incircumscriptus, in loco non est"; PG 94, 851.
50. Giovanni Balbi, of Genoa, *Catholicon*: "Maiestas a maior dicitur. Hec maiestas, tatis, i.e., honor, dignitas, splendor dicta, quia maior potestas." Copy consulted: Biblioteca Vaticana, Ms. Vat. Lat. 1474, f. 206r.

Saint Thérèse's Discovery
of Merciful Love

Thérèse's *Act of Oblation to Merciful Love* is described at the end of manuscript "A," written for her sister Pauline, otherwise known as Mother Agnes. Earlier in the manuscript Thérèse had described her childhood: happy until her mother's death, sad for nine years afterwards until she grew out of her over sensitivity at Christmastime in 1886. She described her trip to Rome, her entrance to Carmel, gave little detail about her life in Carmel, and ended the manuscript praising the merciful love of God.

She traced her soul's growth through contact with the Franciscan Father Prou, the writings of John of the Cross and Thomas à Kempis, but most especially the impact on her of Scripture and particularly the gospels. Similar to her namesake, Teresa of Avila, Thérèse in her abandonment learned to let go even of the ostensibly noble desires to suffer and die. Both Carmelites had learned that what God desires is what is important.

Thérèse knew about God's justice, and she was aware that devout people often offered themselves as victims to that justice so that sinners may be spared and God appeased. This God was not familiar to Thérèse. None of the faces of God in her life demanded appeasement, not her mother, nor her father, not Pauline, nor Céline, nor Marie, not the God of the Hebrew Bible who loved little ones, not Jesus who called little ones to him, not the lover of the Song of Songs or of the poetry of John of the Cross. The cheeky Thérèse recalled praying in her bed, this boast

389

"...contrary to the Bride in the Canticles, I always found my beloved there."[1]

Thérèse did not deny that God was just. On the contrary, God's justice was a source of consolation for her. "What a sweet joy it is to think that God is just, i.e., that He takes into account our weakness, that He is perfectly aware of our fragile nature."[2] Convinced that she was to be love in the heart of the Church and that she was destined to love God with the very love God showed her, she made an act of oblation in 1895, not to God's justice but to God's merciful love. "I desire, in a word, to be a saint," she wrote, "but I feel my helplessness and I beg you, O my God! to be Yourself my *Sanctity*. ...I OFFER MYSELF AS A VICTIM OF HOLOCAUST TO YOUR MERCIFUL LOVE, asking You to consume me incessantly, allowing the waves of *infinite tenderness* shut up within You to overflow into my soul, and that thus I may become a martyr of Your Love, O my God!"[3]

"I offer myself to your merciful love...." Notice her understanding of God, of the Trinity, a tender love overflowing, not able to be contained within God as though God could really be indifferent to us. But, notice too that she understood that this love needed someplace to go, someone to receive it. It is offered freely, gratuitously, not forced, waiting for someone in his or her freedom to be open to that love. God's love awaits reciprocity, calls for relationship. And we, with all our reasons to cower before this immensity, are encouraged by Thérèse to step trustingly into this relationship. Why? Because what we bring to it is not simply our always feeble response. But, we love God back with the very love God gives us.

In this approach, Thérèse found herself at the heart of the Gospel. She learned to speak about her life the way Teresa of Avila spoke about hers: our lives are a story of God's mercies. What is called for is not a cowering, not a crowing, but, as Thérèse wrote, "...to be silent and to weep with gratitude and love."[4] She also wrote that she could sing with the psalmist, "How GOOD is the Lord, his MERCY endures forever!"[5]

The mystery of her whole life is wrapped up in God's mercy. On the very first page of her autobiography she quotes St. Paul: "God will have mercy on whom he will have mercy, and he will show pity to whom he will show pity. So then there is question not of him who wills nor of him who runs, but of God showing mercy."[6] She wrote: "To me the Lord has always been 'merciful and good, slow to anger and abounding in steadfast love.'"[7]

In her last days when she was unable to receive Communion, Thérèse is reported by Pauline to have said, "*No doubt, it is a great grace to receive the sacraments. When God does not permit it, it is good too! Everything is a grace!*"[8]

Hers is a genuinely Christian intuition into the heart of God's relationship with us. Her sound Christian faith allows her to walk confidently over a landscape scarred with ancient battles. The following is a brief rehearsal of some of those battles, allowing us to better appreciate Thérèse's contribution.

Grace in Scripture

That God is merciful and gracious toward us is firmly rooted in Scripture. In the Hebrew Scriptures two words, *hanan* and *hesed*, in particular, influenced the later Christian use of the term grace.[9] The Hebrew word *hanan* means to be gracious, to have mercy on someone, to offer a cordial response to one in need. In wisdom literature *hanan* includes a bestowal of mercy on the poor. It expresses a conviction that God cares for the weak, the poor, and the oppressed. "I give grace (*hanan*) to whom I please, I show mercy (*raham*) to whom I please." (Ex 33:19)

Hesed, a noun, expresses itself in deeds of kindness and friendship, beyond a quid pro quo. *Hesed* is overwhelming, astonishing graciousness, oblivious of itself and solely for the other. In Exodus 34:6 God is "a merciful and gracious God, long-suffering and rich in *hesed* and faithfulness." Here we have what is considered the most adequate language to capture God's relationship or disposition toward humans. It also speaks of the ideal human response.

In sum, *hanan* refers to God's presence among us as a gracious and concerned presence, especially in solidarity with the weak and oppressed. *Hesed* expresses a love which is unmerited, a love transcending duty, a love overflowing in abundance.

In the Christian Scriptures the Greek word *charis* corresponds to *hanan* and *hesed*, means the free, benevolent and merciful love of God for people. English translates *charis* as grace. In the Hebrew Scriptures the fundamental expression of grace is "covenant." In the Christian Scriptures, Jesus Christ is *the* grace of God, the favor, the personified benevolence of God towards the human. Grace is God's own Trinitarian indwelling within us as Father-Son-Spirit. Jesus' favorite symbol for the reality of grace is the reign of God. Many of his parables bring out the love, compassion and forgiveness characteristic of this reigning God. Although used frequently in the Christian Scriptures, especially by Paul, grace was not a special focus of theological reflection until Augustine.

Augustine and Grace

Heresies have a way of returning to haunt us. Aspects of Manichaeism and Pelagianism, foes fought by Augustine, still plague us. Or rather, perhaps, still express in meaningful ways our own experiences. Manichaeism held that matter was evil and sinful. Human beings have no freedom; we are determined. Augustine agreed that we are sinful, but, since we are God's creation, we are fundamentally good. Pelagius taught a very appealing optimism. He agreed that humanity was good because it was created by God. And he went further to say, because God created humanity, that was enough for humanity to be able to do good things on its own. The grace of Christ is secondary, but not a necessary help to do the good.

Augustine said that humanity, even though created good by God, can no longer do the good because of original sin. Adam's disobedience has been passed down to us through procreation, and this original sin has taken away our freedom to do good and love God. Our free will is in bondage, and all we can do, on our own, is sin. Augustine argued that we are so wounded that only the grace of Christ can heal us so that we may once again do good. The solution to our wounded state is grace, the grace of Christ received in Baptism.

So, against Manichaeism, Augustine denied that we are evil by nature. We tend to the evil, not because we are evil, but because of an event, Adam's sin, which we inherit. Against Pelagianism, Augustine maintained that, although we can do good and our free will can love God, as Pelagius taught, this is not possible without the grace of Christ. The healing grace of Christ frees our will to do the good.

Augustine's doctrine on original sin has determined subsequent Christian theology and the official doctrine of the church. We need grace (God, the Holy Spirit) because we are fundamentally flawed and will do evil without it. He simultaneously told us that we are good because we are God's creation, and, at the same time, he left us highly suspicious of our sexual passions. Christianity emerged from these battles with an extreme focus on sin, and a deep distrust of sexuality and the body. But, Christianity gained a greater appreciation for the need for grace and dependence on God.

Aquinas and Grace

Aquinas maintained the absolute necessity of grace. But he had a different reason. For Augustine, grace was necessary to overcome the effects of original sin. For Aquinas, grace was necessary because of the disparity between our human nature and our infinite goal. Influenced by Aristotle, Aquinas dealt in natures, that which makes a thing be what it is. Finite human nature has an infinite goal, the beatific vision. God is humanity's goal, but it is a goal beyond human nature. Consequently, a "new nature," a super-nature is needed. This super-nature is grace. Grace re-makes humanity. We need grace, therefore, not because of sin, but because we are not up to our destiny. For Thomas, grace is a created sharing in God's own divine nature, a finite participation in it. We are doubly gifted by God: once when we are created by God, and a second time when we are graced with divine life.

A problem that has arisen since Aquinas' identification of grace as a new nature is that grace had become thing-like, reified; it becomes a possession I have and can use in order to barter with God. "I have so much grace to show for my life!" Grace is not seen primarily as the indwelling Spirit. A person can lose grace (through mortal sin) and get back into grace (through confession). In this concept of grace, there is little sense of a relationship with God.

Another problem with discussing grace as this new super-nature added on to human nature is that nature and the supernatural become separated into differing realities, leading to dichotomies between religious life and secular life, the profane and the sacred.

Luther and Grace

Luther returned to scriptural language, particularly that of St. Paul. He also returned to an Augustinian focus on sin. Luther discussed grace in the context of human sinfulness. He said: "the proper subject of theology is man guilty of sin and condemned, and God the Justifier and Savior of man the sinner. Whatever is asked or discussed in theology outside this subject is error and poison." In other words, if no sin, then no theology.

For Luther, grace is God's word of forgiveness. It is a relationship with God, specifically a union with Christ in spite of our sinfulness. Luther is totally anti-Pelagian: this forgiveness and union is not our work nor anything initiated by us. We have nothing to bring to the bargaining table. Luther and Thérèse would probably be in great agreement if they were to discuss such matters. Luther did not believe in merit. Thérèse said simply, "I have none."

Catholic theology understands a true change or transformation in us as a result of grace. Luther believed we remain sinners even after God's pardon and forgiveness.

The Council of Trent, in responding to Luther, attempted to differentiate traditional Catholic teaching from the teaching of the Reformation. While Trent also used scriptural language, Rome's usual language in the debates was objective, systematic, emphasizing human freedom and responsibility under grace. Luther's language was subjective, experiential, descriptive and emphasized human passivity before the power of God's spirit, leading to faith and justification through grace.

Post-Tridentine Currents

In the 16th century, Pelagianism returned as semi-Pelagianism, holding that human freedom allows a person to take the first steps, and then God responds and completes the work. The church condemned this view, reaffirming what the Councils of Carthage and Orange said, when they made it clear that we can never win or merit God's favor.

In the 17th century, Jansenism, following the Augustinian view, understood grace as strictly an antidote for sin. Our human nature is so damaged by original sin that anything purely natural is evil. All our actions are from either earthly desire and concupiscence, and hence sinful, or from heavenly desire and efficacious grace, and hence morally good. God gives grace only to those who are saved; Jesus died only for those predestined to be saved, and they are few. And Holy Communion is to be received only rarely, then as a reward for virtue. Jansenism resulted in a pessimistic view of our human situation. It led to a spirituality which denigrated human feeling, human desire, and the body. Marriage was permitted only for procreation.[10]

At the end of the last century, any possible renewal of the theology of grace, especially discussing it in the context of religious experience or any attempt to link it with our human aspirations, became entangled with Modernism and the suspicions and condemnation it engendered. Only in the 1930's and 1940's was there a sustained renewal of the theology of grace, especially through the historical study of patristic and medieval traditions. Names associated with this contemporary renewal are Henri de Lubac, Jean Daniélou, Henri Bouillard, Bernard Lonergan, and Karl Rahner.

Karl Rahner, influenced by Matthias Scheeben and the Eastern theologians, taught that grace is God's self-gift (the Holy Spirit). God's self-gift is the primary meaning of grace in the Scriptures. It is the presence of God to the soul. It is a relationship of love between God and the person. When we talk about grace today we mean uncreated grace, God, the Holy Spirit.

Rahner referred to the supernatural existential in human nature, meaning uncreated grace itself which is offered to all. It is the presence of the Holy Spirit (and Father and Son) to all human beings. It is the situation in which every human being is embraced by uncreated grace. Rahner here helped Pelagius find an orthodox way to state his insights.

"Man is the event of a free, unmerited and forgiving, and absolute self-communication of God."[11] This presence and self-communication of God (or grace) implies both an *offer* and a *response;* hence, grace is not structural but relational.

Thérèse and Grace

Thérèse finds her way intuitively through these issues and takes her stand squarely in the authentically scriptural and truly Christian understanding of grace. It is the presence of God, and hence it is *relational.* God communicates God's self, calling us to life and union, and so it is *loving*. And this loving presence is offered to us before we can do anything to earn or merit it; it is *gratuitous, free!* These three characteristics of grace, as 1) relational 2) loving and 3) free, gratuitous, found expression in Thérèse's autobiography.

Thérèse had various ways of speaking about her experience of being in a relationship with God. She described her experience on the day of her First Communion as a fusion with Christ, as a drop of water in the ocean.[12] "...Was not Jesus my *only Friend*," she wrote. She found it "more valuable to speak to God...."[13] Even the experience of God's inattention, when she was trying to get permission to enter Carmel early, was expressed in a relational image. She was a toy lying on the ground, while Jesus went off to sleep.[14] She learned to surrender as a little child in her Father's arms, noting that perfect victims are required to appease God's justice, but weak creatures are sufficient to respond to God's love.[15]

Her oblation to God's merciful love was the culmination of her life-long conviction that God's presence to us was a forgiving, healing, loving presence. She described her First Communion as a "kiss of *love*; I *felt* that I *was loved*...."[16] When she prayed for the condemned man, Pranzini, she said she was "absolutely confident in the mercy of Jesus."[17] She learned from the still-living pioneer of Lisieux, Sr. Geneviève, that "our God is a God of peace."[18] She credits the Franciscan Fr. Prou for launching her on the "waves of *confidence and love*...."[19] He assured her that her faults caused God no pain. She had an understanding of God's justice, but said that even this justice was clothed in his love.[20]

Over and over Thérèse expresses her conviction that, although she is little and has nothing, she is beloved by God. She knew her desires to be a great saint were God-given, and consequently God would bring it about. She herself was incapable of great things, for example, in the Joan of Arc mold. In her confidence she believed that being a great saint does not depend on merits because "I have *none*," she said.[21]

She referred to her practices as a practice of "nothing." She maintained she did not do "penances" as such; they held no attraction for her. "My mortification," she wrote, "consisted in *breaking my will....*"[22] Even though Thérèse counted on God's fulfillment of her desires, she did what she could to cooperate with and respond to God's grace which was transforming her desires and shaping her will. Her path became that of abandonment, a guide she trusted.[23] She did not concern herself about works to gain merit, only love.[24] She maintained that "Jesus does not demand great actions from us but simply *surrender* and *gratitude.*"[25] A beautiful image captured her trust in God's love. She described herself as a little bird, poor, weak, unfaithful; but she can soar to heaven "with the *Divine Eagle's own wings!*"[26]

Conclusion

Thérèse negotiated her way between competing values.[27] When Pelagius said we can do good on our own without Christ's grace, he was taking a stand for human freedom and autonomy, for self-determination, self-creation and world-fashioning. We define human existence today in those terms. When Augustine argued that we cannot do the good and overcome our concupiscence without the grace of Christ, he was taking a stand for the absoluteness of God and our total dependency on the divine. They were fighting over two symbols or poles of human existence: 1) human autonomy; 2) total dependence on God. These poles must be kept in tension. Augustine does it best.

God and humanity are not in competition. Grace does not undermine freedom and autonomy. Grace is the self-donation of God to human beings. Grace, far from limiting us, guarantees human autonomy and gives liberty. In Augustine, grace expands the horizon of freedom to include the possibility of a decision which transcends the self and this world in its intentionality. Speaking psychologically, as Augustine does, grace re-orients our elemental desire, interest and delight as well as our understanding.

Thérèse's act of oblation to merciful love is simply a wording, an expression, a ritualizing of the reality in which she found herself, embraced by God, loved into ever greater freedom and life, and able to respond, to love in return, through God's own love available to her.

John Welch, O.Carm.

Endnotes

1. Thérèse of Lisieux, *Story of a Soul*, John Clarke, trans. (Washington, DC: Institute of Carmelite Studies, 1976) 71.
2. Ibid., 180.
3. Ibid., 276, 277.
4. Ibid., 188.
5. Ibid., 180.
6. Ibid., 13.
7. Ibid., 15.
8. Ibid., 266.
9. This discussion of grace in Scripture relies on Stephen J. Duffy, *The Dynamics of Grace* (Collegeville, MN: Liturgical Press, 1993) 17-40.
10. More positive aspects of Jansenism were an emphasis on the liturgy, including greater lay participation and the use of Scripture by both clerics and laity. Cf. F. Ellen Weaver-LaPorte, "Jansenism" in *The New Dictionary of Catholic Spirituality*, Michael Downey, ed. (Collegeville, MN: Liturgical Press, 1993).
11. Karl Rahner, *Foundations of Christian Faith* (New York: Seabury, 1978) 116.
12. *Story of a Soul* 77.
13. Ibid., 87.
14. Ibid., 136.
15. Ibid., 195.
16. Ibid., 77.
17. Ibid., 100.
18. Ibid., 169.
19. Ibid., 174.
20. Ibid., 180.
21. Ibid., 72.
22. Ibid., 143.
23. Ibid., 178.
24. Ibid., 189.

25. Ibid., 188.

26. Ibid., 198.

27. For a discussion of the competing values of Pelagius and Augustine, cf. Roger Haight, *The Experience and Language of Grace* (New York: Paulist Press, 1979) 41-51.